The
Bible Knowledge Commentary

EPISTLES & PROPHECY

The Bible Knowledge Commentary

EPISTLES & PROPHECY

John F. Walvoord and Roy B. Zuck
GENERAL EDITORS

THE BIBLE KNOWLEDGE COMMENTARY: EPISTLES & PROPHECY
Published by David C Cook
4050 Lee Vance Drive
Colorado Springs, CO 80918 U.S.A.

David C Cook U.K., Kingsway Communications
Eastbourne, East Sussex BN23 6NT, England

The graphic circle C logo is a registered trademark of David C Cook.

All rights reserved. Except for brief excerpts for review purposes,
no part of this book may be reproduced or used in any form
without written permission from the publisher.

The website addresses recommended throughout this book are offered as a resource
to you. These websites are not intended in any way to be or imply an endorsement
on the part of David C Cook, nor do we vouch for their content.

Unless otherwise noted, all Scripture quotations are taken from the Holy Bible, New
International Version®, NIV®. Copyright © 1973, 1978 by Biblica, Inc.™ Used by
permission of Zondervan. All rights reserved worldwide. www.zondervan.com.
The authors have added italics to Scripture quotations for emphasis.

LCCN 2017955602
ISBN 978-0-8307-7269-8
eISBN 978-0-8307-7288-5

© 1983, 2018 John F. Walvoord and Roy B. Zuck
Previously published as part of *The Bible Knowledge Commentary:
New Testament*, ISBN 978-0-88207-812-0.

Cover Design: Nick Lee
Cover Photo: Getty Images

Printed in the United States of America
First Edition 2018

1 2 3 4 5 6 7 8 9 10

CONTENTS

PREFACE	7
Editors	9
Consulting Editors	9
Series Contributing Authors	9
Abbreviations	11
Transliterations	12
Groupings of New Testament Books	13
Hebrews	15
James	53
1 Peter	75
2 Peter	97
1 John	119
2 John	143
3 John	149
Jude	155
Revelation	163

PREFACE

The Bible Knowledge Commentary series is an exposition of the Scriptures written and edited solely by Dallas Seminary faculty members. It is designed for pastors, laypersons, Bible teachers, serious Bible students, and others who want a comprehensive but brief and reliable commentary on the entire Bible.

Why another Bible commentary when so many commentaries are already available? Several features make this series a distinctive Bible study tool.

The Bible Knowledge Commentary series is written by faculty members of one school: Dallas Theological Seminary. This commentary interprets the Scriptures consistently from the grammatical-historical approach and from the pretribulational, premillennial perspective, for which Dallas Seminary is well known. At the same time, the authors often present various views of passages where differences of opinion exist within evangelical scholarship.

Additionally, this commentary has features that not all commentaries include. (a) In their comments on the biblical text, the writers discuss how the purpose of the book unfolds, how each part fits with the whole and with what precedes and follows it. This helps readers see why the biblical authors chose the material they did as their words were guided by the Holy Spirit's inspiration. (b) Problem passages, puzzling Bible-time customs, and alleged contradictions are carefully considered and discussed. (c) Insights from modern conservative biblical scholarship are incorporated in this series. (d) Many Hebrew, Aramaic, and Greek words, important to the understanding of certain passages, are discussed. These words are transliterated for the benefit of readers not proficient in the biblical languages. Yet those who do know these languages will also appreciate these comments. (e) Throughout the series, dozens of maps, charts, and diagrams are included; they are placed conveniently with the Bible passages being discussed, not at the end of each book. (f) Numerous cross references to related or parallel passages are included with the discussions on many passages.

The material on each Bible book includes an *Introduction* (discussion of items such as authorship, date, purpose, unity, style, unique features), *Outline, Commentary,* and *Bibliography.* In the *Commentary* section, summaries of entire sections of the text are given, followed by detailed comments on the passage verse by verse and often phrase by phrase. All words quoted from the New International Version of the Bible appear in boldface type, as do the verse numbers at the beginning of paragraphs. The *Bibliography* entries, suggested for further study, are not all endorsed in their entirety by the authors and editors. The writers and editors have listed both works they have consulted and others which would be useful to readers.

Personal pronouns referring to Deity are capitalized, which often helps make it clear that the commentator is writing about a Member of the Trinity. The word LORD is the English translation of the Hebrew YHWH, often rendered *Yahweh* in English. *Lord* translates *'Ăḏōnāy.* When the two names stand together as a compound name of God, they are rendered "Sovereign LORD," as in the NIV.

The New Testament Consulting Editor, Dr. Stanley D. Toussaint, has added to the quality of this commentary by reading the manuscripts and offering helpful suggestions. His work is greatly appreciated. We also express thanks to Lloyd Cory, Victor Books Reference Editor, to Barbara Williams, whose careful editing enhanced the material appreciably, to hardworking Production Coordinator Myrna Jean Hasse, and to the many manuscript typists at Scripture Press and Dallas Theological Seminary for their diligence.

This commentary series is an exposition of the Bible, an explanation of the text of Scripture, based on careful exegesis. It is not primarily a devotional commentary, or an exegetical work giving details of lexicology, grammar, and syntax with extensive discussion of critical matters pertaining to textual and background data. May this commentary deepen your insight into the Scriptures, as you seek to have "the eyes of your heart ... enlightened" (Eph. 1:18) by the teaching ministry of the Holy Spirit.

This book is designed to enrich your understanding and appreciation of the Scriptures, God's inspired, inerrant Word, and to motivate you "not merely [to] listen to the Word" but also to "do what it says" (James 1:22) and "also ... to teach others" (2 Tim. 2:2).

John F. Walvoord
Roy B. Zuck

Editors

John F. Walvoord, B.A., M.A., TH.M., Th.D., D.D., Litt.D.
Chancellor Emeritus
Professor Emeritus of Systematic Theology

Roy B. Zuck, A.B., Th.M., Th.D.
Senior Professor Emeritus of Bible Exposition
Editor, *Bibliotheca Sacra*

Consulting Editors

Donald K. Campbell, B.A., Th.M., Th.D.
President Emeritus
Professor Emeritus of Bible Exposition

Stanley D. Toussaint, B.A., Th.M., Th.D.
Senior Professor Emeritus of Bible Exposition

Series Contributing Authors

Louis A. Barbieri, Jr., B.A., Th.M., Th.D.
Professor of Theology
Moody Bible Institute
Chicago, Illinois
Matthew

J. Ronald Blue, B.A., Th.M., Ph.D.
President Emeritus
CAM International
Dallas, Texas
James

Edwin A. Blum, B.S., Th.M., Th.D., D.Theol.
Translator and Editor
Philologos Foundation
Dallas, Texas
John

Donald K. Campbell, B.A., Th.M., Th.D.
President Emeritus
Professor Emeritus of Bible Exposition
Galatians

Thomas L. Constable, B.A., Th.M., Th.D.
Chairman and Senior Professor of Bible Exposition
1 and 2 Thessalonians

Edwin C. Deibler, B.A., Th.M., Ph.D.
Professor Emeritus of Historical Theology
Philemon

Kenneth O. Gangel, B.A., M.A., M.Div., S.T.M., Ph.D., Litt.D.
Scholar in Residence
Toccoa Falls College
Toccoa Falls, Georgia
2 Peter

Norman L. Geisler, Th.B., B.A., M.A., Ph.D.
Provost
Southern Evangelical Seminary
Charlotte, North Carolina
Colossians

John D. Grassmick, B.A., Th.M., Ph.D.
Associate Professor of New Testament Studies
Mark

Zane C. Hodges, B.A., Th.M.
Writer
Kerygma, Inc.
Dallas, Texas
Hebrews, 1, 2, and 3 John

Harold W. Hoehner, B.A., Th.M., Th.D., Ph.D.
  Director of Ph.D. Studies
  Chairman and Distinguished Professor of New Testament Studies
  Ephesians

Robert P. Lightner, Th.B., M.L.A., Th.M., Th.D.
  Professor Emeritus of Systematic Theology
  Philippians

A. Duane Litfin, B.S., Th.M., Ph.D.
  President Wheaton College
  Wheaton, Illinois
  1 and 2 Timothy, Titus

David K. Lowery, B.A., Th.M., Ph.D.
  Professor of New Testament Studies
  1 and 2 Corinthians

John A. Martin, B.A., Th.M., Th.D.
  Provost
  Roberts Wesleyan College
  Rochester, New York
  Luke

Edward C. Pentecost, B.A., M.A., Th.M., D.Miss.
  Professor of World Missions
  Jude

Roger M. Raymer, B.A., Th.M.
  Senior Pastor
  Lake Ridge Bible Church
  Dallas, Texas
  1 Peter

Stanley D. Toussaint, B.A., Th.M., Th.D.
  Senior Professor Emeritus of Bible Exposition
  Acts

John F. Walvoord, B.A., M.A., Th.M., Th.D., D.D., Litt.D.
  Chancellor Emeritus
  Professor Emeritus of Systematic Theology
  Revelation

John A. Witmer, B.A., M.A., M.S.L.S., Th.M., Th.D.
  Associate Professor Emeritus of Systematic Theology
  Romans

*Authorial information based on original edition of the Bible Knowledge Commentary set. At the time of the commentary's first printing, each author was a faculty member of Dallas Theological Seminary.

Abbreviations

A. General

act.	active	n., nn.	note(s)
Akk.	Akkadian	n.d.	no date
Apoc.	Apocrypha	neut.	neuter
Aram.	Aramaic	n.p.	no publisher, no place of publication
ca.	*circa*, about		
cf.	*confer*, compare	no.	number
chap., chaps.	chapter(s)	NT	New Testament
comp.	compiled, compilation, compiler	OT	Old Testament
		p., pp.	page(s)
ed.	edited, edition, editor	par., pars.	paragraph(s)
eds.	editors	part.	participle
e.g.	*exempli gratia*, for example	pass.	passive
Eng.	English	perf.	perfect
et al.	*et alii*, and others	pl.	plural
fem.	feminine	pres.	present
Gr.	Greek	q.v.	*quod vide*, which see
Heb.	Hebrew	Sem.	Semitic
ibid.	*ibidem*, in the same place	sing.	singular
i.e.	*id est*, that is	s.v.	*sub verbo*, under the word
imper.	imperative	trans.	translation, translator, translated
imperf.	imperfect		
lit.	literal, literally	viz.	*videlicet*, namely
LXX	Septuagint	vol., vols.	volume(s)
marg.	margin, marginal reading	v., vv.	verse(s)
masc.	masculine	vs.	versus
ms., mss.	manuscript(s)	Vul.	Vulgate
MT	Masoretic text		

B. Abbreviations of Books of the Bible

Gen.	Ruth	Job	Lam.	Jonah
Ex.	1, 2 Sam.	Ps., Pss. (pl.)	Ezek.	Micah
Lev.	1, 2 Kings	Prov.	Dan.	Nahum
Num.	1, 2 Chron.	Ecc.	Hosea	Hab.
Deut.	Ezra	Song	Joel	Zeph.
Josh.	Neh.	Isa.	Amos	Hag.
Jud.	Es.	Jer.	Obad.	Zech.
				Mal.

Matt.	Acts	Eph.	1, 2 Tim.	James
Mark	Rom.	Phil.	Titus	1, 2 Peter
Luke	1, 2 Cor.	Col.	Phile.	1, 2, 3 John
John	Gal.	1, 2 Thes.	Heb.	Jude
				Rev.

C. Abbreviations of Bible Versions, Translations, and Paraphrases

ASV	American Standard Version
JB	Jerusalem Bible
KJV	King James Version
NASB	New American Standard Bible
NEB	New English Bible
NIV	New International Version
NKJV	New King James Version
Ph.	New Testament in Modern English (J.B. Phillips)
RSV	Revised Standard Version
Sco.	New Scofield Reference Bible
Wms.	The New Testament (Charles B. Williams)

Transliterations

Hebrew

Consonants

א – ʾ	ד – ḏ	י – y	ס – s	ר – r
בּ – b	ה – h	כּ – k	ע – ʿ	שׂ – ś
ב – ḇ	ו – w	כ – ḵ	פּ – p	שׁ – š
גּ – g	ז – z	ל – l	פ – p̄	תּ – t
ג – ḡ	ח – ḥ	מ – m	צ – ṣ	ת – ṯ
ד – d	ט – ṭ	נ – n	ק – q	

Daghesh forte is represented by doubling the letter.

Vocalization

בָּה – bâh	בָּ – bā	בֹּ – bo[1]	בְּ – bĕ
בּוֹ – bô	בֹּ – bō	בֻּ – bu[1]	בְּ – bᵉ
בּוּ – bû	בָּ – bū	בֶּ – be	בָּה – bāh
בֵּי – bê	בֵּ – bē	בִּ – bi[1]	בָּא – bāʾ
בֶּי – bè	בִּי – bī	בַּ – bă	בֵּה – bēh
בִּי – bî	בַּ – ba	בֹּ – bŏ	בֶּה – beh

[1] In closed syllables

Greek

α, ᾳ	— a	ξ	— x	γγ	— ng
β	— b	ο	— o	γκ	— nk
γ	— g	π	— p	γξ	— nx
δ	— d	ρ	— r	γχ	— nch
ε	— e	σ, ς	— s	αἰ	— ai
ζ	— z	τ	— t	αὐ	— au
η, ῃ	— ē	υ	— y	εἰ	— ei
θ	— th	φ	— ph	εὐ	— eu
ι	— i	χ	— ch	ηὐ	— ēu
κ	— k	ψ	— ps	οἰ	— oi
λ	— l	ω, ῳ	— ō	οὐ	— ou
μ	— m	ῥ	— rh	υἰ	— hui
ν	— n	ʿ	— h		

Groupings of New Testament Books

I. **History**
    A. Four Gospels
    B. Acts

II. **Epistles**
    A. Pauline

        Journey Epistles
- Galatians
- 1 and 2 Thessalonians
- 1 and 2 Corinthians
- Romans

        Prison Epistles
- Ephesians
- Philippians
- Colossians
- Philemon

        Pastoral Epistles
- 1 Timothy
- Titus
- 2 Timothy

    B. General

        Hebrew Christians
- Hebrews
- James

        Others
- 1 and 2 Peter
- 1, 2, and 3 John
- Jude

III. **Visions**
    Revelation

HEBREWS
Zane C. Hodges

INTRODUCTION

The Epistle to the Hebrews is a rich part of the New Testament canon. In a unique fashion it exalts the person and work of the Lord Jesus Christ. In doing so, it makes immensely valuable contributions to the doctrines of His Incarnation, His substitutionary death, and His priesthood. Among the other truths to which the epistle effectively contributes are those involving the relationship between the New Covenant and the Old, the interpretation of the Old Testament, and the life of faith. The church would indeed be incalculably poorer without the teaching of this inspired book.

But despite its unquestioned value, little is known with certainty about its occasion, background, and authorship. Ignorance in these matters, however, does not seriously affect the understanding of the epistle's message. That remains timeless and relevant whatever the circumstances out of which it arose.

Date. In considering the background of Hebrews, it is reasonable to begin with the question of its date. This can be fixed within fairly good limits. The epistle can hardly be later than about A.D. 95 since it was known to Clement of Rome and quoted by him in 1 Clement. In addition it can scarcely be dated after A.D. 70, since there is no reference to the destruction of the Jewish temple in Jerusalem. Had this event already occurred, it would have given the author a definitive argument for the cessation of the Old Testament sacrificial system. Instead he seems to regard this system as still in operation (cf. 8:4, 13; 9:6-9; 10:1-3).

There is no need to regard 2:3 as a reference to second-generation Christians, and the epistle was obviously written during the lifetime of Timothy, whom the author knew (13:23). If the author is not Paul (and on the whole it seems likely he is not; see the following discussion on *Authorship*), then 13:23 may suggest he had already died. Otherwise, Timothy might have been expected to join Paul on his release from prison. On balance, a date somewhere around A.D. 68 or 69 seems most likely.

Authorship. Many names have been conjectured for the authorship of Hebrews, but the question remains unsolved. The tradition of Pauline authorship is very old and has never been decisively disproved. From the time of Pantaenus (died ca. A.D. 190) it was held in Alexandria that the epistle was in some sense Pauline. Clement of Alexandria thought Paul had written it originally in the Hebrew language and that Luke had translated it into Greek.

On the basis of style, Origen doubted the Pauline authorship but was not willing to set the tradition aside. In a famous statement he admitted that only God knew who had written the book.

The belief in the Pauline authorship of Hebrews belonged chiefly to the East until a later time. Jerome and Augustine seem to have been responsible for popularizing it in the West. In modern times it has usually been felt that the style and internal characteristics of Hebrews rule out Paul as the author. But arguments built on such considerations are notoriously subjective and have also been used to prove highly untenable propositions. Still it must be admitted that when Hebrews is read in Greek and compared with the known letters of Paul, the total impression is that here one meets a spiritual mind clearly attuned to Paul but in subtle ways quite different. This subjective impression, however, would not have prevailed if the early church's tradition had only mentioned Paul.

In fact the other name with early support is that of Paul's former missionary partner, Barnabas. This tradition appeared first in the West in Tertullian (ca. 160/170–215/220). In a polemical passage he quoted from Hebrews and assigned the quotation to an Epistle by Barnabas. Moreover, he did not talk as if this were his own opinion but simply a fact which his readers would know. The view that Barnabas wrote Hebrews was referred to at a later time by Jerome and reappeared in Gregory of Elvira and Filaster, both writers of the fourth century. There is reason to think that in the ancient catalog of canonical books found in the Western manuscript called Codex Claremontanus, the Book of Hebrews went under the name of the Epistle of Barnabas.

The evidence is not extensive, but the fact that it came from the West is perhaps significant. The only geographical reference in Hebrews is to Italy (13:24), and if the tradition about Barnabas is true it is not surprising that it comes from that part of the world. In other respects, Barnabas fits the requirements for authorship of this epistle. Since he was a Levite (Acts 4:36), an interest in the Levitical system, such as the author of Hebrews displayed, would be natural for him. Since he had close ties with Paul, resemblances in Hebrews to Paul's thought would be naturally explained. Moreover, Timothy had been converted in the area of Paul's first missionary journey (Acts 16:1-3) and was therefore most probably known to Barnabas. If Paul were dead at the time of the writing of Hebrews, it would not be surprising if Timothy were to join Paul's former companion (Heb. 13:23). The rift between Paul and Barnabas (Acts 15:37-39) had long since healed and Paul had later spoken warmly of Barnabas' cousin Mark (cf. Col. 4:10; 2 Tim. 4:11).

Of course authorship by Barnabas cannot be proved, any more than authorship by Paul can be disproved. But it has more to commend it than the other alternative suggestions. Among these it may be mentioned that at one time or another the names of Clement of Rome, Luke, Silvanus, Philip the Evangelist, Priscilla, and Apollos have been offered as possible authors. In particular the name of Apollos has found favor with some modern writers. The suggestion is often traced to Martin Luther. But the evidence is tenuous and does not include the early traditional support that the proposal Hebrews was written by Barnabas does. On balance this seems like the best conjecture. If Hebrews were actually authored by Barnabas, then it can claim apostolic origin since Barnabas was called an apostle (Acts 14:4, 14). In any case its divine authority is manifest.

Background and Setting. The identity of the first readers of Hebrews, like the author, is unknown. Nevertheless they were evidently part of a particular community. This appears from several considerations. The readers had a definite history and the writer referred to their "earlier days" (Heb. 10:32-34); he knew about their past and present generosity to other Christians (6:10); and he was able to be specific about their current spiritual condition (5:11-14). Moreover, the author had definite links with them and expressed his intention to visit them, perhaps with Timothy (13:19, 23). He also requested their prayers (13:18).

In all probability the readers were chiefly of Jewish background. Though this has sometimes been questioned, the contents of the epistle argue for it. Of course the ancient title "To the Hebrews" might be only a conjecture, but it is a natural one. When everything is said for a Gentile audience that can be said, the fact remains that the author's heavy stress on Jewish prototypes and his earnest polemic against the permanence of the Levitical system are best explained if the audience was largely Jewish and inclined to be swayed back to their old faith. The heavy and extensive appeal to the authority of the Old Testament Scriptures also was most suitable to readers who had been brought up on them.

As to the locale of which the readers were a part, nothing can be said definitely. The view that Apollos wrote the letter to the churches of the Lycus valley (where Colosse was situated), or to Corinth, is not independent of this view about authorship. The thesis that the readers were an enclave of Jewish Christians within the church at Rome has also found adherents. But apart from the reference to "those from Italy" (13:24), there is not much to suggest a Roman destination. On the view that Barnabas was the author, Cyprus has been proposed as a destination, since Barnabas was a Cypriot. But none of these proposals carries conviction.

The opinion that the epistle had a Palestinian destination has recently been strengthened by the observation that the polemic of the author may be best explained as directed against a sectarian form of Judaism such as that found at Qumran. Many of the alleged parallels are both interesting and impressive and will be mentioned in the following commentary. In particular the author's concern to show that the wilderness experience of ancient Israel was a time of unbelief and failure can be seen as especially pointed if directed at sectarians such as those at Qumran, who idealized the wilderness sojourn. Though not everyone is equally impressed by the data purporting to link Hebrews with sectarian thought, as far as it goes it adds support to a Palestinian location for the epistle's readership.

But there are problems with this view as well. For one thing, the reference to the readers receiving their knowledge of the Lord from those who originally heard Him (2:3) sounds a bit more natural for readers on a mission field. In Palestine, and especially Jerusalem, many of the readers might have heard Christ in person. In addition the reference to the readers' generosity to the poor (6:10) does not sound like Jerusalem at any rate, since poverty was prevalent there at a later time (cf. Acts 11:27-29; Gal. 2:10). If the statement of Hebrews 12:4 means that no martyrdoms had occurred in the community the writer is addressing, then a Palestinian or at least a Jerusalem locale is excluded. But the writer may only have meant that the people in his audience had not yet made such a sacrifice.

If Barnabas is the author of the epistle, one locale which might fit all the requirements is the ancient Libyan city of Cyrene in North Africa. Cyrene had been founded as a Greek colony around 630 B.C., but in the Roman period had a sizable and influential Jewish community. The origins of Christianity there seem to have been quite early, for the church at Antioch in Syria was founded by missionaries from Cyprus and Cyrene (Acts 11:20). The connection between Cyprus and Cyrene in that account is of interest because of Barnabas' Cypriot background. Two of the men with whom Barnabas later ministered in the Antioch church were "Simeon called Niger" and "Lucius of Cyrene" (Acts 13:1). Since Simeon's other name, Niger, means "black," he may have been from North Africa, as was his companion Lucius. Whether this Simeon was also the man called Simon who bore Jesus' cross (Luke 23:26) is unknown, but he too was from Cyrene. This latter Simon had two sons, Alexander and Rufus (Mark 15:21), who may have been known in the Roman church if that is where that Gospel was first published. In any case, contacts between Christians of the Libyan city of Cyrene and those at Rome and in Italy is most probable. This would explain the reference to Italians in Hebrews 13:24.

If the parallels with some kind of Jewish desert sectarianism are given weight, then the fact that Cyrene stood on the fringes of a wilderness where nomadism was a way of life may also be important. The author's references to the Greek word *oikoumenē* (trans. "world" in 1:6 and 2:5) would have special point in Cyrene. The word was commonly used to denote the Roman Empire and the limits of the Roman *oikoumenē* to the south were not far from Cyrene. Since it is unlikely that the impulse to withdraw from urban life and corrupted Jewish society existed only in Palestine, it would not be surprising if desert enclaves of sectarians existed also in the wilderness of Cyrenaica. That an ascetic Jewish sect had taken up residence on the shores of a lake near Alexandria in Egypt is known from Philo.

On the whole, the most plausible backdrop for the Epistle to the Hebrews might be a Christian church, largely Jewish in membership, in a city such as Cyrene. Under repeated pressures from their unbelieving fellow Jews they were tempted to give up their Christian profession and to return to their ancestral faith. If the form of this faith that allured them particularly was a sectarianism similar to that known at Qumran, then many of the author's appeals would have been especially pertinent, as the commentary will seek to show. The temptation to withdraw from civilized life into a kind of wilderness experience is precisely the kind of temptation the Epistle to the Hebrews would counter so well.

The destiny of the Lord Jesus is precisely to rule the *oikoumenē* (2:5) and

HEBREWS

those who adhere faithfully to Him will share in that rule (cf. 12:28). They must therefore hold fast to their Christian profession.

In the final analysis, however, the exact destination of the epistle is of as little importance as the identity of its author. Regardless of who wrote it, or where it was first sent, the Christian church has rightly regarded it down through the ages as a powerfully relevant message from God, who has definitively spoken in His Son.

OUTLINE

I. Prologue (1:1-4)
II. Part I: God's King-Son (1:5-4:16)
   A. The King-Son exalted (1:5-14)
   B. The first warning (2:1-4)
   C. The King-Son as the perfected Captain (2:5-18)
     1. The destiny of the Captain (2:5-9)
     2. The Captain's link with His followers (2:10-18)
   D. The second warning (chaps. 3-4)
     1. The call for faithfulness (3:1-6)
     2. The admonishment from Israel's failure (3:7-4:11)
     3. God's Word and the throne of grace (4:12-16)
III. Part II: God's Priest-Son (chaps. 5-10)
   A. Introduction: the qualified Priest (5:1-10)
     1. The general requirements for a high priest (5:1-4)
     2. The Son's call to priesthood (5:5-10)
   B. The third warning (5:11-6:20)
     1. The problem of immaturity (5:11-14)
     2. The solution to the problem (6:1-3)
     3. The alternative to progress (6:4-8)
     4. The concluding encouragement (6:9-20)
   C. The greater Priest and His greater ministry (7:1-10:18)
     1. The superior Priest (chap. 7)
       a. The greatness of Melchizedek (7:1-10)
       b. The new priesthood supersedes the old (7:11-19)
       c. The superiority of the new Priest (7:20-28)
     2. The superior service (8:1-10:18)
       a. Introduction to the superior service (8:1-6)
       b. The superior covenant (8:7-9:15)
       c. The superior sacrifice (9:16-28)
       d. The superior effect of the new priesthood (10:1-18)
   D. The fourth warning (10:19-39)
     1. The basic admonition (10:19-25)
     2. The renewed warning (10:26-31)
     3. The renewed encouragement (10:32-39)
IV. Part III: The Response of Faith (chaps. 11-12)
   A. The life of faith (chap. 11)
     1. Prologue (11:1-3)
     2. The divine acceptance of faith (11:4-16)
     3. The variegated experiences of faith (11:17-40)
   B. The final warning (chap. 12)
     1. The introductory admonition (12:1-2)
     2. The reminder that things are not as bad as they seem (12:3-11)
     3. The call to renewed spiritual vitality (12:12-17)
     4. The final warning itself (12:18-29)
V. Epilogue (chap. 13)

COMMENTARY

I. Prologue (1:1-4)

In a majestically constructed opening paragraph, the writer introduced his readers at once to the surpassing greatness of the Lord Jesus Christ. The Son, he declared, is the par excellence vehicle for divine revelation. In asserting this, he implicitly contrasted Him with the prophets of old and explicitly contrasted Him with the angels.

1:1-2a. The central assertion of the Prologue is made here. Though **God** has variously (*polymerōs kai polytropōs,* lit., "by various means and **in various ways**") revealed Himself **in the past,** Old Testament prophetic revelation has now received its end-times climax through God's **Son.** However highly the readership regarded that former revelation, the writer implied they must now listen most closely to the Son.

1:2b-4. In a series of subordinate constructions which are part of a single sentence in the Greek, the author set forth the Son's greatness. The unified structure of the writer's sentence is hidden by the NIV which breaks it down into several sentences. To begin with (v. 2b), the Son is the designated **Heir of all things.** This is obviously as it should be since He is also their Maker—the One **through whom He made the universe** (*tous aiōnas,* lit., "the ages," also rendered "the universe" in 11:3). The reference to the Son's heirship anticipates the thought of His future reign, of which the writer will say much.

But the One who is both Creator and Heir is also a perfect reflection of the God who has spoken in Him. Moreover **His Word** is so **powerful** that all He has made is sustained by that Word. And it is this Person who has **provided purification for sins** and has taken His seat **at the right hand of the Majesty in heaven** (cf. 8:1; 10:12; 12:2). In doing so it is obvious He has attained an eminence far beyond anything **the angels** can claim.

As might easily be expected in the Prologue, the writer struck notes which will be crucial to the unfolding of his argument in the body of the epistle. He implied that God's revelation in the Son has a definitive quality which previous revelation lacked. Moreover the sacrifice for sins which such a One makes must necessarily be greater than other kinds of sacrifices. Finally the Son's greatness makes preoccupation with angelic dignities entirely unnecessary. Though the Prologue contains no warning—the writer reserved those for later—it carries with it an implicit admonition: This is God's supremely great Son; hear Him! (cf. 12:25-27)

II. Part I: God's King-Son (1:5–4:16)

The first major unit of the body of the epistle begins at this point and extends through the dramatic appeal of 4:14-16 for the readers to avail themselves of the resources available to them at "the throne of grace" (4:16). The emphasis of the whole unit is on the sonship of Jesus Christ which the writer viewed as a kingly sonship in accord with the Davidic Covenant.

A. The King-Son exalted (1:5-14)

Drawing heavily on the witness of Old Testament revelation, the writer demonstrated the uniqueness of the Son. The title of Son, and the prerogatives it entails, elevate Him above all comparison with the angels. Those who see in Hebrews ties with sectarian Judaism point to the highly developed angelology of the Dead Sea sect. These verses offer an effective rebuttal against any tendency to give excessive prominence to angels.

1:5. The two questions in this verse show that the name **Son** belongs to Messiah in a sense in which it never belonged to **the angels.** Obviously "Son" is the superior name which Jesus "has inherited" (v. 4). But it is clear that the special sense of this name, in its kingly ramifications, is what basically concerns the writer.

The quotation in verse 5a is drawn from Psalm 2:7, while the quotation in Hebrews 1:5b comes from either 2 Samuel 7:14 or 1 Chronicles 17:13. Psalm 2 is an enthronement psalm in which God "adopts" the Davidic King as His "Son." That this is what the writer to the Hebrews understood is confirmed in Hebrews 1:5a by the quotation from the Davidic Covenant. No doubt the "today" in the expression **today I have become Your Father** was understood by the author of Hebrews to refer to Messiah's sitting at the right hand of God (cf. v. 3).

Of course the Lord Jesus Christ has always been the eternal Son of God. In a collective sense, the angels are called "sons of God" in the Old Testament (Job 38:7, marg.), but the writer was thinking of the title **Son** in the sense of the Davidic Heir who is entitled to ask God for dominion over the whole earth (cf. Ps. 2:8). In this sense the title belongs uniquely to Jesus and not to the angels.

1:6. The prerogatives of the One who bears this superlative title are set forth beginning with this verse. Instead of the NIV's **And again, when God brings**

His Firstborn into the world, it would be preferable to translate, "and when He again brings the Firstborn into the world." The reference is to the Second Advent when the kingly prerogatives of the Son will be recognized with open angelic **worship** (cf. Ps. 97:7 where the LXX rendering **"angels"** correctly renders the text).

1:7-9. In a pair of contrasting quotations, the author juxtaposed the servanthood of **the angels** (v. 7) and the eternal dominion of **the Son** (vv. 8-9). It is possible that, in line with one strand of Jewish thought about angels (cf. 2 Esdras 8:21-22), the writer understood the statement of Psalm 104:4 (quoted in Heb. 1:7) as suggesting that angels often blended their mutable natures with **winds** or **fire** as they performed the tasks God gave them. But in contrast with this mutability, the Son's **throne** is eternal and immutable (v. 8).

The quotation found in verses 8-9 is derived from Psalm 45:6-7 which describes the final triumph of God's messianic King. The writer extended this citation further than the previous ones, no doubt because the statements of the psalmist served well to highlight truths on which the author of Hebrews desired to elaborate. The King the psalmist described had **loved righteousness and hated wickedness.** This points to the holiness and obedience of Christ while He was on earth, to which reference will be repeatedly made later (cf. Heb. 3:1-2; 5:7-8; 7:26; 9:14). And though this King thus deservedly enjoys a superlative **joy,** still He has **companions** in that joy. The reference to "companions" is likewise a significant theme for the writer. The same word *metochoi* ("companions or sharers") is employed in 3:1, 14 of Christians (it is also used in 12:8). Since the King has attained His joy and dominion through a life of steadfast righteousness, it might be concluded that His companions will share His experience by that same means. This inference will later become quite clear (cf. 12:28).

1:10-12. The immutability of the King-Son is further stressed by the statements now quoted from Psalm 102:25-27. A simple "and" (*kai,* disguised a bit by NIV's **He also says**) links the quotation in these verses with that in Hebrews 1:8-9. That the author construed the words of Psalm 102 as likewise addressed to the Son cannot be reasonably doubted. The Son, then, is **Lord** and has created both **earth** and **the heavens** (cf. Heb. 1:2). But even when the present creation wears out like an old **garment** and is exchanged for a new one, the Son will remain unchanged. The reference here of course is to the transformation of the heavens and earth which will occur after the Millennium and will introduce the eternal state (2 Peter 3:10-13). Yet even after those cataclysmic events the Son's **years will never end.** This certainly points to His personal eternality, but it is also likely that the word "years" stands for all that they contain for the Son, including an eternal throne and scepter as well as unending joy with His companions. The writer definitely taught that Messiah's kingdom would survive the final "shaking" of the creation (cf. Heb. 12:26-28).

1:13-14. The writer drew this section to a climax with a final Old Testament quotation, one which is crucial to the entire thought of the epistle. It is taken from Psalm 110 which the author later employed in his elaboration of the Melchizedek priesthood of the Lord Jesus. Here he cited verse 1 of the psalm to highlight the final victory of the Son over His enemies. If the Son is to have an eternal throne (Heb. 1:8), such a victory obviously awaits Him. But the victory is His and not the angels'. Their role, by contrast, is **to serve those who will inherit salvation.**

It should not be automatically assumed that "salvation" here refers to a believer's past experience of regeneration. On the contrary it is something future as both the context and the words "will inherit" suggest. As always, the writer of Hebrews must be understood to reflect the ethos of Old Testament thought, especially so here where a chain of references to it form the core of his argument. And it is particularly in the Psalms, from which he chiefly quoted in this chapter, that the term "salvation" has a well-defined sense. In the Psalms this term occurs repeatedly to describe the deliverance of God's people from the oppression of their **enemies** and their consequent enjoyment of God's blessings. In the Septuagint, the Greek Bible so familiar to the writer, the word "salvation" (*sōtēria*) was used in this sense in Psalms 3:2, 8; 18:2, 35, 46, 50; 35:3; 37:39; 71:15; 118:14-15, 21; 132:16; and elsewhere. This meaning is uniquely suitable here where the Son's own triumph over enemies has just been mentioned.

That the readers were under external pressure there is little reason to doubt. They had endured persecution in the past and were exhorted not to give up now (Heb. 10:32-36). Here the writer reminded them that the final victory over all enemies belongs to God's King and that the angels presently serve those who are destined to share in that victory, that is, to "inherit salvation."

B. The first warning (2:1-4)

The writer now paused in his exposition to address the readers with the first in a series of five urgent warnings. (The others are in chaps. 3-4; 5:11-6:20; 10:19-39; 12.) This one is the briefest and most restrained of all of them, but is nonetheless solemn.

2:1. The truth he had just enunciated has important implications. The **therefore** shows that this admonition arose directly from the preceding material. Since the Son is so supremely great and is destined for final triumph over His enemies, the readers would do well to **pay more careful attention** to these realities. The danger is that, if they would not, they might **drift away** (*pararyōmen*, a word that occurs only here in the NT). The writer's audience was marked by immaturity and spiritual sluggishness (cf. 5:11-12), and if this trait were not eliminated there was danger of their slipping away from what they had heard. The author may have had the Septuagint rendering of Proverbs 3:21 in mind, where the Greek translators used the word for "drift away" that is found here: "My son, do not slip away, but keep my counsel and intent."

2:2-4. Inasmuch as under the Old Covenant, which was instituted through angelic ministration (Gal. 3:19), there were severe penalties for infractions of its demands, the readers could not suppose there would be no penalties for infractions against the New Covenant. On the contrary, with tantalizing vagueness, the author asked, **How shall we escape** (cf. Heb. 12:25) **if we ignore such a great salvation?** If the readers lost sight of the ultimate victory and deliverance that was promised to them in connection with the Son's own final victory, they could expect retribution. What its nature might be the writer did not spell out, but it would be unwarranted to think he was talking about hell. The "we" which pervades the passage shows that the author included himself among those who needed to pay close attention to these truths.

The "salvation," of course, is the same as that just mentioned in 1:14 (see comments there) and alludes to the readers' potential share in the Son's triumphant dominion, in which He has "companions" (cf. 1:9). The Lord Jesus Himself, while on earth, spoke much of His future kingdom and the participation of His faithful followers in that reign (cf., e.g., Luke 12:31-32; 22:29-30). But **this salvation** experience, **which was first announced by the Lord** had also received confirmation through the various miracles and manifestations of the Spirit which His original auditors, **those who heard Him**, were empowered to exhibit. In speaking like this, the writer of Hebrews regarded these **miracles** as the powers of the coming Age (cf. Heb. 6:5) and, in harmony with the early Christians in the Book of Acts, saw them as expressions of the sovereignty of the One who had gone to sit at God's right hand (cf. "signs," "wonders," and/or "miracles" in Acts 2:43; 4:30; 5:12; 6:8; 8:6, 13; 14:3; 15:12; also cf. 2 Cor. 12:12). That the author was indeed thinking throughout of "the world to come" is made clear in Hebrews 2:5.

C. The King-Son as the perfected Captain (2:5-18)

The author here returned to his main train of thought, the destiny of Jesus in the world to come. But now Jesus' intimate involvement through His Incarnation with those who will share that destiny was brought to the fore.

1. THE DESTINY OF THE CAPTAIN (2:5-9)

2:5. It has been claimed that the Dead Sea Scrolls show that the sectarians of Qumran believed that the coming Age would be marked by the dominion of Michael and his angelic subordinates. The statement here by the writer of Hebrews forcefully refutes this view. **Not . . . angels,** but people, will be awarded this dominion in **the world to come.** That the author was not just now introducing this subject is made plain by the expression **about which we are speaking.** It is obvious that the first chapter, with its manifest stress on the kingship and future reign of the Son, was about this very subject.

2:6-8a. A portion of Psalm 8 was now quoted. While the psalm as a whole is often read as a general statement about the role of man in God's Creation, it is clear in the light of Hebrews 2:5 and the application that follows in verses 8b-9 that the author of Hebrews read it primarily as messianic and eschatological. In doing so he stood well within the New Testament perspective on the Old Testament, a perspective directly traceable to Jesus Himself (cf. Luke 24:25-27, 44-45).

2:8b-9. Whatever might have been the general appropriateness of Psalm 8 to man's current standing in the world, in the view of the writer those words do not now describe the actual state of affairs. Instead, he affirmed, **at present we do not see everything subject to Him.** He was thinking here primarily of Jesus (Heb. 2:9). No doubt the familiar messianic designation "Son of Man" (v. 6) contributed to this understanding. Thus, he asserted, while total dominion over the created order is not yet His, Jesus is at last seen as **crowned with glory and honor because He suffered death.** The One so crowned **was made a little lower than the angels** for the very purpose of dying, that is, **that by the grace of God He might taste death for everyone.** This last statement is best understood as the purpose of the Lord's being made lower than the angels in His Incarnation. The words beginning with "now crowned" and ending with "suffered death" are a parenthesis more easily read as such in the Greek text. The focus of the statement, despite its reference to Jesus' present glory, is on the fact that He became a man in order to die.

2. THE CAPTAIN'S LINK WITH HIS FOLLOWERS (2:10-18)

In this section the writer of Hebrews used, for the first time, the Greek word *archēgos* of Jesus (his other use of the word is in 12:2). The word suggests such concepts as "Leader," "Originator," and "Founder" and is almost equivalent in some respects to the English word "Pioneer." The familiar rendering "Captain" (KJV) seems a bit superior to "Author" (2:10). The Lord Jesus, the writer will try to show, is the Captain of that loyal band of people whom God is preparing for glory.

2:10. The author here continued to think of Psalm 8, as his reference to **everything** reveals (cf. Heb. 2:8). Thus the **glory** he mentioned here is also the glory referred to in the psalm, that is, the glory of dominion over the created order (cf. Heb. 2:7-8). Even the expression **many sons** is inspired by the psalmist's mention of "the Son of Man" and suggests that for the writer of Hebrews the messianic title Son of Man probably had a corporate aspect. Jesus is *the* Son of Man, and His brothers and sisters are the many people who are linked with Him in both **suffering** and future glory. They will be the King's "companions" who share His joy in the world to come (cf. 1:9).

In 2:9 the writer had mentioned Jesus' death for the first time. Now he affirmed that such suffering was appropriate for the One who was to serve as the Captain of the many sons. Before He could fittingly lead them to the salvation experience God had in mind for them (i.e., "to glory"), He must be made **perfect** for this role "through suffering." Since His brethren must suffer, so must He if He is to be the kind of Captain they need. By having done so, He can give them the help they require (cf. v. 18).

2:11-13. Accordingly there is a deep unity between the Son and the many sons. By His death He **makes** them **holy,** and those who are thus **made holy are of the same family.** That the writer thought of the sacrifice of Christ as making the many sons holy in a definitive and final way is clear from 10:10, 14 (see comments there). Thus as Psalm 22:22 (quoted in Heb. 2:12) predicts, Jesus can **call them brothers.** He can also speak to them of His own **trust in** God (v. 13a, quoting Isa. 8:17) and can regard them as **the children God has given Me** (Heb. 2:13b, quoting Isa. 8:18). Like an elder brother in the midst of a circle of younger children, the Captain of their salvation can teach them the lessons of faith along the pathway of suffering.

2:14-15. These children, however, were once held in servitude by their enemy, Satan. Since they were human, their Captain had to become human and die for them, in order to rescue them. But by doing so He was able to **destroy . . . the devil**. The author did not mean that Satan ceased to exist or to be active. Rather the word he used for "destroy" (*katargēsē*) indicates the annulment of his power over those whom Christ redeems. In speaking of the devil as wielding **the power of death,** the writer meant that Satan uses people's **fear of death** to enslave them to his will. Often people make wrong moral choices out of their intense desire for self-preservation. The readers were reminded that they were no longer subject to such **slavery** and that they could face death with the same confidence in God their Captain had.

2:16-18. Whatever their needs or trials, their Captain is adequate to help them since He ministers to **Abraham's descendants,** not angels. The expression "Abraham's descendants" (lit., "Abraham's seed") may point to the Jewishness of the writer's audience, but even Gentile Christians could claim to be the "seed of Abraham" in a spiritual sense (Gal. 3:29). The help which the Captain gives to these His followers is again predicated on the fact that **He** was **made like His brothers in every way** (Heb. 2:17), that is, both in terms of becoming incarnate and by virtue of suffering. Here for the first time the writer introduced the thought of His priesthood, which he elaborated on later. For now he was content to affirm that this identification with "His brothers" had made possible a priesthood characterized both by mercy and fidelity **in service to God.** This involved, as its basis, **atonement for the sins of the people.** Of this too the author said more later, but he chose to conclude the section on the profoundly hopeful thought that the Captain, in His role as Priest, is able to aid his readers **who are being tempted** (v. 18) out of the experience of temptation which His own sufferings entailed. Though the discussion of these themes is far from over, the author has already suggested that the Captain has indeed been made perfect for His role in leading them into participation in His future glory.

D. The second warning (chaps. 3–4)

The writer paused again in the course of his exposition to introduce the second warning section. This one is far more extensive and detailed than the brief one in 2:1-4. The real nature of his anxiety for his readers becomes clearer here, as well as the incalculable loss which they faced if they did not attend to his exhortation. The basic text for this section is Psalm 95:7-11 which he quoted (Heb. 3:7-11) and expounded in the remainder of chapter 3 and in 4:1-11. The section closes with a reminder of the judgmental power of God's Word (4:12-13) and with a call to seek the help available through the great High Priest (4:14-16).

1. THE CALL FOR FAITHFULNESS (3:1-6)

3:1. The readers were now addressed as **holy brothers, who share in the heavenly calling.** This form of address gathered up the strands of truth which the author dealt with in chapter 2. They were indeed "brothers" (cf. 3:12; 10:19), not only with one another but with their Captain (2:11-12), and they were "holy" because He had made them so (2:11). They did "share in the heavenly calling" because God was "bringing" them "to glory" (2:10). The words "who share" are rendered "companions" in 1:9 (*metochoi*; this Greek word is also used in this epistle in 3:14; 6:4; 12:8). The author was thinking especially of their high privilege of being invited to participate in the future dominion and joy of God's King-Son.

It was as such people that they were to focus their thinking on the One who is both **the Apostle and High Priest** of their Christian profession. The first of these titles probably points to the Lord Jesus as the One sent forth by God as the supreme Revealer of the Father (cf. 1:1-2), while the second picks up the role just mentioned in 2:17-18.

3:2. The NIV disjoins this verse from the previous one by making it a separate sentence. But connecting it as in the original with verse 1, the statement may read: "Contemplate Jesus . . . being faithful to the One who appointed Him." Taken in this way, the readers are urged to fix their gaze on the person of Christ who is even now **faithful** to God. Thus they would find a model for their own fidelity. The faithfulness of Christ, moreover, has an Old Testament prototype in Moses.

The reference to **Moses** being **faithful in all God's house** was drawn from Numbers 12:7 in which the tabernacle furnished the backdrop. Hence God's "house" in the Old Testament situation would be the tabernacle itself which Moses had constructed in strict obedience to the divine directions. It was a prophetic testimony "to what would be said in the future" (Heb. 3:5).

3:3-6a. But **Jesus** as a **Builder** excels **Moses** in **honor** since Moses was simply a servant carrying out instructions. But what Jesus has built is, in fact, **everything,** for **God is the Builder of** "everything." Implicit here is the Son's role in Creation (cf. 1:2, 10) and indeed His identification as God (cf. 1:8). But beyond this is the thought that **God's house** in which **Moses was faithful** was a kind of miniature representation of "everything," that is, of the greater **house** over which the Son presides at God's right hand in heaven (cf. 1:3 with 4:14). The "holy of holies" in **His** earthly **house** was but a shadow of heaven itself where Christ has now gone "to appear for us in God's presence" (9:24). Moses' fidelity consisted in erecting that shadow house, the tabernacle, so that it could properly prefigure the future order of priestly activity which now has the universe itself as its proper sphere. This is the sphere where the exalted **Christ** sits **faithful** in all His current ministrations as well as past ones, functioning **as a Son over God's house** (3:6a).

3:6b. By a natural semantic shift to which the Greek word for **house** naturally lends itself, the writer moved from the thought of the house as the sphere where priestly activities transpired to the thought of the "house" as consisting of the people who engaged in these activities. His readers, he affirmed, comprise **His** (the Son's) "house" contingent, however, on one important consideration: **if they hold on to** their **courage** (*parrēsian,* used four times in Heb., here and in 4:16; 10:19, 35) **and the hope of which** they **boast.** As in the earlier warning passage (2:1-4), the writer used "we" and thus included himself within the scope of his admonition. As he will shortly state (3:12), he was concerned that there might be in some of his Christian "brothers" an "unbelieving heart that turns away from the living God." Should any of his readers do this, they would forfeit their roles in the Son's priestly house, which is only maintained by holding firmly to their Christian profession (cf. also v. 14 and 10:23-25, 35-36). The author did not mean, of course, that his readers could forfeit their eternal salvation; it is an error to identify the word "house" with the body of Christ, the true universal church. As the context and the Old Testament background show, the author was thinking in priestly terms. He was also thinking functionally. The exalted Son presides over a priestly apparatus which is an operative reality. As long as the readership held firmly to their Christian commitment, they also functioned within this priestly arrangement. But just as one who was a true Levite by birth could withdraw from participation in the tabernacle of Moses' day, so too one who is truly a Christian by new birth may withdraw from his priestly role within the functioning household. It was precisely this danger which concerned the writer, in the present warning passage as well as in later ones.

2. THE ADMONISHMENT FROM ISRAEL'S FAILURE (3:7-4:11)

3:7-11. To drive home his call to fidelity and to warn of the consequences of unbelieving infidelity, the author referred to the classic failure of Israel at Kadesh Barnea which led to their 40-year detour in the wilderness. Far from being an ideal period of Israel's history, as some sectarians seem to have held, it was an era marked by tragic loss and defeat. The readers were not to repeat such an experience in their own lives.

The text chosen by the writer to enforce the lesson he had in mind was taken from Psalm 95. Verses 7-11 of that psalm are quoted here. The choice of this psalm is highly appropriate in a context that is concerned with worship and priestly activity. For Psalm 95 is, in fact, essentially a call to worship (cf. Ps. 95:1-7). The psalmists' invitation, "Come, let us bow down in worship, let us kneel before the Lord our Maker, for He is our God and we are the people of His pasture, the flock under His care" (Ps.

95:6-7), ideally reflects the author's perspective with regard to his readers. The material quoted in Hebrews immediately follows these words and, most naturally, must be understood against this background.

3:12-13. See to it, brothers introduces the author's application of his text to his Christian readership. Neither here nor anywhere else in his letter did the writer betray the slightest suspicion that his audience might contain people who were not real Christians. Instead, they were regarded as "brothers" (as here) or as "holy brothers, who share in the heavenly calling" (v. 1). The widespread view that he was concerned about mere professors of the faith as over against genuine believers is not found in the text.

Each Christian brother, therefore, should be most careful to guard against a **sinful, unbelieving heart** which God's flock in the wilderness displayed, the kind of heart **that turns away from the living God.** One preventative against such a tendency would be a spirit of mutual concern and admonition among the Christian brotherhood. Accordingly they were to **encourage one another daily . . . so that none** would **be hardened by sin's deceitfulness** (v. 13). This exhortation is still completely pertinent to any local congregation at the present time, where the hardening tendencies of sin can often be counteracted by truly concerned fellow Christians. The expression **as long as it is called Today** alludes to the "Today" in Psalm 95:7 and means something like "while you still have opportunity."

3:14. The statement, **we have come to share in Christ** might be more literally rendered, "we are partners with the Christ." The word "the" found in the original probably gives to "Christ" the sense of "the Messiah." In the word "partners" the reader meets again the Greek *metochoi,* used in 1:9 and 3:1 of the "companions" of the messianic King. Once again, the writer reverted to the supreme privilege of being among the "many sons" whom God is bringing to the glory of shared dominion over the created order which Christ is destined to rule. But again too, like the privilege of serving in the priestly house (v. 6), this role is contingent on continuing fidelity: **if we hold firmly to the end the confidence we had at first.** In this connection, Revelation 2:26-27 comes readily to mind: "To him who overcomes and does My will to the end, I will give authority over the nations—he will rule them with an iron scepter."

3:15. The renewed quotation of part of the writer's text in Psalm 95 connects with the caution just uttered in Hebrews 3:6. The readers must hold their confidence firmly to the end and not, like the Israelites of old, **harden** their **hearts as . . . in the rebellion.**

3:16-19. Having alluded again to the passage he wished to expound, the author then began doing so. The questions in verse 16 seem more naturally read as statements: "For some, when they had heard, did provoke; howbeit not all that came out of Egypt by Moses." The writer is aware of the notable exceptions of Joshua and Caleb, who did not take part in the general failure. But then he asked, **With whom was** God **angry for 40 years?** The answer is that He was angry **with those** in the wilderness congregation **who sinned** and who died in that wilderness. Their disobedience in refusing to enter the Promised Land caused **God to swear that they would never enter His rest.** This meant of course that the sinful generation in **the desert** was permanently excluded from taking possession of their inheritance in Canaan. Naturally it had nothing to do with the question of their going to hell, so it would be wrong to allege that the entire Exodus generation was unregenerate. But exclusion from Canaan was a consequence of their lack of faith in the power of God to bring them into it in victory over their enemies, a failure that in principle might be repeated by the readers of Hebrews if they forgot Messiah's ultimate triumph over His enemies and theirs (cf. 1:13-14). The writer wished his readers to take it to heart that **unbelief,** lack of confidence in God, was the reason God's people did not enter the land.

4:1. It follows from the tragic example of Israel that Christians should also take warning. This is true because **the promise of entering His rest still stands.** The NIV rendering of the last half of the verse is, **let us be careful that none of you be found to have fallen short of it.**

This is possible, but the word "found" cloaks a difficulty in the underlying text, involving a word which usually means "to seem" or "to suppose." Some modern writers (Montefiore, Héring) prefer the meaning, "let us be careful that none of you suppose that he has missed it." Since the following context seems dedicated to demonstrating that God's rest is still open, this understanding is probably preferable.

The writer's concept of "rest" must not be separated from its Old Testament roots. The Septuagint includes notable passages where the word for rest (*katapausis*), in connection with Israel's possession of the land, is clearly paralleled with the word for inheritance (*klēronomia*). Moses showed clearly (Deut. 3:18-20; 12:9-11) that for Israel their rest was their inheritance. In the same way it is natural to suppose that the term "rest" for the writer of Hebrews was a functional equivalent for a Christian's inheritance. That Christians are "heirs" he has already affirmed (Heb. 1:14) and will shortly do so again (6:12, 17; cf. 9:15). How exactly he understood their relationship to this inheritance will unfold as his argument proceeds. But the inheritance itself can hardly be divorced from his presentation of Messiah's kingdom and His "partners'" share in that. If this needed explicit confirmation, it could be found in 12:28.

If, as just suggested, the writer was concerned that none of his readers would think they had missed their "inheritance-rest," it is quite conceivable that he was confronting the problem of the delay in the Second Advent, which Paul himself had also already encountered at Thessalonica. The writer of Hebrews' later call to patience that the readers may "receive what He has promised" is followed by the assurance that "in just a very little while, 'He who is coming will come and will not delay'" (10:36-37). If this was God's concern, it was urgent to show that this promised "rest" is still available.

4:2. Here the writer said that **the gospel was preached to us** (lit., "we were evangelized" or "we were given good news"). But this good news does not always refer to the plan of salvation from sin. In some circles the word "gospel" has acquired a sense too technical and narrow to do justice to the writer's ideas here. What was preached to the Israelites of old was, quite clearly, God's offer of rest. This, of course, was "good news" for them just as it is for people now, but it is not exactly what is meant today by "gospel." The Greek verb used, *euangelizomai*, was fully capable of having a nontechnical sense in the New Testament (cf. its use in Luke 1:19; 1 Thes. 3:6), but naturally the writer here did not sharply distinguish the "good news" about rest, which his readers had heard, from the "good news" to which the term "gospel" is more usually applied (cf. 1 Cor. 15:1-4). But as the whole context shows, his concern was with the good news about a future rest for God's people (cf. Heb. 4:10), not with the fundamental facts Paul spoke of in 1 Corinthians 15.

As was already pointed out in reference to the Israelites, **the message they heard** (about rest) **was of no value to them, because** of their lack of **faith** (cf. Heb. 3:19). That is to say, through unbelief they failed to take advantage of God's offer of rest. So it follows that for the readers to profit from this invitation to rest, they had to exercise faith.

4:3. This is precisely what he then affirmed. The words *hoi pisteusantes* should be rendered "we who believe" rather than **we who have believed**. The writer's concern was not about their original faith in the past, but their perseverance in it (cf. 3:6, 14). Faith remains the prerequisite for entrance into rest, since it was to those who failed to exercise faith that God **declared** by **oath** they would not **enter** into His **rest**. This exclusion was definitive despite the fact that this rest had been established as far back as **Creation** itself.

4:4-5. With considerable enrichment of thought, the author then linked God's Sabbath-rest at the time of Creation with the rest that the Israelites missed in the desert. **God rested** when He finished His creative activity and this kind of experience has, ever since, lain open to people who also finish the **work** that is set before them (cf. v. 10). When, as with the nation in the wilderness, a task is left unfinished, of such it must be said, **They shall never enter My rest.**

4:6-7. But the failure of the Israelites did not nullify the truth **that some will**

enter that rest, and accordingly God renewed the offer (in Ps. 95) as late as the time of David. At that time **God again set a certain day, calling it Today,** thus presenting this opportunity to all readers of the psalm for whom the "Today" becomes their own "Today." Already the writer had applied that "Today" to his readers (cf. Heb. 3:14-15).

4:8-10. But the readers were not to suppose that the promise of rest was realized in Joshua's day. Here the author showed himself perfectly aware that the Old Testament might have been quoted to show that the **rest** had already been entered via the conquest of the land in Joshua's time (cf. Josh. 22:4; 23:1). Probably it had been so quoted to his audience. But the writer's rebuttal was simple and sufficient: if this had been so, **God would not have spoken later about another day.** The psalm which forms his text disproves the notion that the rest had already been entered and was no longer open.

Behind this argument lies the undeniable fact that the conquest in Joshua's day did not lead to a permanent possession of the land. Such permanent possession of their promised inheritance had become for Judaism an expectation which would only be realized in Messiah's kingdom. This at least was true in normative Judaism, whatever might have been true in some sectarian thought. It may be suspected that here the author confronted some form of "realized eschatology" which denied the futurity of such a hope. (Cf. the similar view of believers' resurrection which Paul resisted, 2 Tim. 2:17-18.) If so, the Hebrews author regarded Psalm 95 as silencing such a distorted perspective. The rest—the messianic partnership—did indeed lie ahead: **There remains, then, a Sabbath-rest for the people of God.**

But it must now be said clearly that entering into **God's rest** means resting from one's **own work just as God did from His.** The statement is both a reassurance and an admonition. On the one hand it follows up the writer's conclusion (Heb. 4:9) that there is such a rest to be entered. But on the other, it reminds the readers that this is only done by their getting to the end of their task just as did God in His creative activity. In the phrase "rests from His own work," the author employed a kind of word play since the verb for "rest" also signifies "cease" which, against the backdrop of God's own work, clearly suggests successful completion. This thrust is what the writer has had in mind from the beginning of the section. The readers need to model their lives after Jesus Christ who "was faithful to the One who appointed Him" (3:2) and must be careful to "hold firmly till the end the confidence we had at first" (3:14; cf. 3:6). Only thus would they be able to rest from their works *in the joyful possession of their inheritance in the messianic kingdom.*

4:11. It follows logically from this that the readers should, along with the author (note, **Let us**), **make every effort to enter that rest.** Unlike the assurance which all Christians have that they possess eternal life and will be raised up to enjoy it in the presence of God (cf. John 6:39-40), the share of the companions of Messiah in His dominion over creation is attained by doing His will to the end (Rev. 2:26-27). The readers must therefore be warned by Israel's failure in the desert and take care that they not follow Israel's **example of disobedience.**

3. GOD'S WORD AND THE THRONE OF GRACE (4:12-16)

Having completed his exposition of Psalm 95 and Israel's failure to enter rest, the writer brought this section of warning to a conclusion that is both sobering and comforting. God's Word is a solemn instrument of divine judgment, but His throne is both gracious and merciful.

4:12. The lesson he had just taught from the Old Testament Scriptures was not a mere historical tale. Instead, as had already been made clear by much he had said, it was powerfully relevant to his audience. **For the Word of God is living** (*zōn*) **and active** (*energēs*). Not only that, its penetrating power is greater **than any double-edged sword** and reaches the innermost being of a person so that **it judges the thoughts and attitudes of the heart.** In doing this, it is able to discriminate successfully between what is spiritual in man and what is merely "soulish" or natural (**it penetrates even to dividing soul and spirit**), and does so even when these often-contradictory inner elements are interwoven as closely as **joints and**

marrow. The inner life of a Christian is often a strange mixture of motivations both genuinely spiritual and completely human. It takes a supernaturally discerning agent such as the Word of God to sort these out and to expose what is of the flesh. The readers might think that they were contemplating certain steps out of purely spiritual motivations when, as God's Word could show them, they were acting unfaithfully as did Israel of old.

4:13. Let them not suppose, therefore, that their motives would go undetected for **nothing is hidden from God's sight.** Instead, **everything is uncovered and laid bare before . . . Him.** In saying this, the readers were reminded that, like all Christians, they would someday stand before the judgment seat of Christ where they **must give account** to God for their lives (cf. Rom. 14:10-12; 2 Cor. 5:10). If at that time their lives are seen to be marked by the kind of failure they have been warned against, the writer implied they will suffer loss of reward (cf. 1 Cor. 3:11-15). In this context the loss they suffer will be that of their inheritance-rest.

4:14. But this need not be so. On the contrary there is every reason to **hold firmly to the faith we profess** in view of the fact that the believers' **great High Priest . . . has gone through the heavens.** Only once previously (2:1–3:6) had the writer referred explicitly to the priesthood of Jesus, though it was implicit in 1:3, but now he was preparing to undertake an extensive consideration of that truth. But before doing so, he wished to suggest its practical relevance to his readers whom he exhorted to "hold firmly to the faith." They had to know that the priesthood of their Lord offered them all the resources they needed.

4:15. The One who served as **High Priest** on their behalf had been where they were and had **been tempted in every way, just as** they were. Though unlike them He **was without sin** (cf. 7:26; 2 Cor. 5:21; 1 John 3:5), never responding wrongly to any of His temptations (nor could He, being God), yet as a man He could feel their reality (much as an immovable boulder can bear the brunt of a raging sea) and thus He is able to **sympathize** (*sympathēsai*, lit., "to feel or suffer with") **with** their and **our weaknesses.** It may indeed be argued, and has been, that only One who fully resists temptation can know the extent of its force. Thus the sinless One has a greater capacity for compassion than any sinner could have for a fellow sinner.

4:16. With such a High Priest, it follows that believers should **approach the throne of grace with confidence** (*parrēsias;* cf. 3:6; 10:19, 35). In a book filled with lovely and captivating turns of expression, few excel the memorable phrase "throne of grace." Such a conception of the presence of God into which beleaguered Christians may come at any time, suggests both the sovereignty of the One they approach (since they come to a "throne") and His benevolence. At a point of contact with God like this Christians can fully expect to **receive mercy and find grace to help . . . in . . . time of need.**

III. Part II: God's Priest-Son (chaps. 5–10)

In the first major movement of the epistle (1:5–4:16), the author set forth two major truths: (1) the exalted position and destiny of Him who is uniquely God's King-Son and (2) the salvation-inheritance of those who cleave to Him by faith. Included in the consideration of these themes have been solemn warnings not to neglect or forfeit the inheritance that His exalted station makes so attainable. The Son's future kingship has been at the center of all this discussion.

At the same time, it has been made clear that the King-Son is also a High Priest. The importance of this reality has already been briefly pointed out. Now, however, the Son's priestly role would be considered in detail. In doing so the writer as usual interspersed sections of exposition with passages of exhortation and warning.

A. Introduction: the qualified Priest (5:1-10)

Before enlarging on the ramifications of the priesthood of Christ, the writer took the logical step of showing Christ's qualifications for that role. Though His priesthood has already been assumed, its validity must now be asserted if the admonitions based on it are to carry full weight.

1. THE GENERAL REQUIREMENTS FOR A HIGH PRIEST (5:1-4)

5:1. If it be asked what a **high priest** really is, the answer is easily drawn from the Old Testament institution with which the readers were familiar. Such a person is one of mankind's own number: he **is selected from among men** and he is also their representative **in matters related to God.** These "matters" include the offering of both **gifts** (*dōra*) **and sacrifices** (*thysias*) **for sins** (cf. 8:3; 9:9).

5:2-3. The high priest must also be a man of compassion as the word *metriopathein*, which underlies the phrase **deal gently,** implies. This is the capacity to moderate one's feelings to avoid the extremes of cold indifference and uncontrolled sadness. For an ordinary high priest of the Old Testament, this sympathy grew out of an awareness that **he himself** was **subject to weakness,** prone to failures of his own. Hence in his sacrificial activities he must make the necessary offerings **for his own** and the peoples' **sins.** In this respect alone, as the author will show later (cf. 7:27), Christ did not exactly correspond to the characteristics described here, since He "was without sin" (4:15). But it is also possible that the writer thought of the compassion of the Son-Priest as being far richer than the moderate gentleness he ascribed to other high priests.

5:4. But one thing is certain. The high-priestly office was a divine appointment and could not simply be entered because one aspired to that **honor. Just as Aaron was,** this High Priest must also be **called by God.**

2. THE SON'S CALL TO PRIESTHOOD (5:5-10)

5:5-6. No one is to suppose, the author insisted, that Christ began His priestly functions without the appropriate call from **God.** On the contrary, the same One who declared **Christ** to be the King-Son, declared Him also to be **a Priest forever, in the order of Melchizedek.** In uniting as the author did here the text of Psalm 2:7, which he had quoted before (Heb. 1:5), and the text of Psalm 110:4, he skillfully joined the two great truths about the Messiah which lie at the heart of this epistle. The declaration of Psalm 2 had proclaimed Him the Davidic Heir whose destiny was to rule the nations (cf. Ps. 2:8). But Psalm 110 had also been earlier quoted to much the same effect (cf. Heb. 1:13). Now, however, a further statement of this latter psalm was cited to show that the future Conqueror is also a Priest of a special order. In this way the author united in the person of Christ the dual offices of Priest and King. In doing so the author was perhaps conscious of countering a sectarian position like that evidently current at Qumran, where both a lay, or kingly, Messiah and a priestly Messiah seem to have been anticipated. In any case the two quotations given here from Psalms 2:7 and 110:4 furnish the concentrated essence of the author's thought about the Lord Jesus Christ. It is likely enough that the writer assigned the proclamations of both psalms to the moment when the Son "sat down at the right hand of the Majesty in heaven" (Heb. 1:3).

5:7. But also in other respects Jesus is qualified for His priesthood. If it is a question of offerings (cf. v. 1), it can be pointed out that when Jesus was on earth **He offered up prayers and petitions.** In the expression "offered up" the writer employed the same verb (*prospherō*) he had used in verse 1. The added description, **with loud cries and tears to the One who could save Him from death,** has often been thought to refer to the experience of Gethsemane. But the Greek here seems to reflect the Septuagint rendering of Psalm 22:24. Since that psalm is messianic for this author (cf. Heb. 2:12), it is probable that he actually has the sufferings of the Cross in mind, as does the psalm. This would be appropriate since the cries of the Savior would then be linked directly with His sacrificial work.

That these "cries and tears" were accepted by God is evidenced by the observation, **He was heard because of His reverent submission** (*eulabeias*). To this also Psalm 22 bears reference in that its latter half are the words of One who has emerged from suffering in triumph and praises God for that (cf. Ps. 22:22-31). In fact the psalm's first note of triumph has already been quoted (i.e., Ps. 22:22 in Heb. 2:12). Thus the "reverent" Sufferer was indeed saved from death, and this by means of rising from the dead. Hence too the Resurrection furnishes the decisive proof of God's acceptance of **Jesus'** sacrificial activity.

5:8-10. The whole experience just referred to was a form of education for Jesus before He served His suffering people. His unique relation to God notwithstanding (**He was a Son**), He had to experience the true meaning of obedience in terms of the suffering it entailed. Having done so, He was thereby **made perfect** for the role He would play as His people's Captain and High Priest. That there is an element of mystery in all this need not be denied, but it is no greater than that found in Luke's words: "Jesus grew in wisdom and stature, and in favor with God and men" (Luke 2:52). In a real sense not fully comprehensible, the Incarnation gave the already infinitely wise and perfect Son of God the experiential acquisition of knowledge about the human condition. Suffering thus became a reality that He tasted and from it He can sympathize deeply with His followers. (The Gr. has an interesting play on words in the verbs **He learned** [*emathen*] and **He suffered** [*epathen*].)

This is what the writer had in mind when he affirmed that **He became the Source** (*aitios*) **of eternal salvation for all who obey Him.** The salvation here referred to cannot be distinguished from that which is termed an inheritance (Heb. 1:14). It is also to be identified with the "eternal inheritance" mentioned in 9:15. It should not be confused with the acquisition of eternal life which is conditioned not on obedience but on faith (cf. John 3:16, etc.). Once again the writer had in mind final deliverance from and victory over all enemies and the consequent enjoyment of the "glory" of the many sons and daughters. This kind of salvation is explicitly contingent on obedience and indeed on an obedience modeled after that of Jesus who also **suffered.** It is thus closely related to the saying of the Lord in which He declared, "If anyone would come after Me, he must deny himself and take up his cross and follow Me. For whoever wants to save his life will lose it, but whoever loses his life for Me and for the gospel will save it" (Mark 8:34-35).

The High Priest has become the "Source" of this kind of salvation experience for those who are willing to live obediently. In describing Him this way, the author was chiefly thinking of all the resources that flow from Christ's priestly activities that make a Christian's life of obedience possible. Whatever one's suffering, the High Priest understands it, sympathizes, and makes available the "mercy" and "grace" which are needed to endure it successfully. As the writer will later say, "He is able to save completely those who come to God through Him, because He always lives to intercede for them" (Heb. 7:25). With precisely this end in view Christ **was designated by God to be High Priest in the order of Melchizedek.**

B. The third warning (5:11–6:20)

The author had barely begun his consideration of the topic of the Melchizedek priesthood of Christ. But he felt constrained to pause for another warning section before proceeding further. This was due to the immaturity and sluggishness of his audience which made him wonder how much exposition they could digest. No doubt he hoped to arouse them to greater attentiveness to the truth he wished to unfold. But at the same time he wanted them to face squarely the danger of remaining where they were, since this could lead to tragic retrogression.

1. THE PROBLEM OF IMMATURITY (5:11-14)

5:11-12. We have much to say about this, he began, referring to the subject of Jesus' Melchizedek priesthood. As it turned out, his subsequent discussion was indeed lengthy (7:1–10:18) as well as deep. Accordingly he anticipated that it would be **hard to explain because** his readers were **slow to learn.** They had been Christians a long time, he reminded them, so that **by this time** they **ought to be teachers.** Others who had been in the faith less time than they should be profiting from their instruction. Instead they needed someone to instruct them again in the basics.

In alluding to **the elementary truths** the writer employed an expression which could refer to the letters of the alphabet as they might be learned by a school child. "You seem to need your ABCs reviewed," his rebuke suggested, but at the same time he had no intention of going over them (6:1). What he apparently had mainly in view was their wavering state of mind in regard to the error that sought to lure them away from the faith. If they were being urged, whether by sectarians or others, to abandon their Christian profession, then clearly this called into question the fundamental truths they should have been firm in. The result was, to all appearances, **you need milk, not solid food!** But what he would shortly offer them would be solid food indeed, by which he evidently hoped to pull them dramatically forward in their Christian experience.

5:13-14. It is unsatisfactory to remain a baby in spiritual matters. This is true because a spiritual **infant**, living **on milk . . . is not acquainted with the teaching about righteousness.** The words "not acquainted" (*apeiros*) might be better rendered "inexperienced." It is not so much that a spiritual "infant" lacks information—though at first he obviously does—but rather that he has not yet learned to put "the teaching about righteousness" to effective use. He lacks the skill which goes with maturity and which results in the ability to make appropriate moral choices. Such ability is exactly what is possessed by those **who . . . have trained themselves to distinguish good from evil.** That kind of person can handle **solid food.**

Once more the writer betrayed his concern about his readers' ability to reject the false ideas which confronted them. Had they been sufficiently mature they would be able to "distinguish" those ideas as "evil" over against the truths they should have known were "good." But he feared that this capability was not yet really theirs, though he would make every effort to instill it in them.

2. THE SOLUTION TO THE PROBLEM (6:1-3)

6:1-2. Somewhat surprisingly, despite his estimate of their spiritual state, the author declined to go over old ground. Instead he urged them to go beyond **the elementary teachings about Christ and go on to maturity.** To have reviewed the fundamentals would only have left them where they were. The author preferred "radical surgery" and decided to pull them forward as rapidly as he could. Indeed this was the solution to their problem. If they progressed properly, they would avoid the danger of **laying again the foundation of repentance.** If, as verses 4-6 went on to warn, they were to "fall away," then a foundation would have been laid for a new repentance, but such a repentance is "impossible" (cf. vv. 4, 6). So advance was their only real remedy.

Acts that lead to death literally means "dead works," which expression occurs again in a context where it seems to refer to the Levitical ritual (9:14). Here it would be appropriate in the same sense since many of the readers had been converted to Christianity from Judaism. The rituals they had left behind were lifeless ones, incapable of imparting the experiences of life they had found in Christ. The author implied that they should not return to these dead works in any form since to do so would be to lay again a basis for repenting from them—though such repentance would not be easily reached, however appropriate it might be.

But the foundation they would lay in the unhappy event that they fell away would involve other fundamental truths. These are enumerated in the words, **and of faith in God, instruction about baptisms, the laying on of hands, the resurrection of the dead, and eternal judgment.** The author clearly implied that all these matters belong to the "elementary truths" (5:12) on which the readers gave every indication of wavering. It is likely that each of them was a point at issue in one way or another in the readers' confrontation with those of other persuasions. The return to ordinances, whether in normative or sectarian Judaism, would only be a return to "dead works." One who took that backward step would need to be taught all over again that acceptance was obtained by "faith in God," not by rituals.

Moreover the significance of the various "baptisms" which Christianity knew (John's baptism, Christian baptism proper, or even Spirit baptism) would have to be relearned as well as the basic facts about "laying on of hands." In alluding to matters like these, the writer may have been consciously countering sectarian teachings which may well have offered initiations of their own involving "baptisms" and "laying on of hands." If the sectarians or others, in addition to offering their own initiatory rites, likewise denied the normal Christian eschatological expectations (cf. comments on 4:1, 8-10), then the fundamental doctrines of "the resurrection of the dead and eternal judgment" would also have been at issue. To abandon their Christian profession and "fall away" (6:6) would be to abandon all these doctrines. Whatever the readers had previously learned, they would be giving up. In this sense the foundation would have been laid for relearning them all over again, though the writer held out little hope in his subsequent statements for such a process to take place.

6:3. What he wanted them to do was to press forward. But he was perfectly aware that this required more than his effort to challenge his readers to make progress. God must help and He alone could help them achieve these goals. The writer had said, "Let us . . . go on to maturity" (v. 1), but in a spirit of dependence on divine aid he then added, **and God permitting, we will do so.**

3. THE ALTERNATIVE TO PROGRESS (6:4-8)

In an extremely solemn pronouncement, the author then set forth the tragic alternative to the progress he desired his readers to make. If they did not advance, they would retreat. Should anyone so retreat, his situation would be grim indeed.

6:4-6. This passage has been interpreted in four ways: (1) that the danger of a Christian losing his salvation is described, a view rejected because of biblical assurances that salvation is a work of God which cannot be reversed; (2) that the warning is against mere profession of faith short of salvation, or tasting but not really partaking of salvation (*The New Scofield Reference Bible*, p. 1315); (3) that hypothetically *if* a Christian could lose his salvation, there is no provision for repentance (*The Ryrie Study Bible*, p. 1843); (4) that a warning is given of the danger of a Christian moving from a position of true faith and life to the extent of becoming disqualified for further service (1 Cor. 9:27) and for inheriting millennial glory. The latter is the interpretation adopted here. The entirety of these verses constitutes a single sentence in Greek as well as in the English of the NIV. The central assertion is: **It is impossible for those who have . . . to be brought back to repentance.** Following the words "those who" is a description of the persons whom the writer affirmed cannot possibly be brought back to a state of repentance. The description he gave shows that he had Christians in mind.

To begin with, he described them as individuals **who have once been enlightened.** This is a natural way to refer to the conversion experience (cf. 2 Cor. 4:3-6). The writer's only other use of the verb "enlightened," is Hebrews 10:32, where the reference to true Christian experience can hardly be doubted. In also calling them people **who have tasted the heavenly gift,** he again employed familiar concepts related to initial conversion (cf. John 4:10; Rom. 6:23; James 1:17-18). The effort to evade this conclusion by seeing in the word "tasted" something less than full participation fails—in view of the writer's own use of this word (Heb. 2:9)—to describe Jesus' experience of death. One might also compare 1 Peter 2:3, which quotes Psalm 34:8.

The description is continued with the words **who have shared in the Holy Spirit.** The underlying Greek employs again the word *metochoi*, used in Hebrews 1:9 of the "companions" of the messianic King, and in 3:1, 14 of the Christian readers (and is also used in 12:8). The preceding expression evidently led the author to think about those who had received the gift of the Spirit as a result of their conversions. Finally, there are also those **who have tasted the goodness of the Word of God and the powers of the coming Age.** Here the thought naturally applies to converts whose instruction in "the Word of God" had given them a genuine experience of its "goodness" and who likewise had known the reality of miracles. The word rendered "powers" (*dynameis*) in NIV is the usual one in the New Testament for "miracles" and is an apparent allusion back to the experience mentioned in 2:4. In every way the language fits true Christians with remarkable ease. The effort to see here mere professors of the faith as over against true converts is somewhat forced.

There follows, however, the grim expression **if they fall away.** But the translation does not do full justice to the original language, where there is no hint of a conditional element. The Greek word *parapesontas* is in fact a part of the construction to which the preceding descriptive phrases belong. Thus a more accurate translation would be: "It is impossible for those who have once been enlightened, who have tasted . . . who have shared . . . who have tasted . . . and who have fallen away, to be brought back to repentance." Far from treating the question in any hypothetical way, the writer's language sounds as if he knew of such cases.

Naturally the words "fall away" cannot refer to the loss of eternal life which, as the Gospel of John makes perfectly clear, is the inalienable possession of those who trust Christ for it. But the writer evidently has in mind defection from the faith, that is, apostasy, withdrawal from their Christian profession (cf. Heb. 3:6, 14; 10:23-25, 35-39). The assertion that such a failure is not possible for a regenerate person is a theological proposition which is not supported by the New Testament. Paul knew the dangers of false doctrine to a Christian's faith and spoke of a certain Hymenaeus and Philetus who said "that the resurrection has already taken place, and they destroy the faith of some" (2 Tim. 2:17-18). The author of Hebrews was a solid realist who took assaults against the faith of his readers with great seriousness. And he warned that those who succumb, that is, "fall away," after all of the great spiritual privileges they had experienced, could not **be brought back to repentance.**

The reason is expressed in the words **because to their loss they are crucifying the Son of God all over again and subjecting Him to public disgrace.** The words "to their loss" might be better rendered "with respect to themselves." Those who renounce their Christian faith are, with respect to their own conduct and attitude, taking a step that amounts to a fresh public rejection of Christ. When they first trusted Him, they thereby acknowledged that His crucifixion had been unjust and the result of man's sinful rejection of the Savior. But by renouncing this opinion, they reaffirmed the view of Jesus' enemies that He deserved to die on a cross. In this sense, "they [were] crucifying the Son of God all over again." Since the original Crucifixion was especially the work of the Jewish nation, if the readers were Jews being lured back into some form of their ancestral religion, the writer's words made a particular point. Their apostasy would be like stepping back over the line again and once more expressing solidarity with their compatriots who wanted Jesus put on the cross. That this was most serious was precisely the writer's point. Such persons could not be won back to the state of repentance which marked their original conversion to Christianity. In affirming this, the author's words suggested a deep hardening of their hearts against all efforts to win them back, not to Christian conversion, but to Christian commitment.

6:7-8. An illustration from nature now drives home the writer's point. Whenever **rain**-soaked ground is properly productive, it **receives the blessing of God.** Here the writer compared the spiritual privileges he had just enumerated (vv. 4-5) to a heavenly rain descending on the life of a Christian. Their effect should be a **crop useful to those for whom it is farmed**—a reference perhaps to the way other Christians benefit from the lives of fruitful believers (cf. v. 10). Such productivity brings divine blessings on fruitful believers' lives.

But suppose the land that has received this "rain" is unproductive? Though the NIV introduces the word **land** for a second time in verse 8, the original text seems to relate the statement directly to the "land" mentioned in verse 7. A clearer rendering would be: "But when (or, if) it produces thorns and thistles. . . ." The point is that when a plot of ground that has been rained on is productive, God blesses it. But if it only **produces thorns and thistles,** it **is worthless** (*adokimos*, "disapproved"; cf. 1 Cor. 9:27) **and is in danger of being cursed. In the end it will be burned.** The metaphor recalls God's original curse on the ground (Gen. 3:17-19) and suggests that an unproductive Christian life ultimately ("in the end") falls under the severe condemnation of God and is subject to His blazing wrath and judgment (cf. Heb. 10:27).

Naturally the reference to "burned" has caused many to think of hell, but there is nothing in the text to suggest this. God's anger against His failing people in the Old Testament is often likened to the burning of fire (cf., e.g., Isa. 9:18-19; 10:17). Even this writer could say, with intense metaphorical effect, "Our God is a consuming fire" (Heb. 12:29). In fact, to think of hell here is to betray inattention to the imagery employed by the author. The burning of a field to destroy the rank growth it had produced was a practice known in ancient times. Its aim was not the destruction of the field itself (which, of course, the fire could not effect), but the destruction of the unwanted produce of the field. Thereafter the field might be serviceable for cultivation.

By choosing this kind of metaphor, the author showed that he did not totally despair of those who took the backward step he was warning against. To be sure, at least prior to severe divine judgment, all efforts to recall such people to Christian faith are futile (6:4-6), but it cannot be said that the impossibility applies in an absolute sense to God Himself. What the author probably meant is that nothing can deter apostates from the fiery retribution toward which they are headed, but once their "land" has been burned it is another matter. Paul believed that those who "have shipwrecked their faith" could profit by the retributive experiences to which they were exposed as a result (1 Tim. 1:19-20). But of course the writer of Hebrews was reticent about the issue of subsequent restoration. That some might not respond to the chastisement was perhaps in mind, but he was mainly concerned about warning against the course of action which leads to such calamitous divine judgment. Nevertheless his deft choice of this agricultural image serves to disclose that the "burning" is both temporary and essentially hopeful.

4. THE CONCLUDING ENCOURAGEMENT
(6:9-20)

The author knew that his words were both heavy and solemn, though not to the same degree that subsequent exposition has often made them. He felt that a word of encouragement was then in order. This pattern—stern warning followed by warm encouragement—has already appeared in the previous warning section (3:1-4:16) which concluded in a distinctly positive manner (4:14-16). Similarly the writer drew his warning section here to a conclusion that is alive with hope.

6:9. The author did not want his readers to believe that he had despaired of them. Instead he was convinced **of better things in your case.** The words are like those of a pastor who, after warning his congregation of a dangerous course of action, might say: "But I am sure you people would never do that!" The words are not a theological proposition, as they are sometimes wrongly taken, but an expression of hope. The "better things" about which he had confidence were the **things that accompany salvation.** The "salvation" referred to should be understood in congruity with its meaning in 1:14. It is that experience of victory and glory which the persevering companions of the King inherit. It is also the inheritance-rest which the persevering are allowed to enter. The writer insisted here that he had every expectation that the readers would persevere to the end and acquire these blessings, even though he felt constrained to warn them against a contrary course.

6:10. The author knew that **God is not unjust.** His readers would not be forsaken. God would remember their **work and the love** they had **shown Him** in their helping other believers. The author's words were a skilled touch on the hearts of his fellow Christians. In speaking of them, he reminded his readers of what they had done for their fellow Christians and were still doing. He thus encouraged them to keep it up while assuring them that God was conscious of all their aid and available to help them in any needed way.

6:11-12. If they would only diligently hold onto the good course they already were pursuing—and of which God was fully mindful—they would thus guarantee the **hope** which is duly awarded to those who so persevere. He added, **We do not want you to become lazy.** The word "lazy" (*nōthroi*) is the same word rendered "slow" in 5:11 in the phrase "slow to learn." The sluggishness which marked their immaturity was to be shrugged off. (The Gr. of this verse can mean, "We do not want you to *be* lazy" rather than "*become* lazy.") Their real goal should be the inheritance that is set before them. They were to be imitators of **those who through faith and patience inherit** God's promises.

6:13-15. If the readers were searching for models to "imitate," there was the case of **Abraham** who received an oath from **God,** the **promise** that assured the multiplication of his seed. In due time his patience was rewarded in that he (lit.) "received the promise." Since the reference is to the promise given in Genesis 22:17 after the offering of Isaac, the author may have been thinking of the reception of the promise itself as the reward. In that case the idea is that after Abraham had patiently endured (the test involving Isaac), he obtained the promise. **Waiting patiently** translates the participle *makrothymēsas,* related to the noun "patience," *makrothymias* in Hebrews 6:12. This word, common in the New Testament, refers to the ability to hold one's feelings in restraint without retaliation against others (cf., e.g., Col. 1:11; 3:12; James 5:7-8, 10). A synonym, *hypomonē,* "endurance, perseverance," means the ability to remain steadfast in the face of undesirable circumstances; cf. Col. 1:11; Heb. 12:1-3, 7; James 5:11).

6:16-18. At this point Abraham is left behind as a model and **the oath** made to him is treated as for the benefit of Christians generally. That the promise of Genesis 22:18 had messianic aspects is clear from these words: "Through your offspring all nations on earth will be blessed." Then the author of Hebrews affirmed that the messianic hope which the promise entailed was sure, not only to Abraham, but also to the Christian **heirs of what was promised.** As in human affairs an oath **puts an end to all arguments,** so too there can be no argument about this expectation since God **confirmed it with an oath.** If anyone, such as a sectarian, denied this eschatological anticipation, he was flying in the face of the strongest possible divine guarantee. Not only was it **impossible for God to lie,** but His ever truthful Word was supported in this case by His oath. These are the **two unchangeable things,** which encourage those who **take hold of the hope.**

6:19-20. The image suggested in verse 18 by the words "fled to take hold" of hope was that of a fortified refuge. By a swift change in his figure, the writer then suggested the thought of a harbor where **the soul** may securely drop **anchor.** That anchor has been carried to the safest point of all—**the inner sanctuary behind the curtain**—by **Jesus, who went before us.** The Greek *prodromos* ("who went before us") suggests a "forerunner," and if the harbor imagery is still in mind it recalls the role of sailors who leave their ship in a smaller craft in order to carry the anchor forward to a place where it can be firmly lodged. So too the Lord Jesus, by His entrance into the heavenly sanctuary where He functions as **a High Priest forever,** has given to a Christian's hope an anchorage from which it cannot be shaken loose. Since, therefore, the readers' hope was sure, they could cling to it tenaciously right to the very end.

C. The greater Priest and His greater ministry (7:1–10:18)

Here begins the longest single expository passage in the epistle. Its very length suggests its importance. Its theme is the core theme of Hebrews. The real resource of the readership, in the midst of their pressures, is the high priesthood of Christ. They must realize the greatness of that priesthood, its superiority to the Levitical institutions, and the perfect access they have to it on the basis of Christ's death.

1. THE SUPERIOR PRIEST (CHAP. 7)

The writer returned to the theme he had introduced in 5:1-10, but which he doubted his readers would comprehend (cf. 5:11). In the conclusion of his most recent warning (5:11–6:20) he had renewed the subject of the Melchizedek priesthood (6:19-20). The exposition of that theme is now given.

a. The greatness of Melchizedek (7:1-10)

7:1-3. To begin with, the writer set forth the personal greatness of the Old Testament figure **Melchizedek.** As a fit prototype for Christ Himself, Melchizedek was both a **king and a priest.** He both **blessed . . . Abraham** and received his tithes. Melchizedek's name and title suggest the messianic attributes of **righteousness** and **peace.** So far as the Old Testament record is concerned, he was **without father or mother, without genealogy, without beginning of days or end of life.** In saying this, the author is often taken to mean that the silence of the inspired record presents Melchizedek as typologically **like the Son of God.** But though this is possibly true, the statements do not sound like it, particularly the assertion that Melchizedek **remains a priest forever.** The word "forever" translates a phrase (*eis to diēnekes*) that occurs only in Hebrews (here and in 10:12, 14) and means "continuously" or "uninterruptedly."

It seems more natural that the author meant that Melchizedek belonged to an order in which there was no end to the priesthood of those engaged in it. (He later said in 7:8 that Melchizedek "is declared to be living.") If this is correct, Melchizedek may have been an angelic being who reigned for a time at Salem (i.e., Jerusalem). If so, the statement that he was "without beginning of days" would not mean that he was eternal, but simply that he had a pretemporal origin. Nor would this concept of Melchizedek as an angel elevate him to the same level as God's Son, since the author painstakingly asserted the Son's superiority to the angels (1:5-14). There is indeed evidence that, at Qumran, Melchizedek was regarded as an angelic personage. If this is the case in Hebrews, then the Son of God is the *High* Priest in an order in which Melchizedek is simply a priest.

7:4-10. The personal superiority of Melchizedek over the patriarch Abraham is guaranteed by the fact that **Abraham gave him a 10th of the plunder.** And though Melchizedek had no connections with the Levitical order, still he both received this tithe from **Abraham and blessed him.** This act of blessing reinforced his superiority to the patriarch. Moreover, he was evidently superior to the Levites as well, who collected tithes but were nonetheless subject to death. By contrast the tithe collected from Abraham was collected **by him who is declared to be living.** Furthermore, in a sense Levi paid the tithe **through Abraham because . . . Levi was still in the body of his ancestor.** The original expression, rendered **one might even say,** probably means something like "so to speak." The writer knew that Levi did not literally pay tithes to Melchizedek, but on the principle that an ancestor is greater than his descendants, Abraham's act affirmed Melchizedek's superiority even to the Levitical priests themselves. Melchizedek thus has a greatness which the Old Testament record clearly attests.

b. The new priesthood supersedes the old (7:11-19)

Having established Melchizedek's greatness both personally and in comparison with Abraham and Levi, the writer was ready for a new point. This superiority was needed, since the Law was superseded. The inadequacy of the legal and Levitical systems had to be replaced by something better.

7:11-12. In the simplest manner, the author argued for the imperfection of **the Leviticial priesthood** on the basis of God's promise (recorded in Ps. 110:4) that a new Priest would arise belonging to an order other than Aaron's. Since there was **a change of the priesthood,** it follows that the whole legal system on which the Leviticial institutions were predicated also had to be changed. Here the writer virtually affirmed the Pauline truth that "you are not under Law" (Rom. 6:14), though he approached it from a different angle.

7:13-14. Leviticial priesthood was superseded by the fact that **our Lord descended from Judah. That tribe** had no role in the Leviticial institutions, and the things God had said about the new Priest applied to One from Judah, which is proof that a change was made.

7:15-19. A further proof (**and what we have said is even more clear**) is found in the consideration that the new Priest has **an indestructible** (*akatalytou*) **life.** Psalm 110:4 was here quoted again to show that such an unending life is an inherent part of the order of Melchizedek. (The author probably had this text in mind when he made the statement about Melchizedek in Heb. 7:8.) Thus the new Priest does not hold His office **on the basis of a regulation as to His ancestry.** This rendering freely translates the original which is more nearly represented by the words "not after the Law of a carnal commandment." The writer seems to mean that the Law which regulated the priestly institution and succession was "carnal" or "fleshly," not in the sense of being evil, but in the sense that it pertained to people of flesh who died. But this **former regulation** has been replaced because of its inherent weakness and uselessness. What has replaced it is the new priesthood which constitutes **a better hope . . . by which we draw near to God.** Thus the writer established the point that **the Law** which **made nothing perfect** was replaced by a priestly institution which *can* accomplish its objectives in those who approach God through it.

c. The superiority of the new Priest (7:20-28)

If, as the author has shown, Melchizedek was greater than Levi (vv. 4-10) and the new priesthood necessarily abrogates the old (vv. 11-19), then the new Priest has to be greater than the Levitical priests.

7:20-22. The priesthood of Christ differs dramatically from the Levitical priesthood in that it was instituted **with an oath.** By contrast, the descendants of Aaron assumed their jobs **without any oath.** The writer then quoted again the divine oath of Psalm 110:4 whose very solemnity argues for the superiority of the new Priest, who was majestically inducted into His role. Moreover, **because of this oath, Jesus** became **the guarantee** (*engyos*, used only here in the NT) **of a better covenant.** In His own person, Jesus assured the superiority of the new order over the old because His oath secured His permanent installation in the priestly office.

7:23-25. No Old Testament priest ever functioned in this permanent way, **since** all were subject to **death.** But the **permanent priesthood** of Jesus gives Him the capacity to carry His saving work to completion. When the writer asserted that **He is able to save completely,** he continued to have in mind the salvation-inheritance first referred to in 1:14. The readers were to hold fast to their professions of faith and to continue numbering themselves among **those who come to God through Him,** knowing that He can see them through every trial and difficulty right to the end of the road **because He always lives to intercede for them.** In saying this, the author reverted again to a truth he had already enunciated (4:14-16) where he had invited the readers to avail themselves boldly of the mercy and grace accessible to them through Jesus' priesthood. As they did so, they would find that their Captain and High Priest could get the job done! He could lead them victoriously into the glory of the many sons. In this way He saves "completely."

7:26-28. After all, He is the kind of **High Priest** who **meets our need.** His character is utterly without blemish and He has been **exalted above the heavens.** Consequently too, He had no need like the Levitical priests **to offer sacrifices day after day, first for His own sins, and then for the sins of the people.** At first sight verses 27-28 seem to refer to the ritual of the Day of Atonement (Lev. 16), but that was yearly, not "day after day." Probably these verses telescope that ritual with the regular sacrificial routine. There seems to be some evidence from Jewish tradition that a high priest was thought to offer daily sacrifice, and the stipulations of Leviticus 6:12-13 may refer to him.

In any case the new Priest had no need either for sacrifices for Himself or for repeated sacrifices for others. His one act of self-offering was definitive and sufficient. Of this more will be said in Hebrews 9 and 10. Here the author was content to conclude that, in contrast with the Levitical priests, the Son is a perfected High Priest. The reference to the fact that He **has been made perfect forever** recalls 5:8-10. The sufferings of the Son, here referred to as His sacrificial offering of Himself **once for all** (*ephapax*, cf. 9:12; 10:10; also cf. *hapax*, "once" in 9:26, 28), are what have constituted Him "perfect" for His role in God's presence where He intercedes for His followers. Thus **the Law** appointed **as high priests** those **who were weak, but the oath, which came after the Law, appointed** this kind of Priest. Accordingly the readers could go to Him at all times, fully confident of His capacity to serve their every need.

2. THE SUPERIOR SERVICE (8:1–10:18)

In chapter 7, the writer had considered the superiority of the new priesthood. It follows that such a priesthood must have a superior priestly ministry. That it does is unfolded in this section of the epistle. In the process, the letter reveals that the New Covenant underlies this newer priestly service.

a. Introduction to the superior service (8:1-6)

8:1-2. The author of Hebrews opened this passage with a clear transitional statement: **the point of what we are saying is this.** He wished to summarize what he had been teaching and go on to new ideas. By referring to the Lord Jesus as **a High Priest who sat down at the right hand . . . of the Majesty in heaven,** he picked up the wording of 1:3 (cf. 10:12; 12:2). What he meant by this truth is reasonably clear but will be elaborated further in what follows. In the expression **who serves in the sanctuary, the true tabernacle,** he touched on ideas already implicit in his foregoing instruction, yet used new terms to describe them. The idea of service (*leitourgos,* a "minister" in the priestly sense) is in reality the new theme. The "true tabernacle" is the heavenly sphere where that service takes place.

8:3-6. Here is an initial, preliminary elaboration of the new theme. Since the role of a priest involved **gifts** (*dōra*) **and sacrifices** (*thysias;* cf. 5:1; 9:9), it follows that this new High Priest should **have something to offer.** Nevertheless His service cannot be an earthly one since the Levitical ritual of sacrifice continued. (These words imply that the Jewish temple was still standing.) But the **sanctuary** used for that is a mere **copy** (*hypodeigmati;* cf. 9:23-24) **and shadow** (*skia;* cf. 10:1) of the heavenly one in which the new Priest ministers. Its status as a "shadow sanctuary" was secured when Moses erected **the tabernacle** (prototype of the temple) under strict divine direction (8:5). But Jesus' ministry surpasses that of the Levitical priests just as the covenant He mediates supersedes theirs. (The word **Mediator** is used of Jesus by the author three times—8:6; 9:15; 12:24.) The word **ministry** (*leitourgia,* cf. "serves," 8:2) again strikes the pivotal note, but it is now added that the superiority of the new priestly service is related to a superior covenant, which in turn **is founded on better promises.** Both the covenant and its promises will now be considered.

b. The superior covenant (8:7–9:15)

8:7. That there is a promise of a New Covenant the writer will shortly prove by quoting Jeremiah 31:31-34. By doing so, he argued that such a promise demonstrates the inadequacy of the old one.

8:8-12. The promise of a New Covenant was made, the writer pointed out, in a passage where God **found fault with the people.** The Old Covenant failed because of the sinfulness of the nation, for which it had no remedy. The **New Covenant,** however, has such a remedy.

In the passage quoted, there is first the prediction that a New Covenant will be made (v. 8) followed by a strong declaration that it will differ from the previous one (v. 9). Then follows (vv. 10-12) a description of the superior accomplishments, or enablements, of the promised **covenant.** These are: (1) an inner inclination to obey (God will put His **laws in their minds and write them on their hearts),** (2) a firm relationship with God (**I will be their God, and they will be My people**), (3) the knowledge of God (**they will all know Me**), and (4) the forgiveness of sins (**I will forgive their wickedness and will remember their sins no more**). These are the "better promises" alluded to in verse 6.

It is clear that all these benefits belong, in fact, to all the regenerate of every age since the Cross. Though the New Covenant is specifically focused on Israel (cf. **house of Israel** and "house of Judah" in Jer. 31:31), it is clear that Christians of the present time also stand under its blessings (cf. Luke 22:20; 1 Cor. 11:25; 2 Cor. 3:6). This perception does not lead to an inappropriate confusion between Israel and the church. The New Covenant is God's appointed vehicle for fulfilling the Abrahamic blessings to Israel. But the Abrahamic Covenant also promised universal blessing, so the New Covenant becomes as well God's vehicle of salvation for believers since the Cross. To say this is not to say anything more than Jesus did when He declared that "salvation is from the Jews" (John 4:22). In no way should this impede the perception of the Christian church as a unique, interadvent body, closely united to Christ as His bride and significantly distinct from the nation of Israel. But inasmuch as all salvation is through the Cross of Christ, it is also through the blood of the New Covenant.

8:13. From the Old Testament prophecy he had just quoted, the writer then drew the justifiable conclusion that the Old Covenant was **obsolete** (*palaioumenon*) **and aging** and would **soon disappear.** The ceremonies still being conducted under it (cf. vv. 4-5) were spiritually anachronistic and the author's words suggest that he recalled the prophecy of Jesus that the temple in Jerusalem would be destroyed (Matt. 24:1-2). Probably this prophecy was fulfilled soon after Hebrews was written. If so, it was a dramatic confirmation of the writer's thesis about the Old Covenant.

9:1-5. With regard to the "aging" First Covenant, the writer wished to discuss that covenant's **regulations for worship** and its **earthly sanctuary**. These he highlighted in order to contrast them with the superior features of the New-Covenant ministry. How "earthly" (*kosmikon*, v. 1), or mundane, that first sanctuary was, he emphasized by reviewing the material objects associated with it. All these had typological value, but the author could not **discuss these things in detail** at the time (v. 5). He confined himself to the chief features of the comparison he wished to make.

9:6-10. The "regulations for worship" mentioned in verse 1 were now dealt with so that they underlined the insufficiency of the Old-Covenant service. Whereas **the outer room** of the tabernacle could be **entered regularly** by the officiating **priests**, it was only on the Day of Atonement (cf. Lev. 16) that **the high priest entered the inner room** (i.e., the "holy of holies") and then only with sacrificial **blood, which he offered for himself and for the sins the people had committed in ignorance**. This restricted access clearly demonstrated that a true entrance into God's presence (symbolized by **the most holy place**) **had not yet been disclosed**. That at least was the message **the Holy Spirit** intended to communicate by this arrangement. The Levitical arrangements were designed to convey the idea that the true way to God did not lie in them. What this indicates **for the present time** is that the Old-Covenant sacrificial system did not meet human need at its deepest level. It could not **clear the conscience of the worshiper**. Hence the regulations which formed part of the observant worshiper's adherence to this system were chiefly concerned with externals which were only meant to apply **until the time of the new order**.

The words of Hebrews 9:10 probably refer to sectarians for whom **food** laws and **ceremonial washings** retained great importance. The readers must remember the transitory nature of these things under the "aging" covenant and should not return to them.

9:11-12. The author then brought the discussion which began in 8:7 to a fitting conclusion. He had shown that the Old Testament anticipated a better New Covenant (8:7-13) and that the ritual of the Old Covenant, carried on in an "earthly sanctuary," pointed to its own inadequacy (9:1-10). Now he set forth the superiority of Christ's service as Mediator of the New Covenant (vv. 11-15).

The NIV rendering of verse 11 is questionable. It is not likely the writer meant to say that **Christ . . . went through the greater and more perfect tabernacle**, since this cannot be distinguished from "the most holy place" which He entered according to verse 12. It is probably better to take the original word translated "through" (*dia*) and connect it with **came as High Priest of the good things that are already here** (or, per most Gr. mss., "the good things which were to come"). In that case, instead of "through" the word can be translated "in connection with" and the total statement expresses the idea that Christ's high-priesthood is linked with "the greater and more perfect tabernacle" rather than the "earthly" one previously described (vv. 1-5).

When Christ **entered the most holy place once for all by His own blood** (v. 12; cf. Christ's blood in v. 14; 10:19, 29; 13:20) rather than by animal blood, He likewise demonstrated the superiority of His service because His blood had **obtained eternal redemption**. Thus the value of His sacrifice is immeasurably greater than the animal offerings of the Levitical arrangements. A perfect ransom price had been paid for human "redemption," and because it need not be paid again (this sacrificial act was "once for all," *ephapax*; cf. 7:27; 10:10) that redemption is an "eternal" one.

9:13-14. This "eternal redemption" through which the blessings of the New Covenant (cf. 8:10-12) have reached all believers, should affect the way believers serve God. Old-Covenant rituals served for the **ceremonially unclean** and only made them **outwardly clean**. But **the blood of Christ** can do much more. His was a sacrifice of infinite value because **through the eternal Spirit He offered Himself unblemished to God**. With this lovely assertion, the writer of Hebrews involved all three Persons of the Godhead in the sacrifice of Christ, which magnifies the greatness of His redemptive offering. "Unblemished" (*amōmon*) fittingly describes Christ's perfection (cf. 4:15; 7:26) for it is also used of spotless animals brought for sacrifice.

Such a great accomplishment ought to **cleanse our consciences from acts that lead to death,** but the expression "acts that lead to death" is literally "dead works" which in this context seems to refer to the Levitical rituals that, in contrast with the work of Christ, can never impart spiritual life. As also in 6:1, where such "acts that lead to death" are referred to, the writer wished his readers would give up all thoughts of returning to Old-Covenant rituals. Their consciences ought to be perfectly free from any need to engage in such things and, retaining their confidence in the perfect efficacy of the Cross, they should hold fast their profession and **serve the living God** within the New-Covenant arrangements.

9:15. To do so is to retain the hope of an **eternal inheritance** (cf. "eternal redemption" in v. 12 and "the eternal Spirit" in v. 14) which has been **promised** to recipients of New-Covenant life. **Christ is the Mediator** (cf. 8:6; 12:24) of that **covenant,** and the "inheritance" is available to **those who are called** since the death of the Mediator has freed them from all guilt derived **from the sins committed under the First Covenant.**

The author was here perhaps countering the appeal of the sectarians, or others, to the "guilt feelings" of those Jewish Christians who must often have been charged with deserting their ancestral faith. But the blood of Christ ought to quiet their consciences permanently and lead them to pursue the "eternal inheritance" which the New-Covenant relationship brought them. Of course the writer meant here as elsewhere that it is only "through faith and patience" that his readers could "inherit what has been promised" (6:12); but if they would rest their consciences at the Cross, they could pursue this heirship undistractedly.

c. *The superior sacrifice (9:16-28)*

The author has made it clear that Christ's death has instituted a better covenant (vv. 11-15) which is superior to animal offerings (vv. 12-14). But the need for such a sacrifice has yet to be explored. So a key word in this subunit is "necessary" (*anankē,* vv. 16, 23). In the process of exploring this point, the author clearly underscored the measureless superiority of the sacrificial death of Christ.

9:16-17. In opening the new unit of thought, the writer employed a swift semantic shift in which he treated the Greek word for "covenant" (*diathēkē*) in the sense of **a will.** While "covenants" and "wills" are not in all respects identical, the author meant that in the last analysis the New Covenant is really a testamentary disposition. Like human wills, all the arrangements are secured by the testator and its beneficiaries need only accept its terms.

Treating the New Covenant in this way, the author argued that its **force**—like that of all human wills—depends on **the death of the one who made it.** That is when it **takes effect.**

9:18-21. The Old **Covenant** was also **put into effect** with **blood.** Drawing on material that may have partly been derived from traditions known to the writer but not specified in the Old Testament, he described the inauguration of the Old Covenant through ceremonies involving the sprinkling of sacrificial **blood.**

9:22. This verse applies to the Old-Covenant institutions, and the words **nearly everything** leave room for the flour offering which a poor Israelite might bring for his sin (Lev. 5:11-13). But the writer was thinking of the system as a whole and the ritual of the Day of Atonement that pertained to the totality of the nation's sins, which showed that **without the shedding of blood there is no forgiveness.** These words also constitute a principle that is true in the New Covenant.

9:23. In connection with the New Covenant, the writer then enunciated his basic principle: the death of Christ **was necessary.** Mere **copies** (*hypodeigmata;* cf. 8:5; 9:24) **of the heavenly things** might be adequately hallowed by animal sacrifices, **but the heavenly things themselves** required more than that. The expression "heavenly things" referred quite generally to the new priestly arrangements, which have heaven as their focal point. These arrangements involve dealing with people's sin and must thus be inaugurated with a sacrifice adequate to "do away" with that sin (cf. v. 26). The death of Christ meets this requirement.

9:24-26. Christ was appointed as High Priest of the New Covenant to represent sinful people in **heaven itself,** that is, in the presence of God. So His sacrifice had to be greater than that which allowed entrance into a mere **man-made sanctuary that was only a copy** (*antitypa*) **of the true one.** Nor could Christ offer repeated sacrifices as in the Levitical institution, for that would have required Him to die **many times since the Creation of the world.** Instead, as is obvious, the heavenly ministry of Christ called for a thoroughly sufficient, one-time sacrifice. This is precisely why He **appeared once for all** (*hapax*, cf. v. 28; also cf. *ephapax* in 7:27; 9:12; 10:10) **at the end of the ages to do away with sin,** which the priests in the old arrangement could not do. By the phrase "end of the ages" the writer evidently meant the climax of the Old Testament eras as well as the imminency of the climax of all things. He will shortly refer to Christ's second advent.

9:27-28. With this observation, eschatological realities come into focus. Humans are sinful creatures **destined to die once, and after that to face judgment.** But this danger is turned aside by the fact that **Christ was sacrificed once** (*hapax,* cf. v. 26) **to take away the sins of many people.** The recurrence of "once" (9:26, 28) and of "once for all" (7:27; 9:12; 10:10) stresses the finality and the singleness of Christ's sacrificial work in contrast with the repeated Levite ministrations. In addition, the "once"-sacrifice of Christ (vv. 26, 28) compares with the "once"-death of each person (v. 27). Now those **who are waiting** (*apekdechomenois;* used seven times in the NT of the return of Christ: Rom. 8:19, 23, 25; 1 Cor. 1:7; Gal. 5:5; Phil. 3:20; Heb. 9:28) **for Him** can look forward to His coming, not with a fearful expectation of judgment, but with the anticipation of **salvation.**

His first advent was to bear sins away—but His second will be **not to bear sin** (lit., "without [reference to] sins").

Deftly the author implied that "those who are waiting for Him" constitute a smaller circle than those whom His death has benefited. They are, as all his previous exhortations reveal, the ones who "hold firmly till the end the confidence we had at first" (3:14). The "salvation" He will bring them at His second coming will be the "eternal inheritance" of which they are heirs (cf. 9:15; 1:14).

d. The superior effect of the new priesthood (10:1-18)

This is the final subsection of the expository unit that began at 7:1. In chapter 7 the author argued for the superiority of Christ, as a Priest after the order of Melchizedek, over the Levitical priests. In 8:1–10:18 he argued the superiority of Christ's priestly ministry which is based on a superior covenant (8:7–9:15) and entailed a superior sacrifice (9:16-28). Now he argued that the superior sacrifice perfects the New-Covenant worshiper.

10:1. By virtue of its anticipatory character, **the Law could never ... make perfect those who draw near to worship.** By "make perfect" the writer did not mean sinless perfection. As the following discussion shows, he was concerned with that definitive removal of guilt which makes free access to God possible for worshipers who trust in the sufficiency of the Cross.

10:2-4. The continous sacrifices of the old order which are "repeated endlessly year after year" (v. 1) testify to the Law's incapacity to "perfect" its **worshipers.** Far from enabling them to achieve a standing before God in which they **would no longer have felt guilty for their sins,** the yearly rituals (of the Day of Atonement) served as a kind of **annual reminder of sins,** since animal blood has no power **to take away sins.**

10:5-7. It was precisely for this reason that an Old Testament prophecy (Ps. 40:6-8) recorded the words of the One who would do what God really wanted. This psalm prophetically anticipated some of Christ's words at his First Advent. The phrase **a body You prepared for Me** is one Septuagint rendering of the Hebrew expression "You have dug ears for Me." The Greek translator whose version the author of Hebrews used (obviously translating with the help of the Holy Spirit), construed the Hebrew text as a kind of figure of speech (technically called synecdoche) in which a part is put for the whole. If God is to "dig out ears" He must "prepare a body." This interpretation is both valid and correct as its quotation in Hebrews proves. In the "body" which He assumed in Incarnation,

Christ could say that He had **come to** achieve what the Old-Covenant sacrifices never achieved, the perfecting of New-Covenant worshipers. In this sense He did God's will.

10:8-10. The writer then expounded the text he had just quoted. In the words **He sets aside the first to establish the second** (v. 9), the author referred to the setting aside of the Old-Covenant sacrifices which did not ultimately satisfy God. What was established was God's will, and it was **by that will** that **we have been made holy through the sacrifice of the body of Jesus Christ once for all** (*ephapax*; cf. 7:27; 9:12).

The words rendered "made holy" involve a single Greek word (*hēgiasmenoi*) often rendered "sanctify" (cf. 10:14, 29). Here it occurs in a tense that makes it plain, along with the rest of the statement, that the sanctification is an accomplished fact. Nowhere in Hebrews does the writer refer to the "progressive sanctification" of a believer's life. Instead sanctification is for him a functional equivalent of the Pauline concept of justification. By the sanctification which is accomplished through the death of Christ, New-Covenant worshipers are perfected for guilt-free service to God (cf. 2:11).

10:11-14. The truth just stated is reinforced by a contrast with the Levitical priesthood. Levite priests could never sit down on the job since their sacrificial services were never completed. But Christ's sitting **at the right hand of God** (cf. 1:3; 8:1; 12:2) is both a signal that His sacrifice was offered **for all time** and also that He can now confidently await final victory over **His enemies.** The words "for all time" (*eis to diēnekes*) are translated "forever" in verse 14 (see comments on 7:3). Thus by a single sacrifice (**one sacrifice,** 10:12, 14)—in contrast with the many sacrifices offered by the priests **day after day** and **again and again** . . . **He has made perfect forever those who are being made holy.** The translation "are being made holy" sounds like a continuing process. But this ignores the force of the expression "made holy" in verse 10. A better rendering is, "them who are sanctified" (*tous hagiazomenous*; cf. v. 29). "The sanctified" have a status in God's presence that is "perfect" (cf. 11:40; 12:23) in the sense that they approach Him with the full acceptance gained through the death of Christ (cf. 10:19-22).

10:15-18. Reverting to his basic text on the benefits of the New Covenant (cf. 8:8-12), the author requoted a portion of it (in 10:16 he quoted Jer. 31:33; and in Heb. 10:17, Jer. 31:34) to drive home his point. The text is a testimony given by God's **Holy Spirit,** and shows that final forgiveness, such as the New Covenant promised, meant that there was no further need for any **sacrifice for sin.** As the writer will shortly show, a person who turns from the one sufficient sacrifice of Christ has no real sacrifice to which he can turn (cf. Heb. 10:26).

D. The fourth warning (10:19-39)

In some ways this warning section is the most pointed and stern of all. It is also climactic. It follows the completion of the epistle's exposition of the high priestly role and service of Jesus Christ, so it gathers up the implications of these truths and drives them home with full force. But as usual, the writer mingled a solemn warning with his words of consolation and encouragement.

1. THE BASIC ADMONITION (10:19-25)

10:19-22. The central assertion of these verses is in the words, **Therefore, brothers** (cf. 3:1, 12) . . . **let us draw near to God.** The intervening material, beginning with the word **since,** gives the basis for the author's call to approach God. The readers are New-Covenant people ("brothers") who should **have confidence** (*parrēsian*; cf. 3:6; 4:16; 10:35) to come into the very presence of God. This idea is enriched by the use of Old-Covenant imagery. God's presence in **the most holy place** and **the curtain** that once was a barrier to man is now no longer so. It symbolized Christ's **body,** so the writer may have had in mind the rending of the temple curtain at the time of Christ's death (Matt. 27:51). At any rate His death gave believers the needed access and route to God, aptly described as **new** (*prosphaton,* "recent," occurring only here in the NT) **and living,** that is, partaking of the fresh and vitalizing realities of the New Covenant.

But in addition, the call to draw near is appropriate **since we have a great Priest over the house of God** with all that this entails in the light of the writer's previous discussion. So the approach of believers should be **with a sincere** (*alēthinēs*, "true, dependable," from *aletheia*, "truth") **heart in full assurance of faith.** There ought to be no wavering in regard to these superlative realities. Rather each New-Covenant worshiper should approach God in the conscious enjoyment of freedom from guilt (**having our hearts sprinkled to cleanse us from a guilty conscience**) and with a sense of the personal holiness that Christ's sacrifice makes possible (**having our bodies washed with pure water**). The writer's words are probably an exhortation to lay hold consciously of the cleansing benefits of Christ's Cross and to draw near to God in enjoying them, putting away inward guilt and outward impurity. These verses approximate 1 John 1:9.

10:23-25. This kind of confident access to God necessarily entails that believers **hold unswervingly to the hope we profess** with full confidence in the reliability of God's promises. The writer revealed in these verses that his concern for fidelity to the faith is not an abstraction, but a confrontation with real danger. There was an urgent need for mutual concern and exhortation (**toward love and good deeds**) within the church he wrote to. His readers were not to abandon **meeting together, as some** were **doing.** Already there seemed to have been defections from their ranks, though his words might have applied to other churches where such desertions had occurred. In any case their mutual efforts to spur one another on should increase **as** they **see the Day approaching** (cf. v. 37; a well-known NT triology is included in these vv.: faith, v. 22; hope, v. 23; love, v. 24).

In referring again to the Second Advent, the writer left the impression he was concerned that genuine believers might cease to hope for the Lord's coming and be tempted to defect from their professions of faith in Christ (cf. comments on 1:13–2:4; 6:9). They must treat their future expectations as certainties (since **He who promised is faithful**). If they would only lift up their eyes, they could "see the Day approaching."

2. THE RENEWED WARNING (10:26-31)

10:26-27. The KJV translation here, "if we sin willfully," is superior to NIV's **if we deliberately keep on sinning,** as the words "keep on" overplay the Greek tense. As the context shows (cf. v. 23), the author was concerned here, as throughout the epistle, with the danger of defection from the faith. Most sin is "deliberate," but the writer was here influenced by the Old Testament's teaching about sins of presumption (cf. Num. 15:29-31) which lay outside the sacrificial provisions of the Law. Apostasy from the faith would be such a "willful" act and for those who commit it **no sacrifice for sins is left** (cf. Heb. 10:18). If the efficacious sacrifice of Christ should be renounced, there remained no other available sacrifice which could shield an apostate from God's **judgment** by **raging fire.** A Christian who abandons "the confidence [he] had at first" (3:14) puts himself on the side of God's enemies and, as the writer had already said, is in effect "crucifying the Son of God all over again and subjecting Him to public disgrace" (6:6). Such reprehensible conduct can scarcely be worthy of anything but God's flaming indignation and retribution. This, however, as stated earlier (cf. comments on 6:8), is not a reference to hell (cf. comments on 10:29).

10:28-29. Under the Old Covenant, if an Israelite spurned the Mosaic Law and at least **two or three witnesses** verified his actions, he was put to death. This being true, the author then argued from the lesser to the greater. If defiance of an inferior covenant could bring such retribution, what about defiance of the New Covenant which, as he had made clear, is far superior? The answer can only be that the punishment would be substantially greater in such a case.

In order to show that this is so, the writer then placed defection from the faith in the harshest possible light. An apostate from the New Covenant **has trampled the Son of God underfoot** and **has treated as an unholy thing the blood of the covenant** (cf. "blood of the eternal covenant," 13:20) **that sanctified him.** The words "sanctified him" refer to true Christians. Already the writer to the Hebrews has described them as "made holy (Gr. 'sanctified') through the sacrifice of the body of Jesus Christ once for all" (10:10) and as "made perfect forever" through this sanctifying work (v. 14).

Some seek to evade this conclusion by suggesting that Christ is the One referred to here as "sanctified" or that the person only *claims* to be sanctified. But these efforts are foreign to the writer's thought and are so forced that they carry their own refutation. The author's whole point lies in the seriousness of the act. To treat "the blood of the covenant" (which actually sanctifies believers) as though it were an "unholy" (*koinon*, "common") thing and to renounce its efficacy, is to commit a sin so heinous as to dwarf the fatal infractions of the Old Covenant. To this, an apostate adds the offense of insulting **the Spirit of grace** who originally wooed him to faith in Christ. This kind of spiritual rebellion clearly calls for a much worse punishment than the capital penalty that was inflicted under the Mosaic setup.

But again the writer was not thinking of hell. Many forms of divine retribution can fall on a human life which are worse than immediate death. In fact, Jeremiah made just such a complaint about the punishment inflicted on Jerusalem (Lam. 4:6, 9). One might think also of King Saul, whose last days were burdened with such mental and emotional turmoil that death itself was a kind of release.

10:30-31. No one should regard such a warning as an idle threat. God Himself has claimed the right to take vengeance and to **judge His people.** In saying this, the author quoted twice from Deuteronomy (32:35-36), a chapter which most vividly evokes the picture of God's people suffering His retributive judgments (cf. esp. Deut. 32:19-27). Those familiar with this text, as well as other descriptions of God's wrath against "His people," agree: **it is a dreadful thing to fall into the hands of the living God.**

3. THE RENEWED ENCOURAGEMENT
(10:32-39)

But as was his custom after the most severe admonitions, the writer chose to conclude his warning with a distinct note of encouragement.

10:32-34. An effective way to fortify people against future trials is to remind them of the courage they displayed in past ones. This is precisely what the writer did. His readers knew what it was to stand their **ground in a great contest in the face of suffering.** (The words "stood your ground" [*hypemeinate*] render the verb usually translated "persevered," as in, e.g., v. 36). They knew what it was to be publicly shamed and persecuted, and also to support others who had such experiences (v. 33). They had shown sympathy for brethren who had been imprisoned, and they had suffered property loss with joy because they had an assurance of possessing heavenly wealth (v. 34). They would do well to recall now their steadfastness in the past. Whatever they might now be facing—and the writer suggested it might be something similar—they would be helped if they would **remember those earlier days after** they **had received the light** (cf. "received the knowledge" in v. 26 and "enlightened" in 6:4).

10:35-36. This was no time for them, then, to **throw away** their **confidence** (*parrēsia*, cf. 3:6; 4:16; 10:19). As the author's exposition of the eternal inheritance—the glory of the many sons—had sought to show, that confidence, if retained, **will be richly rewarded.** What the readers needed, therefore, was just what the writer had often said and implied: **to persevere** (lit., "you had need of perseverance," *hypomonēs echete chreian*) so that by thus doing God's **will** (cf. v. 9) they would **receive what** God had **promised.** As much as anything, these words express the central exhortation of the Book of Hebrews.

10:37-38. If their concern was about the delay of the Second Advent, they should rest assured that **in just a very little while, He who is coming will come and will not delay.** These words and those that follow were adapted by the author from the Septuagint of Isaiah 26:21 and Habakkuk 2:3-4. But they were used freely and were not intended as a precise quotation, since no words such as "He says" introduced them. In the phrase **My** (or "the") **righteous one** (only a handful of Gr. mss. read "My"), the author employed Paul's description of a person who is justified by faith. It is likely that the writer of Hebrews understood it similarly. A justified person ought to **live by faith,** which is what the writer had been urging his readers to do. But, **if he shrinks back,** that is, if the "righteous one" commits apostasy, denouncing his

Christian profession, God's favor cannot rest on his life. By understating the serious consequences, the writer softened his words so that he would not distract from his predominant note of encouragement.

10:39. Then he affirmed, **But we are not of those who shrink back and are destroyed.** Here the original text has an emphatic "we," which the writer might have intended as an "editorial we," of which he was quite fond (cf. 2:5; 5:11; 8:1; etc.). Then he would mean: "As far as I am concerned, I am determined not to shrink back and experience the ruin which divine retribution would bring." The words "are destroyed" reflect the Greek *apōleia*, which can refer either to temporal or eternal ruin. In this context the former is correct. Instead of the ruin which an apostate invites, the writer intended to be among **those who believe and are saved.** The NIV rendering should not be misread as a reference to conversion. Though the author's own normal word for salvation does not occur here, the expression "and are saved" somewhat freely translates *eis peripoiēsin psychēs*. A viable rendering of the last half of verse 39 would be: "but [we are] of faith leading to the preservation of the soul" (cf. comments on 1 Peter 2:9). But "soul" here should be understood in the Hebraic sense of the person himself, or his life, and refers in this context to the way in which persistence in the faith preserves an individual from the calamities that overtake those who "shrink back." Even if the writer was speaking primarily of his own purpose of heart, he clearly intended that to be shared by his readers. Thus the concluding statement of his warning passage (10:19-39) amounts to a call for determination and perseverance.

IV. Part III: The Response of Faith (chaps. 11–12)

This section—the final major portion of the epistle—constitutes a call to respond in the only appropriate way, namely, by faith, to the realities the writer has discussed. Though the importance of faith has already been made apparent, the thought of the writer is not complete till its value and worth are more fully considered. As before, there is exposition (chap. 11) followed by warning and exhortation (chap. 12).

A. The life of faith (chap. 11)

In concluding the previous warning section, the writer touched on the theme of living by faith (cf. 10:37-39). What this really means he then expounded in terms his readers could fully appreciate, because it is faith that underlies the experience of the heroes of Old Testament history. Since these people experienced faith, so could his readers.

1. PROLOGUE (11:1-3)

11:1-3. In a brief Prologue the author set forth three fundamental considerations about faith: its basic nature, the honor associated with it, and its way of seeing things. In its essence **faith is being sure** (*hypostasis*, rendered "being" in reference to God in 1:3) . . . **and certain** (*elenchos*, from the verb *elenchō*, "to prove or convince") about unseen hopes and realities. That this is honorable is seen in the fact that Old Testament worthies, **the ancients, were commended for** it. **Faith** is also a way of viewing all experience since it is the way in which believers see **the universe** (*tous aiōnas*, lit., "the ages," also rendered "the universe" in 1:2) for what it is—a creation by God.

2. THE DIVINE ACCEPTANCE OF FAITH (11:4-16)

In the first major movement of his exposition, the author stressed the theme suggested in verse 2. Faith wins acceptance and reward from God.

11:4. Abel represents the **righteous man** referred to in 10:38, whose acceptance before God was based on a superior sacrifice. Like Abel, the readers found acceptance before God on the basis of the better sacrifice of the New Covenant. Their unbelieving brethren, like **Cain,** found no such divine approbation. Even death does not extinguish the testimony of a man like Abel.

11:5-6. Enoch, on the other hand, reflected the kind of life that pleases God since he walked with God by faith (as the readers also should). If Christ had come in their lifetimes (cf. 10:37), the readers also would **not** have experienced **death.** In any case they could only please God by continued confidence that **He exists and . . . rewards those who earnestly seek Him.**

11:7. That God does reward those who seek Him is suggested by the career of **Noah,** who became an heir of righteousness by faith. What he inherited was, in fact, the new world after the Flood as the readers might inherit "the world to come" (cf. 2:5). The reference here to Noah saving his household recalls the writer's stress on a Christian's salvation-inheritance. It further suggests that a man's personal **faith** can be fruitful in his family, as they share it together.

11:8-10. That the readers should look forward to "the world to come" and treat their present experience as a pilgrimage is a lesson enforced by the life of **Abraham.** This great patriarch lived **like a stranger** in a land **he would later receive as his inheritance.** So also would the readers inherit if they, like this forefather, kept **looking forward to the city with foundations,** a reference to the heavenly and eternal Jerusalem (cf. Rev. 21:2, 9-27).

11:11-12. The NIV introduces the word **Abraham** into these verses. But its marginal reading is preferable: "By faith even Sarah, who was past age, was enabled to bear children because she. . . ." The NIV interpretation is influenced by the opinion that the phrase **to become a father** (*eis katabolēn spermatos*) can refer only to the male parent, but this need not be so. The writer here chose to introduce his first heroine of faith, one who was able to overlook the physical limitation of her own barrenness to become a fruitful mother. Since "she considered Him faithful who had promised" (NASB) so also should the readers (cf. 10:23). Her **faith** in fact, contributed to the startling multiplication of her husband's seed, when old Abraham was **as good as dead.**

11:13-16. In an impressive summary of his discussion thus far, the writer pointed out that people can be **still living by faith** when they die, even if by that time they do **not receive the things promised.** By faith the old saints saw the promised realities **from a distance** and persisted in their pilgrim character, **looking for a country of their own** and refusing to **return** to the land they had left. So too the readers should renounce the **opportunity** to go back to any form of their ancestral religion and should persist in **longing for a better country—a heavenly one.** If they did so they, like the patriarchs, would be people with whom **God** would **not** be **ashamed** to be associated.

3. THE VARIEGATED EXPERIENCES OF FAITH (11:17-40)

A new movement, the author's exposition of the life of faith, begins here. In a multiplicity of varied experiences faith remains the constant factor by which these experiences are met and understood. Faith constitutes a Christian's true "world view" (cf. v. 3).

11:17-19. The theme of testing emerges here as the writer returned to **Abraham.** The readers can learn from that supreme test in which the patriarch was called on **to sacrifice his . . . son.** Though this seemed to contradict the divine promise, Abraham was able to rise above the trial and trust in the resurrecting power of God. So also Christian readers must sometimes look beyond the experiences of life, in which God's promises do not seem to be fulfilled, and realize that their resurrections will bring those promises to fruition.

11:20-22. The patriarchs mentioned here likewise looked to the future in **faith. Isaac,** trusting God to fulfill His promises to Abraham and his descendants, pronounced blessings on his own two sons **Jacob and Esau** regarding **their future.** So did **Jacob** in regard to **Joseph's sons,** which was for him an act of faith in his old age. The readers too were to maintain their worship right to the end of life, persevering in faith in the future that God had foretold. **Joseph** too, nearing death, expressed confidence that God would in the future deliver **the Israelites from Egypt.** In similar fashion all believers should, in genuine faith, have confidence in the future of God's people.

11:23. With this transition to the life of **Moses,** the writer began to focus on the way faith confronts opposition and hostility, a subject familiar to his readers. It was **by faith** that Moses was hidden by his **parents** and his life was thus preserved. The phrase **because they saw he was no ordinary child** might be better read, "because they saw he was a beautiful child." ("Beautiful" is the Gr. *asteion,* which occurs in the NT only here and in Acts 7:20, which also refers to Moses.) Delighted by the precious gift of a son which God had given them, they evidently believed God had something better for this lovely baby than death. Not fearing Pharaoh's **edict,** they kept him alive, and God rewarded their faith by their son's illustrious career.

11:24-26. In a classic presentation of the way faith chooses between the attractive but temporary **pleasures of sin** and the prospect of **disgrace for the sake of Christ,** the writer showed **Moses** to be a real hero of faith who had an intelligent regard for the eschatological hopes of the nation of Israel. The readers also were to accept "disgrace" and reject "the pleasures of sin," and they would do so if they, like Moses, anticipated their **reward.**

11:27-28. Moreover, at the time of the Exodus, Moses was undeterred by fear of **the king's anger.** By keeping **the Passover,** which included **the sprinkling of blood,** the nation avoided God's judgment. In the same way, the readers should not be afraid of human wrath and should maintain their separateness from the surrounding world. They should persist in the worship experience made possible by the blood of the New Covenant. If they would do so, they would not fall under divine retribution (cf. 10:19-31).

11:29-31. The readers could also look forward to victory over their enemies (cf. 1:13-14). They could learn from the destruction of **the Egyptians** and the collapse of **the walls of Jericho** what triumphs faith can win over its adversaries. If, as seems probable, there were a few Gentiles in the church that received this letter, they could take comfort from the experience of **the prostitute Rahab,** a Gentile who was spared when Jericho was conquered.

11:32-35a. There were far too many heroes of faith for the writer to deal with them all in detail. Swiftly he mentioned the variegated accomplishments of some of them. At the climax of this list stand women who **received back their dead, raised to life again**—a truly superlative victory of faith which does not allow death to defeat it (cf. 1 Kings 17:17-24; 2 Kings 4:17-37).

11:35b-38. In a swift transition of thought, the writer moved from faith's obvious triumphs to what seemed to be its defeats. But these defeats were only apparent, not real. Those who **were tortured and refused to be released** did so because they knew their sufferings would lead to a richer and **better resurrection** experience. So the readers might also endure suffering staunchly and expect reward in the future world. Indeed, all manner of physical suffering (vv. 36-37, 38b cite about a dozen kinds of persecution) has been endured by people of faith, as well as ostracism from their homes and countries, treatment that the readers might also have to endure. But in a lovely touch, the writer commented that **the world was not worthy** of those whom it banished.

11:39-40. In a concluding summary the writer pointed out that the great heroes of faith he had spoken of had not yet realized their eschatological hopes. This fact shows that **God had planned something better for** them and **us.** It is indeed "better for us" that the future hopes they strove toward be delayed, since only thus could believers enjoy the present experience of becoming companions of the Messiah who leads them to glory. As a result, the perfecting (cf. 10:14; 12:23) of the Old Testament worthies—that is, the realization of their hopes—awaits that of all believers.

B. The final warning (chap. 12)

The author concluded the basic argument of the epistle with a final admonition and warning. As usual his hortatory section grew directly out of the expository one which preceded it. His discussion of the life of faith now led to another call for perseverance.

1. THE INTRODUCTORY ADMONITION (12:1-2)

12:1-2. The life of faith has been amply attested by this **great cloud of** Old Testament **witnesses.** (This does not mean that they watch believers today.) Hence believers ought to **run with perseverance** (*hypomonēs*; cf. 10:32, 36; 12:2-3,7) **the race marked out** in their Christian lives, setting aside whatever **hinders and the sin that so easily entangles** (*euperistaton*, "ambushes or encircles"). Their supreme Model for this continued to be **Jesus,** however admirable any Old Testament figure might be. He is both the **Author and Perfecter of our faith.** The word "author" (*archēgon*) was used in 2:10 (see comments there) and suggests that Jesus "pioneered" the path of faith Christians should follow. He also "perfected" the way of faith since He reached its end successfully. He kept His eye on **the joy set before Him**, the "joy" alluded to in 1:9 wherein He obtained an eternal throne. The believers' share in that joy must also be kept in view. After enduring (*hypemeinen*, the verb related to the noun *hypomonē* in 12:1; cf. vv. 3, 7) **the cross** and **scorning its shame**, Jesus assumed that triumphant position **at the right hand of the throne of God** (cf. 1:3; 8:1; 10:12) which presages His and the believers' final victory (cf. 1:13-14).

2. THE REMINDER THAT THINGS ARE NOT AS BAD AS THEY SEEM (12:3-11)

Nothing is more natural for a person than to overestimate the severity of his trials. The writer did not want his audience to do that.

12:3-4. If they would **consider the opposition from sinful men** which Jesus confronted and **endured** (*hypomemenēkota*; cf. vv. 1-2, 7), they would be encouraged. After all, unlike Him, they had **not yet resisted . . . sin . . . to the point of** bloodshed. By "sin" the author probably primarily meant that of "sinful men" who opposed them, but doubtless also had their own sin in mind, which they had to resist in order to maintain a steadfast Christian profession.

12:5-8. The readers also seemed to **have forgotten** the **encouragement** found in Proverbs 3:11-12, which presents divine **discipline** as an evidence of divine love. Thus they should not **lose heart** (cf. Heb. 12:3) but should **endure hardship** (*hypomenete*, lit., "persevere"; cf. vv. 1-3) **as discipline** and regard it as an evidence of sonship, that is, that they are being trained for the glory of the many sons (cf. 2:10 and comments there). All God's children are subject to His discipline, and in the phrase **everyone undergoes discipline** the writer for the last time used the Greek *metochoi* ("companions," "sharers"), also used in 1:9; 3:1, 14; 6:4. (Lit., the Gr. reads, ". . . discipline, of which all have become sharers.") In speaking of those who **are not disciplined** and **are thus illegitimate children**, he was probably thinking of Christians whose disloyalty to the faith resulted in their loss of inheritance (i.e., reward) which is acquired by the many sons and daughters. (In the Roman world, an "illegitimate child" had no inheritance rights.) What such Christians undergo, the author had shown, is severe judgment. On the other hand believers who undergo God's "discipline" are being prepared by this educational process (*paideia*, "discipline," lit., "child-training"; cf. Eph. 6:4) for millennial reward.

12:9-11. Drawing on the analogy of the discipline of earthly **fathers**, the author encouraged a submissive spirit to the discipline of **the Father of our spirits** which is life-preserving (**and live**) as well as productive of an experience of **His holiness,** which involves a rich **harvest of righteousness and peace.** But Christians must let this discipline have its full effect and be **trained by it.**

3. THE CALL TO RENEWED SPIRITUAL VITALITY (12:12-17)

12:12-13. The author sensed the tendency to spiritual weakness in his readers, and in the light of the truths he had expounded he encouraged them to renew their strength. If they would do this and would pursue the **level paths** which real righteousness entails, the weakest among them (**the lame**) would not be further **disabled, but rather healed.** Their own strength would benefit weaker Christians.

12:14. Peace with all men as well as personal holiness must be vigorously sought since **without holiness** (*hagiasmos*) **no one will see the Lord.** Since no sin can stand in God's presence, Christians must—and will be—sinless when they see the Lord (cf. 1 John 3:2). That realization offers motivation for pursuing holiness here and now. But the author may also have had in mind the thought that one's perception of God even now is conditioned by his real measure of holiness (cf. Matt. 5:8).

12:15-17. As a grim reminder of what can happen among believers, the writer warned that **one who misses the grace of God** may become like a **bitter root** whose infidelity to God affects others. Here the author had in mind Deuteronomy 29:18 where an Old-Covenant apostate was called a "root . . . that produces such bitter poison." Such a person would be **godless** (*bebēlos*, "profane, unhallowed, desecrated") **like Esau,**

Jacob's brother, whose loose and profane character led him to sell **his inheritance rights as the oldest son** for the temporary gratification of **a single meal.** He warned the readers not to yield to transitory pressures and forfeit their inheritances. If some did, they would ultimately regret the foolish step and might find their inheritance privileges irrevocably lost as were Esau's. This would of course be true of one who ended his Christian experience in a state of apostasy, which the writer had continually warned against.

4. THE FINAL WARNING ITSELF (12:18-29)

12:18-21. Vividly the writer pictured the situation at Mount Sinai where the Old Covenant was given and its awesomeness and fearful nature were described (cf. Ex. 19:9-23; Deut. 9:8-19).

12:22-24. The realities that pertain to New-Covenant people and to which they **have come** are even more impressive because they are **heavenly.** Not only is there the heavenly **city,** but there are also heaven-related beings, both **angels** and people, associated with it. The term **church of the firstborn** may mean the assembly of those whose inheritance rights are already won (since under the OT Law the "firstborn" was the primary heir; cf. v. 16). They have already gone on to the heavenly regions where the angels are. But above all, it is to **God, the Judge of all men,** that they have come—and there are some who indeed can stand His searching scrutiny of their lives (**the spirits of righteous men made perfect;** cf. 10:14; 11:40)—and **to Jesus the Mediator** (cf. 8:6; 9:15) **of a New Covenant** whose atoning **blood** does not cry for judgment as did Abel's but secures the acceptance of all New-Covenant persons.

If the readers would contemplate these things properly, they would be awed by them and more inclined to fulfill their call to the highest privileges that the New Covenant can provide.

12:25. The contrast between the two covenants is now focused as a contrast between a warning given **on earth** and one that issues **from heaven** itself. Since those who refused the Old Covenant **did not escape,** how could those of the New Covenant who **turn away** expect to do so? (cf. 2:3) Here no doubt the author thought of the Speaker as none other than the Originator of the New Covenant who now sits "at the right hand of the Majesty in heaven" (1:3).

12:26-27. This is the divine **voice** which once **shook** only **the earth,** but will ultimately **shake not only the earth but also the heavens.** The reference to Haggai 2:6 was understood by the author as speaking of the ultimate remaking of the heavens and earth which will follow the millennial kingdom (cf. Heb. 1:10-12). What remains after this cataclysmic event will be eternal.

12:28-29. And such is the character of the **kingdom** which **we are receiving.** The words **let us be thankful** may be rendered "let us have [or, 'obtain'] grace" (*echōmen charin*) and are likely a final reference to the resources of grace available from the great High Priest (cf. 4:14-16). This is confirmed by the words **and so** (lit., "through which," *di' ēs*) which remind the readers that this grace is required in order to **worship** (better, "serve," *latreuōmen,* also used in 8:5; 9:9; 10:2; 13:10) **God acceptably** within the New-Covenant community. Failure to do so should be deterred by the concluding solemn thought that **our God is a consuming fire** (cf. 10:26-27). A believer who departs from his magnificent privileges will invite God's retribution.

V. Epilogue (chap. 13)

The Epilogue can be distinguished from the body of the epistle in that the latter contains only broad, general admonitions, while the Epilogue contains specific ones. In some ways these specific instructions suggest ways "to worship God acceptably" (cf. 12:28). The Epilogue also contains the writer's personal comments to his readers and his farewell to them.

13:1-6. The first section of the Epilogue contains moral directions for the readers. Obeying these would inculcate personal kindness to **brothers** (v. 1), **strangers** (v. 2), and **prisoners** (v. 3). The writer then called for sexual purity in which **marriage** is held in high regard (v. 4). The readers were also to avoid monetary greed and to **be content with what they have** (v. 5; cf. Luke 12:15; Phil. 4:11; 1 Tim. 6:6-10). Even if they had little on the material level, they had the Lord (Heb. 13:5) and His help (v. 6).

13:7-8. Religious directions follow the moral ones and this segment of the

Epilogue extends through verse 17. The call, **Remember your leaders,** perhaps referred to former leaders who had passed away. The **outcome of their way of life** could be contemplated with good effect and the readers were to **imitate their faith.** Those leaders were gone, but **Jesus Christ** of whom they spoke remains continuously **the same.**

13:9. That is why new doctrines which conflict with the unchanging message about Jesus Christ should be rejected. The author's reference here to **all kinds of strange teachings** does not sound at all like a reference to normative Judaism but as if the readers were confronting a peculiar, sectarian variation of that religion (cf. comments under "Background and Setting" in the Heb. *Introduction*).

13:10-14. If those who hawked "strange teachings" tended to idealize the wilderness experience and the tabernacle, the writer's words now make a special point. A Christian has a special **altar** (probably a figure of speech for the sacrifice of Christ) from which he derives spiritual sustenance. **Those who minister at the tabernacle** were not entitled to partake of that kind of spiritual food. If some people preferred a desert way of life and considered themselves "servants" of the ancient tabernacle they were, the writer pointed out, debarred from Christian privileges. Under the old institution the **blood** from sacrifices made on the Day of Atonement was brought **into the most holy place, but the bodies** were **burned outside the camp** (v. 11), a location deemed unholy in the years of the wilderness sojourn. But **Jesus also suffered outside the city gate** (i.e., outside Jerusalem), but the effect of His sacrifice was **to make the people holy.** Far from association with Him being unholy, as some unbelieving Jews regarded it, the readers were in fact "holy" (or sanctified; cf. 2:11; 10:10, 14) and should not hesitate to share in **the disgrace He bore** (cf. 12:2) by abandoning **the camp** of Judaism and identifying with Him. If the readers actually were acquainted with sectarian encampments in their region this exhortation would have had special force. The readers' true home was no camp or city that then existed, but **the city that is to come** (cf. 11:10, 16; 12:22).

13:15-16. No blood sacrifices were needed in the light of Jesus' death, but to **offer . . . praise** and **to do good and to share with others** were indeed **sacrifices** that God desired (cf. 10:25).

13:17. If former **leaders** were to be remembered and their teachings retained (vv. 7-8), present ones were to be obeyed. Their responsibility before God was to be recognized and their shepherding tasks should not be complicated by disobedience. (**So that their work will be a joy** possibly should be, "so their accounting [to God for you] may be with joy.")

13:18-19. With that same sense of spiritual humility that led him to use "we" in most of his warning sections, the writer requested the prayers of his readers, and **particularly** that he might **be restored to** them **soon.** His interest in them was personal, and he was eager to see them.

13:20-21. In a lovely benediction which captures a number of the major themes of the epistle (e.g., **peace, blood, covenant,** Resurrection, **Shepherd, equip**), the writer expressed confidence in **our Lord Jesus** as the **Great Shepherd** of New-Covenant people, through whom God was able to effect His will (equip is *katartisai*, "to prepare, make ready for use"; cf. Eph. 4:12) in the readers and in himself. This indeed is what he prayed for his readers.

13:22-25. Urging once again that his readers **bear with** his **word of exhortation,** he expressed the hope that he and **Timothy** would soon **see** them. After giving them greetings, he committed them to God's **grace.**

BIBLIOGRAPHY

Bruce, F. F. *The Epistle to the Hebrews: The English Text with Introduction, Exposition and Notes.* Grand Rapids: Wm. B. Eerdmans Publishing Co., 1964.

Griffith Thomas, W.H. *Hebrews: A Devotional Commentary.* Grand Rapids: Wm. B. Eerdmans Publishing Co., n.d.

Héring, Jean. *The Epistle to the Hebrews.* Translated by A.W. Heathcote and P.J. Allcock. London: Epworth Press, 1970.

Hewitt, Thomas. *The Epistle to the Hebrews: An Introduction and Commentary.* The

Tyndale New Testament Commentaries. Grand Rapids: Wm. B. Eerdmans Publishing Co., 1961.

Hughes, Philip Edgcumbe. *A Commentary on the Epistle to the Hebrews.* Grand Rapids: Wm. B. Eerdmans Publishing Co., 1977.

Kent, Homer A., Jr. *The Epistle to the Hebrews: A Commentary.* Grand Rapids: Baker Book House, 1972.

Montefiore, Hugh. *A Commentary on the Epistle to the Hebrews.* London: Adam & Charles Black, 1964.

Newell, William R. *Hebrews Verse by Verse.* Chicago: Moody Press, 1947.

Pfeiffer, Charles F. *The Epistle to the Hebrews.* Everyman's Bible Commentary. Chicago: Moody Press, 1968.

Westcott, Brooke Foss. *The Epistle to the Hebrews: The Greek Text with Notes and Essays.* London: Macmillan & Co., 1892. Reprint. Grand Rapids: Wm. B. Eerdmans Publishing Co., 1974.

Wiersbe, Warren W. *Be Confident.* Wheaton, Ill.: Scripture Press Publications, Victor Books, 1982.

JAMES

J. Ronald Blue

INTRODUCTION

Few books of the Bible have been more maligned than the little Book of James. Controversy has waged over its authorship, its date, its recipients, its canonicity, and its unity.

It is well known that Martin Luther had problems with this book. He called it a "right strawy epistle." But it is only "strawy" to the degree it is "sticky." There are enough needles in this haystack to prick the conscience of every dull, defeated, and degenerate Christian in the world. Here is a "right stirring epistle" designed to exhort and encourage, to challenge and convict, to rebuke and revive, to describe practical holiness and drive believers toward the goal of a faith that works. James is severely ethical and refreshingly practical.

Considered one of the General Epistles, James, like the epistles of Peter, John, and Jude, is an encyclical addressed not to individual churches or persons but to a larger sphere of believers. The teaching in these general letters complements the doctrine of Paul. Paul emphasized faith; James stressed conduct; Peter, hope; John, love; and Jude, purity.

Authorship. The human author of this epistle is not easily identified. The New Testament mentions at least four men named James: (1) the son of Zebedee and brother of John (Mark 1:19), (2) the son of Alphaeus (Mark 3:18), (3) the father of Judas (not Iscariot; Luke 6:16), and (4) the half brother of the Lord (Gal. 1:19). Which one wrote the epistle?

James, the son of Zebedee, could not be the author since he suffered martyrdom under Herod Agrippa I before this epistle was written (Acts 12:2).

It is unlikely that the little-known son of Alphaeus was the author though some, especially Roman Catholics, equate the son of Alphaeus with the Lord's brother. They claim that James was really Jesus' cousin through Mary of Cleopas (Alphaeus), the Virgin Mary's sister. This contention, however, violates a literal interpretation of "brother" and is clearly an attempt to support the invention of the perpetual virginity of Mary. It seems clear from Scripture that children were born to Joseph and Mary after the virgin birth of the Lord Jesus Christ. Jesus is called "her firstborn" (Luke 2:7), implying that others were born thereafter. The Scriptures state that Joseph had no union with Mary, that is, no normal physical relationship, "until" (*heōs*) after the birth of Jesus (Matt. 1:25). Repeated references are made to the Lord's half brothers and half sisters and four of His brothers are named: James, Joseph, Simon, and Judas (Matt. 13:55).

James, the father of Judas (not Iscariot) did not figure as an important person in the early church. He could hardly be the author of this epistle.

It seems clear therefore that the author is James, the half brother of the Lord, who became the recognized leader in the Jerusalem church. This conclusion is supported by the authoritative tone of the letter and by the marked similarities in Greek between this epistle and the speech by James recorded in Acts 15.

Though James was reared in the same home with the Lord Jesus, he apparently did not become a believer until after Christ's resurrection. John wrote, "For even His own brothers did not believe in Him" (John 7:5).

James' encounter with the risen Lord may have brought him to saving faith. Christ "appeared to James, then to all the apostles" (1 Cor. 15:7). Paul later listed James, Peter, and John as "those reputed to be pillars" of the church (Gal. 2:9).

The strongest evidence for the authorship of the Epistle of James clearly favors the half brother of Christ. Furthermore, Origen, Eusebius, Cyril of Jerusalem, Athanasius, Augustine, and many other early writers support this view.

Date. The date of the epistle is related to its authorship. Some deny that James wrote this letter because of its excellent Greek. They place the writing between A.D. 80 and 150. This is hardly justified. James was obviously a gifted Galilean, fluent in both Aramaic and Greek.

Flavius Josephus, first-century historian, records that James was martyred in A.D. 62, so the epistle must have been written prior to that date. Since no mention is made of the Jerusalem Council (A.D. 49) in which James took so active a role, it is likely that the letter was written between A.D. 45 and 48.

James is probably the earliest of the writings of the New Testament and therefore can hardly be seen as a polemic against Paul's letter to the Romans, which was written later. Romans, however, is not a refutation of James. It is apparent from Paul's relationship with James (Acts 15:13; 21:18) and his recognition of James (Gal. 1:19; 2:9, 12) that Paul held James in high respect. Together Paul and James give the full dimension of faith. Paul wrote about inner saving faith from God's perspective. James wrote about outward serving faith from man's perspective. The true seed of saving faith is verified by the tangible fruit of serving faith. James' point is that biblical faith works.

Recipients. Clearly addressed to "the 12 tribes scattered among the nations" (James 1:1), this letter has a marked Jewish flavor. The book has the substance and authority of the Prophets and the style and beauty of the Psalms. He refers to "firstfruits" (1:18; cf. Lev. 23:10), the synagogue or "meeting" (James 2:2), "our ancestor Abraham" (2:21), Gehenna or "hell" (3:6), "the Lord Almighty" (5:4; cf. Gen. 17:1), and to the early and latter or "fall and spring rains" (James 5:7; cf. Deut. 11:14). Though some suggest that the "12 tribes" may be taken metaphorically as the Gentile church scattered throughout the Roman Empire, it is far more logical to take the statement in its normal sense. The letter is definitely to a Jewish constituency. Though the letter demonstrates careful Greek diction, it is nonetheless filled with extensive Hebrew symbolism.

It is likely that Peter wrote to the Jewish Christians scattered to the West (cf. 1 Peter 1:1) and that James addressed the Jewish Christians scattered to the East, in Babylon and Mesopotamia.

Canonicity. It is interesting to note that James was omitted from some of the early versions and collections of sacred books. The earliest known collection, the Muratorian fragment of the second century, does not include Hebrews, James, and the epistles of Peter. It was not until the fourth and fifth centuries that James appears to be consistently included in the canon. It appears that while the churches of Rome and Carthage doubted the canonicity of James, it was nonetheless in use from an early date by the churches of Jerusalem and Alexandria and is included in the collections of scriptural books in Asia Minor. The reason is rather obvious. Written at Jerusalem and addressed to the Jews of the Eastern dispersion, those of the West were not so ready to accept the letter as Scripture. It is clear, however, that God not only superintended the writing of Scripture but its acceptance and authority as well.

Style. The Book of James is as much a lecture as it is a letter. Though it opens with the customary salutation of an epistle, it lacks personal references common in a letter and it has no concluding benediction.

This so-called "epistle" was obviously prepared for public reading as a sermon to the congregations addressed. The tone is clearly authoritative but not autocratic. James included 54 imperatives in his 108 verses—an average of one call for action in every other verse!

James' style is both energetic and vivid, conveying profound concepts with crisp, well-chosen words. The sentences are short, simple, and direct. He used many metaphors and similes with a touch of poetic imagination. In fact, the Book of James probably has more figures of speech, analogies, and imagery from nature (see the chart) than all Paul's epistles together. Exhortations, rhetorical questions, and illustrations from everyday life give spice to this little book.

A striking literary technique employed by James is the practice of linking together clauses and sentences by the repetition of a leading word or one of its cognates. For example, "perseverance" (1:3) and "perseverance" (v. 4); "not lacking anything" (v. 4) and "if any of you lacks" (v. 5); "he should ask" (v. 5) and "when he asks" (v. 6); "he must . . . not doubt" (v. 6) and "he who doubts" (v. 6). (For others see W. Graham Scroggie, *Know Your Bible*, 2 vols. London: Pickering & Inglis, n.d., 2:293.)

In addition to his unique and innovative style, James furnishes an unusual number of references or parallels to other writings. He makes reference to Abraham, Rahab, Job, Elijah, to the Law and the Ten Commandments, and includes allusions to passages in 21 Old Testament books: Genesis through Deuteronomy, Joshua, 1 Kings, Psalms, Proverbs, Ecclesiastes, Isaiah, Jeremiah, Ezekiel, Daniel, and 7 of the 12 Minor Prophets.

James' teaching strongly resembles that of John the Baptist (e.g., cf. James 1:22, 27 with Matt. 3:8; James 2:15-16 with Luke 3:11; James 2:19-20 with Matt. 3:9; James 5:1-6 with Matt. 3:10-12). Probably James, like Peter, John, and Andrew, had heard John the Baptist preach. Amazing parallelisms exist between James' letter and the Sermon on the Mount in Matthew 5–7 (see the chart on the next p.). James did not actually quote the Lord's words, but he obviously had internalized His teachings and reproduced them with spiritual depth.

In its expressive abruptness and eloquent austerity, James' epistle stands as a literary masterpiece. This book is

References to Nature in the Book of James

1:6	"wave of the sea"
1:6	"tossed by the wind"
1:10	"wild flower"
1:11	"sun . . . with scorching heat"
1:11	"the plant . . . blossom falls"
1:17	"the heavenly lights"
1:17	"shifting shadows"
1:18	"firstfruits"
3:3	"bits into the mouths of horses"
3:4	"ships . . . driven by strong winds"
3:5	"a great forest is set on fire by a small spark"
3:6	"a fire"
3:7	"animals, birds, reptiles, and creatures of the sea"
3:8	"deadly poison"
3:11	"fresh water and salt water"
3:12	"can a fig tree bear olives, or a grapevine bear figs?"
3:18	"sow in peace [and] raise a harvest of righteousness"
4:14	"you are a mist"
5:2	"moths have eaten your clothes"
5:3	"gold and silver are corroded"
5:4	"workmen who mowed your fields"
5:4	"the cries of the harvesters"
5:5	"fattened yourselves in the day of slaughter"
5:7	"the farmer waits for the . . . crop"
5:7	"how patient he is for the fall and spring rains"
5:14	"anoint him with oil"
5:17	"prayed . . . that it would not rain"
5:17	"it did not rain on the land"
5:18	"the heavens gave rain"
5:18	"the earth produced its crops"

James' References to Jesus' Sermon on the Mount

James	Sermon on the Mount
1:2	Matthew 5:10-12
1:4	5:48
1:5; 5:15	7:7-12
1:9	5:3
1:20	5:22
2:13	5:7; 6:14-15
2:14-16	7:21-23
3:17-18	5:9
4:4	6:24
4:10	5:3-5
4:11	7:1-2
5:2	6:19
5:10	5:12
5:12	5:33-37

both picturesque and passionate. It combines the rhythmic beauty of Greek with the stern intensity of Hebrew. This letter is beautiful in its expression and bombastic in its impression.

Unity. The alleged lack of unity in James has been a prevalent complaint. Some contend the book bears a loose format like that of Hebrew wisdom literature of the type found in Proverbs. One commentator contends that there is "no discernible plan in the epistle" (C. Leslie Mitton, *The Epistle of James*, p. 235). Another argues that what James wrote "is not so much a reasoned argument as a series of sententious sayings clustered round certain recurring themes" (Frank E. Gaebelein, *The Practical Epistle of James*, p. 14). "Lack of continuity of thought" (Martin Dibelius, *A Commentary on the Epistle of James*, Philadelphia: Fortress Press, 1976, p. 1); "a series of loosely connected paragraphs" (Clayton K. Harrop, *The Letter of James*, p. 14); and "altogether informal and unsystematic" (E.H. Plumptre, *The General Epistle of St. James*, p. 43) are other expressions of commentators' frustrations. However, there is little need for confusion. The epistle demonstrates a marked unity and a clear goal.

The purpose of this potent letter is to exhort the early believers to Christian maturity and holiness of life. This letter deals more with the practice of the Christian faith than with its precepts. James told his readers how to achieve spiritual maturity through a confident stand, compassionate service, careful speech, contrite submission, and concerned sharing. He dealt with every area of a Christian's life: what he is, what he does, what he says, what he feels, and what he has.

With his somewhat stern teaching on practical holiness, James showed how Christian faith and Christian love should be expressed in a variety of actual situations. The seemingly unrelated parts of the book can be harmonized in light of this unified theme. The pearls are not rolling around in some box; they are carefully strung to produce a necklace of priceless beauty.

OUTLINE

I. Stand with Confidence (chap. 1)
  A. Salutation and greeting (1:1)
  B. Rejoice in diverse trials (1:2-12)
    1. Attitude in trials (1:2)
    2. Advantage of trials (1:3-4)
    3. Assistance for trials (1:5-12)
  C. Resist in deadly temptation (1:13-18)
    1. Source of temptation (1:13-14)
    2. Steps in temptation (1:15-16)

3. Solution for temptation (1:17-18)
D. Rest in divine truth (1:19-27)
1. Receptivity to the Word (1:19-21)
2. Responsiveness to the Word (1:22-25)
3. Resignation to the Word (1:26-27)
II. Serve with Compassion (chap. 2)
A. Accept others (2:1-13)
1. Courtesy to all (2:1-4)
2. Compassion for all (2:5-9)
3. Consistency in all (2:10-13)
B. Assist others (2:14-26)
1. Expression of true faith (2:14-17)
2. Evidence of true faith (2:18-20)
3. Examples of true faith (2:21-26)
III. Speak with Care (chap. 3)
A. Control talk (3:1-12)
1. The tongue is powerful (3:1-5)
2. The tongue is perverse (3:6-8)
3. The tongue is polluted (3:9-12)
B. Cultivate thought (3:13-18)
1. Wisdom is humble (3:13)
2. Wisdom is gracious (3:14-16)
3. Wisdom is peaceable (3:17-18)
IV. Submit with Contrition (chap. 4)
A. Turn hatred into humility (4:1-6)
1. Cause of conflict (4:1-2)
2. Consequence of conflict (4:3-4)
3. Cure for conflict (4:5-6)
B. Turn judgment into justice (4:7-12)
1. Advice for justice (4:7-9)
2. Advantage of justice (4:10-11)
3. Author of justice (4:12)
C. Turn boasting into belief (4:13-17)
1. Statement of boasting (4:13)
2. Sentence on boasting (4:14)
3. Solution for boasting (4:15-17)
V. Share with Concern (chap. 5)
A. Share in possessions (5:1-6)
1. Consternation from wealth (5:1)
2. Corrosion of wealth (5:2-3)
3. Condemnation in wealth (5:4-6)
B. Share in patience (5:7-12)
1. Essence of patience (5:7-9)
2. Examples of patience (5:10-11)
3. Evidence of patience (5:12)
C. Share in prayer (5:13-20)
1. Sensitivity to needs (5:13)
2. Supplication for needs (5:14-18)
3. Significance of needs (5:19-20)

COMMENTARY

I. Stand with Confidence (chap. 1)

A. Salutation and greeting (1:1)

1:1. The letter begins with a conventional opening: the name of the writer, the people to whom the letter is addressed, and a word of greeting. James was content with a simple introduction.

The writer introduced himself modestly. He did not indicate his status in the church or that he was the Lord's brother. The lack of title suggests that he was well known and had the authority to send a letter of this kind.

James was actually Jacob (*Iakōbos*). It is not certain why the English translators chose "James" rather than "Jacob." "James," "Jake," and "Jacob" all come from the same root. Bible translations in other languages tend to utilize the transliterated name from the actual Hebrew "Jacob" (*ya'ăqōb*). Could it be that King James desired to see his name in the English translation he authorized?

James, or Jacob, described himself simply as **a servant of God and of the Lord Jesus Christ.** James considered himself a bond-slave (*doulos*). He was the property of God and of the One he could have called his "Brother," the Lord Jesus Christ. Obviously James recognized the deity of Christ by placing Him coequal with God. Furthermore, James used His full name, "the Lord Jesus Christ." "Jesus" means "Savior" and "Christ" is the Greek for "Messiah," the "Anointed." The eternal "Lord" became the Savior, "Jesus," and rose again as everlasting Sovereign, "Christ." The Lord of lords is King of kings (1 Tim. 6:15; Rev. 17:14; 19:16).

The letter is addressed **to the 12 tribes scattered among the nations.** James was writing to the Jews dispersed from their homeland. The technical term "scattered" (*diaspora*) occurs in only two other places in the New Testament (John 7:35; 1 Peter 1:1). It refers to the Jews who were scattered among the Gentiles as their ancestors had been in the days of the Captivity. Though the 12 tribes of Israel are scattered, they are never lost. They are again listed at the close of biblical history in the Book of Revelation: Judah, Reuben, Gad, Asher, Naphtali, Manasseh, Simeon, Levi, Issachar, Zebulun, Joseph, and Benjamin (Rev. 7:5-8; cf. 21:12).

The idiom, **Greetings,** common in thousands of ancient papyri letters, does not stand alone in any other New Testament letter. This is the Greek salutation much like the English "Hello" or "Welcome." (See comments on 2 John 10-11.) It is interesting that James did not add the Jewish salutation "Peace" (*šālôm*). Paul usually included both the Greek and Hebrew greetings, which are translated "grace and peace." James undoubtedly sought to maintain a crisp style and the simple elegance of good Greek even though he wrote to fellow Jews. Furthermore, the play on words between "greetings" (*chairein*) in James 1:1 and "joy" (*charan*) in verse 2 is thus more evident.

In order to attain Christian maturity and holy conduct it is essential to have a firm foundation. The believer must be able to stand with confidence. He dare not be pushed down by trials. He must not be pulled over by temptation. "Push, pull—stick, stick" must be his motto. How can such stamina be achieved? A believer can stand by pursuing, perceiving, and practicing the Word of God. Trials from without and temptations from within are no match for a Christian who stands in the truth from above.

B. *Rejoice in diverse trials (1:2-12)*

All too often trials prompt groanings and complaints. This kind of response does not contribute to Christian maturity. It only makes matters worse. Trials are not to be seen as tribulations but testings. A test is given to see if a student can pass, not pass out. James gave sound advice on how to score high on every test. One who brings the right attitude to the trial, who understands the advantage of the trial, and who knows where to obtain assistance in the trial will certainly end up on God's honor roll.

1. ATTITUDE IN TRIALS (1:2)

1:2. To persecuted Jewish believers scattered among pagan peoples, James gave the surprising advice, **Consider it pure joy, my brothers, whenever you face trials of many kinds.** Trials should be faced with an attitude of joy. Trials should not be seen as a punishment, a curse, or a calamity but something that must prompt rejoicing. Furthermore they should produce "pure joy" (lit., "all joy"; i.e., joy that is full or unmixed), not just "some joy" coupled with much grief.

Though James' command was direct and forceful, he did not preach at his audience. He identified with them. He addressed them warmly as "my brothers." This mode of address is characteristic of the epistle. He used this familiar form no less than 15 times. James' direct commands are coupled with deep compassion.

It is important to note that James did *not* say that a believer should be joyous *for* the trials but *in* the trials. The verb translated "face" might more literally be expressed as "fall into," *peripesēte*, much as the poor man "fell among robbers" (Luke 10:30). The "trials of many kinds" (*peirasmois . . . poikilois*) were also referred to by Peter, who used the same Greek words, though in reverse order (1 Peter 1:6). When surrounded by these trials, one should respond with joy. Most people count it all joy when they *escape* trials. James said to count it all joy in the midst of trials (cf. 1 Peter 1:6, 8).

It is clear that the reference here is to external trials, or tests of stamina (*peirasmois*) whereas later in the same chapter (James 1:13) the verb form (*peirazomai*) of that noun is used to speak of inner temptations, or solicitations to sin.

Obviously the question arises: How can a person find joy in trials?

2. ADVANTAGE OF TRIALS (1:3-4)

1:3. Christians can face trials with joy because there are rich advantages from these testings. Trials, rightly taken, produce the sterling quality of endurance.

This is no new revelation. It is a simple reminder. James wrote, **because you know,** literally "knowing through experience" (*ginōskontes*). Everyone has experienced both the pain of problems and the ensuing profit of persistence. There is no gain in endurance without some investment in trials.

It is the true part or approved portion of faith that produces perseverance. **The testing** refers more to "approval" than to "proving." The word (*dokimion*) appears only here and in 1 Peter 1:7. **Faith** is like gold; it stands in the test of fire. Without this approved standard of faith, trials would not yield perseverance. There would only be ashes. True faith, like pure gold, endures, no matter how hot the fire. True faith therefore **develops**, or more literally "works" (*katergazetai*), **perseverance** or staying power. The noun "perseverance" (*hypomonēn*; cf. the verbal form in James 1:12) means steadfastness or endurance in the face of difficulties (cf. 5:11).

1:4. Perseverance is only the beginning of benefits. There are more advantages to trials. **Perseverance must finish its work.** Just as tested and true faith works to produce perseverance, so perseverance must be allowed to continue its perfect or finished work to produce the ultimate by-products of maturity and spiritual fulfillment. This, of course, is the lofty goal that serves as this epistle's unifying theme. James' main point was to show how to achieve spiritual maturity.

Two words describe the goal: **mature and complete.** "Mature" (*teleioi*), often translated "perfect" or "finished," is coupled with "complete" (*holoklēroi*, from *holos*, "whole," and *klēros*, "part") to give the idea of perfected all over or fully developed in every part.

Trials can be faced with joy because, infused with faith, perseverance results, and if perseverance goes full-term it will develop a thoroughly mature Christian who lacks nothing. He will indeed be all God wants him to be.

James' argument may seem logical, but it is still difficult to see how trials can be welcomed with an attitude of joy. Where does one turn for help to understand this paradox?

3. ASSISTANCE FOR TRIALS (1:5-12)

1:5. To those who feel confused and frustrated by the high goal of "not lacking anything," James wrote, If **any of you lacks wisdom, he should ask God.** Assistance is readily available from "the giving God" (*tou didontos theou*). To those who lack wisdom, this valuable resource is available for the asking. James assumed his readers would feel the need for wisdom (*sophias*), not just knowledge. God will not only provide wisdom, but will do so generously, not grudgingly.

1:6-8. However, God's provision has some prerequisites. To receive God's wisdom in trials, the believer must be wise in asking. First, he must ask in faith. **He must believe and not doubt** (*diakrinomenos*, the word for "doubt," suggests vacillating). He dare not come to God **like a wave of the sea,** blown [horizontally] **and tossed** [vertically] **by the wind.** God is not pleased with **a double-minded** (lit., "two-souled," *dipsychos*; cf. 4:8) **man** who is **unstable in all he does,** like an unsteady, staggering drunk. The answer from God depends on assurance in God.

1:9-11. Furthermore one who asks for wisdom needs to evidence hope. Whatever his social or economic position, the believer must see eternal advantages. **The brother in humble circumstances** can be glad in his **high** standing spiritually, and **the one who is rich** can be glad for his human frailty (knowing that he has "eternal glory" in Christ, 2 Cor. 4:17). Social prominence passes away, wealth withers away **like a wild flower** in the hot **sun,** and fame will **fade.** Hope in the eternal is evidence of believing faith.

1:12. Finally, the one who asks for wisdom must be steadfast and infused with love. God blesses someone **who perseveres under trial.** In this verse James returned to the theme with which he opened this passage in verses 2-3; both refer to "trials," "testing," and "perseverance." The Christian who steadfastly endures (*hypomenei*) trials (*peirasmon*) and **has stood the test** (*dokimos genomenos*; cf. *dokimion* in v. 3) . . . **will receive the crown of life.** This "crown" consists of life, that is, the crown *is* life (cf. Rev. 2:10). "The life which is promised is probably life here and now, life in its fullness, life in its completeness" (cf. James 1:4) (Curtis Vaughan, *James: Bible Study Commentary,* p. 28). (Other crowns are referred to in 1 Thes. 2:19; 2 Tim. 4:8; 1 Peter 5:4.) **God** promises such life **to those who love Him.** Love for God enables believers who undergo trials to rest confidently in Him. Their steadfastness reveals their love. (Some, however, say the crown refers not to full life now but to eternal life, for all true believers do in fact love God; 1 John 4:8.) Asking for wisdom with faith (James 1:6-8), hope (vv. 9-11), and love (v. 12) brings not only the blessing of wisdom but also the blessing of winning.

To have the right attitude in trials, one must see the advantage of trials, but if it is difficult to see the advantages, one can ask for aid and, if one asks correctly, God will give him the right attitude in trials. He can rejoice in trials (v. 2) and be **blessed** (v. 12) by enduring them.

C. Resist in deadly temptation (1:13-18)

Believers are in danger of falling before the attacks and pressures of trials. But they are also subject to falling before the attractions and pleasures of temptation. Just as a wrong reaction to testing will obstruct spiritual growth and maturity, so will a wrong response to temptation. James outlined the source of temptation, the steps in temptation, and the solution for temptation.

1. SOURCE OF TEMPTATION (1:13-14)

1:13. James offered a sharp rebuke to those who find an easy excuse for their sinning. To free themselves from responsibility they say, "I am tempted by God," or "from God" (*apo theou*), denoting the origin, not merely the agency. James made it abundantly clear **God cannot be tempted.** There is nothing in God to which evil can make an appeal. He is literally "untemptable" (*apeirastos;* cf. comments on Heb. 4:15). Furthermore, He tempts no one. God often tests, but He never tempts.

1:14. The source of temptation is from within a person; it is **his own evil desire,** lust, or inner craving. **He is dragged away and enticed.** This inner craving draws a person out (*exelkomenos*) like a fish drawn from its hiding place, and then entices him (*deleazomenos,* from the verb *deleazō* "to bait, to catch a fish with bait, or hunt with snares"). So a person both builds and baits his own trap.

2. STEPS IN TEMPTATION (1:15-16)

1:15-16. The biological imagery is vivid. The lust or **desire** conceives and from this conception **sin** is born. The unmentioned father is most certainly Satan. The grotesque child, **sin,** then matures and produces its own offspring, death. The steps are all too clear: unchecked lust yields sin, and unconfessed sin brings death. How strange that sin **gives birth to death.** It may seem strange, but James warned his dear brothers and sisters who were to read this "genealogy" not to be **deceived** or led astray. Just as a right response to trials can result in growth to full spiritual maturity, so a wrong response to lust will result in decline to abject spiritual poverty and ultimately to death itself.

3. SOLUTION FOR TEMPTATION (1:17-18)

1:17-18. In stark contrast with the morbid scene of death that descends from unbridled lust is the bright scene of new life that emanates from **the Word of truth** (v. 18; cf. Eph. 1:13; Col. 1:5). The father of darkness—Satan (Acts 26:18; Col. 1:13)—generates the offspring of sin and death. **The Father of the heavenly lights** (i.e., God, who created the starry universe) gives salvation and life and is unchanging. Shadows from the sun shift, but not the One who made the sun! The words, **every good and perfect gift is from above,** have a poetic cadence in Greek. They are literally, "every good act of giving (*dosis*) and every perfect gift (*dōrēma*) is from above."

The solution for temptation is to be found in a close relationship with the Father and a constant response to His Word. One must rest in the unchangeable Lord of light and rely on His life-giving "Word of truth" (cf. Eph. 1:13; Col. 1:5; 2 Tim. 2:15).

There is no reason why one of God's chosen **firstfruits,** or regenerated believers, has to yield to temptation. He must learn to resist its deadly force, or he can never grow into the spiritual maturity God desires of His children of light (Eph. 5:8; 1 Thes. 5:5).

D. Rest in divine truth (1:19-27)

Ultimately the key both to responding to trials and resisting temptation is to be found in one's reaction to God's Word. Receptivity to the Word, responsiveness to the Word, and resignation to the Word are essential to spiritual growth. One must accept God's Word, act on it, and abide by it.

1. RECEPTIVITY TO THE WORD (1:19-21)

1:19-20. Again James identified with his audience, **My dear brothers,** and then made it clear that what was to follow was of great importance: **take note of this,** or "know this" (*iste*). A threefold injunction follows: let **everyone . . . be quick to listen, slow to speak, and slow to become angry.** In an argument, of course, the one who is listening rather than lambasting is the one who is slow to anger (cf. 3:1-12). Anger fails to yield **the righteous life that God desires,** the goal to which this epistle is committed.

1:21. Consequently it is essential to put away, or remove, **all moral filth** (*ryparian,* used only here in the NT; cf. *rypara,* "shabby," in 2:2) and all the abundance of **evil,** and **humbly** (lit., "in meekness") receive **the implanted Word.** "Planted" (*emphyton,* used only here in the NT) contrasts with grafted. The Word is to be ingrown or inborn, rooted in the fertile soil of the soul. It is that Word of God **which can save.**

2. RESPONSIVENESS TO THE WORD (1:22-25)

1:22. It is not sufficient, however, to receive the Word; one must respond to it in active obedience. The command is clear, **Do not merely listen to the Word. . . . Do what it says.** One must "become," or "keep on becoming" (*ginesthe*), a doer of the Word and not just a hearer. The growing numbers of sermon-sippers who flit from one doctrinal dessert to another like helpless hummingbirds are deceiving themselves. "Deceiving" is from a verb used in the New Testament only here and in Colossians 2:4. *Paralogizomai* means "to cheat or deceive by false reasoning." The deception comes from thinking they have done all that is necessary when actually listening to the Word is only the beginning. A fitting illustration of the "sit, soak, and sour" crowd follows.

1:23-24. The one **who listens** and does nothing **is like a man who** glances at **his face in a mirror and** then **forgets what he** saw. It is interesting that James cited a man (*andri*) in this illustration. A woman would probably not give just a cursory glance, and if she saw a flaw she would probably do what she could to cover it or correct it. Not so this man who sees the "face of his birth" (*prosōpon tēs geneseōs*) and then forgets about it.

1:25. To look into the mirror of the Word of God involves an obligation. One must look **intently into the perfect Law that gives freedom.** The intent and sustained look with a ready response is the key to spiritual strength and continued maturity. The word for "looks intently into" (*parakypsas*) literally means "to stoop down" in order to have a good close look.

The "Law that gives freedom" seems like a paradox. Law seems to imply restraint and therefore a lack of freedom. Not so with God's Law. His perfect Law provides true freedom. "Hold to My teaching," Christ said, "then you will know the truth, and the truth will set you free" (John 8:31-32). One who does what God decrees will find full liberty and **will be blessed in what he does.**

3. RESIGNATION TO THE WORD (1:26-27)

Receptivity to the Word and responsiveness to its revelation must be coupled with a new approach to life. One must be resigned to continued obedience and perpetual practice.

1:26. One who is truly **religious** will demonstrate it by controlled speech. The word "religious" (*thrēskos*) refers to external observances. The outward ritualistic practices which a person may think are commendable are considered to be **worthless** (*mataios,* "futile, fruitless, useless") if there is no parallel control, or **tight rein on the tongue,** a theme elaborated more fully in 3:1-12. Such a person **deceives himself** (*apatōn kardian heautou,* lit., "misleads or seduces his own heart"; cf. a different word for deceive in 1:22).

1:27. A clean and undefiled religion is one in which one's conduct and character are disciplined in accordance with God's Word. The Greek word *thrēskeia* (**religion**) appears only four times in the New Testament and two of those occurrences are here (cf. Col. 2:18; Acts 26:5). It is apparent that God's emphasis is not on religious ritual but on right living.

James outlined what **God the Father** (cf. "Father" in James 1:17) stresses: **look after orphans and widows**—referring to one's conduct, and **keep oneself from being polluted**—referring to one's character. "From being polluted" translates one word *aspilon,* "spotless" (cf. 1 Tim. 6:14; 1 Peter 1:19; 2 Peter 3:14), in contrast with moral filth (James 1:21). A believer with God-pleasing "religion" helps others in need—and thus is **faultless** (lit., "pure, undefiled"), and keeps himself **pure** (lit., "clean"). This is not a definition of religion but rather a contrast to mere acts of worship and ritualistic observances that are commonly called "religion." Again, the goal is a mature Christian walk and practical holiness. What does it take to achieve that goal? The first step is to stand with confidence. Trials or temptations will not topple one who is anchored in God's truth and is applying that truth to his life.

II. Serve with Compassion (chap. 2)

One who is properly related to the Bible is also properly related to the body of Christ. He who stands with confidence serves with compassion. James just made it clear that true religion finds an outlet in service, a service which demands that a believer learn to accept others without prejudice and to assist others without presumption.

A. Accept others (2:1-13)

James became increasingly specific and direct in his admonitions and instructions. He was obviously displeased with the inconsistencies among the brethren. He attacked the attitudes these believers displayed toward others and then complained of their failures to act as they should. He first condemned the attitude of favoritism and gave suggestions on how to combat this obstacle to spiritual maturity. One must learn to accept others, whatever their status or class. He must show courtesy to all, compassion for all, and consistency to all. Equity, love, and fidelity are the vital ingredients.

1. COURTESY TO ALL (2:1-4)

2:1. A transition to a new consideration is evident by James' use of **my brothers.** By "brothers" he meant fellow **believers in our glorious Lord Jesus Christ.** The NIV has done well in showing that it is the faith *in* Christ, not the faith *of* Christ, that is here considered, and in taking the word "glorious" (*doxēs*) in apposition to, and therefore descriptive of, Christ. The key command is likewise clear: **don't show favoritism.** God shows no favoritism (Rom. 2:11; Eph. 6:9; Col. 3:25); therefore neither should Christians. James condemned prejudice and preferential treatment.

2:2-3. The issue addressed is then illustrated. The illustration's hypothetical nature, evident in the Greek "if clause," is shown with the word **suppose.** The specific situation is then presented. A **gold**-fingered and brilliantly clothed man comes **into** the **meeting** place, here designated as a synagogue which emphasizes the Jewish character of both the epistle and this scene. A **poor man** in dirty **clothes** also enters. The word **shabby** (*rypara*, "dirty" or "vile") is found only here and in Revelation 22:11. (Cf. the word *ryparian*, "moral filth," which James used in 1:21.) **Special attention** (lit., "to gaze upon") and preferential seating is given to the rich man, and standing room only or an inferior seat **on the floor** (lit., "under my footstool") is afforded the **poor man.**

2:4. The illustration is followed by a penetrating inquiry: **Have you not discriminated among yourselves?** The question in Greek assumes an affirmative answer. James' brethren must plead guilty not only to discriminatory divisions but also to assuming the role of **judges with evil thoughts** of partiality.

2. COMPASSION FOR ALL (2:5-9)

2:5-7. With the plea, **Listen, my dear brothers,** James went on to explain why their preferential judgment was wrong. He made his point through four questions, each of which anticipated an affirmative answer. First, **Has not God chosen those** who appear **poor** materially, but are **rich** spiritually, **to inherit** His promised **kingdom?** (cf. 1:9) Second, Are not **the rich** the ones who are consistently guilty of oppression, extortion, and slander (*blasphēmousin*, 2:7, lit., "blasphemy"). Third, **Are they not the ones who are dragging you into court?** Fourth, **Are they not the ones who** slander Jesus' **noble name?** Believers **belong** to **Him,** not to the rich exploiters. James' readers would have to agree with these contentions, and to recognize that insulting **the poor** and favoring the rich was wrong and totally unreasonable.

2:8-9. The alternatives are clear. Love is right. Favoritism is sin. James was optimistic; the "if-clause," **if you really keep the royal law,** was written in Greek in such a way that an obedient response was anticipated. The "royal law" was given in Leviticus 19:18 and affirmed by Christ (Matt. 22:39): **Love your neighbor as yourself.** The law is royal or regal (*basilikon*, from *basileus*, "king") because it is decreed by the King of kings, is fit for a king, and is considered the king of laws. The phrase reflects the Latin *lex regia* known throughout the Roman Empire. Obedience to this law, nonpreferential love, is the answer to the evident disobedience to God's **Law**, prejudicial **favoritism**.

3. CONSISTENCY IN ALL (2:10-13)

2:10-11. James was aware there would be some who would tend to dismiss their offense of prejudice as a trivial fault. They would hardly consider themselves as lawbreakers. James went on to make it clear that this was no small offense. **Whoever keeps the whole Law and yet stumbles at just one point is guilty of breaking all of it.** There are no special indulgences. Utilizing the extreme instances of **adultery** and **murder,** James showed the absurdity of inconsistent obedience.

2:12-13. Total obedience is the key. One must both habitually **speak and act** (Gr. pres. tense imper.) as those **to be judged by the Law.** God's Law, because of its wise constraints, brings true **freedom** (cf. 1:25). Disobedience to God's Law brings bondage; and to those who have **not been merciful,** God's **judgment** is **without mercy.** Just as love triumphs over prejudice, **mercy triumphs over judgment.** The verb "triumphs" or "exults over" (*katakauchatai*) appears only here, in 3:14, and in Romans 11:18.

God has ordained unalterable laws. Complete and consistent obedience is required if spiritual maturity is to be attained. The believer is commanded to accept his brother with courtesy, compassion, and consistency.

B. *Assist others (2:14-26)*

Just as the law of love gives no excuse for respect of persons, so the possession of faith gives no license to dispense with good works. A believer must not only demonstrate his love by ready acceptance of others, but he must also demonstrate his faith by responsible aid to others. James went on in his letter to emphasize the expression of true faith, to outline the evidence of true faith, and finally to cite examples of true faith.

1. EXPRESSION OF TRUE FAITH (2:14-17)

2:14. Another shift in the argument of the epistle can be seen by James' use of **my brothers.** He introduced this paragraph with a rhetorical question, **What good is it . . . if a man claims to have faith but has no deeds?** The emphasis is not on the true nature of faith but on the false claim of faith. It is the spurious boast of faith that James condemned. Such "faith" does no "good"; there is no "profit" (*ophelos,* used in the NT only here and in v. 16; 1 Cor. 15:32). It is worthless because it is all talk with no walk. It is only a habitual empty boast ("claims" is in the pres. tense). **Can such faith save him?** A negative answer is anticipated in the Greek. Merely claiming to have faith is not enough. Genuine faith is evidenced by works.

2:15-16. The rhetorical question is followed by a hypothetical but realistic illustration: **Suppose a brother or sister is without clothes and daily food.** (James frequently wrote about the poor: 1:9, 27; 2:2-6, 15.) For one in need of the basics of life, sentimental good wishes do little good, like the common Jewish farewell, **Go, I wish you well** (lit., "Go in peace," cf. Jud. 18:6; 1 Sam. 1:17; 2 Sam. 15:9; Mark 5:34; Luke 7:50). If nothing is done to fill the pressing need for warm clothes and satisfying food, **what good is it?** The same phrase that James used to introduce this paragraph (James 2:14) is repeated for emphasis.

2:17. The vain boast, **faith by itself,** or faith in and of itself with no evidence of **action, is dead.** Workless faith is worthless faith; it is unproductive, sterile, barren, dead! Great claims may be made about a corpse that is supposed to have come to life, but if it does not move, if there are no vital signs, no heartbeat, no perceptible pulse, it is still dead. The false claims are silenced by the evidence.

2. EVIDENCE OF TRUE FAITH (2:18-20)

2:18. This may be one of the most misunderstood sections of the entire epistle. **But someone will say, You have faith; I have deeds.** An imaginary respondent, "someone," was introduced.

He did not object to James' conclusion. He agreed that faith without works is dead. But he wrongly disparaged faith while stressing works (see comments on v. 19).

What follows, **Show me your faith without deeds, and I will show you my faith by what I do,** may be the continuation of the respondent's words. If so, they should be included within quotation marks. (If this were James' response to a contender's "I have deeds," James would have written, "Show me your *deeds* without *faith*.") Though recent translations do not include the second half of verse 18 in the quotation of the respondent (e.g., NEB, NIV, RSV), the NASB correctly considers this entire verse part of his remarks. The Greek, of course, does not include quotation marks, which accounts for the variations in English. It seems, however, that the respondent is throwing down the challenge, "Show me your faith apart from (*chōris*, 'without') works, and I will show you my faith by (*ek*, 'emerging from') my works" (author's trans.).

2:19. It may be well to include even verse 19 as part of the respondent's argument: **You believe that there is one God. Good! Even the demons believe that—and shudder.** If so, he may be a typical Gentile believer who attacked the creedal belief of monotheism accepted by all Jews. He was saying, to "believe" in one God may be good so far as it goes, but it does not go far enough. The demons do that. In fact not only do they believe (the same verb, *pisteuō*); they even "shudder," or "bristle up" (*phrissousin*, an onomatopoeic verb used only here in the NT). The "belief" in one God may not be "trust" in that God. Unless it is "trust," it is not true faith and will not be evidenced in good works.

In other words the respondent is saying, "Faith is not the key; what counts is works." Thus the respondent has gone too far. James did not say that works are *essential* to faith, or that faith is unimportant. His argument was that works are *evidence* of faith.

Other writers understand this passage to mean that James (v. 18b) challenged the "someone" to show his faith without deeds—the point being that it cannot be done! James, however, said that faith can be demonstrated (only) by what one does (v. 18c). The demons' "belief" in God is inadequate. Such a so-called but unreal faith is obviously unaccompanied by deeds on their parts.

2:20. James did not launch into a lengthy refutation of the respondent. The apostle simply addressed him forcefully, **You foolish man,** and returned to his original argument **that faith without deeds is useless** (*argē*, "lazy, idle, negligent"). The adjective "foolish" (*kene*) is usually translated "vain," "empty," or "hollow" (cf. *mataios*, "worthless, fruitless, useless," in 1:26). Flimsy faith is dead; so are empty, faithless works. James' argument is not pro-works/anti-faith or pro-faith/anti-works. He has simply said that genuine faith is accompanied by good works. Spiritual works are the evidence, not the energizer, of sincere faith.

3. EXAMPLES OF TRUE FAITH (2:21-26)

As a final proof of his thesis, James gave two biblical examples: Abraham, the revered patriarch, and Rahab, the redeemed prostitute. He presented each example in the form of a question, anticipating the reader's ready agreement.

2:21. Was not our ancestor Abraham considered righteous for what he did when he offered his son Isaac on the altar? This question is often held to be directly opposed to Paul's statement that Abraham's faith, not his works, caused God to declare him righteous (Rom. 4:1-5). Paul, however, was arguing for the *priority* of faith. James argued for the *proof* of faith. Paul declared that Abraham had faith, and was therefore justified, or declared righteous (Gen. 15:6), prior to circumcision (Gen. 17:11; cf. Rom. 4:9). James explained that Abraham's faith was evident in his practice of Isaac's sacrifice (Gen. 22:12), and he was therefore justified, or declared righteous. Works serve as the barometer of justification, while faith is the basis for justification.

2:22-24. James emphasized the joint role of **faith and ... actions ... working together.** Faith is the force behind the deed. The deed is the finality of the faith. The verb translated **was made complete** (*eteleiōthē*) means to "carry to the end." Faith finds fulfillment in action. So it was with **Abraham.** James and Paul quoted the same passage—Genesis 15:6—to prove their points (cf. Rom. 4:3). Paul said that Abraham was **justified** by faith, and James said that Abraham was justified by faith evidenced **by what he did.**

2:25. In the same way (lit., "and likewise also"; *homoiōs de kai*) **was not even Rahab** declared **righteous for** her actions in welcoming **the spies** (*angelous*, "messengers") and helping them escape? (Josh. 2; 6)

2:26. The conclusion is most clear. **Faith** and **deeds** are as essential to each other as **the body** and **the spirit.** Apart from (*chōris*) the spirit, or the "breath" (*pneumatos*) of life, the body **is dead.** Apart from (*chōris*) the evidence of works, faith may be deemed **dead.** It is *not* the real thing. True faith continually contributes to spiritual growth and development.

Not only is a believer to stand confidently on God's Word even in the midst of trials and temptations (chap. 1), but also he must serve his brothers and sisters in Christ (chap. 2). He is to accept all members of God's family without favoritism (vv. 1-13) and to aid the family with a working faith (vv. 14-26). To gain spiritual maturity a believer must be what God wants him to be and do what God wants him to do.

III. Speak with Care (chap. 3)

Another measure of spiritual maturity is a believer's speech. James devoted a good portion of his letter to attacking a careless and corrupt tongue. He appealed, however, not only for controlled tongues (3:1-12) but also for controlled thoughts (3:13-17). The mouth is, after all, connected to the mind. Winsome speech demands a wise source. Both controlled talk and cultivated thought are necessary.

A. Control talk (3:1-12)

From his discourse on idle faith, James proceeded to discuss idle speech. The failure to bridle the tongue, mentioned earlier (1:26), is now expanded. As disturbing as those who have faith with no works are those Christians who substitute words for works. One's tongue should be controlled. Small though it is, the tongue is powerful and all too prone to perversion and pollution.

1. THE TONGUE IS POWERFUL (3:1-5)

3:1. Again addressing **my brothers,** a sign that a new topic is being considered, James suggested moderation and restraint in the multiplication of **teachers.** Obviously too many of the new Jewish Christians aspired to teach and thereby carry some of the rank and admiration given to Rabbis. It is doubtful that the reference here is to official teachers of the apostolic or prophetic status. These are the unofficial teachers (*didaskaloi*) in the synagogue meetings of the church family where much latitude was given for even strangers to speak. Paul frequently used this courtesy given visitors. James' complaint was simply that too many believers were overly anxious to speak up and show off (cf. John 3:10; 9:40-41).

Teaching has to be done, but those who teach must understand their responsibility, as those **who teach will be judged more strictly.** A teacher's condemnation is greater because, having professed to have a clear knowledge of duty, he is all the more bound to obey it.

3:2. James did not point a finger at the offenders without including himself: **We all stumble in many ways.** Nothing seems to trip a believer more than a dangling tongue. If a believer **is never at fault** (lit., "stumbles not") **in what he says** (lit., "in word"), **he is a perfect,** fulfilled, mature, complete person (*teleios anēr*). He is **able to** "bridle" **his whole body.** Spiritual maturity requires a tamed tongue.

3:3-5. The tongue may be small but it is influential. Three illustrations make this point clear: the bit and the horse, the rudder and the ship, and the spark and the forest. James' use of imagery drawn from natural phenomena is similar to the Lord's. It is likewise characteristic of Jewish thought. The Greek used in this passage is both ancient and eloquent. James was both steeped in Jewish tradition and well-versed in Greek classics.

The argument is clear. Just as little **bits** . . . **turn** grown **horses,** small rudders guide large **ships,** and **a small spark** consumes an entire **forest,** so **the tongue is a small part of the body, but it makes great boasts.** The tongue is petite but powerful!

2. THE TONGUE IS PERVERSE (3:6-8)

3:6. The tongue is not only powerful; it is also perverse. It is small and influential but, worse by far, it can be satanic and infectious. **The tongue** . . . **is a**

fire (cf. Prov. 16:27; 26:18-22), **a world of evil.** The tongue sets itself up *(kathistatai)* among the members, or **parts** of one's anatomy, corrupting, spotting, or staining *(spilousa;* cf. *aspilon,* "spotless," in James 1:27) the whole **body** and inflaming **the whole course of . . . life** (lit., "the wheel of existence" or "wheel of birth," *ton trochon tēs geneseōs).* It is as though the tongue is at the center or hub of the wheel of nature and, like a fireworks display, the wheel is **set on fire** at the center. The more it burns, the faster it revolves until the whole wheel spins in a blaze, spitting fire in all directions. But the tongue is only the fuse; the source of the deadly fire is **hell** itself (lit., "Gehenna," a place in the Valley of Hinnom south of Jerusalem where human sacrifice had been offered [Jer. 7:31] and where continuous burning of rubbish made it a fit illustration of the lake of fire).

3:7. The tongue is not only like an uncontrolled fire. It is also like an untamed beast. Every kind, or all nature *(physis),* of wild beasts—**birds** of the air, **reptiles** on land, and **creatures of the sea**—all **are being tamed and have been tamed by man** (lit., "human nature," *physis;* thus "beastly nature" is tamed by "human nature"). But no human is able to tame the tongue!

3:8. No one **can tame the tongue** because **it is a restless evil,** an unruly, unsteady, staggering, reeling evil (like the "unstable" man of 1:8). Worse yet, the tongue is **full of deadly poison** (cf. Ps. 140:3). Like the poison of a serpent, the tongue is loaded with the venom of hate and death-dealing gossip.

3. THE TONGUE IS POLLUTED (3:9-12)

3:9-10. Similar to the forked tongue of a snake, man's uncontrolled **tongue** both emits **praise** and spews out curses. "Praise," or "saying a good word" *(eulogoumen)* of **our Lord and Father** (this is the only place where the NT uses this title of God) is polluted by a "curse," or "wishing evil" *(katarōmetha)* on **men . . . made in God's likeness** (cf. Gen. 1:27; 9:6; Col. 1:10). That both **praise and cursing** should **come** from **the same mouth** is incongruous. **My brothers, this should not be.**

3:11-12. Again James turned to the natural elements to illustrate his point. Anticipating a negative response, James asked, **Can both fresh** (lit., "sweet," *glyky*) **water and salt** (lit., "bitter," *pikron*) **water flow,** or "bubble up," **from the same spring? Can a fig tree bear olives, or a grapevine bear figs?** Of course not. **Neither** does **salt** *(halykon)* make **water** sweet *(glyky).* The point is clear: a believer's tongue should not be an instrument of inconsistency.

Small and influential, the tongue must be controlled; satanic and infectious, the tongue must be corralled; salty and inconsistent, the tongue must be cleansed.

B. *Cultivate thought (3:13-18)*

A key to right talk is right thought. The tongue is contained in a cage of teeth and lips, but it still escapes. It is not intelligence that keeps the lock on that cage; it is wisdom—a wisdom that is characterized by humility, grace, and peace.

1. WISDOM IS HUMBLE (3:13)

3:13. James asked the rhetorical question, **Who is wise and understanding among you?** "Wise" *(sophos;* cf. *sophias* in 1:5) describes one with moral insight and skill in the practical issues of life. "Understanding" *(epistēmōn)* refers to intellectual perception and scientific acumen.

Let him show it. Here is an original "show and tell." Wisdom is not measured by degrees but by deeds. It is not a matter of acquiring truth in lectures but of applying truth to life. The **good life** and **deeds** are best portrayed **in the humility** of **wisdom,** or "wise meekness" *(prautēti sophias).* The truly wise man is humble.

2. WISDOM IS GRACIOUS (3:14-16)

3:14. True wisdom makes no room for **bitter envy** ("zealous jealousy") or for **selfish ambition** ("factious rivalry," *erithian,* from *eritheuō,* "to spin wool," thus working for personal gain). This is nothing to glory about. To **boast** (lit., "exult," *katakauchasthe*) in such attitudes is to **deny,** or "lie against," **the truth.**

3:15-16. Envy and strife are clear indicators that one's so-called **wisdom** is not from above (cf. 1:17), **but is earthly, unspiritual** ("natural, sensual," *psychikē*), and **of the devil** ("demonic," *daimoniōdēs*). **Envy and selfish ambition,** or rivalry, can only produce **disorder,** or confusion, and **every evil practice.** A truly wise person does not seek glory or gain; he is gracious and giving.

3. WISDOM IS PEACEABLE (3:17-18)

3:17. Wisdom that comes from heaven (lit., "wisdom from above"; cf. "from above" in 1:17) **is first ... pure** or "holy" (*hagnē*), then **peace-loving, considerate** or "forbearing," **submissive** or "easy to be entreated" (*eupeithēs*, only used here in the NT), **full of mercy and good fruit, impartial** (lit., "without uncertainty"; cf. "not doubt" in 1:6), **and sincere** ("without hypocrisy").

3:18. Peace is the seed sown that yields **a harvest** (lit., "fruit") **of righteousness.** The truly wise man is a man of peace.

To achieve "righteousness," spiritual maturity, practical holiness—the theme of this book—a believer must learn to speak with care. Winsome speech comes from a wise spirit. A controlled tongue is possible only with cultured thought. A mouth filled with praise results from a mind filled with purity.

A believer should stand confidently (chap. 1), serve compassionately (chap. 2), and speak carefully (chap. 3). He should be what God wants him to be, do what God wants him to do, and speak as God wants him to speak.

IV. Submit with Contrition (chap. 4)

Fights, quarrels, lust, hate, envy, pride, and sin are words that stain this portion of James' letter like inkblots. In stark contrast with the closing words of chapter 3, "peacemakers who sow in peace raise a harvest of righteousness," chapter 4 opens with "fights and quarrels." James confronted this despicable behavior with valor. Furthermore he gave clear advice on how to quell the storms that are so detrimental to spiritual growth and maturity. A believer must turn hatred into humility, judgment into justice, and boasting into belief.

A. *Turn hatred into humility (4:1-6)*

The appearance of conflict among the followers of Jesus stirred James to intense indignation. The severity of his tone in this section is accented by the absence of the words "my brothers," which James used so frequently in other parts of the letter. He revealed the cause of conflict, outlined the consequences of conflict, and proposed a cure for conflict.

1. CAUSE OF CONFLICT (4:1-2)

4:1. Characteristically, James introduced this new section with a rhetorical question, **What causes fights and quarrels among you?** Where do "fights" (lit., "state of war," *polemoi*) and "quarrels" (lit., individual disputes or "battles," *machai*) come from? James answered his own question: **from your desires that battle within you.** Conflict comes out of (*ek*) inner sensual lusts or pleasures (*hēdonōn*; cf. v. 3). Hedonism, the playboy philosophy that makes pleasure mankind's chief end, still wages battles in people's hearts.

4:2. War is the fruit of illicit wants. Lust brings about murder. Covetousness results in the frustration of not obtaining the hotly pursued desires. It all leads to the "quarrels" and "fights," that "battle" against people, mentioned in verse 1. The last part of verse 2, **You do not have, because you do not ask God,** is best taken with what follows. James did not contend that the reason lust was not gratified was because people failed to ask God to fill those desires. He simply revealed the clear source of conflict deep in covetous human hearts.

2. CONSEQUENCE OF CONFLICT (4:3-4)

4:3. The correct way for Christians to have their legitimate needs met is by asking God. One reason a believer does not receive what he asks for is that he asks **with wrong motives** (lit., "evilly" or "amiss," *kakōs*). The verb **ask** is in the middle voice, meaning, "ask for yourself." The purpose clause that follows further clarifies, **that you may spend what you get on your pleasures.** "Spend" could be translated "squander." "Pleasures" is again the Greek word *hēdonais* (cf. v. 1). God will never provide for "hedonistic squandering"!

4:4. Instead of the customary "my brothers," James bristled with **you adulterous people.** Again he asked a pointed question: **Don't you know that friendship** (*philia*) **with the world** (cf. "world" in 1:27) **is hatred toward God?** Then he added, **Anyone who chooses to be a friend of the world becomes** (lit., "is constituted") **an enemy of God.** The consequence is worse than ending up empty-handed; a rebellious Christian who has an illegitimate relationship with the world is at enmity with God!

3. CURE FOR CONFLICT (4:5-6)

4:5. This is one of the most difficult verses to translate in the entire letter. A very literal translation would be, "Or think you that vainly the Scripture says to envy yearns the spirit which was made to dwell in you, but He gives great grace." Is the "spirit" the Holy Spirit or the human spirit? Is the spirit to be taken as the subject of the verb "yearns" or as its object? Is "envy" to be seen as "unrighteous desire" or as "righteous jealousy"? Numerous translations are possible: (a) "The Spirit who indwells you jealously yearns [for you] and He gives more grace." (b) "He [God] yearns jealously for the Holy Spirit which indwells you and He gives more grace." (c) "The [human] spirit which indwells you yearns to envy, but He [God] gives more grace." The NIV favors the latter idea: **Or do you think . . . that the spirit He caused to live in us tends toward envy,** but "He gives us more grace?" (v. 6)

Not only is the translation of the sentence a problem, but also the apparent indication that it is a part of Scripture poses difficulties. James' question, typically rhetorical, "or do you think Scripture says without reason" (*kenōs*, lit., "vainly"), introduces the section. The ambiguous sentence that follows is not a direct quotation of any passage in Scripture. Rather than assume that James quoted some other sacred book, or some unknown Greek translation of the Old Testament, or that he simply referred to the general sense of Scripture, it seems more reasonable to assume that he focused on the quotation in verse 6, a statement clearly taken from Proverbs 3:34: "God opposes the proud but gives grace to the humble" (also quoted in 1 Peter 5:5).

4:6. Whatever questions remain unresolved about verse 5, there is no question about the clear truth of verse 6. **God opposes the proud.** The word "opposes," or "resists," is *antitassetai*, a military term meaning "to battle against." **To the humble,** however, God **gives grace.** Whether a believer is called to resist his human spirit which tends toward envy or to rejoice in the Holy Spirit who jealously yearns for each believer's edification, the call is to shun pride and to submit humbly to God's authority. The cure for conflict is a humble spirit which is rewarded by God's unmerited favor. James continued by showing in verses 7-12 how humility is related to peaceful justice.

B. Turn judgment into justice (4:7-12)

Apparently the Jewish believers to whom James wrote tended not only to conflict and jealousy but also to condemnation and judgment. Justice, not judgment, is what God requires. Upright, righteous relationships are essential to spiritual growth. Pointed advice for justice is given, the clear advantage of justice is revealed, and the divine author of justice is named.

1. ADVICE FOR JUSTICE (4:7-9)

4:7. In verses 7-9 a whole series of commands (10 aorist imperatives) are given which, if followed, contribute to harmony and holiness. James called for commitment (v. 7), cleansing (v. 8), and contrition (v. 9).

Like a magnet, the call for commitment has both positive and negative poles: **submit . . . to God** and **resist the devil.** "Submit" is a military term "to be subordinated" or "to render obedience." "Resist" (*antistēte*) means "take a stand against." Take a stand against the devil, **and he will flee.**

4:8. On the other hand draw **near to God and He will come near** in response. To draw near to God, however, demands His cleansing. **Wash your hands, you sinners, and purify your hearts, you double-minded.** Both "wash" and "purify" are verbs that refer to ceremonial cleansing, a figure that spoke eloquently to Jewish converts. The need for cleansing is clear from the way James addressed his readers, "you sinners" and "you double-minded" (*dipsychoi*; cf. 1:8).

4:9. Recognition of the tremendous need for cleansing allows no room for merriment. **Grieve** (lit., "be afflicted"), **mourn, and wail** was James' candid advice. Exchange merriment for **mourning** and gaiety for **gloom** (lit., "a downcast look, lowered eyes"). A contrite spirit of confession is essential for God's cleansing.

2. ADVANTAGE OF JUSTICE (4:10-11)

4:10. The key is humility. **Humble yourselves before the Lord, and He will lift you up.** The way up is down. The lowly one becomes the lifted one. There is a marked advantage to humility—eventually it brings honor.

4:11. To **slander** and **judge one another** is totally incongruous to the humble spirit God desires. Furthermore, to judge another is actually a judgment of God's **Law** itself. His Law is a mandate over all people. No one dares assume a haughty position over the Law. The slanderer is sentenced by the Law; the self-styled judge is jeopardized by the Law; only the humble person is honored. True justice is rendered when a believer subjects himself to God in humility and obedience.

3. AUTHOR OF JUSTICE (4:12)

4:12. Only One is above the Law. He alone has the right to modify or overrule it. God is the **one Lawgiver and Judge.** "Lawgiver" is a compound noun used only here in the New Testament (*nomothetēs*, from *nomos*, "law," and *tithēmi*, "to set, place, constitute, or lay down"). God not only authored the Law; He also administrates the Law. He serves as both the executive and judicial branches of the divine government. God is King; He institutes and declares His Law. God is Judge; He upholds and enforces His Law. He is **the One who is able to save and destroy.** There is one Author of the Law, one Judge over the Law, and but one Savior from the Law's condemnation. This reminder of a truth well known by James' Jewish readers was also a rebuke to their haughty attitudes and judgmental actions. **But you—who are you to judge your neighbor?** is another of James' typical penetrating rhetorical questions. A humble attitude and just actions are essential for spiritual growth. James then went on to show how these qualities of life militate against empty boasting.

C. Turn boasting into belief (4:13-17)

In addition to conflict and a judgmental spirit among the brethren, bragging was also apparently prevalent. James gave an example of a boastful statement, struck a condemnatory sentence on such boasting, and offered a practical solution for boasting.

1. STATEMENT OF BOASTING (4:13)

4:13. James' attack was direct. **Now listen** is literally, "Go now." It is the same construction found in 5:1, a colloquial phrase used only by James in the New Testament. The interjection both goads the reader and gains his undivided attention. The offender attacked by James is a fairly typical businessman who makes his plans apart from God. He is self-assertive in his travel plans: **we will go to this or that city;** self-confident in his time schedule, **spend a year there;** and self-centered in his trade relationships, **carry on business and make money.** "Carry on business" is from a compound verb (*emporeusometha*, from *en*, "in," and *poreuomai*, "to go") from which the English word "emporium" has come. It is related to the noun (*emporos*) which could be translated "merchant," "trader," "drummer," or "one who goes in and gets the trade." A vivid picture of the Jewish merchant James tried to correct is a go-getter salesman out drumming up business for the bottom-line objective: "Make money!"

2. SENTENCE ON BOASTING (4:14)

4:14. To the selfish hustlers James simply stated, **Why, you do not even know what will happen tomorrow.** Man's plans are always tentative. His plans are not his own. Time is not his own. In fact, life is not his own. James then fired another of his famous questions: **What is your life?** The answer is **a mist** ("vapor, a puff of steam"). Believers need this godly perspective on their earthly sojourn. Among other things, it blasts boasting right out of the selfish, proud quagmire from which it emerged.

3. SOLUTION FOR BOASTING (4:15-17)

4:15. The key to avoiding boasting is to maintain a godly perspective. Instead of making big plans on the human plane, one must expand his view to include God in the picture. In place of vain boasting one should **say, If it is the Lord's will, we will live and do this or that.** These are not so much words to be used like some charm but a realistic attitude that affects all of one's being and behavior.

4:16. To make sure his readers understood, James reiterated that to **boast and brag . . . is evil.** Self-centered bragging must be replaced by God-honoring trust. The cure for boasting is belief.

4:17. It is likely that chapter 4's concluding sentence, **Anyone, then, who knows the good he ought to do and doesn't do it, sins,** is related not only to the matter of boasting but also to all the advice given thus far in the epistle. "Then" (lit., "therefore," *oun*) supports this contention. James' readers could not plead ignorance. The letter abounds with exhortations to do good. To fail to comply is clearly sin.

To attain spiritual maturity a believer must do the good he now knows. He must stand confidently on God's Word even in trials and temptations. He must compassionately serve his brethren without prejudicial favoritism but with practical faith. He must speak carefully with a controlled tongue and wise, cultivated thought. He must submit in contrition to his all-powerful Father, Lawgiver, and Judge with a humble spirit, just action, and a trusting heart. He must be what God wants him to be, do what God wants him to do, speak as God wants him to speak, and sense what God wants him to sense.

V. Share with Concern (chap. 5)

James continued his attack on self-centered merchants who seem to succeed in their business plans and not only turn a profit but are considered rich with their hoarded wealth. Such wealth James declared waste. Spiritual access is found in sharing, not hoarding, possessions. To those who may have been the victims of the heartless conduct of the rich, or who may have been tempted to turn to similar shortsighted goals, James recommended patience. Finally, to all believers, whether blessed, burdened, or backslidden, James appealed for praise, prayer, and persuasion.

James' concluding remarks center on sharing—sharing one's possessions, sharing with patience, and sharing in prayer.

A. Share in possessions (5:1-6)

The attack begun in the concluding section of chapter 4 is carried into chapter 5 but with greater concentration and condemnation. The rich are denounced. James appears to have included all rich people, both believers (cf. 1:10) and unbelievers (cf. 2:6). There is no plea for reform, only a grim warning that hoarded wealth brings consternation, ends up in corrosion, and results in condemnation.

1. CONSTERNATION FROM WEALTH (5:1)

5:1. The same exclamatory interjection used in 4:13 introduces this section: **Now listen** (lit., "Go now"). The **rich people,** so often the object of envy, were the object of James' scorn and condemnation. He put down those who placed their arrogant trust in things which were doomed to decay. **Weep and wail,** could be elaborated as "burst into tears" (*klausate;* also in 4:9) and "howl with grief" (*ololyzontes,* an onomatopoeic verb used only here in the NT). Money brings merriment only temporarily; wealth eventually results in **misery** (*talaipōriais,* from *talaō,* "to undergo, endure," and *pōros,* "a callus" or "hardened concretion").

2. CORROSION OF WEALTH (5:2-3)

5:2-3. Riches rot, and fine **clothes** may be chewed up by **moths.** The story is not from "rags to riches" but from "riches to rags." **Gold and silver** are the most sought-after metals and have long been considered the material standards for the world. Though they do not rust, they do become **corroded.** Gold can darken and silver tarnishes. **Their corrosion** (*ios,* or "poison," as in 3:8 and Rom. 3:13) is a testimony to the rich man's folly and will consume his **flesh like fire.** As metals lose their luster, the poison of greed eats up people. The corrosion of **wealth** is testimony to this sickness of the wealthy. Hoarding for **the last days** only gives more fuel for the fire that will consume the lost.

3. CONDEMNATION IN WEALTH (5:4-6)

5:4-5. It is not the wealth itself that is condemned, but the greedy attitude toward it and the grisly actions with which it was obtained. God is not deaf to the cries of injustice that rise both from **wages** withheld in fraud and from the laborers who have been oppressed by the rich. The Jewish converts were well aware of God's Law forbidding holding back on wages (Lev. 19:13; Deut. 24:15) and oppressing the poor (Prov. 3:27-28; Amos 8:4-6; Mal. 3:5). The life of **luxury** (*etryphēsate*, "to lead a soft life," used only here in the NT) **and self-indulgence** (*espatalēsate*, "to live voluptuously or wantonly," used only here and in 1 Tim. 5:6), is like so much fat for the **slaughter.** The sarcastic illustration was vivid for Jewish believers who had seen many fattened sheep and oxen meet their fates in sacrifice.

5:6. In the scramble for more wealth, the rich used their influence in courts of justice, and in the process were guilty of bringing condemnation and even death to **innocent men** who offered no resistance ("innocent men" is lit., "the righteous one" though it probably refers to a class of people rather than to one individual). What began as an interest in money ended as an insensitivity to murder.

A believer who seeks spiritual growth dare not become caught up in the accumulation of wealth for himself. He should share his possessions for God's glory and the good of others.

B. *Share in patience (5:7-12)*

From the rich, James turned to the restless. For these he again used the friendly address, "brothers." The tone turns from stark condemnation to sensitive consolation. James excoriated the rich but encouraged the receptive. He appealed to his brethren to be patient. He defined the essence of patience, gave some examples of patience, and indicated an evidence of patience.

1. ESSENCE OF PATIENCE (5:7-9)

5:7. Be patient, then (lit., "therefore"), said James as a direct corollary to the coming judgment on the wicked rich. "Be patient" (*makrothymēsate*) comes from a compound of "long" (*makros*) and "temper" (*thymos*). The idea is to set the timer of one's temper for a long run. Think long. Focus on the final lap in the race of life. Have a long fuse. Look ahead to **the Lord's coming.** The essence of patience is furthermore seen in **the farmer** who **waits** patiently (*makrothymōn*) for the needed **rains** and the ultimate **valuable** (lit., "precious") **crop.**

5:8. The application is clear. Just like the farmer, every believer should **be patient and stand firm, because the Lord's coming is near.** The Lord's return (*parousia*) should stimulate every believer to patience and persistence.

5:9. James called for the believers to stop groaning lest they be judged, because **Jesus the Judge is standing at the door!** In view of the hope of Christ's soon return, believers should cease the petty conflicts to which James alluded in chapter 4. As children in a school classroom look out for their teacher's soon return, God's children should be on guard for Christ's return. In so doing, good behavior and mutual harmony are essential.

2. EXAMPLES OF PATIENCE (5:10-11)

5:10. James reminded his Jewish **brothers** of **the prophets** who endured much **suffering** with **patience** (*makrothymia*, lit., "long-temperedness"; cf. v. 7) as they spoke out **in the name of the Lord.**

5:11. As you know (lit., "behold"), **we consider blessed** (lit. "happy or fortunate"; *makarizomen*) **those who have persevered.** James then presented another well-known and highly revered example of patience, Job. The Lord honored **Job's perseverance** with multiplied blessings (cf. Job 42:12). Interestingly, James did not say that Job had *makrothymia*, "patience," but that he had *hypomonēn*, "steadfastness, endurance, perseverance" (cf. James 1:3; Col. 1:11). Job endured and he was steadfast, though he was impatient with God!

James summed it up: **The Lord is full of compassion and mercy.** "Full of compassion" is a compound adjective (*polysplanchnos*, from *polys*, "much," and *splanchna*, "innermost parts" or "seat of affections"), used only here in the New Testament). "Mercy," also rare (*oiktirmōn*, from the verb *oikteirō*, "to pity") is found only here and in Luke 6:36.

3. EVIDENCE OF PATIENCE (5:12)

5:12. Above all, my brothers, concluded James, **do not swear** or take an empty oath. For those who truly demonstrate the persistence and patience prescribed for believers, there is no need to invoke an oath, whether **by heaven or by earth,** that their word is certain. ("Swear" does not refer to profanity but

JAMES

to taking an oath.) The testimony should be such that when one says **yes,** it means **yes,** and when he says **no,** that is just what he means (cf. Matt. 5:37). The soon return of the Lord, the Judge who stands at the door (James 5:9), is motivation enough for this kind of honesty and trustworthiness, lest one **be condemned** (lit., "fall under judgment").

C. Share in prayer (5:13-20)

A fitting climax to James' letter is his emphasis on prayer. The greatest assistance any believer can offer another is faithful prayer. Prayer is clear evidence of care. Prayer is the "hotline" to the One who can provide for any need no matter how complex or impossible it may seem. To share in prayer, a believer must have a sensitivity to someone's needs, engage in diligent supplication for those needs, and recognize the significance of those needs.

1. SENSITIVITY TO NEEDS (5:13)

5:13. Perhaps the two greatest weaknesses in the average church today are the areas of prayer and praise. The reason for these weaknesses may be traced to insensitivity. There is much need for prayer and much cause to praise. Suffering should elicit prayer. Sufficiency should elicit praise. James used several questions to stress these points. **Is any one of you in trouble?** "In trouble" (*kakopathei*, "suffering ill"; cf. v. 10) relates to suffering from any source. **Is anyone happy? Let him sing songs of praise.** "Praise" (*psallētō*) originally meant "to play on a stringed instrument." The verb is used only four times in the New Testament (cf. Rom. 15:9; 1 Cor. 14:15; Eph. 5:19).

2. SUPPLICATION FOR NEEDS (5:14-18)

5:14-15. James asked a third question and then answered it fully. **Is any one of you sick?** A great deal of misunderstanding has resulted from these verses. Some seem to teach from this passage that full physical health is always just a prayer away. Others have found in this passage justification for "extreme unction" (a practice begun in the eighth century). Still others have tried to relate the process outlined by James to the modern practice of invoking God ("pray over him") and using medicine ("anoint him with oil")—prayer plus a physician.

The heart of the problem lies in just what James meant when he referred to the "sick." Actually there is no reason to consider "sick" as referring exclusively to physical illness. The word *asthenei* literally means "to be weak." Though it is used in the Gospels for physical maladies, it is generally used in Acts and the Epistles to refer to a weak faith or a weak conscience (cf. Acts 20:35; Rom. 6:19; 14:1; 1 Cor. 8:9-12). That it should be considered "weak" in this verse is clear in that another Greek word (*kamnonta*) in James 5:15, translated **sick person,** literally means "to be weary." The only other use in the New Testament (Heb. 12:3) of that word clearly emphasizes this same meaning.

James was not referring to the bedfast, the diseased, or the ill. Instead he wrote to those who had grown weary, who had become weak both morally and spiritually in the midst of suffering. These are the ones who **should call** for the help of **the elders of the church.** The early church leaders were instructed (1 Thes. 5:14) to "encourage the timid" and "help the weak" (*asthenōn*).

James said that the elders should **pray over him and anoint him with oil.** It is significant that the word "anoint" is *aleipsantes* ("rub with oil") not *chriō* ("ceremonially anoint"). The former is the "mundane" word and the latter is "the sacred and religious word" (Richard Chenevix Trench, *Synonyms of the New Testament,* ninth ed. Reprint. Grand Rapids: Wm. B. Eerdmans Publishing Co., 1950, pp. 136-7). "Therefore James is not suggesting a ceremonial or ritual anointing as a means of divine healing; instead, he is referring to the common practice of using oil as a means of bestowing honor, refreshment, and grooming" (Daniel R. Hayden, "Calling the Elders to Pray," *Bibliotheca Sacra* 138. July–September 1981:264). The woman "poured" (*aleiphō*) perfume on Jesus' feet (Luke 7:38). A host "put oil" (*aleiphō*) on the head of his guest (Luke 7:46). A person who is fasting should not be sad and ungroomed, but should "put oil" (*aleiphō*) on his head, and wash his face (Matt. 6:17). Thus James' point is that the "weak" (*asthenei*) and "weary" (*kamnonta*) would be refreshed, encouraged, and uplifted by the elders who rubbed oil on the despondents' heads and prayed for them.

For the fallen, discouraged, distressed weary believer, restoration is assured and the elders' **prayer offered in faith will make the sick person** (lit., "weary one") **well** (i.e., will restore him from discouragement and spiritual defeat), and **the Lord will raise him up**.

That the restoration is spiritual, not physical, is further clarified by the assurance, **if he has sinned, he will be forgiven**. Many physically ill Christians have called on elders to pray for them and to anoint them with oil, but a sizable percentage of them have remained sick. This fact suggests that the passage may have been mistakenly understood as physical restoration rather than spiritual restoration.

5:16. The conclusion is clear: **therefore confess your sins to each other and pray for each other**. A mutual concern for one another is the way to combat discouragement and downfall. The cure is in personal confession and prayerful concern. The healing **(that you may be healed)** is not bodily healing but healing of the soul (*iathēte*; cf. Matt. 13:15; Heb. 12:13; 1 Peter 2:24). It is the **powerful and effective ... prayer of a righteous** person that brings the needed cure from God. This of course relates to the closing verses of James' letter. If James 5:14-16 refer to physical healing, then those verses seem disjointed with the verses before and after them.

5:17-18. James again gave an example well known to his Jewish audience. First, it was the prophets (v. 10), then Job (v. 11), and now **Elijah**. James identified Elijah as a fellow sufferer. **A man just like us** could be translated "a man of like feeling" or "of similar suffering" (*homoiopathēs*; cf. *kakopathei* in vv. 10, 13). Elijah knew all the frailties of human nature but "in prayer he prayed" (*proseuchē proseýxato*), that is, **he prayed earnestly,** and **rain** was withheld and later restored (1 Kings 17:1; 18:41-46). Earnest and persistent prayer, of course, is essential, whereas halfhearted prayer is self-defeating (cf. James 1:6-8).

3. SIGNIFICANCE OF NEEDS (5:19-20)

5:19-20. James' last appeal to his readers has a touch of tenderness and a clear note of encouragement to those who have helped others who have grown weary and have fallen from the way. **My brothers,** he wrote, "if any one among you strays from the truth, and someone turns him around, let him know that the one who turns him back from his error will save his soul from death and will hide a multitude of sins" (author's trans.).

These who have lost their way are the "sick ones" of the church family. They have wandered away. The Greek word here (*planēthē*) suggests one who has missed his path and is hopelessly lost. "Planet" was taken from this Greek word to convey the idea that the luminaries were "wandering stars" (cf. Jude 13), not "fixed" like the rest.

Wandering ones need to be brought back to the fold. James referred here not to evangelism but to restoration. Revival, not redemption, is in view. The rescue action is of great significance. A lost sheep is saved from destruction and his **sins** (the sins of the restored one, not the restorer) are covered as if a veil were thrown over them (cf. 1 Peter 4:8). He can move ahead again on the path toward spiritual maturity.

James has given clear instructions about how to achieve practical holiness and spiritual maturity. His pointed exhortations were designed to stab the consciences and stir the souls of his beloved Jewish brothers. Stand with confidence, serve with compassion, speak with care, submit with contrition, and share with concern. A believer should be what God wants him to be, do what God wants him to do, say what God wants him to say, sense what God wants him to sense, and share what God wants him to share. Spiritual maturity involves every aspect of life.

BIBLIOGRAPHY

Adamson, James B. *The Epistle of James*. The New International Commentary on the New Testament. Grand Rapids: Wm. B. Eerdmans Publishing Co., 1976.

Barclay, William. *The Letters of James and Peter*. 2d ed. Philadelphia: Westminster Press, 1960.

Davids, Peter H. *The Epistle of James*. The New International Greek Testament Commen-

JAMES

tary. Grand Rapids: Wm. B. Eerdmans Publishing Co., 1982.

Gaebelein, Frank E. *The Practical Epistle of James.* Great Neck, N.Y.: Doniger and Raughley, 1955.

Harrop, Clayton K. *The Letter of James.* Nashville: Convention Press, 1969.

Hiebert, D. Edmond. *The Epistle of James.* Chicago: Moody Press, 1979.

Manton, Thomas. *A Practical Commentary or An Exposition with Notes on the Epistle of James.* London: John Gladding, 1840.

Mayor, Joseph B. *The Epistle of St. James: The Greek Text with Introduction Notes and Comments.* Reprint. Grand Rapids: Baker Book House, 1978.

Mitton, C. Leslie. *The Epistle of James.* London: Marshall, Morgan & Scott, 1966.

Motyer, J.A. *The Tests of Faith.* London: InterVarsity Press, 1970.

Oesterley, W.E. "The General Epistle of James." In *The Expositor's Greek Testament*, vol. 4. Reprint. Grand Rapids: Wm. B. Eerdmans Publishing Co., 1976.

Plumptre, E.H. *The General Epistle of St. James.* The Cambridge Greek Testament for Schools and Colleges. Cambridge: University Press, 1893.

Reicke, Bo. *The Epistles of James, Peter, and Jude.* The Anchor Bible. Garden City, N.Y.: Doubleday & Co., 1964.

Robertson, A.T. *Studies in the Epistle of James.* New York: George H. Doran, 1915.

Ropes, James H. *A Critical and Exegetical Commentary on the Epistle of St. James.* The International Critical Commentary. Edinburgh: T. & T. Clark, 1916.

Ross, Alexander. *The Epistles of James and John.* The New International Commentary on the New Testament. Grand Rapids: Wm. B. Eerdmans Publishing Co., 1954.

Strauss, Lehman. *James Your Brother.* New York: Loizeaux Brothers, 1956.

Tasker, R.V.G. *The General Epistle of James.* The Tyndale New Testament Commentaries. Grand Rapids: Wm. B. Eerdmans Publishing Co., 1957.

Vaughan, Curtis. *James: Bible Study Commentary.* Grand Rapids: Zondervan Publishing House, 1974.

1 PETER
Roger M. Raymer

INTRODUCTION

First Peter was written to Christians who were experiencing various forms of persecution, men and women whose stand for Jesus Christ made them aliens and strangers in the midst of a pagan society. Peter exhorted these Christians to steadfast endurance and exemplary behavior. The warmth of his expressions combined with his practical instructions make this epistle a unique source of encouragement for all believers who live in conflict with their culture.

Authorship. First Peter 1:1 clearly identifies the author as "Peter, an apostle of Jesus Christ." His given name was Simon, but Jesus, on meeting him, said he would be called Cephas (John 1:42). The Greek translation of the Aramaic word *Cephas* is "petros," and the word in both languages means "stone" or "rock." Jesus' description of Simon's future strength of character became his personal name. Interestingly he is the only man in the New Testament called Peter.

Until relatively recent times the authenticity of the epistle's claim to apostolic authorship went unchallenged. Then some modern scholars noted that Peter was considered by Jewish religious leaders as "unschooled" and "ordinary" (Acts 4:13). The superb literary style and sophisticated use of vocabulary in 1 Peter seem to indicate that its author must have been a master of the Greek language. Those who deny Peter's authorship say that such an artistic piece of Greek literature could not possibly have flowed from the pen of a Galilean fisherman.

Though Peter could be called "unschooled" and though Greek was not his native tongue, he was by no means ordinary. The Jewish leaders saw Peter as unschooled simply because he had not been trained in rabbinical tradition, not because he was illiterate. Luke also recorded (Acts 4:13) that these same leaders were astonished by Peter's confidence and the power of his Spirit-controlled personality. Peter's public ministry spanned more than 30 years and took him from Jerusalem to Rome. He lived and preached in a multilingual world. It is reasonable to believe that after three decades Peter could have mastered the language of the majority of those to whom he ministered.

The rhetorical style and use of metaphor employed in 1 Peter could just as easily be credited to an accomplished public speaker as to a literary scholar. Certainly Peter had the time and talent to become an outstanding communicator of the gospel via the Greek language.

Any further doubts of Petrine authorship based on linguistic style may be answered by the fact that Peter apparently employed Silas as his secretary (1 Peter 5:12). Silas, though a Jerusalem Christian, was a Roman citizen (Acts 16:36-37) and may have had great facility in the Greek language. But whether or not Silas aided Peter with the grammatical Greek nuances, the epistle's content still remains Peter's personal message, stamped with his personal authority.

The parallels between this letter and Peter's sermons recorded in Acts are significant (cf. 1 Peter 1:20 with Acts 2:23 and 1 Peter 4:5 with Acts 10:42). One of the more striking examples is the similarity between 1 Peter 2:7-8 and Acts 4:10-11. In each passage Psalm 118:22 is quoted and applied to Christ. It is interesting that Peter was present when Christ Himself used Psalm 118:22 to refer to His rejection by the Jewish leaders (Matt. 21:42).

Another allusion to Jesus' ministry that strongly supports Peter's authorship is the command to elders in 1 Peter 5:2 to "be shepherds." The only other place in the New Testament where this word is used as a command is in John 21:16, where Jesus gave Peter the same charge. In several other passages the author referred to being an eyewitness of Christ's earthly ministry (1 Peter 1:8; 2:23; 5:1).

This epistle exerted a wide influence on early Christian writings. The letters of Polycarp, Clement, and Irenaeus (to name only a few) show that the early church unquestionably accepted the authenticity of 1 Peter. The letter's content and the witness of church history support beyond any reasonable doubt the simple affirmation made in verse 1. The letter indeed comes from "Peter, an apostle of Jesus Christ."

Date. Peter wrote this epistle apparently just before or shortly after the beginning of Nero's persecution of the church in A.D. 64. Since Peter referred to the government as still functioning (an institution which commends those who do right and punishes those who do wrong; 2:13-14), some believe that the church was not yet facing an organized Roman persecution. Evidently repressive laws had not yet been enacted specifically against Christians. It was still possible for Peter's readers to "honor the king" (2:17). The persecution and suffering that Peter did refer to was primarily social and religious rather than legal. A hostile pagan society would slander, ridicule, discriminate against, and even inflict physical abuse on those whose lifestyles had radically changed because of their faith in Christ.

However, Peter seemed to indicate that greater persecution was imminent. He assured his readers (1:6) that they could rejoice though they "may have had to suffer grief in all kinds of trials." Peter exhorted them to prepare, to be self-controlled (1:13), possibly to suffer as Christians according to God's will (4:19). So perhaps Nero's severe persecution had already begun in Rome and was spreading to the provinces to which Peter was writing. This would place the date of the letter in late A.D. 64 or early 65.

The suggestion that the persecution had already begun in Rome also explains why Peter would refer cryptically to his location as "Babylon" (5:13). Peter was in Rome during the last decade of his life. His martyrdom is dated about A.D. 67. At the time of the writing of 1 Peter he was not in the custody of the Roman officials, and evidently wished to conceal his true location. (Other scholars, however, say that Peter was in the literal city of Babylon, where a Jewish community then flourished.)

Destination. First Peter is addressed to Christians scattered throughout five Roman provinces of the peninsula of Asia Minor. That area today is northern Turkey. The churches in those provinces were made up of both Jews and Gentiles. This epistle is rich in references to and quotations from the Old Testament. Jewish Christians would have found special significance in the term *diasporas*, translated "scattered," used in the salutation (1:1). Jews who lived outside of Jerusalem were referred to as living in the diaspora.

Gentile readers would have noted Peter's exhortation to holy living in light of their background of complete ignorance of God's Word (1:14). Gentile Christians also would have been greatly encouraged by the fact that though they *were* in ignorance, they were now considered "the people of God" (2:10). Clearly Peter carefully included both Jewish and Gentile Christians in his letter of encouragement to the churches of Asia Minor.

Purpose. This epistle could be understood as a handbook written for ambassadors to a hostile foreign land. The author, knowing persecution would arise, carefully prescribed conduct designed to bring honor to the One they represented. The purpose then of 1 Peter was to encourage Christians to face persecution so that the true grace of Jesus Christ would be evidenced in them (5:12).

This epistle gives a theology of practical exhortation and comfort for believers' daily needs. Peter concretely linked doctrine with practice. The *new birth* gives a living hope to those in the midst of persecution. *New conduct* is prescribed because Christ endured unjust suffering. *New behavior* is required to demonstrate the grace of God to an unbelieving and hostile world. And *new responsibilities* are placed on the leaders and members of the body of Christ since they should stand together as living stones against the onrushing tide of persecution.

Those who read 1 Peter are encouraged to lift their eyes from present problems and trials and behold the vistas provided by an eternal perspective. For though believers may for a while suffer grief in trials, they wait for an inheritance that can never perish, spoil, or fade.

OUTLINE

I. Customary Salutation (1:1-2)
   A. Identification of the author (1:1a)
   B. Identification of those addressed (1:1b-2)
II. Chosen for New Birth (1:3-2:10)
   A. The new birth's living hope (1:3-12)
      1. The future inheritance (1:3-5)
      2. The present joy (1:6-9)
      3. The past revelation (1:10-12)
   B. The new birth's holiness (1:13-2:10)
      1. The preparation (1:13-16)
      2. The price (1:17-21)
      3. The purification (1:22-2:3)
      4. The practice (2:4-10)
III. Challenged to New Behavior (2:11-3:7)
   A. New behavior before the world (2:11-25)
      1. Christian conduct as witnesses (2:11-12)
      2. Christian conduct as citizens (2:13-17)
      3. Christian conduct as slaves (2:18-25)
   B. New behavior in the family (3:1-7)
      1. Christian conduct as wives (3:1-6)
      2. Christian conduct as husbands (3:7)
IV. Cautioned for New Persecution (3:8-4:19)
   A. Overcoming injustice (3:8-22)
      1. A compassionate conduct (3:8-12)
      2. A clear conscience (3:13-22)
   B. Enduring suffering (chap. 4)
      1. Christlike attitude (4:1-6)
      2. Christlike service (4:7-11)
      3. Christlike faith (4:12-19)
V. Charged with New Responsibility (5:1-11)
   A. Elders are to shepherd (5:1-4)
   B. Young men are to submit (5:5-7)
   C. All are to stand firm (5:8-11)
VI. Conclusion (5:12-14)

COMMENTARY

I. Customary Salutation (1:1-2)

The introductory greeting is the common form of salutation used in first-century correspondence. Paul's letters usually began in the same manner, identifying both the author and those to whom the letters were addressed.

A. Identification of the author (1:1a)

1:1a. Peter is the Greek translation of the Aramaic Cephas, the name Jesus gave Simon when he was called to be a disciple (John 1:42). Nobody else in the New Testament could be identified as Peter, **an apostle of Jesus Christ.** This bold statement of apostolic authority is supported both by internal evidence in the text and by its early and universal acceptance as a part of the canon of Scripture.

B. Identification of those addressed (1:1b-2)

1:1b-2. Peter immediately, using a careful choice of words, began to comfort and encourage his readers. Christians are **God's elect** not by chance or human design but by God's sovereign, unconditional choice. Once only the nation of Israel could claim this title.

It is not surprising that those who have been **chosen** by God are seen as **strangers in the world** (from the one word *parepidēmois*, that emphasizes both foreign nationality and temporary residence; cf. 2:11). Christians, whose citizenship is in heaven (cf. Phil. 3:20), live in the midst of a pagan society as aliens and sojourners, displaced persons whose thoughts should often turn toward their true home.

The readers were **scattered throughout Pontus, Galatia, Cappadocia, Asia, and Bithynia,** sprinkled like salt throughout five of Asia Minor's Roman provinces. The letter was evidently meant to circulate among the churches in this area. "Scattered" (*diasporas*) had special meaning to the Jewish Christians in these churches. The diaspora referred to Jews who were separated from their homeland. Peter adapted this word which previously described Israel to emphasize the condition of the early church.

Peter elaborated on the descriptive term "God's elect" (cf. 2:9) **who have been chosen according to the foreknowledge of God.** God's choice is part of His predetermined plan, and is not based on any merit in those who are elected, but solely on His grace and love for them before their creation.

As the Williams translation puts it, God's choosing is "in accordance with" (*kata*) or in keeping with His foreknowledge. This seems preferable to the view that election follows or is based on foreknowledge. Moreover the word for foreknowledge (*prognōsin*) means more than a passive foresight; it contains the idea of "having regard for" or "centering one's attention on" (cf. Kenneth S. Wuest, *First Peter in the Greek New Testament for the English Reader*, p. 15). The same word is used in 1:20 of Christ who was "chosen" by the Father before Creation. The Father did more than merely know about His Son ahead of time; He knew Him completely. Thus God chose all those on whom He focused His attention (by His grace, not because of their merit).

The sanctifying work of the Spirit has set these chosen ones apart for service, putting God's choice and purpose into effect. The result of the Spirit's work is **obedience . . . and sprinkling by His blood.** "Obedience" (*hypakoēn*, from *hypakouō*, "to hear under, to hearken") is man's responsibility to be submissive to God's Word (cf. Ex. 24:7; Rom. 1:5; 15:18; 16:26). One living in obedience is constantly being cleansed with Christ's blood and is thus "set apart" from the world (cf. 1 John 1:7, 9). The blood sprinkling is redolent of the Old Testament priestly work at the tabernacle (Lev. 7:14; 14:7, 16, 51; 16:14-15; cf. Heb. 9:13; 12:24), which required obedience on the part of the offerers. However, the only time *people* were sprinkled with blood was at the inauguration of the Mosaic Covenant (Ex. 24:8).

In these words (1 Peter 1:2) Peter laid the theological foundations for this letter of encouragement. "God" **the Father** in His grace had chosen them and God the "Spirit" had sanctified them through the atoning blood of God the Son, **Jesus Christ.** (All three Persons of the Trinity are mentioned in this verse.) Thus Peter greeted his readers with the prayerful wish that they might experience **in abundance** God's **grace** (*charis*) **and peace** (*eirēnē*, equivalent of the Heb. *šālôm*; cf. 5:14). The words (lit.) "Grace to you and peace be multiplied" are also used in 2 Peter 1:2. God's grace was dear to Peter, for he referred to it 10 times in this epistle (1 Peter 1:2, 10, 13; 2:19-20 [trans. "commendable" in these two verses]; 3:7; 4:10; 5:5, 10, 12).

II. Chosen for New Birth (1:3–2:10)

Peter continued to present the theological basis for encouragement in persecution. The stress throughout this section is on God's grace toward believers, evidenced by His sovereign call to salvation and its results in a believer's life. In the midst of trials one's new birth is the source of a living hope and a lifestyle of holiness.

A. The new birth's living hope (1:3-12)

In a doxology of praise to God, Peter encouraged his readers by reminding them that the new birth gave them a living hope in an imperishable future inheritance. The inheritance is sure because believers are shielded by the power of God till it is ready to be revealed. Consequently Christians may rejoice even when they face trials, since trials will prove their faith genuine and thus bring greater glory to Christ. Finally the new birth's hope is based not only on a future inheritance and present blessings but also on the written Word of God.

1. THE FUTURE INHERITANCE (1:3-5)

1:3. The contemplation of God's grace caused Peter to praise God, the Author of salvation and the Source of hope. The words **Praise be to the God and Father of our Lord Jesus Christ** are identical to 2 Corinthians 1:3. The phrase **in His great mercy** refers to God's unmerited favor toward sinners in their hopeless condition. **He has given us new birth;** people can do nothing to merit such a gift. The words "has given . . . new birth" translate *anagennēsas*, from the verb "beget again" or "cause to be born again." It is used only twice in the New Testament, both times in this chapter (1 Peter 1:3, 23). Peter may have been recalling Jesus' interview with Nicodemus (John 3:1-21). The "new birth" results in **a**

living hope through the resurrection of Jesus Christ from the dead. The "living hope" is based on the living resurrected Christ (cf. 1 Peter 1:21). The Christian's assurance in Christ is as certain and sure as the fact that Christ is alive! Peter used the word "living" six times (1:3, 23; 2:4-5; 4:5-6). Here "living" means that the believer's hope is sure, certain, and real, as opposed to the deceptive, empty, false hope the world offers.

1:4. The sure hope is of a future **inheritance** (*klēronomian*). This same word is used in the Septuagint to refer to Israel's promised possession of the land (cf. Num. 26:54, 56; 34:2; Josh. 11:23); it was her possession, granted to her as a gift from God. A Christian's inheritance cannot be destroyed by hostile forces, and it will not spoil like overripened fruit or fade in color. Peter used three words, each beginning with the same letter and ending with the same syllable, to describe in a cumulative fashion this inheritance's permanence: **can never perish** (*aphtharton*), **spoil** (*amianton*), **or fade** (*amaranton*). This inheritance is as indestructible as God's Word (cf. 1 Peter 1:23, where Peter again used *aphtharton*). Each Christian's inheritance of eternal life is **kept in heaven** or "kept watch on" by God so its ultimate possession is secure (cf. Gal. 5:5).

1:5. Not only is the inheritance guarded, but heirs who have been born into that inheritance **are shielded by God's power.** "Shielded" (*phrouroumenous*) is a military term, used to refer to a garrison within a city (Phil. 4:7 uses the same Gr. word). What greater hope could be given to those undergoing persecution than the knowledge that God's power guards them from within, to preserve them for an inheritance of salvation that will be completely **revealed** to them in God's presence. Believers possess salvation now (pres. tense) but will sense its full significance at the return of Christ **in the last time.** This final step, or ultimate completion of "the salvation of their souls" (1 Peter 1:9), will come "when Jesus Christ is revealed," a clause Peter used twice (vv. 7, 13).

2. THE PRESENT JOY (1:6-9)

1:6. A living hope results in a present joy. **In this** likely refers to the truths mentioned in verses 3-5. Peter encouraged his readers to put their knowledge into practice. Their response to the tremendous theological truths taught so far should be that they would **greatly rejoice.** Knowledge alone cannot produce the great joy of experiential security and freedom from fear in the face of persecution. God's omnipotent sovereignty needs to be coupled with human responsibility. Christians are responsible to respond in faith. Faith turns sound doctrine into sound practice. Faith acts on the content of theology and produces conduct that corresponds to that content. Faith makes theological security experiential. The Apostle John wrote, "This is the victory that has overcome the world, even our faith" (1 John 5:4). This kind of faith or living hope can enable believers to rejoice even when they are called on **to suffer grief in all kinds of trials.**

Peter stressed that a Christian's joy is independent of his circumstances. James used the same two Greek words (*poikilois peirasmois*, trans. here "all kinds of trials"). The trials themselves are seen as occasions for joy (James 1:2). Though trials may cause temporary grief, they cannot diminish that deep, abiding joy which is rooted in one's living hope in Christ Jesus.

1:7. These various trials—which seem to refer to persecution rather than life's normal problems—have two results: (a) they refine or purify one's faith—much as **gold** is **refined by fire** when its dross is removed, and (b) trials prove the reality of one's **faith.** Stress deepens and strengthens a Christian's faith and lets its reality be displayed. The word *dokimazomenou*, rendered **proved genuine,** means "to test for the purpose of approving" (cf. *dokimion*, "testing," in v. 7 ["the trial of your faith," kjv] and James 1:3, and *dokimon*, "test," in James 1:12).

In addition to *comparing* faith to gold, Peter *contrasted* purified faith with purified gold. Faith is more precious, **of greater worth, than gold.** Even refined gold, though it lasts a long time, eventually perishes (cf. 1 Peter 1:18; cf. James 5:3). It will be valueless in the marketplace of eternity. But faith "purchases" an inheritance that can never perish.

Genuine faith is not only of ultimate value to its possessor, but it will also bring **praise, glory, and honor** to the One whose name Christians bear, when He will return (**is revealed;** cf. 5:1) to claim them as His own. "Is revealed" translates *apokalypsei*, from which comes "apocalypse" (cf. 1:5, 12, and comments on v. 13).

1:8. Here is the climax of the experiential joy that results from faith. God accomplished salvation through the work of His Son Jesus Christ. So the focus of a believer's faith is not on abstract knowledge but on the person of Christ. The apostle's warm heart overflowed as he spoke of the love and belief in Christ of those who, unlike himself, did not see Jesus when He walked on earth. Peter may have had in mind Jesus' words: "Blessed are those who have not seen and yet have believed" (John 20:29). Yet, though Christians **do not** now **see Him,** like Peter they love and **believe in Him,** and are also **filled with an inexpressible and glorious joy.** The verb *agalliasthe* ("are filled with . . . joy") was used by Peter in 1 Peter 1:6, "you greatly rejoice," and *agalliōmenoi* is used in 4:13.

1:9. Believers can rejoice because they **are** (pres. tense) **receiving** (*komizomenoi*, "to receive as a reward") what was promised, namely **salvation,** the **goal** or culmination (*telos*, "end") **of . . . faith.** For those who love and believe in Jesus Christ, salvation is past ("He has given us new birth," v. 3), present ("through faith are shielded by God's power," v. 5), and future (it is their "inheritance," v. 4, which will "be revealed in the last time," v. 5, and is "the goal of your faith," v. 9). Since each day brings believers closer to that final day, they are now "receiving" it. All of this—in spite of persecution which deepens and demonstrates one's faith—is certainly cause for "inexpressible and glorious joy"! (v. 8)

3. THE PAST REVELATION (1:10-12)

1:10-12. The living hope of the new birth springs not only from believers' future inheritance and present experience but also from their faith in God's written Word (v. 11). Peter iterated that faith is not based on the mere writings of men but on the Word of God. **Concerning this salvation** (cf. "salvation" in vv. 5, 9) **the prophets . . . searched intently and with the greatest care** their own Spirit-guided writings. They longed to participate in this salvation and coming period of grace and tried to discover the appointed **time and circumstances to which the Spirit of Christ in them was pointing.** They pondered how the glorious Messiah could be involved in suffering. Again Peter echoed the teachings of Christ (cf. Matt. 13:17).

In 1 Peter 1:10-12 the apostle gave a practical illustration of the doctrine of the inspiration of Scripture he clearly stated in 2 Peter 1:20-21. The prophets did not fully understand all that the Holy Spirit had authored through them. It was the Spirit who predicted **the sufferings of Christ** (Isa. 53) **and the glories that would follow** (Isa. 11). Peter's readers would be encouraged by this reminder that Christ's suffering was followed by glory. They too would experience glory after their suffering (cf. 1 Peter 5:10).

Peter gave further encouragement (1:12), stating that the prophets understood they were not writing for themselves but for those who would live later, those who would hear **the gospel** proclaimed **by the Holy Spirit** (cf. "the Spirit of Christ," v. 11), and consequently follow Christ. In the ultimate stage of believers' salvation they will experience glory, not suffering. The writer of Hebrews also referred to this "ultimate" salvation (Heb. 1:14; 2:3).

The reality of the Christian's living hope was held in awe and wonder by the angelic hosts of heaven. Prophets and angels alike wondered about "this salvation" in **the grace that was to come** (v. 10).

B. *The new birth's holiness (1:13-2:10)*

The believers' living hope based on their new birth should lead to a lifestyle of holiness. Those chosen for new birth are also called to be holy. Peter exhorted his readers to prepare to meet the challenge of obedience by adopting a new mind-set. The price paid for a believer's redemption calls for reverence and obedience. Obedience involves purifying oneself and practicing holy living, while offering spiritual sacrifices as a royal priest.

1. THE PREPARATION (1:13-16)

1:13-16. Peter now gave five pointed exhortations: **prepare your minds for action; be self-controlled; set your hope.**

... do not conform to ... evil desires. ... be holy. Actually in the Greek the first, second, and fourth are participles, which are subordinate to *two* commands: "have hope" and "be holy." The participles either support the commands (i.e., have hope, with a prepared mind and self-control; and be holy, not conforming to evil desires) or they take the role of commands, as in the NIV.

(1) "Prepare your minds for action" (v. 13). Obedience is a conscious act of the will. Christians in conflict need a tough-minded holiness that is ready for action.

(2) "Be self-controlled" (v. 13; cf. 4:7; 5:8; 1 Thes. 5:6, 8). This word *nēphontes*, from the verb *nēphō* ("be sober") is used only figuratively in the New Testament. It means to be free from every form of mental and spiritual "drunkenness" or excess. Rather than being controlled by outside circumstances, believers should be directed from within.

(3) "Set your hope fully" (1 Peter 1:13). Holy living demands determination. A believer's hope is to be set perfectly (*teleiōs*, completely or unchangeably), and without reserve **on the grace** (cf. v. 10) to be bestowed **when Jesus Christ is revealed** (lit., "in the revelation [*apokalypsei*] of Jesus Christ"; cf. the same phrase in v. 7; also cf. the verb "be revealed" [*apokalyphthēnai*] in v. 5). Four times Peter has already spoken of the Savior's return and the accompanying ultimate stage of salvation (vv. 5, 7, 9, 13).

The strenuous mental preparation suggested by the three admonitions in verse 13 is needed so that Christians (4) **do not conform to** (*syschēmatizomenoi*, also used in Rom. 12:1) **the evil desires** (1 Peter 1:14) of their past sinful lives (cf. Eph. 2:3), when they were ignorant of God (cf. Eph. 4:18). Rather **as obedient children** (lit., "children of obedience") they were to mold their characters to (5) "**be holy**" **in all** they did (1 Peter 1:15). Their lifestyle was to reflect not their former **ignorance** (*agnoia*), but the **holy** (*hagioi*) nature of their heavenly Father who gave them new birth and called them (cf. "called" in 2 Peter 1:3) to be His own. First Peter 1:15-16 do not speak of legal requirements but are a reminder of a Christian's responsibility in his inner life and outer walk. Though absolute holiness can never be achieved in this life, all areas of life should be in the process of becoming completely conformed to God's perfect and holy will. The quotation in verse 16 was familiar to all who knew the Old Testament (Lev. 11:44-45; 19:2; 20:7).

2. THE PRICE (1:17-21)

The high cost of salvation—the beloved Son's precious blood—calls for believers to live in reverent fear before God. Holy living is motivated by a God-fearing faith which does not take lightly what was purchased at so great a cost.

1:17-19. Obedient children know the holy nature and just character of this One who **judges ... impartially.** Their right to call God **Father** leads to their obeying Him **in reverent fear.** So they are to live according to His absolute standards, **as strangers** (cf. "aliens" in 2:11) to the world's shifting, situational ethics. "Reverent fear" is evidenced by a tender conscience, a watchfulness against temptation, and avoiding things that would displease God. Children of obedience should also be strangers to their former **empty way of life** (cf. v. 14) **handed down** from their forebears, since they have been **redeemed** (*elytrōthēte*, from *lytroō*, "to pay a ransom") **with the precious** (cf. 2:4, 6-7) **blood of Christ** (cf. 1:2). That redemption is a purchasing from the marketplace of sin, a ransom not paid by silver or gold, which perish (cf. v. 7), but with the priceless blood of a perfect **Lamb.** Similar to the sacrificial lambs which were to be **without ... defect,** Christ was sinless, uniquely qualified as "the Lamb of God, who takes away the sin of the world" (John 1:29; cf. Heb. 9:14).

1:20-21. This payment for sin was planned **before the Creation of the world** and **revealed** for people's sake through the Incarnation of Jesus Christ. (The pres. Age is **these last times** [v. 20] whereas the coming Age is "the last time" [v. 5].) It is through Christ, whom the Father resurrected (cf. v. 3) and **glorified** in His Ascension (John 17:5; Heb. 1:3) that people may come to know and trust **in God.** As a result of God's eternal plan and priceless payment for sin, **faith and hope** can be placed in Him. (Cf. "faith" in 1 Peter 1:5, 7, 9; and "hope" in vv. 3, 13.)

3. THE PURIFICATION (1:22–2:3)

The response of holy living that should result from the new birth is now applied to three areas. Obedience to the truth purifies and produces (a) a sincere love for the brethren (1: 22-25), (b) repentance from sin (2:1), and (c) a desire for spiritual growth (2:2).

1:22. Holy living demands purification. A positive result of **obeying the truth** is a purified life (cf. v. 2b). "How can a young man keep his way pure? By living according to Your Word" (Ps. 119:9). As trials refine faith, so obedience to God's Word refines character. One who has **purified** himself by living according to God's Word has discovered the joy of obedience.

A changed life should also be evidenced by a changed relationship with God's other children. A purified life allows one to love purely those who share the same faith. **Sincere** (*anypokriton*) could also be rendered "without hypocrisy." All evil thoughts and feelings regarding one's **brothers** and sisters in Christ must be removed, for His followers **are to love ... deeply, from the heart.** This kind of loving (*agapēsate*, from *agapē*) can come only from a changed heart, from one whose motives are pure, and who seeks to give more than he takes. This love is to be expressed not shallowly but "deeply" (*ektenōs*, "at full stretch" or "in an all-out manner, with an intense strain"; cf. *ektenē* in 1 Peter 4:8).

1:23-25. Peter again reminded his readers that they had experienced the new birth (cf. v. 3): **For you have been born again.** This supernatural event made it possible for them to obey the truth, purify themselves, and love the brethren. This change in their lives would not die, because it took place through God's **Word,** which is **imperishable** (*aphthartou*, the word in v. 4 that described a believer's inheritance), **living and enduring.** Peter supported his exhortation (v. 22) by quoting Isaiah 40:6-8 (1 Peter 1:24-25). All that is born of perishable seed withers and falls, but God's Word **stands forever.** This imperishable Word was the content of Peter's preaching (cf. v. 12). His hearers must be affected by its life-changing power, as indicated in 2:1-3.

2:1. Repentance was called for: **Therefore, rid yourselves.** Peter then listed five sins of attitude and speech, which if harbored would drive wedges between believers. **Malice** (*kakian*) is wicked ill-will; **deceit** (*dolon*) is deliberate dishonesty; **hypocrisy** (*hypokriseis*), pretended piety and love; **envy** (*phthonous*), resentful discontent; and **slander** (*katalalias*), backbiting lies. None of these should have any place in those who are born again. Rather, in obedience to the Word, believers are to make decisive breaks with the past.

2:2. Peter wanted his readers to be as eager for the nourishment of the Word as babies are for **milk.** After believers cast out impure desires and motives (v. 1), they then need to feed on wholesome **spiritual** food that produces growth. (**Pure** [*adolon*] is deliberately contrasted with "deceit" [*dolon*] in v. 1. God's Word does not deceive; neither should God's children.) Christians should approach the Word with clean hearts and minds (v. 1) in eager anticipation, with a desire to **grow** spiritually. The words **in your salvation** (lit., "unto salvation") recall the ultimate fulfillment of salvation spoken of in 1:5, 7, 9, 13.

2:3. Quoting Psalm 34:8, Peter continued the milk analogy used in 1 Peter 2:2 and likened their present knowledge of Christ to tasting. They had taken a sample, having experienced God's grace in their new birth, and had found that indeed **the Lord is good.**

4. THE PRACTICE (2:4-10)

Peter then used a new metaphor in his exhortation to holy living. His readers, having purified themselves, were ready for the practice or ministry of holiness. No longer babies, they were to grow up together to offer spiritual sacrifices as a chosen "royal priesthood."

2:4. As you come to Him does not refer to the initial response of a sinner who comes to Christ for salvation. The participle's tense and voice indicate that this coming is a personal, habitual approach. It is an intimate association of communion and fellowship between believers and their Lord.

The first step in practicing holiness is fellowship with Jesus Christ, **the living Stone.** Here Peter used a unique figure of speech. In 1:3 he referred to a "living hope" and in 1:23 to the "living ... Word"; then in 2:4 he referred to Christ as "the living Stone." Peter developed and explained the metaphor of the stone in the following verses. Here he said this Stone is living. It has life in itself and gives life to others. People may enter into personal, vital relationships with this "living Stone." Whereas Christ was **rejected by men . . . God** had **chosen** Him (cf. 1:20) and held Him **precious** (cf. 1:19; 2:4, 7). Christians rejected by the world may take heart in the knowledge that they are the elect (1:1), valued (1:18) by God.

2:5. Believers are identified with Christ, for He is *the* living Stone and they are **like living stones.** And as they become more like Him, further conformed to His image, they **are being built into a spiritual house.** Jesus told Peter, "On this rock I will build My church" (Matt. 16:18). Now Peter (1 Peter 2:4-5) clearly identified Christ as the Rock on which His church is built. Paul called the church a "temple" (1 Cor. 3:16; Eph. 2:21) and "a dwelling" (Eph. 2:22). Believers not only make up the church but serve in it, ministering as **a holy priesthood, offering spiritual sacrifices.** All believers are priests (cf. 1 Peter 2:9; Heb. 4:16; Rev. 1:6) and need no mediator other than Jesus Christ to approach God directly. Such priestly service requires holiness (cf. 1 Peter 1:16, 22). Praise to God and doing good to others are spiritual sacrifices that please Him (Heb. 13:15). However, "living stones" may also offer themselves as "living sacrifices" (Rom. 12:1), **acceptable to God through Jesus Christ.**

2:6. In verses 6-8 Peter marshaled Old Testament support about the stone from three passages. His first source is Isaiah 28:16, where Christ is the **chosen and precious** (cf. "precious" in 1 Peter 1:19; 2:4, 7) **cornerstone.** A cornerstone is the visible support on which the rest of the building relies for strength and stability. Believers trust in Christ much as a building rests on its cornerstone. Moreover, they **will never be put to shame.** The Greek double negative *ou mē* used here in the subjunctive mood indicates an emphatic negative assertion referring to the future: never indeed will they be shamed. So Peter encouraged his readers with a sure scriptural promise of ultimate victory for those who trust Christ.

2:7-8. These verses present a sharp contrast between those who believe and those who do not. Christ is "precious," of ultimate value, to those who believe. But those who have **rejected** Christ, the Stone (Peter's second quotation is from Ps. 118:22) **stumble** because of their disobedience. This happened to the chief priests and Pharisees Jesus referred to when He quoted Psalm 118:22 (Matt. 21:42; cf. 21:43-46).

Peter's third quotation is from Isaiah 8:14. Rejection of Jesus Christ is fatal and is connected with disobeying **the message** of God's Word (1 Peter 2:8b). To **disobey** the message (cf. 4:17) is to reject it; and to obey it is to believe (cf. obedience in 1:14, 22 and "obedient to the faith" in Acts 6:7). All who do not receive Christ as their Savior will one day face Him as their Judge. Because of sin, all disobedient unbelievers are **destined for** a "stumbling," which will lead to eternal condemnation.

2:9-10. Peter closed this portion of his letter of encouragement with a moving exhortation for his readers to practice holiness. He reminded them that, in contrast with the disobedient who are destined for destruction, they were a **chosen** (*eklekton*; cf. "elect," *eklektois*, 1:1) **people.** Peter again echoed the Old Testament, specifically Isaiah 43:20. "Chosen people," which used to apply only to Israel, was now used of both Jewish and Gentile believers. The responsibility once solely trusted to the nation of Israel has now, during this Age of Grace, been given to the church. At Sinai, God told Moses to tell the people, "You will be for Me a kingdom of priests and a holy nation" (Ex. 19:6). Now believers in the Church Age are called **a royal priesthood, a holy nation, a people belonging to God.** Peter called Christians "a holy priesthood" (1 Peter 2:5) and "a royal priesthood" (2:9; cf. Rev. 1:6). The words "belonging to God" loosely render the words *eis peripoiēsin*, which are literally "unto obtaining or preserving" (also used in Heb. 10:39, where the NIV has "are saved"). Christians are a special people because God has preserved them for Himself. While these descriptions of the church are similar to those used of Israel in the Old Testament, this in no way indicates that the church supplants Israel and assumes the national blessings promised to Israel (and to be fulfilled in the Millennium). Peter just used similar terms to point up similar truths. As Israel was "a chosen people, a royal priesthood, a holy nation, a people belonging to God," so too believers today are chosen, are priests, are holy, and belong to God. Similarity does not mean identity.

God's purpose in choosing believers for Himself is so that they may **declare the praises of Him** before others. "Praises" could also be translated "eminent qualities," "excellencies," or "virtues" (*aretos*, used only four times in the NT: Phil. 4:8; 1 Peter 2:9; 2 Peter 1:3, 5). Believer-priests should live so that their heavenly Father's qualities are evident in their lives. They are to serve as witnesses of the glory and grace of God, who called them **out of darkness into His wonderful light.** Peter (1 Peter 2:10) explained this figure with a quotation from Hosea 2:23. "Darkness" refers to the time when his readers were pagans, ignorant of God's provision of salvation (cf. Col. 1:13), when they were **not a people,** when they **had not received mercy.** His "wonderful light" now illumines **the people of God** because they **have received mercy.** The practice of holiness, in which God's people serve as a holy and royal priesthood offering spiritual sacrifices and extolling His excellencies, is the proper response to the mercy (cf. 1 Peter 1:3) they have received.

III. Challenged to New Behavior (2:11–3:7)

How can Christians, as a people belonging to God, declare His praises before others? In this section Peter answered this question by suggesting specific ways Christians can behave differently before the world, as citizens, as slaves, and as wives and husbands. Even in familiar situations, their conduct should be different.

A. New behavior before the world (2:11-25)

The world Peter had in view refers to the people his readers faced daily as witnesses, citizens, and slaves. Peter challenged Christians to take a stand against sin, to submit to lawful authority, and to endure harsh masters patiently. This kind of conduct would win others to belief, silence the tongues of foolish people, and bring commendation from God.

1. CHRISTIAN CONDUCT AS WITNESSES (2:11-12)

2:11. Peter warmly addressed his readers as **dear friends** or better, "beloved" (*agapētoi*). Those who are loved by God are exhorted to live **as aliens** (*paroikous*, "those who live in a place that is not their home," used figuratively of Christians, whose real home is in heaven) **and strangers in the world** (cf. comments on "strangers" in 1:1). Just as their Christian values and beliefs are rejected by the world, so they are to live apart from the immorality and **sinful desires** that surround them. **Abstain** (*apechesthai*) is literally "hold oneself constantly back from." Christians are to resist the sinward pull of those worldly desires **which war against** (cf. James 4:1) their spiritual lives. In this real spiritual battle a demonic strategy is to attack believers at their weakest points.

2:12. Christians are to abstain from sinful desires not only for their own spiritual well-being but also in order to maintain an effective testimony before unbelievers. The negative exhortation of verse 11 is now followed by positive instruction. A positive Christian lifestyle is a powerful means of convicting the world of its sin (cf. Matt. 5:16). Peter used the word **good** (*kalos*) twice in this verse to define both Christians' **lives** and their works. A "good" life is composed of **good deeds** (cf. Matt. 5:16; Eph. 2:10; Titus 3:8; James 2:18). Before the critical eyes of slanderous people and their false accusations, the "good deeds" of believers can **glorify God** (cf. Matt. 5:16; Rom. 15:6; 1 Cor. 6:20) and win others to belief. **On the day He visits** is literally "in the day of [His] visitation" (*en hēmera episkopēs*; cf. Luke 19:44). Some say this refers to God's "visiting" or looking on the wicked in judgment, but it probably refers to their salvation (i.e., when God looks in on them in His mercy and brings them to conversion; cf. *epeskepsato*, Acts 15:14).

2. CHRISTIAN CONDUCT AS CITIZENS (2:13-17)

2:13-15. Christians are responsible to obey the law (cf. Rom. 13:1-7; Titus 3:1-2). Peter exhorted his readers to abide by governmental laws, **to submit . . . to every authority** (*ktisei*, lit., "creation" or here "institution" or "law") **instituted among men** (*anthrōpinē*, "made by man, human"). The motivation for obedience is not avoiding punishment but is **for the Lord's sake.** To honor God who ordained human government, Christians are to observe man-made laws carefully as long as those laws do not conflict with the clear teaching of Scripture (cf. Acts 4:19). The general purpose of legal authority is to **punish . . . wrong and to commend . . . right.** Evidently Christians were being slandered and falsely accused of evil, for Peter stressed that **it is God's will** (*thelēma*, a term expressing the result of one's purpose or desire; cf. "God's will" in 1 Peter 3:17; 4:2, 19) that through excellent behavior they **silence** (*phimoun*, lit., "muzzle") **the ignorant talk of foolish men.** Each of the three Greek words rendered "ignorant talk of foolish men" begins with the letter alpha, as do the three Greek words in 1:4 rendered "never perish, spoil, or fade." Apparently Peter enjoyed alliteration!

This section of Peter's argument leads many to believe that the organized persecution through oppressive Roman laws either had not begun or had not yet reached the provinces of Asia Minor. Christians were then facing lies and verbal abuse, not torture and death. Christians were still enjoying the protection of a legal system which commended those who obeyed the law. So a believer's best defense against slanderous criticism was good behavior.

2:16. Submission to lawful authority does not negate Christian liberty (cf. Gal. 5:1, 18). Civil laws should be freely obeyed, not out of fear but because doing so is God's will. Christian freedom is always conditioned by Christian responsibility (cf. Gal. 5:13) and must never be used **as a cover-up** (*epikalymma*, lit., "veil") **for evil.** Christians enjoy true freedom when they obey God and **live as servants** (*douloi*, lit., "slaves"; cf. Rom. 6:22) **of God.** Though living **as free men**, they should also live as God's slaves.

2:17. This section concludes with a four-point summary of Christian citizenship. First, Christians are to **respect** (*timēsate*, "honor, value, esteem"; cf. *timēn*, "respect, honor," in 3:7) . . . **everyone** (cf. Rom. 12:10; 13:7). Believers should be conscious of the fact that each human has been uniquely created in God's image. Second, Christians are to **love the brotherhood of believers,** their brothers and sisters in Christ. God's family members should love each other. Third, Christians are to **fear God.** The verb "fear" (*phobeisthe*) here does not mean to be in terror, but awe and reverence that leads to obedience (cf. *phobō* in 1 Peter 1:17, *phobou* in 3:16, and *phobon* in 2 Cor. 7:11). One will never truly respect people until he reverences God. Fourth, believers are to **honor the king.** "Honor" is from *timaō*, the verb used at the beginning of this verse. The respect or "honor" due to all is especially to be given to those God has placed in authority (cf. "the king" in 1 Peter 2:13 and "governors" in v. 14; cf. Rom. 13:1).

3. CHRISTIAN CONDUCT AS SLAVES (2:18-25)

Peter's instruction to slaves included two reasons why they should patiently endure personal injustice. First, this found favor with God, and second, it faithfully followed Jesus Christ's example.

2:18. The Greek word for **slaves** here is not *douloi*, the common term for slaves (cf. v. 16), but *oiketai*, which refers to household or domestic servants (cf. Luke 16:13; Rom. 14:4). The word translated **submit** (*hypotassomenoi*) is a nominative participle that continues the idea of submission expressed in 1 Peter 2:13 through the aorist imperative *hypotagēte*. This word of exhortation was relevant to a large number of Peter's first readers. Servants and slaves made up a high percentage of the early church, and undeserved punishment and suffering was common for the underlings. To be sure, there were some **good and considerate** masters. Certainly Christian masters were to be numbered in that category. However, Peter challenged Christian slaves to a new behavior which required them to submit to and respect even **those who are harsh.** "Harsh" is from the Greek *skolios* (lit., "curved," "bent," or "not straight"). The medical term "scoliosis," referring to curvature of the spine, comes from this word.

2:19-20. Peter set forth a principle here that may be applied to any situation where unjust suffering occurs. The **commendable** (lit., "for this is grace") motivation for patiently bearing **up under . . . unjust suffering** is a believer's **conscious** awareness of God's presence. No **credit** accrues for enduring punishment for **doing wrong**. It is respectful submission to *undeserved* suffering that finds favor with God because such behavior demonstrates His grace.

2:21-22. Peter powerfully supported his exhortation to slaves by citing Christ's example of endurance in unjust suffering. The Williams translation renders the opening phrase of this verse, "For you have been called for this purpose," referring to suffering for doing good. Christians are **called** (*eklēthēte*; cf. 1:15; 2:9) to **follow** Christ, to emulate His character and conduct, because He **suffered for** them. The word rendered **an example** (*hypogrammon*, lit., "underwriting"), appearing only here in the New Testament, refers to a writing or drawing that a student reproduces. Peter delineated Christ's example in verse 22 by quoting from Isaiah 53:9. Jesus **committed no sin,** either before or during His suffering (cf. 2 Cor. 5:21; Heb. 4:15; 1 John 3:5). He was completely innocent in both deed and word: **no deceit** (*dolos*; cf. 1 Peter 2:1) **was found in His mouth.**

2:23-25. Christ was the perfect example of patient submission to unjust suffering. **He did not retaliate . . . He made no threats** (cf. Rom. 12:19-20). Humanly speaking, the provocation to retaliate during Christ's arrest, trial, and crucifixion was extreme. Yet He suffered in silence, committing Himself to God. Peter explained (1 Peter 2:24) why the One who could have destroyed His enemies with a word patiently endured the pain and humiliation of the Cross. God was justly judging **our sins** which His Son **bore** (cf. 2 Cor. 5:21). In the Greek the words "our sins" are near the beginning of the verse and thus stand out emphatically, while **He Himself** stresses Christ's personal involvement. His death makes it possible for believers to be free from both the penalty and the power of sin and to live for Him: **so that we might die to sins and live for righteousness** (cf. Rom. 6:2, 13). Christ suffered so it would be possible for Christians to follow His example, both in suffering and in righteous living. Peter made a general reference to salvation: **by His wounds you have been healed** (Isa. 53:5). This does not refer to physical healing for the verb's past tense indicates completed action, the "healing" is an accomplished fact. The reference is to salvation. Christ's suffering (lit., "wound"; *mōlōpi*, "stripe left by a lash," referred to Jesus' scourging) and death accomplished "healing," the salvation of every individual who trusts Him as his Savior.

Christ not only set the example and provides salvation, but He also gives guidance and protection to those who were headed away (**like sheep going astray**) from Him, but who then "turned about" (rather than **returned**) **to the Shepherd and Overseer** (*episkopon*) **of their souls.** "Shepherd" and "Overseer" stress Christ's matchless guidance and management of those who commit themselves to His care (cf. Ezek. 34:11-16).

B. New behavior in the family (3:1-7)

Peter extended the principles of respect and submission to authority, from Christian conduct in the world to Christian conduct in the family. He challenged his readers to new behavior as submissive wives and considerate husbands.

1. CHRISTIAN CONDUCT AS WIVES (3:1-6)

3:1-4. The participle translated **be submissive** (*hypotassomenai*, lit., "being under authority") carries the force of a command (cf. 2:18). This command is for **wives** to submit to their *own* **husbands** (cf. Eph. 5:22; Col. 3:18). The command does not require women to be subordinate to men in general but to their husbands as a function of order within the home. A wife is to accept her place in the family under the leadership of her husband whom God has placed as head in the home. Wives are to be submissive even if their husbands are unbelievers, so those men might be saved **by the behavior of their wives.** The powerful **purity** of a godly woman's life can soften even the stoniest male heart without a word (cf. Titus 2:5).

A woman who wins this kind of victory has a winsome loveliness that comes not **from outward adornment** but from her **inner self, the unfading beauty of a gentle and quiet spirit** (cf. 1 Tim. 2:9-11). This adornment of the spirit **is of great worth in God's sight.** While the world prizes costly clothing and gold jewelry, a woman with a gentle and quiet spirit is precious to God. Peter did not state that women should not wear jewelry and nice clothes, but that Christian wives should not think of outer attire as the source of genuine beauty.

3:5-6. Examples of **holy women** in the Old Testament support Peter's exhortation. Purity of life (v. 2) and a submissive spirit (v. 5) have always been a godly woman's lasting source of beauty and attractiveness. **Sarah** is chosen as a specific example of a woman who was **submissive to** her husband. She **obeyed Abraham and called him her master.** That is, she recognized him as the leader and head of their household (Gen. 18:12). Like other holy women of the past, Sarah put her **hope in God.** This kind of conduct gives women the spiritual heritage of Sarah: **You are her daughters if you do what is right and do not give way to fear** (*ptoēsin*, "terror"—used only here in the NT). Wives who are fearful (perhaps because of disobeying their husbands) are not putting all their trust in God.

2. CHRISTIAN CONDUCT AS HUSBANDS (3:7)

Peter exhorted Christian husbands to give their wives two gifts of love: understanding and respect.

3:7. The words (*kata gnōsin*) translated **considerate** (more lit., "according to knowledge" or "with understanding") point out that husbands should understand and be considerate of their wives' spiritual, emotional, and physical needs. Paul also elaborated on the husband's responsibility to protect and care for his wife, "just as Christ does the church" (Eph. 5:28-30).

Also husbands are to **treat** their wives **with respect as the weaker partner.** "Weaker" (*asthenesterō*) refers to physical or emotional weakness, not intellectual inferiority, for wives are their husbands' fellow **heirs** of God's **gift of life.** If Peter referred here to Christian husbands whose wives were Christians, then "the gracious gift of life" could refer to salvation (cf. Rom. 8:17; Eph. 3:6). If, however, the exhortation were directed to Christian husbands whose wives were unsaved (as 1 Peter 3:1-2 was written to wives with unsaved husbands), then "the gift of life" would refer to sharing the gift of physical life together. Peter added that husbands who do not treat their wives with consideration and respect (*timēn*, "honor"; cf. 2:17) cannot expect to have their **prayers** answered.

IV. Cautioned for New Persecution (3:8-4:19)

In the first two chapters Peter referred to "all kinds of trials" (1:6), accusations of "doing wrong" (2:12), "the ignorant talk of foolish men" (2:15), and "the pain of unjust suffering" (2:19). All these persecutions seem to have resulted from the natural reactions of a pagan society against Christians who faithfully obeyed Jesus Christ.

Peter then warned that a time of more severe persecution and suffering was close at hand. He cautioned Christians to keep clear consciences when facing injustice, to endure the inevitable suffering with Christlike courage.

A. *Overcoming injustice (3:8-22)*

Peter used both Christ and Noah to illustrate the principle that in times of rising persecution the right response to injustice results in blessing.

1. A COMPASSIONATE CONDUCT (3:8-12)

3:8-12. Finally introduces a new section rather than giving a summary of the previous exhortations to specific groups (cf. "finally" in Phil. 3:1; 1 Thes. 4:1). Peter now addressed all his readers **(all of you)** and gave practical principles for living peacefully in a hostile pagan culture. First Peter 3:8-9 is Peter's exposition of Psalm 34:12-16, which he then quoted (1 Peter 3:10-12). Peter constructed his thoughts around the three exhortations in the psalm.

Whoever would love life . . . must first **keep his tongue from evil** (3:10). Verse 8 is a listing of Christian characteristics that keep a tongue from evil. **Harmony** (*homophrones*) could be translated "like-minded." Christians are urged to **be sympathetic** (*sympatheis*), to **love as brothers** (*philadelphoi*), to **be compassionate** (*eusplanchnoi*; cf. *splanchna* in Phil. 2:2; Phile. 7, 20), **and humble** (*tapeinophrones*). Of these five characteristics listed in 1 Peter 3:8 only the word for "compassionate" is found more than once in the New Testament and it is only used twice (here and in Eph. 4:32). This unique vocabulary stresses the importance of these Christian virtues which keep one

from deceitful (*dolon;* cf. 1 Peter 2:1, 22) **speech.**

The second exhortation, taken from Psalm 34:14, is foreshadowed by 1 Peter 3:9, **do not repay evil with evil** (cf. Rom. 12:17). Turning **from evil** (1 Peter 3:11) requires that there be no retaliation for ill treatment. Jesus taught this same law of love: "If someone strikes you on the right cheek, turn to him the other also" (Matt. 5:39).

Third, rather than returning evil, Christians are to **seek peace** (*eirenēn;* cf. 1 Peter 1:2; 5:14) **and pursue it** (Ps. 34:14). Peace is pursued by returning a **blessing** (1 Peter 3:9) when an insult is given. "Blessing" (*eulogountes*) here means to speak well of someone. This differs from the word "blessed" (*makarioi,* "fortunate or privileged" in verse 14; cf. 4:14; Matt. 5:3-11). Jesus said, "Pray for those who persecute you" (Matt. 5:44), and Paul wrote, "When we are cursed, we bless" (1 Cor. 4:12). This is the compassionate way that Christians should pursue peace. As a result, believers **inherit a blessing** (1 Peter 3:9; cf. 1:4; 3:7), **for the eyes of the Lord** (v. 12) watch over **the righteous and His ears are attentive to their prayer.** The "eyes" and "ears" of the Lord are figures of speech, anthropomorphisms which attribute human physical characteristics to God. Here the figures emphasize God's watchful oversight and careful attention to His people's needs (cf. 2:25).

2. A CLEAR CONSCIENCE (3:13-22)

Persecution occurred, however, in spite of believers' desires to live peacefully and their eagerness to do good. Peter encouraged his readers with the fact that the right response to undeserved suffering results in blessing. He presented the principle in verses 13-17 and provided examples in verses 18-22.

3:13-14. **Who is going to harm you . . .?** The context of Peter's question makes it almost rhetorical. Though the adversary, through physical suffering or material hardship, would distress those who were **eager** (*zēlōtai,* lit., "zealots") **to do good,** no real harm can come to those who belong to Christ. For even if suffering should occur, Christians **are blessed** and thus should **not be frightened.** The word here translated "blessed" (*makarioi;* cf. 4:14) was used by Jesus (Matt. 5:3-11). To be "blessed" in this context does not mean to "feel delighted" but to be "highly privileged." Christians are not to be afraid of what men can do to them (cf. Matt. 10:28). Consequently 1 Peter 3:14 concludes with a quotation from Isaiah 8:12 which, in context, is part of an exhortation to fear God rather than men.

3:15. In their **hearts** Christians are to **set apart Christ as Lord.** Alexander Maclaren wrote, "Only he who can say, 'The Lord is the strength of my life' can go on to say, 'Of whom shall I be afraid?'" (*Expositions of Holy Scriptures,* 16: 42) Christians should overcome fear by sanctifying (*hagiasate,* "make separate from others") Christ as their Lord (*kyrion*). As a result Christians should **always be prepared** (*hetoimoi,* "ready"; cf. 1:5) **to give . . . the reason** (*apologian,* the "defense" which a defendant makes before a judge; cf. Acts 22:1; 25:16) **for** their **hope** in Christ. Such an oral defense should be consistent with one's "set-apart" conduct.

3:16. A believer's testimony should not be given in an arrogant manner but **with gentleness and respect.** ("Respect" here is from *phobos,* "fear," whereas "respect" for one's wife [v. 7] is *timē,* "honor.") Christians who are not afraid in the face of persecution are able to witness respectfully to their faith in Christ. They then keep **a clear** (*agathēn,* "good") **conscience** (*syneidēsin;* cf. 2:19; 3:21). Peter may have been alluding to the occasion when he denied Christ out of fear, in words that were neither gentle nor respectful.

Christians who suffer unjustly and keep a clear conscience put to shame those who **slander** their **good behavior in Christ.** Once again Peter encouraged his readers with the fact that good behavior is their best defense against unjust punishment and persecution.

3:17. However, Peter pointed out that it may be **God's will** (*thelēma;* cf. 2:15; 4:2, 19) for them **to suffer for doing good** (cf. 1:6; 2:15; 4:16, 19). This, as he told them earlier, "is commendable before God" (2:20) and so is **better** than deserved suffering **for doing evil** (cf. 2:14). First Peter 3:17 is an effective summary of the content of 2:15, 19-20.

3:18. In verses 18-22 Peter illustrated the principles given in verses 13-17. Once again Christ provided the perfect example. He suffered for doing what was right

(2:14). His sinless life provoked the unjust hostilities of evil men. However, He did not fear men but trusted Himself to God. Christ clearly stated His purpose and committed Himself to a course of action. He died in mankind's place, keeping His conscience clear (cf. 2:23). As a result He received tremendous blessing and reward in His own resurrection and exultation.

J.M.E. Ross wrote that verse 18 is "one of the shortest and simplest, and yet one of the richest summaries given in the New Testament of the meaning of the Cross of Jesus" ("The First Epistle of Peter," in *A Devotional Commentary*. London: Religious Tract Society, n.d., pp. 151-52). **Christ died for sins** (cf. 2:21, 24). The phrase "for sins" (*peri hamartiōn*) is used in the Septuagint in regard to the sin offering for atonement. However, **once for all** (cf. Rom. 6:10; Heb. 9:26, 28; 10:10) is clearly a contrast with the Old Testament yearly sacrifice on the Day of Atonement and declares the complete sufficiency of Christ's death. The substitutionary nature of Christ's death is indicated by the phrase **the righteous for the unrighteous** (*dikaios hyper adikōn*). Christ, the "righteous One" (*dikaios*), uniquely qualified to die as the substitute for (*hyper*, "for," "in place of," or "instead of") the "unrighteous ones" (*adikōn*). The divine purpose for Christ's sacrificial death was man's reconciliation, **to bring** people **to God**.

Peter concluded his summary of Christ's redemptive work by referring to His resurrection. Though Christ **was put to death in the body** (*sarki*, "flesh"), He **was made alive by the Spirit**. "By the Spirit" translates one word, *pneumati*, which could refer to the third Person of the Trinity as the agent of Christ's resurrection. Or it may refer to Christ's human spirit in contrast with His human body (cf. 1 Peter 4:6).

3:19-20. Through whom ... He ... preached to the spirits in prison has been subject to many interpretations. Some believe Peter here referred to the descent of Christ's Spirit into hades between His death and resurrection to offer people who lived before the Flood a second chance for salvation. However, this interpretation has no scriptural support.

Others have said this passage refers to Christ's descent into hell after His crucifixion to proclaim His victory to the imprisoned fallen angels referred to in 2 Peter 2:4-5, equating them with "the sons of God" Moses wrote about (Gen. 6:1-2). Though much commends this view as a possible interpretation, the context seems more likely to be referring to humans rather than angels.

The "spirits" (*pneumasin*, a term usually applied to supernatural beings but also used at least once to refer to human "spirits"; cf. Heb. 12:23) are described in 1 Peter 3:20 as those who were disobedient **when God waited patiently for** Noah to finish building **the ark**. They had rebelled against the message of God during the 120 years the ark was being built. God declared He would not tolerate people's wickedness forever, but would extend His patience for only 120 more years (Gen. 6:3). Since the entire human race except Noah (Gen. 6:5-9) was evil, God determined to "wipe mankind ... from the face of the earth." The "spirits" referred to in 1 Peter 3:20 are probably the souls of the evil human race that existed in the days of Noah. Those "spirits" are now "in prison" awaiting the final judgment of God at the end of the Age.

The problem remains as to *when* Christ preached to these "spirits." Peter's explanation of the resurrection of Christ (3:18) "by the Spirit" brought to mind that the preincarnate Christ was actually in Noah, ministering through him, by means of the Holy Spirit. Peter (1:11) referred to the "Spirit of Christ" in the Old Testament prophets. Later he described Noah as "a preacher of righteousness" (2 Peter 2:5). The Spirit of Christ preached through Noah to the ungodly humans who, at the time of Peter's writing, were "spirits in prison" awaiting final judgment.

This interpretation seems to fit the general theme of this section (1 Peter 3:13-22)—keeping a good conscience in unjust persecution. Noah is presented as an example of one who committed himself to a course of action for the sake of a clear conscience before God, though it meant enduring harsh ridicule. Noah did not fear men but obeyed God and proclaimed His message. Noah's reward for keeping a clear conscience in unjust suffering was the salvation of himself and his family, who **were saved through** water, being brought safely through the Flood.

3:21. And this (*ho*, relative pronoun—"water" is the understood antecedent) **water symbolizes baptism** (*baptisma*). Baptism represents a complete break with one's past life. As the Flood wiped away the old sinful world, so baptism pictures one's break from his old sinful life and his entrance into new life in Christ. Peter now applied to his readers the principle he set forth in verses 13-17 and illustrated in verses 18-20. He exhorted them to have the courage to commit themselves to a course of action by taking a public stand for Christ through baptism. The act of public baptism would "save" them from the temptation to sacrifice their good consciences in order to avoid persecution. For a first-century Christian, baptism meant he was following through on his commitment to Christ, regardless of the consequences.

Baptism does not save from sin, but from a bad conscience. Peter clearly taught that baptism was not merely a ceremonial act of physical purification, **but** (*alla*, making a strong contrast) **the pledge** (*eperōtēma*, also trans. "appeal"; cf. NASB) **of a good conscience** (*syneidēseōs*; cf. v. 16) **toward God.** Baptism is the symbol of what has already occurred in the heart and life of one who has trusted Christ as Savior (cf. Rom. 6:3-5; Gal. 3:27; Col. 2:12). To make the source of salvation perfectly clear Peter added, **by the resurrection of Jesus Christ** (cf. 1 Peter 1:3).

3:22. Mentioning Christ's resurrection returned Peter's thoughts to his original example, so he concluded his digression and completed his first illustration with a reference to Christ's reward and blessing. Having witnessed Christ's physical Ascension (cf. Mark 16:19; Luke 24:51; Acts 1:6-11), Peter wrote that Christ **has gone into heaven.** The reward for Christ's faithfulness is seen in His exaltation over all things. He is enthroned **at God's right hand** (cf. Ps. 110:1; Heb. 1:13; 8:1; 10:12; 12:2), the seat of supreme honor, to rule and reign over all creation (cf. Col. 1:15-16; 2:14-15).

B. Enduring suffering (chap. 4)

This chapter is the heart of Peter's encouragement for endurance. Here is practical instruction based on Christ's example in undergoing suffering. In order to endure suffering, Christians are to arm themselves with Christlike courage, minister to one another with Christlike service, and commit themselves to God with Christlike faith.

1. CHRISTLIKE ATTITUDE (4:1-6)

Maintaining proper conduct in suffering requires that Christians maintain a Christlike attitude, living for the present in God's will, knowing that they will live for eternity in His presence.

4:1. Therefore (*oun*, an inferential conjunction) Peter referred back to Christ's suffering in 3:18 and applied the principles of patient endurance in unjust suffering to his readers' immediate situation. He exhorted believers to **arm** themselves with **the same** courageous **attitude** or mind-set Christ had regarding suffering. The word translated "arm yourselves" (*hoplisasthe*, used only here in the NT) referred to a soldier putting on armor (cf. Eph. 6:13). With the same determination and care with which a soldier puts on his armor, Christians are to adopt Christ's "attitude" (*ennoian*, lit., "thought"; Heb. 4:12 has the only other biblical usage of this word) toward persecution, an unswerving resolve to do God's will.

Identification with Christ, arming oneself with His attitude, also means sharing in His suffering and death. Christ **suffered in His body,** and a believer suffers **in his body** also. One who has suffered in this way **is done with sin,** that is, his being identified with Christ demonstrates (as does baptism) his break with a sinful life. Because of Christ's death, "we should no longer be slaves to sin, because anyone who has died has been freed from sin" (Rom. 6:6-7).

4:2. As a result Christians who have adopted Christ's mind-set have counted themselves dead to sin. They **live the rest** of their lives not **for evil human desires, but rather for the will of God** (cf. 2:15; 3:17; 4:19).

4:3. Christians were exhorted to live for the present in God's will because old habits were a thing of **the past.** In blunt language Peter stressed that there must be a definite break from **what pagans choose to do** (*boulēma tōn ethnōn*, lit., "desire of the Gentiles"), the wasted years of debauchery, lust, drunkenness, orgies, carousing, and . . . idolatry** (cf. Gal. 5:19-21). This exhortation probably had a strong impact on Gentile Christians who used to live in gross sin.

4:4. Christians are to live in the present for the will of God because old acquaintances are now persecutors. Godless men are genuinely surprised by the changed lives of those who once were like they are. **They think it strange** (*xenizontai*, from *xenos*, "stranger"; cf. v. 12). A changed life provokes hostility from those who reject the gospel. Consequently **they heap abuse on** (*blasphēmountes*, lit., "blaspheme") believers.

4:5. Those who have spent their lives in indulgence and idolatry will someday **give account** (*apodōsousin logon*, lit., "give back a word or an account"; cf. Matt. 12:36; Luke 16:2; Acts 19:40; Heb. 13:17). Peter warned that these people must one day face the One **who is ready** (i.e., willing) **to judge.** No one will escape this final judgment of the words and works of his earthly life, when Christ will judge both **the living** (*zōntas*) **and the dead** (*nekrous*) (cf. Acts 10:42; Rom. 14:9; 1 Thes. 4:15; 2 Tim. 4:1).

4:6. For this . . . reason, because everybody must give an account to God, **the gospel was preached even to those . . . now dead.** This has been interpreted as referring to (a) those who are spiritually "dead in sin," (b) those who heard and believed the gospel but have since died, (c) those who died without hearing or believing the gospel. Barclay preferred the third interpretation, assuming that 3:19 refers to Christ's preaching to the dead. Consequently he believed that here "was a breathtaking glimpse of a gospel of a second chance." This interpretation has no scriptural support and is contrary to orthodox Christian doctrine (cf. v. 5).

In verse 6 Peter, in contrast with verse 5, encouraged his readers with the fact that rather than facing judgment for their sins, those who had heard and believed the gospel of Jesus Christ faced an altogether different future. The penalty for their sin has been paid by Christ on the cross. The last earthly effect of sin is physical death. Believers still die physically; they are **judged . . . in regard to the body** (cf. suffering in this life "in his body," v. 1). But for Christians physical death does not lead to judgment but to eternal life. They **live . . . in regard to the Spirit.** Those armed with a Christlike attitude will live forever in God's presence.

2. CHRISTLIKE SERVICE (4:7-11)

Encouragement to endure suffering comes not only from a believer's future hope but also from the Christlike service of others within His body.

4:7. The end . . . is near (*ēngiken*, lit., "draws near"; the same form is used in James 5:8 to refer to the Second Coming). After mentioning Christians who had died (1 Peter 4:6), Peter then referred to the imminent return of Christ for His church. The shortness of the time remaining is motivation to live for and serve Jesus Christ (v. 2). As a result, Christians are to **be clear-minded** (*sōphronēsate*, lit., "be of sound mind"; cf. Mark 5:15) **and self-controlled** (*nēpsate*, lit., "be sober"; cf. 1 Peter 1:13; 5:8) **so that** they are able to **pray** (cf. Eph. 6:18). Prayer, of high priority in persecution, is to be clear, reasonable, sober communication with God.

4:8-9. Love (*agapēn . . . echontes*) **each other deeply.** "Deeply" (*ektenē*, "stretched" or "strained") was used to describe the taut muscles of an athlete who strains to win a race (cf. *ektenōs* in 1:22). A Christian's unselfish love and concern for others should be exercised to the point of sacrificially giving for others' welfare. **Love covers over** (*kalyptei*, lit., "hides") **a multitude of sins.** This kind of strenuously maintained love is not blind but sees and accepts the faults of others (cf. Prov. 10:12; 1 Cor. 13:4-7). Christian love may be displayed through extending free food and lodging, offering **hospitality** (*philoxenoi*, lit., "being friendly to strangers") **without grumbling** to those who are traveling. During times of persecution, hospitality was especially welcomed by Christians who were forced to journey to new areas.

4:10. Believers should be diligent in using their spiritual gifts. Each **gift** (*charisma*) is to be used **to serve** (*diakonountes*; cf. *diakonos*, "deacon") or "minister to" **others.** The phrase **faithfully administering** (*hōs kaloi oikonomoi*) could also be translated "as good stewards." A "steward" was one who served as a house manager; he had no wealth of his own, but distributed his master's wealth according to his master's will and direction. The "gift" (*charisma*) stems from **God's grace** (*charitos*). His grace is manifested to His church as believers exercise their spiritual gifts in service to each other. His grace is evident **in its various forms,** that is, it is "manifold" (NASB), variegated, rich in variety (*poikilēs*; cf. 1:6, where Peter said trials are *poikilois*, or varied).

4:11. Peter divided Christian service into two general categories: the one who **speaks** (*lalei*) and the one who **serves** (*diakonei*; cf. v. 10). This division relates to the distinction God's leaders made between ministry roles (Acts 6:2-4). These two general ministry functions often overlap. Both groups function through dependence on God's gracious provision. The reason for relying on God's words (cf. Acts 7:38; Rom. 3:2; Heb. 5:12) and **strength** (*ischyos*, "power") is that **God** will receive the praise **through Jesus Christ.** At the mention of Christ's name Peter offered an appropriate word of praise as a benediction: **To Him be the glory and the power** (*kratos*, "might") **forever and ever. Amen.** (Cf. the similar benediction in 1 Peter 5:11.) The praise and credit for Christian ministry should always be given to Christ.

3. CHRISTLIKE FAITH (4:12-19)

Anticipating hardships the believers in Asia Minor were about to undergo, Peter encouraged his readers to endure suffering with Christlike faith so that they might be further identified with Christ, receive a blessing, and trust God completely.

4:12. Peter warned his readers about the coming of a more intense period of persecution. He again stressed mental readiness (cf. 1:13; 4:7): **Do not be surprised** (*xenizesthe*, "amazed"; cf. v. 4) **at the painful trial you are suffering.** The NASB translates this last phrase "the fiery ordeal among you." Literally rendered it could read "the among you burning." The verb *pyrōsei* is from *pyroō,* "to burn." The meaning may be metaphorical as in 1:7 where the context is quite similar. However, the verse could also be aptly applied to the historical reality of the Neronian persecution. Christians were blamed for the burning of Rome. Some were covered with pitch and used as living torches to light the imperial gardens at night. Peter may have believed that the provincial officials were likely to follow their emperor's example and stake-burn Christians in Asia Minor. Such persecution should not take the Christians by surprise **as though something strange** (*xenou*) were befalling them.

4:13. But rejoice that you participate (*koinōneite,* from *koinōneō,* "to share"; related nouns are *koinōnia,* "communion, fellowship, close relationship," and *koinōnos,* "sharer"; cf. 5:1). Suffering for Christ's sake should cause rejoicing because through suffering Christians further identify with Christ. Sharing in **the sufferings of Christ** results in (a) joy with Christ (the word **overjoyed** is trans. "rejoice" in 1:6), (b) fellowship with Him (Phil. 3:10), (c) being glorified with Him (Rom. 8:17), and (d) reigning with Him (2 Tim. 2:12). The New Testament is clear that those who take part in the suffering of Christ also will take part in **His glory,** when it **is revealed** (*apokalypsei*; cf. 1 Peter 1:7; 5:1). Peter presented this truth as a cause for future hope and present rejoicing while enduring persecution.

4:14. Peter again referred to Jesus' teaching (Matt. 5:11). If a Christian was **insulted** (cf. 1 Peter 3:9) **because of the name of Christ,** he should be considered **blessed** (*makarioi*; cf. 3:14). Anything that we suffer for the sake of Christ is a privilege, not a penalty. **The Spirit of glory and of God** (cf. Isa. 11:2; Matt. 3:16) refers to the Holy Spirit's indwelling presence within all who are identified by "the name of Christ" and thus suffer persecution (cf. 1 Peter 4:16).

4:15. Peter stressed that persecution was no excuse for lawlessness. Christians were not to retaliate (3:9). Physical violence was not to be met by murder. Confiscation of property was not to be compensated for by theft. No matter what their trials, Christians were to do nothing that would justify punishing them as criminals (cf. 2:19; 3:17). They were not to suffer **as a murderer or thief or any other kind of criminal, or even as a meddler.** Even interfering in other people's affairs is out of place for Christians (cf. 1 Tim. 5:13).

4:16. There is no shame if one **suffer**(s) **as a Christian** rather than as a criminal. On the contrary, **that name** should be a source of praise to God for it identifies the bearer with the blessings of salvation (cf. v. 11). The term "Christian" (*Christianos*) occurs only three times in the Bible (here and Acts 11:26; 26:28). It may have been used derisively by unbelievers, as an insult.

4:17-18. Peter had referred to persecution and suffering as trials that refine and prove one's faith (1:6-7) if reacted to in the will of God (3:17). Now he added that God allows persecutions as disciplinary judgment to purify the lives of those in **the family of God.** If believers need disciplinary earthly judgments (**if it begins with us,** a first-class condition which assumes the reality of the premise), how much more will **those who do not obey the gospel** (cf. 2:7) **the ungodly and the sinner,** deserve everlasting judgment? Peter quoted the Septuagint rendering of Proverbs 11:31, **If it is hard for the righteous to be saved,** to emphasize God's disciplinary demands on His children. The vicissitudes of life are a part of God's constant care, yet from a human perspective discipline is always "hard." Peter is not teaching that salvation is earned through personal trials or works, but simply that those who are saved are not exempt from temporal disciplinary judgments which are the natural consequences of sin. The writer of Hebrews also supports Peter: "Endure hardship as discipline; God is treating you as sons" (Heb. 12:7).

4:19. Believers could be sure that they were being called on to **suffer according to God's will** (cf. 2:15; 3:17; 4:2) if, having committed no crimes, they were suffering solely because they bore Christ's name. Peter encouraged suffering saints to endure through the exercise of Christlike faith. Just as Christ trusted Himself to His Father who judges justly (2:23), so should believers **commit** (*paratithesthōsan,* an accounting term, "to deposit or entrust") **themselves** (*psychas autōn,* lit., "their souls") **to their faithful Creator and continue to do good** (cf. 2:15, 20).

V. Charged with New Responsibility (5:1-11)

In the final chapter Peter emphasized new responsibilities within the church in light of the troubled times. He exhorted the elders to shepherd the people, the young men to submit to the elders, and everyone to stand firm in the faith.

A. Elders are to shepherd (5:1-4)

Peter's charge to elders was given in three pairs of negative and positive exhortations. The exhortations reflect Ezekiel (34:1-16), where false shepherds were contrasted with the True Shepherd.

5:1. Peter, in addressing the **elders** (*presbyterous;* cf. Acts 11:30; 20:17), also used a word that identified himself as one who held the same office (*sympresbyteros,* "fellow-presbyter"). As an elder, Peter was speaking from experience. However, Peter's authority came from the fact that he was an apostle (1 Peter 1:1), and **a witness** (*martys;* cf. Acts 3:15; 10:39) **of Christ's sufferings.** Peter also referred to himself as **one who . . . will share** (*koinōnos;* cf. 1 Peter 4:13) **in the glory to be revealed.** Peter had just made the point that those who share in Christ's sufferings will also share in His glory (4:13). Peter further identified with his readers by referring to his own suffering for Christ's sake (Acts 5:40).

5:2. The command **Be shepherds** was also given by Jesus to Peter (John 21:16) The word *poimanate* means "to tend." Besides feeding, it includes caring, leading, guiding, and protecting—all duties and responsibilities a shepherd has for his flock. Related to the participle **serving as overseers** (*episkopountes*) is the noun "overseer" (*episkopos,* used five other times: Phil. 1:1; 1 Tim. 3:1-2; Titus 1:7; 1 Peter 2:25). "Overseer" seems to be interchangeable with "elder" and connotes both a spiritual and physical guardianship. ("Serving as overseers" is not in some Gr. mss.)

Peter, through contrasting exhortations, presented both the motive and the manner of one's ministry. An elder's motive must be from willingness, not from a sense of external compulsion: **not because you must, but because you are willing.** Social or financial pressures should not be substituted for the pure motivation to do God's will and to serve Him freely and eagerly: **not greedy for money, but eager to serve** (cf. 1 Tim. 3:8; Titus 1:7, 11). Shepherds who serve with false motives care only for themselves and devour the flock (Ezek. 34:2-3).

5:3. The word translated **lording it over** (*katakyrieuontes*) includes the idea of domineering as in the rule of a strong person over one who is weak (cf. Matt. 20:25; Mark 10:42; Acts 19:16). Ezekiel indicted false shepherds: "You have ruled them harshly and brutally. So they were scattered because there was no shepherd" (Ezek. 34:4-5). Peter exhorted the elders to be **examples** (*typoi*, "types or patterns"), to serve as models for the people to follow. They were not to drive God's people, but to lead them by their examples of mature Christian character.

5:4. Christ, **the Chief Shepherd** (*archipoimenos*), is "the True Shepherd" (Ezek. 34:11-16), "the Good Shepherd" (John 10:11, 14), and "the Great Shepherd" (Heb. 13:20). When Christ returns, His faithful undershepherds will share in His glory (1 Peter 5:1) and receive unfading crowns (cf. 1:4).

B. Young men are to submit (5:5-7)

Peter then turned his attention from the shepherds to the sheep. Good leaders deserve good followers. Those who are led are responsible to be in subjection to men and to God.

5:5. Young men . . . be submissive (*hypotagēte*; cf. 3:1) **to those who are older.** Church leaders were usually older members. The younger members were to place themselves willingly under the authority of those who had been given the responsibility of leadership. Peter exhorted both young and old alike to **clothe** (*enkombōsasthe*, "clothe or tie on oneself"; an *enkombōma* was the apron of a slave) **yourselves with humility.** True humility is attractive dress (cf. 3:8). Peter may have alluded to Christ's girding Himself with a towel and teaching the disciples that humility is the prerequisite for service and service is the practice of humility (John 13:4-15).

Peter quoted Proverbs 3:34 to emphasize God's different attitudes toward the proud and the humble. **God opposes** (lit., "sets Himself against") the arrogant **but** grants favor and acceptance **to the humble.**

5:6-7. Knowing God's attitude should cause Christians not only to be subject to others but also to subject themselves deliberately to **God's** sovereign rule. The command **humble yourselves** (*tapeinōthēte*) could be translated "allow yourselves to be humbled." Those who were suffering persecution for Christ's sake could be encouraged by the fact that the same **mighty hand** that let them suffer would one day **lift** (*hypsōsē*, "exalt") them **up** (cf. James 4:10).

Peter then referred to Christ's classic words of encouragement in the Sermon on the Mount (Matt. 6:25-32), while quoting Psalm 55:22: "Cast your cares on the Lord and He will sustain you." All a believer's anxieties can be **cast . . . on Him.** Christ sustains **because He cares.** A Christian's confidence rests in the fact that Christ is genuinely concerned for his welfare.

C. All are to stand firm (5:8-11)

Though believers should place their confidence in God, they should not be careless. Christians in conflict are to be on the alert, made strong and steadfast by Christ Himself.

5:8. Be self-controlled (*nēpsate*; cf. 1:13; 4:7) **and alert** (*grēgorēsate*; cf. 1 Thes. 5:6, 10). Christians should be constantly alert because the **enemy** (*antidikos*, "adversary"), **the devil** (*diabolos*, "slanderer"), is always actively seeking an opportunity for a vicious attack. This verse could also be a veiled allusion to the horrors of the Neronian persecution in the Roman Coliseum, in which lions mauled and devoured Christians. Satan desired to do the same thing spiritually, to defeat believers' testimonies.

5:9. The devil can be and should be resisted. **Resist** (*antistēte*) means "withstand," used also in James 4:7 (cf. *antidikos*, "enemy" in 1 Peter 5:8). It is a term of defense rather than attack. Christians may stand firm against Satan only if they depend wholly on Christ, **standing firm in the faith** (cf. v. 12; Col. 2:5). Peter also encouraged his readers by reminding them that they were not alone in their suffering. The knowledge that other Christians, **your brothers throughout the world,** were suffering, would strengthen their resolve to continue to stand firm.

5:10. Peter had encouraged his readers to endure suffering in such a way that the grace of God would be made manifest in their lives. Now in a closing word of benediction he committed them to **the God of all grace** (cf. 4:10). The benediction briefly summarizes Peter's message of encouragement. Christians' suffering will last only **a little while,** while their **glory in Christ,** to which they were **called,** will be eternal (cf. Rom. 8:17-18; 2 Cor. 4:16-18). (This is Peter's last of eight uses of "glory" in this epistle: 1 Peter 1:7,11, 21, 24; 2:20; 4:14; 5:1, 10.) God Himself would **restore** them **and make** them **strong** (*stērixei*; cf. 2 Thes. 2:17), **firm** (*sthenōsei*, used only here in the NT), **and steadfast** (*themeliosei,* "established"; cf. Eph. 3:17; Col. 1:23).

5:11. To Him be the power (*kratos,* "might") **forever and ever. Amen.** In this benediction, similar to the one in 4:11, Peter praised Christ who has all power for all time (cf. Rom. 11:36; 1 Tim. 6:16). Certainly He has the power to strengthen His own as they undergo persecution.

VI. Conclusion (5:12-14)

5:12. As Paul often did at the close of his epistles, Peter may have penned these last verses himself. Silas served as Peter's amanuensis (**with the help of Silas . . . I have written to you**), and probably personally delivered the letter to the churches of Asia Minor along the predetermined route specified in 1:1. This was probably the same Silas who accompanied Paul on his second missionary journey (Acts 15:40). In the words **encouraging** (*parakalōn,* "exhorting, appealing"; cf. 1 Peter 5:1) **. . . and testifying** (*epimartyrōn,* "bearing witness"), Peter summarized the purpose of his letter. He wrote to encourage Christians to endure persecution, to **stand fast,** so that **the true grace of God** (cf. 1:13; 4:10) would be evidenced to the unbelieving world. They were to "stand fast" in His grace (cf. 5:9).

5:13. Some scholars suggest that **she who is in Babylon** refers to Peter's wife (cf. 1 Cor. 9:5). However, since Peter was writing to churches and said she is **chosen together with you,** probably "she" refers to the church (which is a feminine noun *ekklēsia*). If so, Peter was sending greetings from the church in "Babylon" to the churches in Asia Minor. According to historical evidence, Peter was in Rome during the final years of his life. "Babylon" here might be a disguised reference to Rome, used in order to protect both the Roman church and Peter from the Neronian persecution. (Others suggest, however, that he wrote from the literal city of Babylon on the Euphrates River.) Greetings were also sent from Peter's **son** in the faith, **Mark.** Paul (Col. 4:10) placed John Mark in Rome on an earlier occasion. Consequently most would agree that John Mark, the cousin of Barnabas, was in Rome at the time 1 Peter was written. This strengthens the view that "Babylon" referred to Rome.

5:14. The number of New Testament references to **a kiss** indicate that it was a common sign of fellowship and Christian love (cf. Rom. 16:16; 1 Cor. 16:20; 2 Cor. 13:12; 1 Thes. 5:26).

Peter closed as he began (1 Peter 1:2), encouraging Christians in the midst of persecution by praying for **peace** (*eirēnē*), which is abundantly available to all **who are in Christ,** the Prince of Peace.

BIBLIOGRAPHY

Barbieri, Louis A. *First and Second Peter.* Everyman's Bible Commentary. Chicago: Moody Press, 1977.

Barclay, William. *The Letters of James and Peter.* The Daily Study Bible. Rev. ed. Philadelphia: Westminster Press, 1976.

Bigg, Charles. *A Critical and Exegetical Commentary on the Epistles of St. Peter and St. Jude.* The International Critical Commentary. Edinburgh: T. & T. Clark, 1902.

Blum, Edwin A. "1 Peter." In *The Expositor's Bible Commentary,* vol. 12. Grand Rapids: Zondervan Publishing Co., 1981.

Cranfield, C.E.B. *The First Epistle of Peter.* London: S.C.M. Press, 1950.

Johnstone, Robert. *The First Epistle of Peter: Revised Text, with Introduction and Commentary.* Edinburgh: T. & T. Clark, 1888. Reprint. Minneapolis: James Family Publishers, 1978.

Lenski, R.C.H. *The Interpretation of the Epistles of St. Peter, St. John, and St. Jude.* Minneapolis: Augsburg Publishing House, 1966.

Maclaren, Alexander. *Expositions of Holy Scripture,* vol. 16. Reprint. Grand Rapids: Baker Book House, 1975.

Robertson, A.T. *Word Pictures in the New Testament,* vol. 6. Nashville: Broadman Press, 1933.

1 PETER

Selwyn, E.G. *The First Epistle of Peter.* New York: Macmillan Co., 1964.

Stibbs, Alan M. *The First Epistle General of Peter.* Grand Rapids: Wm. B. Eerdmans Publishing Co., 1959.

Wiersbe, Warren W. *Be Hopeful.* Wheaton, Ill.: Scripture Press Publications, Victor Books, 1982.

Wuest, Kenneth S. *First Peter in the Greek New Testament for the English Reader.* Grand Rapids: Wm. B. Eerdmans Publishing Co., 1942.

2 PETER
Kenneth O. Gangel

INTRODUCTION

This epistle may be titled "The Believer's Conflict in the Latter Days." The apostle opened and closed 2 Peter with the theme of victory. But within the epistle he focused primarily on how to live when surrounded by the problems and perplexities of the end time. After painting a landscape (in 2:1-3:10) replete with false teachers, fallen angels, flagrant immorality, and flaccid scoffers, Peter charged his readers "to live holy and godly lives as you look forward to the day of God and speed its coming" (3:11-12). Faithful living in difficult times—that is the lesson Peter would have believers learn through this dynamic letter.

Authorship and Canonicity. For more than 17 centuries this brief but poignant epistle has withstood the blasts of skeptical scholars who have denied the authenticity of its claim to Petrine authorship. The first verse names Simon Peter who stood with James and John as one of the unique eyewitnesses to Christ's transfiguration (1:17-18; cf. Mark 9:2-7). This Peter who had written earlier (1 Peter 1:1), now addressed the same readers (2 Peter 3:1). He was numbered as one of the Twelve (1:1; 3:2), and he knew the Apostle Paul as a "dear brother" (3:15). Peter had heard the manner of his own death foretold by his Lord as they walked together along the shore of the Sea of Galilee (1:14; cf. John 21:18). Yet, despite this internal evidence, as early as the third century Origen (died ca. 253) noted that there was some doubt concerning the true identity of the author of 2 Peter.

During the fourth century, the great church historian Eusebius (260?-340?) listed 2 Peter, along with 2 and 3 John and James, as antilegomena, books whose canonicity was under dispute. Eusebius noted that no long line of church tradition seemed to support the acceptance of 2 Peter.

Jerome (346-420) included 2 Peter in his well-known translation of the Bible, the Latin Vulgate. Though Jerome accepted the authenticity of the book, he stated that many questioned its Petrine authorship because of the marked difference of style between 1 and 2 Peter.

Through the centuries scholars have added to these early arguments. Some have attempted to identify 2 Peter with the apocryphal or pseudonymous writings which claim apostolic authorship (i.e., the Apocalypse of Peter, the Gospel of Peter, and the Acts of Peter). The strong similarity between 2 Peter and Jude has caused some to doubt Petrine authorship.

Others have pointed out that the mention of Paul's writings (3:16) and the problems raised by the false teachers (specifically the delay of the Lord's return [3:4]), argue for a later author writing sometime during the second century, long after Peter's death. As a result of those and other related arguments, most nonconservative scholars reject the apostolic authorship of 2 Peter.

Yet, while modern opinion may run against the acceptance of the traditional position, none of these problems is insurmountable and none of the arguments is unanswerable.

External evidence. The church literature of the second century includes no direct references to 2 Peter. Consequently critics have stated that there is less external attestation for 2 Peter than for any other book in the New Testament. However, silence argues neither for nor against Petrine authorship. The epistle is short and was probably not widely circulated. Its acceptance may have come slowly because of the suspicion the early church had for letters bearing the names of apostles. The extent of early forgeries is emphasized by Paul's admonition to beware of certain false epistles (2 Thes. 2:2). Also since 2 Peter was written just shortly before the author's death, he could not have been around long to verify its authenticity. However, the silence of second-century authors does not indicate that the church did not accept 2 Peter.

During the third century three men referred directly to the Petrine authorship of 2 Peter. Methodius of Olympus, martyred in the Diocletian persecution, quoted 2 Peter 3:8 to support his argument in *De Resurrectione*. He definitely referred to the Apostle Peter as the author. Firmilian, a bishop of Caesarea in Cappadocia, referred to the Apostle Peter's denunciation of false teachers. First Peter does not refer to false teachers, but 2 Peter devotes an entire chapter to the subject. Thus Firmilian may have been ascribing Petrine authorship to 2 Peter. Finally, Origen, though pointing out a current trend of doubt, seems from the content and frequent references in his other writings to have accepted 2 Peter as authoritative. Though the first statement questioning Petrine authorship was made in the third century, both Methodius and Firmilian affirmed 2 Peter as genuine—and, most likely, Origen did as well.

In the fourth century the Petrine authorship of 2 Peter was strongly affirmed. Two of the great theologians of the early church, Athanasius and Augustine, considered 2 Peter as canonical. The Council of Laodicea (A.D. 372) included the epistle in the canon of Scripture. Jerome placed 2 Peter in the Latin Vulgate (ca. A.D. 404). Also the great third Council of Carthage (A.D. 397) recognized the intrinsic authority and worth of 2 Peter and formally affirmed that it was written by the Apostle Peter.

Though 2 Peter is the least attested book in the New Testament, its external support far surpasses that of many of the other Bible books. The absence of early church tradition supporting 2 Peter certainly could have been due to the letter's brevity and the lack of communication among Christians during times of heavy persecution. Consequently the silence of the second century and the caution of the third century posed no insurmountable problems for the careful scholarship of the canonical councils of the fourth century.

Internal evidence. The question of stylistic differences between 1 Peter and 2 Peter has been debated since Jerome first recorded the problem in the fourth century. Jerome himself explained that the difference in style could easily be attributed to the fact that Peter most likely used an amanuensis other than Silvanus who served Peter in writing his first letter (1 Peter 5:12). If Jerome is right, the differences in style are no greater than might have been expected, considering the different subject matter and different purposes for writing the two letters.

The similarities in style between the two books are just as striking as the differences. Both books are filled with *hapax legomena*, words that occur only once in the New Testament. Of the 686 *hapax legomena* in the New Testament, 1 Peter contains 62 and 2 Peter has 54—more, proportionately, than most New Testament books their size (Homer K. Ebright, *The Petrine Epistles.* Cincinnati: Methodist Book Concern, 1917, pp. 70-5, 121-3; cf. Charles Bigg, *A Critical and Exegetical Commentary on the Epistles of St. Peter and St. Jude,* pp. 224-5). Ebright concludes that the noticeable differences are not between the two Petrine Epistles but between these Epistles and the rest of the New Testament. The prominence of *hapax legomena* in both books may point to a common author who had a rich vocabulary and a public speaker's flare for fresh creative expression.

It should not be considered remarkable, then, that a number of words and phrases are found only in these two epistles. Both books include the unusual salutation, "Grace and peace be yours in abundance" (1 Peter 1:2; 2 Peter 1:2). The term *aretas* ("praises") in 1 Peter 2:9, and *aretē* ("goodness") in 2 Peter 1:3 are forms of the same unique word and refer to the moral excellence and goodness of God. The word *apothesis* is used in the New Testament only in 1 Peter 3:21 and 2 Peter 1:14 and is translated "removal" and "put . . . aside," respectively. The graphic phrase *amōmou kai aspilou,* used in 1 Peter 1:19 to refer to the sinlessness of Christ as One without "blemish or defect," is artfully rephrased in 2 Peter 2:13 as *spiloi kai mōmoi* ("blots and blemishes") to refer to the character of the false teachers. The phrase is used again in 3:14, *aspiloi kai amōmētoi* "spotless and blameless"), to challenge Christians to moral excellence in light of Christ's return. The use of these and other unique words and phrases in these two epistles provides strong evidence of their common authorship.

Second Peter also reflects the unique vocabulary of Peter's sermons recorded in the Book of Acts. One of the best examples is the verb *kolasōntai* ("punish"), found only in Acts 4:21, and *kolazomenous* ("punishment") in 2 Peter 2:9. Other similarities may be noted between 1:3 and Acts 3:12 ("power" and "godliness") and between 2 Peter 2:13, 15 (*misthon adikias*, lit., "wages of wickedness") and Acts 1:18 (*misthou tēs adikias*, lit., "reward of wickedness").

Though differences in style exist between 1 and 2 Peter, the frequent use of *hapax legomena*, the unique vocabulary shared by both books, and the strong resemblance between words in 2 Peter and words in Peter's sermons recorded in Acts, all argue strongly for Petrine authorship.

The problem of other apocryphal or pseudonymous literature bearing Peter's name has caused some scholars to reject the authenticity of 2 Peter. In fact, as already mentioned, the early church was slow in giving 2 Peter unqualified acceptance because of the circulation of spurious pseudonymous epistles. Some have tried to argue that pseudonymity was an accepted second-century literary device (e.g., James Moffatt, *The General Epistles: James, Peter, and Judas*, pp. 173-5, and Montague Rhodes James, *The Second Epistle General of Peter and the General Epistle of Jude*, pp. xxxii-iv). However, the fact that 2 Peter was eventually accepted and that the Apocalypse of Peter, the Gospel of Peter, and the Acts of Peter were rejected as pseudonymous books clearly indicates that pseudonymity was not tolerated. The early church recognized the distinctive character and authority of 2 Peter, as opposed to works of lesser quality that merely copied Petrine thought, mixed in later Jewish and Greek ideas, and added a distinctly Docetic view of the person of Christ (that He only *seemed* to have a human body).

The external and internal evidence, though subject to heavy critical attack, has withstood the test of time. No argument against Petrine authorship is conclusive and no new evidence has successfully refuted the epistle's claim to apostolic authorship.

Relationship to Jude. Even a cursory reading of 2 Peter 2 and Jude 4-18 confirms their striking similarity. However, the exact nature of their dependence on each other and the effect of that dependence on their canonicity and authenticity has been the subject of much debate. Scholars of the early church thought that 2 Peter was written first, and that Jude borrowed from it. The results of German higher criticism have swayed scholars in modern times to the opposite view. Some have even posited that the authors of 2 Peter and Jude used a common third source. All three positions face significant difficulties.

If Jude were written first, it is questioned whether an apostle of Peter's standing would have borrowed so extensively from a writer of lesser reputation. However, perhaps Peter viewed Jude's warning against false teachers as important enough to be reemphasized and reinforced by his own apostolic authority. The priority of Jude does not pose a problem to Petrine authorship as long as it is not dated later than A.D. 68, the traditional date of Peter's martyrdom. The Book of Jude does not provide enough evidence for conclusive dating.

If 2 Peter is given priority, the problem arises as to why Jude would merely repeat what was already available and include so little new material. However, Jude may have abbreviated and clarified Peter's letter or some unknown common source to meet the particular needs of churches that had not yet received the earlier epistle. (Cf. Charles Bigg, *A Critical and Exegetical Commentary on the Epistles of St. Peter and St. Jude*, pp. 216-24.)

Donald Guthrie points out that the order of priority of 2 Peter and Jude need not have any particular bearing on their authenticity, authorship, or inspiration (*New Testament Introduction*. Downers Grove, Ill.: InterVarsity Press, 1970, p. 926). The evidence is inconclusive and either position may be held consistently with a conservative view of the inspiration and authority of Scripture.

2 PETER

Date and Place of Writing. Since Peter mentions Pauline literature and deals with questions regarding the Lord's return, some feel the book demands a second-century date and thus could not have been written by the Apostle Peter.

The mention of Paul's letters in 2 Peter 3:16 has given rise to the assumption that the author was referring to an organized collection of epistles that were recognized by the church at large as authoritative. F. H. Chase has written, "It is impossible to suppose that a collection of St. Paul's epistles had been made and that they were treated as Scripture during the lifetime of St. Peter" (*A Dictionary of the Bible*, ed. James Hastings. New York: Charles Scribner's Sons, 1902, s.v. "Peter," 3:810). However, Peter's statement (2 Peter 3:16) need not refer to the entire body of Pauline literature but merely to those letters with which Peter was familiar. Certainly Peter, living the last few years of his life in Rome itself, would have had occasion to read several of Paul's letters as they circulated among churches throughout the Roman world.

Two references in 2 Peter give some indication of the date of the epistle. In 2 Peter 1:13-15, Peter indicated that the time of his death was near. The traditional date for Peter's death is late A.D. 67 or early A.D. 68. The reference to Paul's epistles in 3:16 would seem to indicate a date some time after A.D. 60. Since 1 Peter is normally dated around A.D. 64, 2 Peter may be conservatively placed some time after the writing of 1 Peter and before Peter's death, between A.D. 64 and 68.

The text of 2 Peter suggests no specific place for its composition. However, since 1 Peter was written in Rome and Rome is traditionally held to be the place of Peter's crucifixion, it is reasonable to assume that 2 Peter was written in Rome as well.

Destination. Peter was writing to Christians (1:1) to whom he had written before (3:1). If 2 Peter 3:1 refers to 1 Peter, then he was writing to the mixed Jewish and Gentile churches of "Pontus, Galatia, Cappadocia, Asia, and Bithynia" (1 Peter 1:1). If, however, he referred to a letter no longer extant, then the destination of 2 Peter cannot be determined.

Occasion and Purpose. Peter was both a concerned pastor and a champion of theological orthodoxy. This final impassioned plea to grow in Christian maturity and guard against false teachers was precipitated by the fact that His time was short (1:13-15) and that these congregations faced immediate danger (2:1-3). He desired to refresh their memories (1:13) and stimulate their thinking (3:1-2) so that they would remember his teaching (1:15). He carefully described the characteristics of mature believers and challenged them to make every effort to grow in grace and knowledge (1:3-11). Credentials of true teachers were given to help the readers be discerning students of God's Word (1:12-21). Peter cautioned them against false teachers and exposed their evil characteristics (chap. 2). And he encouraged his readers with the certainty of Christ's return (3:1-16).

The purpose of 2 Peter is to call Christians to spiritual growth so that they can combat apostasy as they look forward to the Lord's return.

OUTLINE

I. Introduction (1:1-2)
   A. The salutation (1:1)
      1. The author (1:1a)
      2. The audience (1:1b)
   B. The blessing (1:2)
II. The Christian's Nature: The Work of God (1:3-11)
   A. The fact of the divine nature (1:3-4)
      1. Divine power (1:3)
      2. Divine promises (1:4a)
      3. Divine participation (1:4b)
   B. The function of the divine nature (1:5-9)
      1. Characteristics of the function (1:5-7)
      2. Consequences of the function (1:8)
      3. Contrasts of the function (1:9)
   C. The finality of the divine nature (1:10-11)
      1. Experiential finality (1:10)
      2. Eternal finality (1:11)
III. The Christian's Nurture: The Word of God (1:12-21)
   A. Memory of God's Word (1:12-15)

B. Majesty of God's Word (1:16-18)
  C. Meaning of God's Word (1:19-21)
IV. The Christian's Warfare: The Attack of False Teachers (chap. 2)
  A. Deliverance from false teachers (2:1-9)
    1. Exposure of false teaching (2:1-3)
    2. Examples of historic judgment (2:4-6)
    3. Explanation of divine deliverance (2:7-9)
  B. Description of false teachers (2:10-16)
    1. They are rebellious (2:10-12a)
    2. They are animalistic (2:12b)
    3. They are deceitful (2:13)
    4. They are chronic sinners (2:14)
    5. They are mercenary (2:15-16)
  C. Destruction by false teachers (2:17-22)
    1. The targets of destruction (2:17-18)
    2. The techniques of destruction (2:19)
    3. The termination of destruction (2:20-22)
V. The Christian's Hope: The Lord's Return (3:1-16)
  A. Believers remember it (3:1-2)
  B. Scoffers laugh at it (3:3-7)
  C. God guarantees it (3:8-9)
  D. Peter describes it (3:10-13)
  E. Behavior is changed by it (3:14-16)
VI. Conclusion (3:17-18)

COMMENTARY

I. Introduction (1:1-2)

A. The salutation (1:1)

1. THE AUTHOR (1:1A)

1:1a. The author is identified as **Simon Peter.** It is ironic that this letter, whose authorship has been so disputed, begins with a textual problem concerning the spelling of its author's name. Some manuscripts have the common Greek spelling (*Simōn*), whereas others have the direct transliteration of the Hebrew (*Symeōn*). The best textual evidence supports the more unusual Hebrew spelling, used elsewhere only in Acts 15:14. This detail provides support for the authenticity of Petrine authorship, for an impostor probably would have used the more widely accepted spelling.

"Peter," the Greek translation of "Cephas" and the name given to Simon by Jesus, is discussed in the *Introduction* of 1 Peter (see also 1 Peter 1:1).

Peter's combining these distinctly Hebrew and Greek names may be an indication of the mixed audience (Hebrew and Greek Christians) he addressed.

Peter adds the term **servant** (*doulos*, lit., "slave"; cf. Matt. 23:11) to his title **apostle of Jesus Christ** (cf. Rom. 1:1; Titus 1:1). Near the close of his life, at the apex of his apostolic authority, he was Christ's servant first, and His apostle second.

2. THE AUDIENCE (1:1B)

1:1b. The recipients of the letter are described only in general terms (cf. 3:1). They are **those who . . . have received a faith as precious as ours.** "Received" is from the unusual verb *lanchanō*, "to obtain by lot" (cf. Luke 1:9; John 19:24). This implies God's sovereign choice rather than anything they might have done to deserve such a gift. The words "as precious" translate the compound word *isotimon*, used only here in the New Testament. It comes from *isos* ("equal") and *timē* ("honor, value"). The word *isotimon* was used for foreigners who had been granted the privileges of citizenship which were equal to those of the native born. The faith given them by God was of equal honor or privilege with that of the apostles' faith. Here Peter foreshadowed his purpose by stressing that the faith of the apostles was no different from the faith of any believer. This contrasted with the pre-Gnostic doctrines of the false teachers who spoke of an inner circle of special knowledge attainable by and available only to a privileged few.

The word "faith" (*pistin*) is used without the article; thus it could refer to the objective content of faith (cf. Jude 3) or, more likely, to the subjective ability to believe. This faith is given **through** (or, on the basis of) **the righteousness** (*dikaiosynē*, "justice" or "uprightness"; cf. Rom. 1:17; 3:22) **of our God and Savior** (Peter called Jesus Savior [Acts 5:31]) **Jesus Christ.** The grammar here clearly indicates that "God and Savior" are one Person, not two (i.e., there is one Gr.

article with two substantives). This passage ranks with the great Christological passages of the New Testament which plainly teach that Jesus Christ is coequal in nature with God the Father (cf. Matt. 16:16; John 1:1; 20:28; Titus 2:13). "Savior" is used of Christ five times in this short epistle (2 Peter 1:1, 11; 2:20; 3:2, 18).

B. The blessing (1:2)

1:2. The first half of this verse corresponds exactly with 1 Peter 1:2b: **Grace and peace** (*charis . . . kai eirēnē*; cf. Pauline usage in Rom. 1:7; 1 Cor. 1:3; 2 Cor. 1:2; etc.) were the characteristic Greek and Hebrew greetings (*eirēnē* being the Gr. trans. of the Heb. *šālôm*). The verb translated **be . . . in abundance** (*plēthyntheiē*; also used in 1 Peter 1:2; Jude 2) is in the optative mood, thus stressing a sincere, prayerful wish for his readers.

This blessing of grace and peace is more than a mere formula of greeting. These virtues come **through the knowledge of God and of Jesus our Lord.** In each of his first two verses Peter mentioned God and Jesus as equal. "Knowledge" (*epignōsei*, "full [*epi*, additional] knowledge") implies an intimate and personal relationship. It is the means by which God's grace and peace may be received and experienced. Peter used this term *epignōsis* again in 2 Peter 1:3, 8; and 2:20. The shorter form (*gnōsis*) is found in 1:5-6 and 3:18. Christians are urged to take advantage of the "full knowledge" available to them through Christ Jesus (each occurrence of *epignōsis* in 2 Peter is related to Christ). In this way they could combat false teachers who claimed to have special knowledge (*gnōsis*) but who openly practiced immorality (cf. Paul's usage of *epignōsis* to combat incipient Gnosticism: Col. 1:9-10; 2:2; 3:10).

II. The Christian's Nature: The Work of God (1:3-11)

Peter challenged believers to take full advantage of the divine power and promise of God which made it possible to *participate* in the divine nature and thus overcome the corruption caused by evil desires (vv. 3-4). Based on this promised power, Peter further challenged Christians to *practice* the characteristics of the divine nature so that they would experience the assurance of eternal rewards (vv. 5-11).

A. The fact of the divine nature (1:3-4)

1. DIVINE POWER (1:3)

1:3. Christ's **divine power** has provided **everything** believers **need for life and godliness.** "Divine" translates *theias*, which is from *theos* ("God") and is used only three times in the New Testament (here and in Acts 17:29; 2 Peter 1:4). "Power" (*dynameōs*) is one of Peter's favorite words (cf. 1 Peter 1:5; 3:22; 2 Peter 1:16; 2:11). All that believers need for spiritual vitality (life) and godly living (*eusebeian*, "godliness," "piety"; cf. comments on 1:6; 3:11) is attainable **through our knowledge of Him** (Christ). An intimate "full knowledge" (*epignōseōs*; cf. 1:2) of Christ is the source of spiritual power and growth (cf. Phil. 1:9; Col. 1:9-10; 2:2).

Christ **called** (cf. 1 Peter 1:15) **us** to this life of godliness **by His own glory and goodness** (*aretē*, "moral excellence"; trans. "praises" in 1 Peter 2:9 and "goodness" in 2 Peter 1:5). Christ attracts people enslaved by sin (cf. 2:19) by His own moral excellence and the total impact of His glorious Person.

2. DIVINE PROMISES (1:4A)

1:4a. Through these, that is, Christ's "glory and goodness" (v. 3), **He has given** believers **His very great and precious promises.** The Greek verb translated "has given" (*dedōrētai*) means "to bestow, to endow." Not the usual word for "give," it carries with it the idea of the worth of the gift. Peter used the same verb in verse 3. In Mark 15:45 the word is used to describe Pilate's "giving" of Jesus' body to Joseph of Arimathea.

The word for "promises" (*epangelmata*, from *epangellō*; used only in 2 Peter 1:4 and 3:13) implies an emphatic public announcement. The promises are appropriately described as "very great and precious" (*timia*, from *timē*, "value"). Peter used "precious" to describe a Christian's faith (1 Peter 2:7; 2 Peter 1:1), Christ's blood (1 Peter 1:19), and here, Christ's promises. The promises Peter had previously written about related to a believer's inheritance (1 Peter 1:3-5) and the return of Christ (1 Peter 1:9, 13).

3. DIVINE PARTICIPATION (1:4B)

1:4b. These promises enable Christians to **participate in the divine nature.** "Participate" is literally "become partners" (*genēsthe . . . koinōnoi*). "Participate" in 1 Peter 4:13 and "share" in 1 Peter 5:1 are from the same word *koinōnoi* ("partners" or "sharers"). "Divine" is *theias,* also used in 2 Peter 1:3. Believers take on God's very nature; each one is a "new creation" (2 Cor. 5:17).

Because they are "partakers" (KJV) of God's nature, Christians can share in His moral victory over sin in this life and share in His glorious victory over death in eternal life. Because of the promise of the new birth (1 Peter 1:3), the promise of God's protecting power (1 Peter 1:5), and the promise of God's enabling power (2 Peter 1:3), believers can "participate in the divine nature," that is, become more like Christ (cf. Rom. 8:9; Gal. 2:20). In addition they can **escape the corruption** (*phthoras,* "moral decay") **in the world** (cf. 2 Peter 2:20; 1 John 2:15-17) **caused by evil desires** (*epithymia,* lit., "lust").

In 2 Peter 1:3-4 Peter employed graphic vocabulary borrowed from the false teachers he warned against. His language must have arrested his readers' attention as he invested words from the pagan and philosophic worlds with new Christian meaning: "godliness" (*eusebeia*), "virtue" (*aretē*), "nature" (*physis*), and "corruption" (*phthoras*).

B. The function of the divine nature (1:5-9)

In this beautiful paragraph Peter orchestrates a symphony of grace. To the melody line of faith he leads believers to add harmony in a blend of seven Christian virtues which he lists without explanation or description. A carnal Christian has spiritual myopia (v. 9), but a spiritual Christian is both effective and productive (v. 8) in his understanding of the Lord Jesus and his application of biblical principles to daily life.

1. CHARACTERISTICS OF THE FUNCTION (1:5-7)

1:5-7. Peter referred back to the divine nature by beginning this new paragraph with the words **for this very reason.** The words **make every effort** translate a participle (*pareisenenkantes,* "applying, bringing to bear alongside of"; used only here in the NT) and *spoudēn pasan* ("all diligence" or "all zeal"; *spoudē* in Rom. 12:11 is rendered "zeal"). It takes every bit of diligence and effort a Christian can muster, along with the enabling power of the Holy Spirit, to "escape the corruption in the world caused by evil desires" (2 Peter 1:4) and to bring in alongside of his faith a complement of virtue. He should work hard at cultivating the seven qualities Peter listed in verses 5-7. As a Christian does so, he becomes more like Christ, participating more fully in God's divine nature.

The word **add,** in the imperative, translates *epichorēgēsate,* from which come the English words "chorus," "choreograph," and "choreography." In ancient Greece the state established a chorus but the director, the *chorēgys,* paid the expenses for training the chorus. Then the word came to be used of one who provides for or supports others or supplies something for them in abundance. A believer is to "furnish, supply, or support" his life with these virtues. (The same word is trans. "supplies" in 2 Cor. 9:10 and "supported" in Col. 2:19. Peter used it again in 2 Peter 1:11 where the NIV renders it "receive.")

Faith in Jesus Christ is what separates Christians from all other people. *Pistis,* trust in the Savior which brings one into the family of God, is the foundation of all other qualities in the Christian life.

1. **To** his faith each believer should add **goodness** (lit., "moral excellency," or "virtue"). In Greek the word is *aretēn,* which Peter also used at the end of verse 3 and in 1 Peter 2:9 ("praises" in the NIV).

2. **Knowledge** (*gnōsin;* cf. 2 Peter 1:2; 3:18) comes not from intellectual pursuits, but is spiritual knowledge which comes through the Holy Spirit and is focused on the person and Word of God.

3. Faith, **goodness,** and spiritual **knowledge** are not enough for a Christian's walk. He must also make every effort to practice **self-control** (*enkrateian;* used only two other times in the NT, in Acts 24:25; Gal. 5:23). This means to have one's passions under control. It contrasts sharply with the anarchy and lack of control on the part of the false teachers whom Peter exposed (chap. 2). In an increasingly anarchistic society Christians

do well to let the music of **self-control** be played in their lives.

4. Believers living in the latter days, especially when surrounded by scoffers and false teachers, also need **perseverance**. This word *hypomenēn* means "staying under." It is frequently used in the New Testament to refer to constancy or steadfast endurance under adversity, without giving in or giving up (cf. Rom. 5:3-4; 15:4-5; 2 Cor. 1:6; 6:4; Col. 1:11; 1 Thes. 1:3; 2 Thes. 1:4; James 1:3).

5. **Godliness** (*eusebian*, also used in 2 Peter 1:3 and 3:11 and 10 times [in the Gr.] in the Pastoral Epistles) refers to piety, man's obligation of reverence toward God. The fourth-century church historian Eusebius was named for this lovely Greek word. How unfortunate that the words "piety" and "pious" have fallen on hard times in current usage.

6. The first five virtues pertain to one's inner life and his relationship to God. The last two relate to others. **Brotherly kindness** translates the Greek *philadelphian*, a fervent practical caring for others (1 John 4:20). Peter already urged this attitude on his readers in his first epistle (1 Peter 1:22; cf. Rom. 12:10; 1 Thes. 4:9; Heb. 13:1).

7. Whereas **brotherly kindness** is concern for others' needs, **love** (*agapēn*) is desiring the highest good for others. This is the kind of love God exhibits toward sinners (John 3:16; Rom. 5:8; 1 John 4:9-11).

Interestingly this "symphony" begins with faith and ends with love. Building on the foundation of faith in Christ, believers are to exhibit Christlikeness by supplying these seven qualities that climax in love toward others (cf. faith and love in Col. 1:4-5; 1 Thes. 1:3; 2 Thes. 1:3; Phile. 5).

2. CONSEQUENCES OF THE FUNCTION (1:8)

1:8. Christian growth (vv. 5-7) results in spiritual effectiveness and productivity. The word **possess** (*hyparchonta*, lit. "possessing") emphasizes that these spiritual qualities "belong to" Christians. However, Christians are to do more than merely possess these virtues. Effective and productive spirituality comes as **these qualities** are held **in increasing measure**. There is to be a growth in grace. A believer who does not progress in these seven areas is **ineffective** (*argous*, "idle" or "useless") **and unproductive** (lit., "unfruitful") **in his knowledge** (*epignōsin*, "full personal knowledge"; cf. vv. 2-3; 2:20) **of our Lord Jesus Christ**. Unfortunately many Christians know the Lord in salvation but lack the "fruit" of the Spirit and are not advancing spiritually. They remain "infants in Christ" (1 Cor. 3:1), still in need of spiritual "milk" (Heb. 5:12-13). But as Peter urged, believers should "grow in the grace and knowledge (*gnōsei*) of our Lord and Savior Jesus Christ" (2 Peter 3:18).

3. CONTRASTS OF THE FUNCTION (1:9)

1:9. In contrast with a growing Christian, a carnal believer is **blind** (*typhlos*) and **nearsighted** (*myōpazōn*). (The NIV reverses these two words; in Gr. the word "blind" comes first.) *Myōpazōn* (from which comes the word "myopia"), occurs only here in the New Testament. A believer with spiritual myopia is not magnifying the grace of Christ. Since his life is not evidencing the qualities cited in verses 5-7, he seems to be just like a spiritually blind (or unsaved) person (2 Cor. 4:4; cf. John 9:39). Such a person **has forgotten that he has been cleansed from his past** (preconversion) **sins**. Some commentators say this refers to unbelievers. But it seems preferable to say that Peter wrote of Christians who are spiritually immature. After all, they had been cleansed from their sins (cf. Titus 3:5), but had not grown spiritually.

C. *The finality of the divine nature (1:10-11)*

In order to be an effective and productive Christian avoiding spiritual myopia, one must be sure that he is genuinely saved. This is demonstrated by his new life in Christ, which provides evidence that he will reach his eternal home.

1. EXPERIENTIAL FINALITY (1:10)

1:10. Being **eager** (*spoudasate*, also used in vv. 1, 15; 3:14 ["make every effort"]; cf. *spoudēn* in 1:5) **to make** one's **calling and election sure** focuses on the confidence a Christian has about his standing with God. A believer hardly has the authority to assure God of his status; actually the reverse is true. The Greek word for "sure" (*bebaian*) was used in classical Greek to refer to a warranty deed somewhat like those people use today on houses and other pieces of property. One's godly behavior is a warranty deed for himself that Jesus Christ has cleansed him from his past sins and therefore that he was in fact called and elected by God. *Bebaian* is rendered "secure" (Heb. 6:19), "guaranteed" (Rom. 4:16), "firm" (2 Cor. 1:7), "courage" (Heb. 3:6), "confidence" (Heb. 3:14), and "in force" (Heb. 9:17).

"Calling" refers to God's efficacious work in salvation (cf. Rom. 1:7; 8:30; 1 Cor. 1:9), and "election" is God's work of choosing some sinners (by His grace, not their merits) to be saved (Rom. 8:33; 11:5; Eph. 1:4; Col. 3:12; 1 Peter 1:1). Election, of course, precedes calling. A believer shows by his godly life and his growth in the virtues mentioned in 2 Peter 1:5-7 that he is one of God's chosen. Such a believer **will not fall** (or "stumble," *ptaisēte*). This word "stumble" does not suggest that a believer loses his salvation, for salvation does not depend on one's spiritual growth. The Greek word for stumble means "to trip up" or "to experience a reversal." Certainly one who is maturing in Christ will not trip up in his spiritual life as readily as one who is immature and nearsighted.

2. ETERNAL FINALITY (1:11)

1:11. The ultimate reward of a growing, Christ-honoring life is the personal "welcome" by the Savior into His kingdom. Stephen experienced it (Acts 7:56); Paul knew when it was imminent for him (2 Tim. 4:7-8, 18); and every believer will experience such a welcome when he enters the Lord's presence in heaven. **You will receive a rich welcome** is, literally, "the entrance will be supplied richly for you." "Supplied" is from the verb *epichorēgeō*, translated "add" in 2 Peter 1:5. The entrance **into the eternal kingdom of our Lord and Savior Jesus Christ** will be supplied with richness; it will be a wonderful "welcome home."

III. **The Christian's Nurture: The Word of God (1:12-21)**

As Peter made a transition from focusing on the work of God in believers' lives (vv. 3-11) to the Word of God as the instrument of nurture (vv. 16-21) he began with a parenthetical personal note about his readers' need to remember what he wrote (vv. 12-15). His section on the Word of God climaxes in a major statement on revelation and inspiration, reaching a high-water mark in verse 21, Peter's tribute to the Holy Spirit's role in God-breathed Scripture.

A. *Memory of God's Word (1:12-15)*

1:12. Peter, knowing his days were numbered, wanted his readers to retain all he would write in this epistle. Three times he spoke of this: **I will . . . remind you** (v. 12), "I . . . refresh your memory" (v. 13), "you will . . . be able to remember" (v. 15; cf. 3:1).

Peter was almost apologetic in the second half of 1:12; he did not want his readers to misunderstand his intention. He was not being critical nor did he suggest they were wavering. Instead, he said they did **know** the truths he wrote about **and he was aware that they were firmly established in the truth.** He wanted them to stay that way. ("Established" is from *stērizō*, which means "strengthen" or "be firm"; cf. 1 Thes. 3:2, 13; 2 Thes. 2:17; 3:3; 1 Peter 5:10.) A problem in many churches today is not that believers do not know what God expects of them, but they either forget (cf. 2 Peter 1:9) or are unwilling to live out the truth they **now have.**

1:13-14. Expecting he would **soon** be with the Lord, Peter wanted **to refresh** (lit., "keep on refreshing," pres. tense) their memories **as long as** he was allowed by the Lord of life to **live in the tent of his body** (cf. "the earthly tent" and "this tent," 2 Cor. 5:1, 4). Peter would **put that tent aside, as the Lord** had **made clear to** him. This could refer to Jesus' words to Peter about his death by crucifixion (John 21:18-19) or to his awareness that through old age or the threat of persecution, his life was almost at an end. The image of this earthly body being like a tent fits well with Peter's pilgrimage theme (1 Peter 1:1, 17; 2:11).

1:15. Peter deliberately repeated himself, perhaps for emphasis: **I will make every effort** translates the one word *spoudasō*, also used in verse 10 ("be . . . eager") and in 3:14 ("make every effort"). The word **departure** (*exodon*), though not the usual word for "death," does not veil the clarity of Peter's suggestion that he is about to die. On the Mount of Transfiguration, Jesus, Moses, and Elijah spoke of Jesus' "departure" (*exodon;* Luke 9:31). Interestingly this "exodus" (lit., "going out," i.e., from this body) contrasts with a believer's "entrance" into (*eisodos,* "going into") God's kingdom (2 Peter 1:11).

How could Peter guarantee that after his death his readers would **always be able to remember these things?** Some suggest this is a subtle reference to Peter's aid in preparing the Gospel of Mark, but this is only speculation. More obviously he was laboring to complete this second epistle which, when joined with the first, would provide ongoing written testimony of the truths so close to his heart. Still another possibility is that he referred to his own life and ministry extending into the lives of others, as Silas and Mark, who would carry on his work after he died. One thing is clear—Peter wanted to be sure that the Lord's people would not forget God's work and God's Word.

B. Majesty of God's Word (1:16-18)

1:16. It is important to distinguish between the written Word (the Bible) and the incarnate Word (Christ). They are both major avenues of God's revelation (cf. Ps. 19:7-11; John 1:18; Heb. 1:2) and therefore both come into focus throughout the remainder of this chapter. A Christian's faith does not rest on clever **stories** (*mythois*) as did the doctrines of the false teachers Peter attacked (2 Peter 2). Instead, true faith is founded on historical facts, which **eyewitnesses** corroborated. It appears that Peter introduced a new theme here. He plunged quickly into a mention of the Lord's return: **the power and coming of our Lord Jesus Christ.** He had already talked about that welcome into the eternal kingdom (1:11), and had written about his own departure from this life. His defense of the doctrine of the Second Coming therefore is based on his eyewitness experience on the Mount of Transfiguration at which time he truly saw Christ's **majesty.** Several times in his earlier epistle he spoke of Christ's return (1 Peter 1:5, 13; 4:13). Obviously Peter considered this doctrine of great importance, one his readers should always keep in mind.

But how does the transfiguration argue that the Lord will come again with power? The transfiguration was designed to show the three apostles, Peter, James, and John, what Christ would be like in His glory, to give them a foretaste of His kingdom (cf. Matt. 16:28–17:2; Mark 9:1-8; Luke 9:28-36). This was a glorious demonstration they could never forget.

1:17-18. Peter's lofty language may stem from his burning desire to communicate the true majesty of the Savior which he, a member of the inner band of disciples, was uniquely privileged to see. Peter wanted his readers to look beyond Christ's first coming to the time when He will return with that same **honor and glory** He demonstrated on the mountain. In Peter's preaching during the days of the early church he was firmly committed to the doctrine of the Second Coming (Acts 2:32-33, 36; 3:16, 20-21).

Interestingly Peter was more profoundly impressed by what he **heard** than what he saw **on** that **sacred mountain.** The **voice that came from heaven,** the **voice** of God the Father, called **the Majestic Glory** (an unusual name for God), spoke approvingly of the **Son.**

C. Meaning of God's Word (1:19-21)

1:19. As Peter wrote of that unforgettable transfiguration experience, he was reminded of another form of God's Word, the written Word, given by the prophets. In fact, God's voice on the mountain made **the word of the prophets . . . more certain** (*bebaioteron;* cf. *bebaian,* v. 10) because the transfiguration pictured the fulfillment of their words. Both the prophets and the transfiguration pointed to Jesus' kingdom on earth.

In an exhortation Peter told how to derive meaning from God's Word—**pay attention to it. As** a Light, God's written Word has validity and authority. In today's experience-oriented societies many people, including some Christians, seek to determine or assess truth by the particular way God has worked in their own lives. But for Peter the splendor of his experience (with Christ at His transfiguration) faded as he spoke of the surety of the written revelation of the prophets.

The apostle wrote of illumination (v. 19), revelation (v. 20), and inspiration (v. 21). Old Testament prophecy is a light compared with the darkness of a squalid room. God's prophetic Word is **a Light** (*lychnō,* "an oil-burning lamp"; cf. Ps. 119:105) **shining in a dark place.** Though the world is darkened by sin (cf. Isa. 9:2; Eph. 6:12), God's Word, pointing to the future, enlightens believers about His ways. But **the day** (Christ's return, Rom. 13:12) is coming. In the daytime, lamps are no longer needed. And a lamp is nothing compared with **the Morning Star** (*phōsphoros*, "Light-Bringer"; used only here in the NT). Much as a lamp at night anticipates and is outshined by the bright morning star, so Old Testament prophecy looks ahead to the coming of Christ, "the bright Morning Star" (*astēr*; Rev. 22:16). Until He comes, believers are to let the Scriptures illumine their hearts (though the light which it brings on that great day will be greatly exceeded by the understanding which will be **in their hearts**).

1:20. Peter then wrote about revelation. The statement, **No prophecy of Scripture came about by the prophet's own interpretation,** has been interpreted several ways: (1) Scripture should be interpreted only in context, that is, a prophecy cannot stand alone without other prophecies to aid in its understanding. (2) Scripture should not be interpreted according to one's own individual liking. (3) Scripture cannot be correctly interpreted without the Holy Spirit. (4) The prophecies did not originate with the prophets themselves. The word *epilyseōs* ("interpretation," lit., "unloosing") and the word *ginetai* ("came about") favor the fourth view. The Scriptures did not stem merely from the prophets themselves; their writings came from God. Verse 20, then, speaks not of interpretation, but of revelation, the source of the Scriptures.

1:21. This verse also supports the view that Peter wrote in verse 20 about prophecies being born of God, not originating from the prophets themselves. **Prophecy** came not from **the will of man, but men spoke from God as they were carried along by the Holy Spirit.**

As the authors of Scripture wrote their prophecies, they were impelled or borne along by God's Spirit. What they wrote was thus inspired by God (2 Tim. 3:16). "Borne along" or "carried along" translates the word *pheromenoi*. Luke used this word in referring to a sailing vessel carried along by the wind (Acts 27:15, 17). The Scriptures' human authors were controlled by the divine Author, the Holy Spirit. Yet they were consciously involved in the process; they were neither taking dictation nor writing in a state of ecstasy. No wonder believers have a word of prophecy which is certain. And no wonder a Christian's nurture must depend on the Scriptures. They are the very words of God Himself!

IV. The Christian's Warfare: The Attack of False Teachers (chap. 2)

When the Edict of Milan was passed in A.D. 313 the church was then free to move into the world, legally and openly propagating its doctrines. But at the same time, the world also began to move into the church, diluting its message for the next 1,200 years until the Reformation broke forth on the scene. But it is obvious from 2 Peter 2 that the world was already in the church well before the time of Constantine. Believers in all ages must be constantly on guard against its attack.

A. Deliverance from false teachers (2:1-9)

The word "rescue" in verses 7 and 9 speaks of God's willingness and ability to deliver His people from assorted difficulties and dangers even when they themselves (like Lot) do not overtly seek deliverance. But depending on the Lord's ability to rescue is no excuse for failing to enter the warfare against false teachers and false prophets.

1. EXPOSURE OF FALSE TEACHING (2:1-3)

2:1. Satan's counterfeits with their insidious activities are always present. They appeared in Israel during the days of the writing prophets spoken of in 1:19-21, and they were present in the first-century church. Though Peter switched from writing about **false prophets** of the past to **false teachers** in the present, their teaching was the same—heresy. False prophets often rose out of Israel (cf. Jer. 5:31; 23:9-18), not from surrounding peoples. Similarly false teachers appear from the midst of the church. They **secretly introduce** their false teachings which are **destructive heresies.** "Secretly introduce" translates *pareisaxousin*, "bring in alongside" (cf. "infiltrated," which translates the related noun *pareisaktous*, in Gal. 2:4). "Heresies" transliterates the Greek word *haireseis*, which in classical Greek simply meant schools of philosophy. But New Testament writers used it to describe religious parties or sects (e.g., the Sadducees [Acts 5:17] or the Pharisees [Acts 15:5]), or factions probably based on false doctrine (e.g., 1 Cor. 11:19, "differences," NIV; "factions," NASB). Such heresies are "destructive," for they lead people away from Christ and thus to spiritual ruin (*apōleias*).

The focus of their heresies was **the sovereign Lord,** Christ, whom they denied (cf. Jude 4). This in turn led to their own spiritual **destruction** or ruin (*apōleian*; cf. 2 Peter 2:3; 3:16), which will be **swift** (*tachinēn*, "sudden"; cf. *tachinē* ["soon"] in 1:14). How can these false teachers, who were said to be **among the people,** and whom the Lord had **bought** (*agorasanta,* "redeem"), end up in everlasting destruction? Several suggestions have been offered: (1) They were saved but lost their salvation. But this contradicts many other Scriptures (e.g., John 3:16; 5:24; 10:28-29). (2) "Bought" means the Lord created them, not that He saved them. But this stretches the meaning of *agorazō* ("redeem"). (3) The false prophets merely *said* they were "bought" by Christ. This, however, seems to read into the verse. (4) They were "redeemed" in the sense that Christ paid the redemptive price for their salvation, but they did not apply it to themselves and so were not saved. Christ's death is "sufficient" for all (1 Tim. 2:6; Heb. 2:9; 1 John 2:2), but is "efficient" only for those who believe. This is a strong argument for unlimited atonement (the view that Christ died for everyone) and against limited atonement (the view that Christ died only for those whom He would later save).

2:2. The tragic fact about **many** false teachers is that they are successful—people listen to them and **follow** them and **their shameful ways** (*aselgeiais*, which Peter also used in 1 Peter 4:3 ["debauchery"]; 2 Peter 2:7 ["filthy"]; v. 18 ["lustful"]). (Cf. *aselgeia* in Rom. 13:13; 2 Cor. 12:21; Gal. 5:19; Eph. 4:19; Jude 4.) It refers to debased sexually immoral practices.

2:3. Ministerial charlatans and quacks have often troubled the flock of God. **In their greed** (cf. v. 14) they use others for their own mercenary purposes and turn the church into a dirty marketplace. **Exploit** (*emporeusontai*) means to commercialize ("buy, sell, trade"; cf. *emporeusometha,* "carry on business," in James 4:13). **Stories they have made up** is literally, "fabricated words" (*plastois* [whence the Eng. "plastic"] *logois*). They are artificial, not genuine. And **their** end is **condemnation** (*krima*, "judgment") and **destruction** (*apōleia*; used twice in 2 Peter 2:1 and also in 3:16). They fall into the same doom which God has planned for other violators of truth and righteousness (as Peter stated in vv. 4-6). Their destruction **has not been sleeping** (*ou nystazei*, used only one other time in the NT, to describe the sleepy virgins in Matt. 25:5). God's justice does not sleep and it is never late.

2. EXAMPLES OF HISTORIC JUDGMENT (2:4-6)

In verses 4-10a, Peter gave several illustrations to demonstrate both the Lord's judgment and His deliverance. After citing three examples of punishment (vv. 4-6), Peter then cited a case of deliverance (Lot, v. 7). In fact, verses 4-9 are a single sentence, one of the longest in the New Testament. Peter was intent on demonstrating that God will judge false teachers and others who sin against Him and His Word. History, Peter wrote, gives ample verification of this truth.

2:4. The first example is that of fallen **angels.** This refers either to their fall with Satan in his rebellion against God (Ezek. 28:15) or to the sin of angels in Genesis 6:1-4. Since Peter's other two illustrations in this section are from Genesis (chaps. 7; 19), perhaps this one is too, though it is difficult to be sure. **If God** in His justice punished angels, surely He would not hesitate to punish people. He plunged the angels into **hell,** literally, "tartarus" apparently a prison of custody (**gloomy dungeons**) between the time of the **judgment** and their ultimate consignment to the eternal lake of fire. There will be no future trial for their doom is already sealed. False prophets, Peter argued, will taste the same judgment as the rebellious angels.

2:5. Peter was greatly impressed by the significance of **the Flood** for he referred to it three times in his two epistles (1 Peter 3:20; 2 Peter 2:5; 3:6). **Noah . . . and seven others** is the NIV's rendering of the Greek "Noah, the eighth person." The others were his wife, his three sons (Shem, Ham, and Japheth), and their wives (Gen. 6:10, 18). Noah was a righteous man (Gen. 6:9), an obedient servant of God, and a shipbuilder (Gen. 6:13-22). Peter added that he was also **a preacher** (*kēryka*, "herald") **of righteousness**, who spoke out against the vile corruption all around him.

The primary focus of 2 Peter 2:5 is the unsparing hand of God on the antediluvian civilization, **the ancient world** with **its ungodly people**. Do false teachers today think they can escape God's judgment because of their large numbers? Peter reminded them and those who are the targets of their delusions that God can judge evil even when it involves the entire human race (with the exception of only eight people). The word **brought** (*epaxas*, past part. from *epagō*, "to bring on") suggests the suddenness of God's judgment in the Flood. Peter used the same verb in verse 1 in speaking of heretics who are "bringing" destruction on themselves.

2:6. God's destruction of **Sodom and Gomorrah by** fire is a classic example of universal destruction of the ungodly (Gen. 10:15-29). The participle *tephrōsas* (**burning them to ashes**), used only here in the New Testament, means "reduce to ashes" or "cover with ashes." Peter concluded this illustration by saying that God **made them an example** (*hypodeigma*, "model, pattern") **of what is going to happen to the ungodly** (cf. Jude 7). The apostle's purpose here was to cite this historical incident of judgment, not to elaborate on the cause for such severe destruction. In the present day homosexuality, which is scarring so much of Western culture, recalls the same shameful conduct in those two ancient cities (Gen. 19:4-5; cf. Gen. 13:13; Rom. 1:27).

3. EXPLANATION OF DIVINE DELIVERANCE (2:7-9)

2:7-9. Peter had spoken (v. 5) of one deliverance (of Noah and his family); now he cited another, God's rescue of **Lot**. Here again is an interesting New Testament commentary on a familiar Old Testament passage (cf. comments on v. 5). In Genesis 19 Lot hardly comes across as **a righteous man**; possibly godliness was not a consistent mark in his daily conduct. But in his standing before God he was a justified man ("righteous," occurring three times in 2 Peter 2:7-8, is *dikaion*, "justified"). This is evidenced by the fact that Lot **was distressed** (*kataponoumenon*, "tormented, oppressed"; used only here and in Acts 7:24 in the NT) by the enormity of iniquity all around him. The people in those twin cities were **filthy** (*en aselgeia*, "in sexual debauchery"; in 2 Peter 2:2 *aselgeia* is trans. "shameful"), **lawless** (*athesmōn*, "unprincipled"; used only twice in the NT: here and in 3:17), and involved in **lawless** (*anomois*, "without any standard or law") **deeds**. Besides being distressed, Lot **was** also **tormented** (*ebasanizen*, "tortured, tormented"; cf. Matt. 8:29) **in his righteous soul** (lit., "he tormented [his] righteous soul"). Seeing and hearing about all their vile ways **day after day** grieved Lot to the point of inner torture.

In 2 Peter 2:9 the point of his words in verses 4-9 unfolds. **The Lord knows how to rescue** the righteous **and to** punish **the unrighteous**. That God can deliver the **godly . . . from trials** is a source of comfort to believers, exemplified by Noah and his seven family members and Lot and his wife and daughters. On the other hand God holds (*tērein*, "keeps under guard") **the unrighteous for the** coming **day of judgment** (cf. 3:7), the great white throne judgment and the lake of fire (Rev. 20:11-15). Meanwhile God continues their punishment in this life (cf. Rom. 1:27b) and in hades after death (Luke 16:23). The participle *kolazomenous* ("punishing, injuring") is another of Peter's words that occurs only once in the New Testament.

B. *Description of false teachers (2:10-16)*

False teachers will be judged by God, as certainly as were the angels, the world in Noah's day, and the sinful people of Sodom and Gomorrah. In verses 10-16 (also v. 17) Peter described the true nature of the false teachers plaguing the church in the first century.

1. THEY ARE REBELLIOUS (2:10-12A)

2:10-12a. The apostles and teachers emphasized purity and cleanliness before God. But the false teachers in the church who denied these standards demonstrated their desire to be indulging the flesh (**follow the corrupt** [*miasmou*, "pollution, defilement"] **desire of the sinful nature**), like the people of Sodom and Gomorrah, and did so in a spirit which held **authority** in contempt (cf. Jude 16, 18). But this was not just any authority; these reckless antinomians **despise**(d) (*kataphronountas*, "think down on") "lordship." *Kyriotētos*, "authority," refers either to angelic powers (Eph. 1:21; Col. 1:16) or perhaps more likely, to the authority of the Lord (*kyrios*) Himself (cf. 2 Peter 2:1). One would expect people of this mentality—who are **bold** (*tolmētai*, "presumptuous") **and arrogant** (*authadeis*, "self-willed"; cf. Titus 1:7)—**to slander** (*blasphēmountes*) even to the point of deliberately speaking untruth about **celestial beings** (*doxas*, possibly fallen angels). It is possible that their blaspheming was the teaching that lustful indulgence is angelic and that God wills man to live under no restraints whatever.

False teachers were doing things **even angels** would not do, namely, slander **such beings**. One might expect **stronger and more powerful** beings (good angels) to criticize less powerful beings (fallen angels), but that is simply not allowed **in the presence of the Lord** (cf. Jude 8-9). Yet so great was the pride of these slanderers that it knew no bounds in their attack on all who disagreed with their teachings. Even so, they were totally ignorant of the very things they blasphemed (2 Peter 2:12a; cf. Jude 10).

2. THEY ARE ANIMALISTIC (2:12B)

2:12b. The false teachers of the first century were **like brute beasts.** They operated from instinct, which was locked into their sin nature, rather than from rational choice. **Creatures of instinct** translates the one Greek word *physika*, "belonging to nature." They followed their natural desires. Like animals in a jungle, their only value was in being **caught and destroyed** (cf. Jude 10). This harsh language from Peter is an indication of how serious he considered these heresies to be. **Like beasts they too will perish** is literally, "in their corruption (*phthora*) they too shall be corrupted" (*phtharēsontai*), an interesting play on words (cf. "corrupted" in Eph. 4:22). Corruption here probably means eternal punishment.

3. THEY ARE DECEITFUL (2:13)

2:13. The wordplay in verse 12b sets up Peter's point in verse 13a, namely, that these false teachers will be caught in their own webs. **They will be paid back with harm** (*adikoumenoi* ["being damaged," or "suffering injustice"] *misthon* ["wages"]) **for the harm** (*adikias*, "injustice" or "wickedness"; cf. v. 15) **they have done.** God will give them what they have done to others (cf. Gal. 6:7). Though the false teachers tried to pass themselves off as spiritual leaders possessing a special level of knowledge, they did not even hide their orgies under the cover of darkness but would **carouse in broad daylight,** while **reveling in their pleasures** (*apatais*, perhaps better trans. "deceptions"). And they did all this while obviously joining in the love feasts of the church (NIV marg.; cf. Jude 12). **They** were **blots** (*spiloi*) **and blemishes** (*mōmoi*; cf. 2 Peter 3:14). Like a stain on a clean shirt or a scratch on a tiny ring, they marred the Lord's Supper by their very presence. This was one of the injustices they did to others.

4. THEY ARE CHRONIC SINNERS (2:14)

2:14. Invective poured from Peter's pen as he summoned staccato phrases to condemn these heretics. Had there been any doubt up to this point about the salvation of these false teachers, Peter closed the door by indicating they were habitual sinners, their eyes consistently looking toward sinning. **With eyes full of adultery** is literally, "having eyes full of an adulteress," that is, thinking only of adultery when they see women. **They never stop sinning** is literally, "unceasing in sin," probably referring to their sinning with their eyes (Matt. 5:28). That such persons should be viewed as believers is diametrically opposed to the Johannine idea that habitual sinning does not mark one who is born of God (1 John 3:9).

Their deceit was aimed at seducing (from *deleazō*, "bait, entice"; used only here and in 2 Peter 2:18) **the** unwary or unsteadfast (cf. 3:16), and **they** had become specialists **in** greed (cf. 2:3; lit., "having a heart exercised in greed"). **Experts** ("exercised," KJV) translates *gegymnasmenēn*, from which comes "gymnasium." They "work out" in covetousness, practicing and sharpening greedy skills. Yet they never have enough. No wonder Peter called them **an accursed brood** (lit., "children of a curse," a Hebraism denoting certain destruction from the hand of God). Sensuality, deception, greed—all are deserving of God's wrath.

5. THEY ARE MERCENARY (2:15-16)

2:15-16. Here Peter invoked a fourth Old Testament illustration, but this time he moved from Genesis to Numbers (chaps. 22-24). These false prophets were like animals (2 Peter 2:12), and their prototype, **Balaam son of Beor,** was reproved by an animal (Num. 22:28, 30). In addition to his mercenary mentality (he **loved the wages** [*misthon*] **of wickedness** [*adikias*]; cf. the same Gr. words in 2 Peter 2:13), Balaam actually urged the Moabites to trick Israelite men into illicit relationships with Moabite women, thereby introducing immorality into the camp (Num. 31:16; cf. Num. 25:1-3; Rev. 2:14). The **donkey . . . spoke** (*phthenxamenon,* "was making a sound"; also used in 2 Peter 2:18), stopping **the** prophet in his **madness** (*paraphronian,* lit., "being apart or away from right thinking"; used only here in the NT). A mere donkey, a dumb animal, was smarter than Balaam! The false teachers, like Balaam, had sinned so long and so intensely that their sin had become a form of insanity. Also today many people have so thoroughly given themselves over to avarice and debauchery that their lifestyles are spiritually insane. Money and sex (even in the name of religion) continue to bring spiritual ruin to many people. This is "the error of Balaam" (Jude 11), his **way** which is diverse from **the straight way.**

C. *Destruction by false teachers (2:17-22)*

Though the ultimate judgment of heretics is assured, Peter wrote as he did because of the damage they continued to wreak in the church. Certain types of people seemed to be especially selected for recruitment by false teachers. Having explained the avenues of God's *deliverance* from ungodly people and offered a vivid *description* of false teachers, Peter now explained the *destruction* that such false teaching can bring into the church.

1. THE TARGETS OF DESTRUCTION (2:17-18)

2:17-18. The "accursed brood" (v. 14) is able to make an impact because of the deceptive nature of its approach and the vulnerability of its targets. False teachers **are springs without water and mists driven by a storm** (cf. Jude 12-13). In both cases one would look for some benefit or blessing (a cool drink from the spring; a refreshing shower from the clouds) but in each case he is disappointed. The very nature of hypocrisy is that one does not have what he pretends to have. Once again (cf. 2 Peter 2:1, 3, 9, 12-13) Peter wrote of their coming judgment. The **blackest darkness** (lit., "blackness" or "gloominess" [*zophos*; cf. "gloomy" in v. 4] of darkness) **is reserved for them** (cf. Jude 13). This blackness is presumably hell. As in the propagation of all heresy, human speech is the weapon that false teachers aim at their targets: **they mouth** (*phthengomenoi,* "make a sound"; also used in 2 Peter 2:16) **empty** (*mataiotētos,* "futile, worthless, without results"; cf. Eph. 4:17) **boastful** (*hyperonka,* "swollen"; still another *hapax legomenon* by Peter) **words.** Such high-sounding words by which they sought to impress and deceive people were actually worthless, being no different from the sound a donkey makes! These false teachers sought to lure the unstable **by appealing to** (*deleazousin,* "baiting, enticing," also used in 2 Peter 2:14) **the lustful** (*aselgeiais;* cf. v. 7) **desires of sinful human nature.** The teachers themselves were licentious and they tried to encourage Christians to be the same.

Such propaganda and sensual license appeals to some people who are **just** learning the gospel and weighing its claim on their lives. The enticed **people who are . . . escaping from those who live** (lit., "are constantly living," pres. part.) **in error** are not believers, according to most commentators. Some Bible students, however, say the ones enticed by the heretics are already converts to Christ, who by their conversions have recently escaped from their pagan companions who live in falsehood.

2. THE TECHNIQUES OF DESTRUCTION (2:19)

2:19. The techniques of false teachers are only workable with the naive, for the heretics are like a 300-pound man selling diet books—**they promise . . . freedom** but are **themselves** hopelessly enslaved by **depravity** (John 8:34-36). Their empty and boastful promises of liberty are reminiscent of Satan's words to Eve (Gen. 3:5). Slavery is not merely chattel ownership but is the mastery of one's will by any person, idea, or substance (Rom. 6:16; 1 Cor. 6:12b).

3. THE TERMINATION OF DESTRUCTION (2:20-22)

Of whom are these verses speaking? Four views are possible.

(1) Some suggest that the word "they" refers to the false teachers rather than the targets of their attack (e.g., Edwin A. Blum, "2 Peter" in *The Expositor's Bible Commentary*, 12:282).

(2) But the connection between the end of verse 18 ("people who are just escaping from those who live in error") and the beginning of verse 20 ("if they have escaped the corruption of the world") seems to favor a reference to the unstable, unsaved people who were "listeners" of the gospel (v. 18).

(3) Others think the reference might encompass both the false teachers and their "converts," who can lose their salvation. This, however, runs counter to many passages that assure believers of eternal salvation.

(4) Another view is that *new* believers are warned against being "caught up into a life of carnality . . . only to find that there is even less pleasure, less fulfillment than before they were saved" (Duane A. Dunham, "An Exegetical Study of 2 Peter 2:18-22," *Bibliotheca Sacra* 140. January-March, 1983:51).

2:20-21. Whether **they** in verse 20 refers to the teachers or their victims, both groups had available to them knowledge about **Jesus Christ,** which could produce liberty and life. But when that knowledge was rejected, their end was deeper corruption (**again entangled in it and overcome**) and presumably a more severe degree of punishment. Indeed, they **would have been better** off never **to have known** the gospel, **the way of righteousness,** and **the sacred** (holy) **commandment** (i.e., the apostolic message) **than to have known** the truth **and** have deliberately violated it.

2:22. Jews considered both dogs and pigs among the lowest of creatures (cf. Matt. 7:6) so Peter chose these animals to describe people who knew the truth and turned away from it. The first proverb, **A dog returns to its vomit,** is taken from Proverbs 26:11. The second proverb, **A sow that is washed goes back to her wallowing in the mud,** was presumably commonly known by Jews in the first century. The underlying principle of both is the same: these apostates (whether false teachers, their victims, or both) never were what they seemed to be and returned to what they had been all along. Dogs and pigs can be scrubbed but not kept clean, for it is in their very nature to return to unclean living. Such apostates are in a tighter bondage, they are farther from the truth, and they are deeper in spiritual filth than ever before.

Believers today do well to heed Peter's warning against false teachers, to learn how to discern truth for themselves, and to teach it to others. The false teachers will themselves meet destruction and others will be destroyed by them. But Christians can wage spiritual warfare more effectively if they know their spiritual enemies, the techniques that heretics use, and the end result of their deception.

V. The Christian Hope: The Lord's Return (3:1-16)

Few people like to wait, but that is precisely what God calls believers to do as they anticipate the Lord's return. Three times the word *prosdokaō*, "look(ing) forward," appears in this chapter (vv. 12-14). This is the same Greek word translated "expect" in Luke 12:46. Waiting is to be coupled with watching.

First-century Christians were close to the words of the Old Testament prophets about Christ's second coming, to which were added the promises of the Lord Himself and the constant reminders of apostles such as Peter in letters like this. Second Peter 3:1-16 presents five facts about or perspectives on the Lord's return.

A. *Believers remember it (3:1-2)*

3:1. Addressing his readers as **Dear friends** (*agapētoi*, "beloved, loved ones"; the first of four occurrences in this chapter: vv. 1, 8, 14, 17; cf. Jude 17-18), Peter called this his **second letter to** this group, and said **both** letters are **remind-**

ers. Many scholars assume that the earlier letter is 1 Peter. But some suggest that calling 1 Peter a "reminder" does not suit its contents. Of greater importance, however, is Peter's purpose: **to stimulate you to wholesome thinking.** "As reminders to stimulate you" translates the same Greek words which are rendered "to refresh your memory" in 2 Peter 1:13. The phrase *eilikrinē dianoian* ("wholesome thinking") may also be rendered "sincere mind" or "pure disposition." (*Eilikrinēs* occurs elsewhere in the NT only in Phil. 1:10, where it is trans. "pure.") The English "sincere" is from the Latin words *sine cera*, "without wax." Some pottery salesmen would use wax to cover cracks and weak places in pottery. Such a cover-up could be detected only by holding the jug up to the sun to see if any weaknesses were visible. Such a vase was "sun-judged" (the lit. meaning of the Gr. *eilikrinēs*). God wants His people to have sun-judged minds, not those in which their sin spots have been covered over.

3:2. Peter again reminded his readers of the need to remember (cf. 1:12-15). Others, like Peter, referred to **the holy prophets** (cf. Luke 1:70; Acts 3:21; Eph. 3:5), whose **words** were oracles regarding the day of the Lord and related topics. **The command** of **our Lord and Savior** refers to His teachings, which were then proclaimed by the **apostles** (cf. Jude 17). Peter's linking the prophets and apostles placed them on the same level of authority (cf. Eph. 2:20). This also suits Peter's earlier purpose of distinguishing the true servants of the Lord from the false. Believers do well **to recall the** writings of both Testaments regarding the Lord's return.

B. Scoffers laugh at it (3:3-7)

3:3. Peter understood that he and his readers were living **in the last days,** the period of time between the Lord's First and Second Advents. **First of all** means "above all" (as in 1:20), foremost in importance. **Scoffers** are the false teachers who deny Jesus Christ (2:1) and His return (3:4). Jesus had said these heretics would come (Matt. 24:3-5, 11, 23-26), and Paul had written the same (1 Tim. 4:1-3; 2 Tim. 3:1-9). Peter echoed the warning, adding that their **scoffing** is accompanied by **their . . . evil desires** (*epithymias,* also used in 2 Peter 1:4; 2:10, 18; Jude 16, 18). Arrogant snobbery and disdain for the idea of a coming judgment led to sexual perversion.

3:4. Their mocking took the form of a stinging question: **Where is this "coming" He promised?** Rejecting this promise, so often repeated in the New Testament (John 14:1-3; Acts 1:11; 1 Cor. 15:23; 2 Cor. 1:14; Phil. 1:6; 1 Thes. 3:13; 4:14-18; 2 Thes. 1:10; 2:1; 1 Tim. 6:14; 2 Tim. 4:8; Titus 2:13; Heb. 9:28; James 5:7) rests on the principle of uniformitarianism. This is the view that the cosmic processes of the present and the future can be understood solely on the basis of how the cosmos has operated in the past. There is almost an incipient deism here which rules out divine intervention in the universal order. In a universe governed by natural laws miracles, mockers argue, simply cannot happen. Therefore they say Jesus Christ could not come again.

The scoffers wanted to push their argument as far back as possible. So they referred to **our fathers** (lit., "the fathers"), that is, Old Testament patriarchs (John 7:22; Acts 3:13; 13:32; Rom. 9:5; 11:28; Heb. 1:1), and to **the beginning of Creation.** Since nothing has happened in all this time, mockers reasoned, why expect the Lord's return now?

3:5-6. Peter met those arguments head on by reviewing some ancient history. Just as water by God's command played a significant role in the early formation of the earth, so **water** also was the agent for destruction of the earth at God's command. **The heavens existed** refers to the expanse or sky created on the second day of Creation (Gen. 1:6-8); **and the earth was formed out of water and with water** refers to the land appearing from the water on the third day of Creation (Gen. 1:9-10).

God the Creator is also God the Judge. In His sovereign will, any change in process can occur at any time for He designed and controls these "natural" processes. The scoffers **deliberately** (*thelontas,* "willingly") **forget** God's Creation and the Flood, an interesting contrast with Peter's constant reminders to his readers to "remember" (2 Peter 1:12-13, 15; 3:1-2, 8). The scoffers deliberately put aside **God's Word** and then complained that God was not doing anything. Interestingly Peter was both a creationist and a believer in the universal Flood (cf. his other references to the Flood: 1 Peter 3:20; 2 Peter 2:5).

At the beginning of 3:6 the words "by water" are literally, "through which." This may refer back to "God's Word" (at the end of v. 5 in Gr.), or it may refer to both water and the Word. But God's use of water in both Creation and destruction seems to lend credence to the NIV rendering. **The world** (*kosmos*) refers to inhabitants, since the earth itself was not destroyed in the Flood. Similarly in John 3:16 "the world" (*kosmos*) means the globe's inhabitants (cf. John 1:9; 3:17, 19; 4:42; 6:33; 7:7; 15:18-19; 17:14, 21, 23, 25; 1 John 2:2; 3:13; 4:14).

3:7. Verses 7, 10, and 12 are the only places where the New Testament depicts the future destruction of the world by fire. In the past the world was destroyed in the Flood by God's Word and by water; in the future it will be destroyed **by the same Word** and by **fire.** Having decided to judge the world (cf. 2:3-4, 9, 17), God is simply holding the earth on layaway. It is **reserved** (*tethēsaurismenoi,* "being stored up like a treasure") **for fire and kept** (*tēroumenoi*, "guarded" or "held") for judgment. Isaiah (66:15-16) and Malachi (4:1) associated fire with the return of the Lord. References to it are also found in the Qumran literature (Dead Sea Scrolls) as well as other sources shortly before and after Christ's birth. "The day of the Lord" (2 Peter 3:10) includes the Tribulation, the Millennium, the great white throne judgment, and the destruction of **the present heavens and earth.** At the great white throne after the Millennium, **ungodly men** (i.e., the wicked dead) will be judged and then thrown into the lake of fire (Rev. 20:11-15). This, as Peter wrote, will be their **day of judgment** (cf. 2 Peter 2:9) **and destruction.** After they are cast into fire, the heavens and the earth will be destroyed by fire. God intervened catastrophically before (in the Flood), and He will do so again.

C. God guarantees it (3:8-9)

3:8-9. Why should the Lord be so long in coming? Peter offered two answers. First, God counts time differently than does man. Once again Peter appealed to their memories (**do not forget this one thing**). The scoffers forget (v. 5), but believers should not. Christians should recall Psalm 90:4, which Peter quoted. People see time against time; but God sees time against eternity. In fact time only seems long because of man's finite perspective. **With the Lord a day is like a thousand years, and a thousand years are like a day.**

Some suggest that this statement argues against premillennialism. They point out that the concept of 1,000 years is not to be taken literally since it is merely a comparative time reference. However, the literal 1,000-year reign of Christ on earth is strongly affirmed in Revelation 20:1-6 (see comments there). Peter was simply using a simile. What to people, including scoffers, may seem like a long time is to the Lord very short. The present Church Age has lasted, in God's eyes, not quite two days!

The second reason the Lord's return seems to be so long in coming is that God wants as many people to be saved as possible (2 Peter 3:9). **The Lord is not slow in keeping His promise.** The words "is . . . slow" translate *bradynei* ("hesitate, linger, delay"), used only here in the New Testament. Again Peter gave a divine-human comparison (cf. v. 8). God's so-called "tardiness" as viewed by some people (**as some understand slowness**) is only a delay with respect to their time schedules, not His. In fact God's time schedule is modified by patience, a major attribute of the heavenly Father (cf. v. 15; Rom. 2:4; 9:22).

The words **not wanting** (*mē boulomenos*) **anyone to perish** do not express a decree, as if God has willed everyone to be saved. Universal salvation is not taught in the Bible. Instead those words describe God's wishes or desires; He longs that all would be saved (cf. 1 Tim. 2:4) but knows that many reject Him.

D. Peter describes it (3:10-13)

3:10. When the Lord does **come**, it will be both surprising and catastrophic: **like a thief.** This simile was used by Jesus (Matt. 24:42-44) and repeated by others (1 Thes. 5:2; Rev. 3:3; 16:15). **The day of the Lord** describes end-time events that begin after the Rapture and culminate with the commencement of eternity. In the middle of the 70th week of Daniel the Antichrist will turn against the people of God in full fury (Dan. 9:24-27; see comments on 1 Thes. 5:2; 2 Thes. 2:2-12).

In the catastrophic conflagration at the end of the Millennium, **the heavens** (the earth's atmosphere and the starry sky, not God's abode) **will disappear with a roar,** which in some way will involve fire (2 Peter 3:7, 12). **The elements** (*stoicheia*, either stars or material elements with which the universe is made) **will be destroyed by fire** (and will melt, v. 12), **and the earth and everything in it will be laid bare** (*eurethēsetai*). This Greek word could mean that everything will be exposed for what it really is. Or it could suggest a question: "The earth and everything in it—will they be found?" Others (on the basis of some Gr. mss.; NIV marg.) say the word *eurethēsetai* should be substituted with *katakaēsetai*, "shall be burned up." Perhaps the first of these views is preferable (as rendered in the NIV).

3:11. Peter sees all this as a strong motivational expectation which should provoke holy living. The question, **What kind of people ought you to be?** is rhetorical. But in case someone should miss the point, Peter answered it: **You ought to live holy and godly lives.** "Holy lives" (*en hagiais anastrophais,* lit., "in holy conduct") refers to Christian separation and sanctification—apart from the world, apart toward God. "Godly" (*eusebeiais;* also in 1:3, 6-7) refers to piety before God. The word "live" (*hyparchein*) is in the present tense, indicating that these qualities are to be constantly present in light of the Lord's return. Scoffers, questioning the Lord's coming with its ensuing judgment on them, lead ungodly lives (2:7, 10, 12-15, 18-20; 3:3). By contrast, Jesus' followers, anticipating His return, are to be godly (v. 14; cf. Titus 2:12-14; 1 John 3:3).

3:12. Holiness and piety (v. 11) not only cause God's people to **look forward to** (from *prosdokaō,* "expect and anticipate"; cf. vv. 13-14) the Lord's return but also to **speed its coming.** How do believers hasten it? The godly lives of the Lord's people, their praying, and their witnessing help bring others to repentance. Peter then repeated for emphasis the fact that at the commencement of eternity (here called **the day of God**) **the heavens** will be destroyed **by fire and the elements will melt** (cf. comments on v. 10). That event concludes "the day of the Lord" (v. 10) and commences "the day of God."

3:13. The old cosmic system will then give way to **a new heaven and a new earth** and this is what believers **are looking forward to** (cf. vv. 12, 14), not to the earth's destruction. The new heaven and new earth, given by the **promise** of God, will finally be **the home** or dwelling place **of righteousness** (lit., "in which righteousness dwells permanently"). It will be the home of righteousness because the Righteous One will be there (Jer. 23:5-7; 33:16; Dan. 9:24; Rev. 21:1, 8, 27). What a contrast this will be to the world's unrighteousness!

E. Behavior is changed by it (3:14-16)

3:14. To show that one's behavior is linked to his expectation of the Lord's coming, this paragraph begins with **So then** (*Dio*). What kind of people should believers be? They are to be holy and godly (v. 11), and they also are to **make every effort** (*spoudasate;* cf. 1:10, 15; also cf. *spoudēn,* 1:5) **to be ... spotless** (*aspiloi,* also used in 1 Tim. 6:14; James 1:27 ["pure"]; 1 Peter 1:19 ["without ... defect," referring to Christ]), **blameless** (*amōmētoi,* "without [moral] defect" like a sacrificial animal without a blemish; used also in Eph. 1:4; 5:27; Phil. 2:15; Col. 1:22; Heb. 9:14; 1 Peter 1:19; Jude 24; Rev. 14:5), **and at peace with Him** (cf. Rom. 5:1). The false teachers, Peter said, "are blots (*spiloi*) and blemishes" (*mōmoi;* 2 Peter 2:13), but believers are to make it their business to be morally clean (cf. 1:4) like Christ the spotless One (1 Peter 1:19). This is the practical result of the implantation of the divine nature (2 Peter 1:4) in the members of God's family; it is the ringing encore to the symphony of grace described in 1:5-7.

3:15. The Lord's patience is because of His desire that people come to **salvation** (cf. v. 9). The seeming procrastination of the Second Coming, far from being negative inaction on God the Father's part is rather a demonstration of His *makrothymian* ("long-suffering"). Now the world has time to repent, but this will not be so when "the day of judgment" (2:9; 3:7) comes. The Lord's patience leads toward repentance, which is precisely the point **Paul** made in Romans 2:4, though this may or may not be the passage Peter had in mind (cf. comments on 2 Peter 3:16). Interestingly Peter called Paul **our dear** (*agapētos,* "beloved"; cf. vv. 1, 8, 14, 17) **brother.** Years before Paul had severely rebuked Peter (Gal. 2:11-14), but this did not sever their love and respect for each other.

3:16. Peter said that Paul wrote about **the same** thing **in all his letters.** Though written with God's "wisdom" (v. 15), Paul's **letters contain some things that are hard to understand.** The Greek word for **hard to understand** (*dysnoēta,* only here in the NT) was sometimes applied in secular Greek literature to oracles that were ambiguous and obscure. Peter himself, as well as the **ignorant** (*amatheis,* "unlearned"), who were neophytes in New Testament doctrine, found some of Paul's statements obscure. These difficult passages (which Peter did not specify) had caused the **unstable** (*astēriktoi;* cf. 2:14) to pervert and **distort** (*streplousin,* "twist, torment"; another word occurring only here in the NT) their real meaning. But that was to be expected since that is how they handled **the other Scriptures.**

The fact that Peter referred to Paul's letters and then to "the other Scriptures" indicates that Paul's writings were then considered authoritative Scripture. Such behavior—twisting the Scripture to suit their own purposes—is met with God's judgment which, in this case, the ignorant and unstable bring on themselves in the form of **destruction** (*apōleian;* cf. 2:1, 3). Believers may not fully understand all the Scriptures, but they certainly ought not twist their obvious meanings.

VI. Conclusion (3:17-18)

3:17. In a warm and loving style (**dear friends** occurs here for the fourth time in this chap.; cf. vv. 1, 8, 14) the Apostle Peter closes this public yet personal epistle with a word of warning (v. 17) and a word of encouragement (v. 18). Both are based on an assumption: **You already know this.** These words translate one Greek word (*proginōskontes*), from which comes the English word "prognosis." When a medical prognosis is made, a patient is better able to prepare himself for what is ahead and if possible, to correct himself. When a doctor says, "If you continue to eat as much as you do now, you will have serious heart problems in a few years," the patient "knows beforehand" and can therefore change his life in accord with the information he has.

Peter then warned, **Be on your guard** (*phylassesthe*). If Peter were writing today, he might say, "Don't say I didn't warn you." If his readers were not careful they could **be carried away by the error of lawless men** (*athesmōn;* cf. 2:7). The verb "carried away" (*synapachthentes;* trans. "led astray" in Gal. 2:13) emphasizes a group or corporate movement. False teachers are not satisfied with ambushing one or two, now and then, here and there; they want to sweep large groups of people away from the correct doctrine of Christ. Those who keep company with such people are in danger of being led astray (referred to as "falling"; cf. 2 Peter 1:10; Gal. 5:4). This does not refer to losing one's salvation. On the other hand those who have paid attention to the warnings, carefully heeding the prognosis, can maintain their **secure position** in the truth. "Secure position" translates *stērigmou* ("firm position"; cf. the adjective *astēriktos,* "unstable," in 2 Peter 2:14; 3:16, and the verb *stērizei,* "make strong or firm" in 1 Peter 5:10).

3:18. To **grow in . . . grace** is not subjective, based merely on experience and emotional happenings. It is objectively related to Peter's key word **knowledge** (cf. 1:2-3, 5-6, 8, 20 ["understand"]; 2:20-21 [twice in v. 21]; 3:3). This is not just any knowledge; it is knowledge about **our Lord and Savior Jesus Christ** (cf. 1:1-2, 11; 2:20). The verb "grow" is a present imperative, which could be rendered "be continually growing." Believers are to grow "in grace," that is, in the sphere of God's unmerited favor, and in the exercise of spiritual graces which Peter spoke of in 1:5-7. This process of spiritual growth begins by knowing Christ initially in regeneration (cf. John 17:3) and it continues in one's deepening relationship with Him (Eph. 4:15; Phil. 3:10; 1 Peter 2:2). Both are necessary. Without the initial knowledge there is no opportunity for growth. But if there is only that initial knowledge, the struggling new believer forgets "that he has been cleansed from his past sins" (2 Peter 1:9).

Now the apostle, at one time more comfortable in fishing boats than with the parchments of biblical texts, affirmed the oneness of the Father and the Son in a splendid doxology. The One who is "our Lord" is also "our Savior." And glory, which belongs only to God (Isa. 42:8), is also the Son's (cf. 2 Peter 1:17). **To Him be glory** (lit., "the glory") is Peter's praise and prayer (cf. 2 Tim. 4:18). The glory of redemption, the glory of spiritual growth, the glory of manifesting the symphony of grace, the glory of escape from the false teachers, and the glory of His ultimate return—*all* glory belongs to Jesus. And He receives that glory **both now and forever.** "Forever" is literally, "to the day of the Age"—from the moment of the Cross, on through the days of the New Testament, throughout the history of the church, to the present hour, and throughout eternity! No wonder Peter concluded with the affirmative word of praise, **Amen!**

BIBLIOGRAPHY

Barbieri, Louis A., Jr. *First and Second Peter.* Everyman's Bible Commentary. Chicago: Moody Press, 1977.

Barnes, Albert. *Barnes' Notes on the New Testament.* 1962. Reprint. Grand Rapids: Kregel Publications, 1966.

Bigg, Charles. *A Critical and Exegetical Commentary on the Epistles of St. Peter and St. Jude.* The International Critical Commentary. Edinburgh: T. & T. Clark, 1901.

Blum, Edwin A. "2 Peter." In *The Expositor's Bible Commentary,* vol. 12. Grand Rapids: Zondervan Publishing House, 1981.

Calvin, John. "Commentaries on the Second Epistle of Peter." In *Calvin's Commentaries,* vol. 22. Translated by John Owen. Reprint. Grand Rapids: Baker Book House, 1981.

DeHaan, Richard W. *Studies in 2 Peter.* Wheaton, Ill.: Scripture Press Publications, Victor Books, 1977.

Demarest, John T. *Commentary on the Second Epistle of the Apostle Peter.* New York: Sheldon & Co., 1862.

Green, Michael. *The Second Epistle of Peter and the General Epistle of Jude.* The Tyndale New Testament Commentaries. Grand Rapids: Wm. B. Eerdmans Publishing Co., 1968.

James, Montague Rhodes. *The Second Epistle General of Peter and the General Epistle of Jude.* Cambridge: At the University Press, 1912.

Lenski, R.C.H. *The Interpretation of the Epistles of St. Peter, St. John and St. Jude.* Minneapolis: Augsburg Publishing House, 1966.

Lillie, John. *Lectures on the 1st and 2nd Epistles of Peter.* Reprint. Minneapolis: Klock & Klock Christian Publishers, 1978.

Mayor, Joseph B. *The Epistle of St. Jude and the Second Epistle of St. Peter.* London: Macmillan & Co., 1907. Reprint. Minneapolis: Klock & Klock Christian Publishers, 1978.

Moffatt, James. *The General Epistles: James, Peter, and Judas.* New York: Harper & Bros. Publishers, n.d.

Reicke, Bo. *The Epistles of James, Peter, and Jude.* The Anchor Bible. Garden City, N.Y.: Doubleday & Co., 1964.

Ward, J.W.C. *The General Epistles of St. Peter and St. Jude.* Westminster Commentaries. London: Methuen & Co., 1934.

Wuest, Kenneth S. *In These Last Days.* Grand Rapids: Wm. B. Eerdmans Publishing Co., 1954.

1 JOHN
Zane C. Hodges

INTRODUCTION

The First Epistle of John is an intensely practical letter addressed to Christian readers. It warns against the dangers of false teaching and exhorts believers to lives of obedience to God and love for their brothers and sisters. Its controlling theme is fellowship with God the Father and with His Son Jesus Christ (1:3).

Authorship. The epistle has been traditionally ascribed to John the Apostle. The author's name, however, does not occur in the letter. Yet it is plain from the tone of the letter as a whole that the writer possessed spiritual authority. Moreover, he placed himself among the eyewitnesses to the incarnate life of the Lord Jesus (1:1-2). Early Christian writers including Irenaeus, Clement of Alexandria, and Tertullian cited the epistle as John's. There is thus no good reason for denying the traditional belief that the letter is of apostolic authorship.

Background. The letter contains no hint about the identity or location of the readers beyond the fact that they are Christians. Since early church tradition associates John with the Roman province of Asia (in western Turkey), it has often been thought that the readers lived there. This may well be true especially since this association is confirmed by Revelation 2 and 3.

The readers had been confronted with false teachers, whom John called antichrists (1 John 2:18-26). The exact character of these false teachers has been much discussed. Many have thought they were Gnostics who held to a strict dualism in which spiritual and material things were sharply distinguished. Others have seen the letter as directed against Docetism, the belief that Jesus' humanity was not real and that He only appeared to have a physical body. Often too, the letter is thought to refute the heresy of Cerinthus. According to church tradition, Cerinthus lived in Roman Asia and was strongly opposed by the Apostle John. Cerinthus taught that Jesus was only a man and that the divine Christ descended on Jesus at His baptism and left Him before the Crucifixion.

It is not possible to be precise about the exact character of the false teaching which John opposed in his letter. The only certain data is what is found in the epistle itself. It is clear that the antichrists denied that Jesus is the Christ (2:22). The statements in 5:6 may well be intelligible against the backdrop of a teaching like that of Cerinthus. The strong claims made in 1:1-2 about the physical reality of the Incarnation would be appropriate if Docetism were in view. The emphasis on "knowing" God fits the view that the heretics made special claims to "knowledge" as the Gnostics did. But Gnosticism is chiefly known from sources much later than 1 John and many characteristics of later Gnostic thought do not find reflection in the epistle.

It is probably a mistake to attempt to systematize the thought of the heretics whom John opposed in this letter. According to his own statements, he had "many" false teachers in view (2:18; 4:1). There is no reason to think that all of them held exactly the same views. The ancient Greco-Roman world was a babel of religious voices, and it is likely that the readers were confronted by a variety of ideas. Still, the heretics had in common their denials of the person of Christ, though they could have done so in different ways. On the basis of 2:19 it may be suggested that they had originated chiefly in Judea (see comments on 2:19). But beyond this little can be said with certainty about the exact nature of the heresy or heresies that gave rise to John's epistle.

That the initial readers were indeed Christians is clear from 2:12-14, 21; and 5:13. The reference to "the anointing" which they possessed (2:20, 27) that is, the Holy Spirit, might also suggest that the addressees were principally the leaders of the church or churches to which John wrote. In the Old Testament the leaders of Israel—prophets, priests, and kings—were often anointed to their offices. While it is conceivable that 1 John 2:20 and 27 refer to an "anointing" which is true of all Christians, this kind of idea is rare in the New Testament. Even 2 Corinthians 1:21 may refer to Paul's apostolic office. Possibly therefore, in 1 John 2:20 and 27 the writer sought to affirm the competency of the church leaders in the area of spiritual understanding and thus to shore up their authority as over against the false teachers. The leaders did not need to be taught by any human teachers since they were taught by their "anointing," that is, by the Holy Spirit.

It is impossible to be dogmatic on this point. No doubt John knew the addressees when he wrote the epistle. Even if the leaders were primarily in view, the letter would naturally have been read to the entire congregation(s) since only in this way could it perform its purpose of supporting the established teachers' authority. The larger audience could then receive the instruction which the letter contained while at the same time being encouraged to rely on the guidance offered by their Spirit-taught leadership. In the early church one of the chief responsibilities of the elders was to protect the flock from spiritual "wolves" (Acts 20:28-29; Titus 1:9-11). If the false teachers made grandiose claims to spiritual wisdom and authority, it would make good sense for the inspired author to affirm his confidence in the regular church leaders. This would strengthen their hands with their congregation(s) in resisting the inroads of heretical ideas.

It might be thought, however, that the references to "children," "fathers," and "young men" (1 John 2:12-14) point to an audience of people of varying levels of spiritual attainment. If so, the leadership alone can hardly be considered as the principal addressees. On the other hand all the readers were addressed by this writer as "children" (e.g., 2:1, 18) and the terms used in 2:12-14 may simply be ways of addressing the same people viewed from different standpoints. (For further discussion, see the comments on those verses.)

In any case the letter was no doubt intended ultimately for the warning and instruction of the whole church or churches to which it was sent. And its truths are richly applicable to every Christian's experience.

Date. Virtually nothing in the epistle indicates a specific date or period for its writing. Many conservatives suggest a date late in the first century A.D., about the time of or shortly after the writing of the Fourth Gospel. But a good case can be made for dating the Gospel of John sometime prior to A.D. 70. If this is done, there is no particular reason why 1 John may not be assigned to the same period of time. If 2:19 suggests that the false teachers had seceded from the Palestinian churches which the apostles supervised, then this perhaps can be taken to indicate a time before the calamities of the Jewish revolt against the Romans in A.D. 66-70. After this period the influences (both good and bad) of Palestinian Christianity on the Gentile churches must have greatly decreased. If the reference of 2:19 is indeed to Palestine, then John may well have been writing from Jerusalem when he stated, "They went out from us."

These deductions are far from firm, but they might be taken to point to a date for the epistle somewhere between A.D. 60 and 65. But it must be admitted that an even earlier date cannot be excluded. Whatever the actual date of writing, the epistle gives truths of timeless value to the Christian church.

OUTLINE

The First Epistle of John is notoriously difficult to outline. Many different approaches have been offered. The justification for the following outline must be sought in the exposition which the commentary contains.

I. Prologue (1:1-4)
II. Introduction: Basic Principles (1:5-2:11)
   A. Basic principles of fellowship (1:5-2:2)

B. Basic principles of knowing God (2:3-11)
III. The Purpose of the Epistle (2:12-27)
  A. In light of the readers' spiritual conditions (2:12-14)
  B. In light of the world's allurements (2:15-17)
  C. In light of the deceptions of the last hour (2:18-23)
  D. In light of the readers' responsibilities to abide (2:24-27)
IV. The Body of the Epistle (2:28-4:19)
  A. The theme stated (2:28)
  B. Discerning the children of God (2:29-3:10a)
  C. Discerning love for the brethren (3:10b-23)
    1. What love is not (3:10b-15)
    2. What love is (3:16-18)
    3. What love does for believers (3:19-23)
  D. Discerning the indwelling God (3:24-4:16)
    1. Discerning the Spirit of truth (3:24-4:6)
    2. Discerning the God of love (4:7-16)
  E. The theme realized (4:17-19)
V. Conclusion (4:20-5:17)
  A. Love clarified (4:20-5:3a)
  B. Love empowered (5:3b-15)
  C. Love practiced (5:16-17)
VI. Epilogue (5:18-21)

COMMENTARY

I. Prologue (1:1-4)

The first four verses of the epistle constitute its prologue. Here the writer affirmed the tangible reality of the Incarnation of Christ and announced that the goals of his letter were fellowship and joy.

1:1. The apostle declared his subject to be **that which was from the beginning.** Many have thought that he referred here to an absolute beginning, such as described in Genesis 1:1 and John 1:1. This is possible, but in view of the epistle's concern with the original message about Jesus Christ, it seems more likely that John referred to the beginning of the gospel proclamation. If so, the usage is similar to that found in 1 John 2:7, 24; and 3:11. The writer was then asserting that what he proclaimed was the truth about God's Son that was originally witnessed by the apostles who had direct contact with Him. Numbering himself among these apostolic eyewitnesses, the author described this proclamation as one **which we have heard, which we have seen with our eyes, which we have looked at and our hands have touched.**

With these introductory words, the apostle directed his first shafts at the heresy with which he was concerned. The antichrists brought new ideas, not those which were "from the beginning" of the gospel era. Moreover, their denial of the reality of the incarnate life of Christ could be countered by the experiences of the eyewitnesses whose testimony was founded on actual hearing, seeing, and touching (cf. "look" and "touch" in Luke 24:39). John's message is solidly based on a historical reality.

The exact meaning of the expression **concerning the Word of life** has been variously explained. By capitalizing the term "Word," the NIV interprets this as a title for the Lord like that found in John 1:1, 14. But there this title has no qualifying phrase such as the expression "of life," which is used here. It seems more natural to understand the phrase in the sense of "the message about life" for which Philippians 2:16 furnishes a parallel (see also Acts 5:20). Indeed, as 1 John 1:2 shows, "life," not "word," is personified. Thus John was saying that his subject matter in this epistle deals with the original and well-attested verities that concern "the message about Life"—that is, about God's Son, who is Life (cf. 5:20).

1:2. The Life which the apostles proclaimed is intensely personal. Not only has that Life **appeared,** but it is nothing less than **the eternal life, which was with the Father and has appeared to** people. The Incarnation is unquestionably in view.

1:3. The objective John had in mind in writing about these significant realities was **that you,** the readers, **may have fellowship with us,** the apostles. Since he later, in 2:12-14, made it perfectly clear that he regarded the readers as genuine Christians, his goal was obviously not their conversions. It is an interpretive mistake of considerable moment to treat the term "fellowship" as though it meant little more than "to be a Christian." The readers were already saved, but they needed this letter if they were to enjoy real fellowship with the apostolic circle to which the author belonged. In the final analysis that apostolic **fellowship is with the Father and with His Son, Jesus Christ.**

Probably the false teachers denied that the readers possessed eternal life (see comments on 2:25; 5:13). If so, and if the readers would begin to doubt God's guarantees on that point, their fellowship with the Father and the Son would be in jeopardy. This, of course, is not the same as saying that their salvation would be in jeopardy. As believers they could never lose the gift of life which God had given them (cf. John 4:14; 6:32, 37-40), but their fellowship depended on walking in the light (1 John 1:7). The danger to the readers was that they might be allured into darkness by the siren song of the antichrists. How seductive their godless appeal was emerges in this letter. John's aim, therefore, was to furnish his readership with a necessary reaffirmation of the basic truths of their faith so that their fellowship with God would be sustained.

1:4. John rounded off the prologue with a delicate personal touch. If this letter would succeed in fulfilling its aim for the readership, the writer himself (and his fellow apostles) would reap spiritual joy. **We write this to make our joy complete.** This statement is similar to one the same author made in 3 John 4: "I have no greater joy than to hear that my children are walking in the truth." The apostles so shared the heart of Christ for His people that their own joy was bound up in the spiritual well-being of those to whom they ministered. If the readers retained their true fellowship with God and with His apostles, no one would be any happier than John himself.

II. Introduction: Basic Principles (1:5–2:11)

Since fellowship is the objective of John's letter, it was natural for him to begin with a discussion of this subject. So in 1:5–2:11 he enunciated some fundamental principles which lie at the root of all genuine fellowship with God. These principles are of immense practical value to the everyday lives of all Christians. By these principles believers may test the reality of their personal communion with God. They may also discern whether they have come to know the God with whom they commune.

A. Basic principles of fellowship (1:5–2:2)

1:5. In the prologue the author asserted that he was writing about things he had heard, seen, and touched. Here he began with something he had heard. **This is the message we have heard from Him and declare to you.** By the words "from Him," John no doubt meant from the Lord Jesus Christ whose Incarnation he had just referred to (vv. 1-2). The content of this "message," as John expressed it, is that **God is Light; in Him there is no darkness at all.** This precise statement is not found in the recorded words of Jesus, but the author was an apostle who heard much more than was "written down" (cf. John 21:25). There is no reason to think that John did not mean just what he said. This is a truth he had learned from the Lord.

In describing God as Light, which John frequently did (John 1:4-5, 7-9; 3:19-21; 8:12; 9:5; 12:35-36, 46; Rev. 21:23), he was no doubt thinking of God as the Revealer of His holiness. Both aspects of the divine nature figure in the discussion of sin and fellowship in 1 John 1:6-10. As Light, God both exposes man's sin and condemns it. If anyone walks in darkness, he is hiding from the truth which the Light reveals (cf. John 3:19-20). Thus revelatory terms such as "the truth" and "His Word" are prominent in 1 John 1:6, 8, 10.

It is important that the "message" John had heard is the one he had directed to his readers ("we . . . declare to you"). Some scholars have maintained that the false assertions which are condemned in verses 6, 8, and 10 are those of the false teachers, or antichrists, about whom John wrote later. But there is no proof of this. The writer continued to use the word "we" throughout as though both he and his readership were in view. When carefully considered, the kind of claims which John refuted are precisely the kind which may be made by Christians who lose touch with spiritual realities and with God. The effort to find in verses 6-10 the doctrinal beliefs of heretical teachers lacks adequate exegetical foundation.

1:6. Since "God is Light," it follows that a Christian cannot truly claim communion with Him while living in the darkness. As John warned, **If we claim to have fellowship with Him yet walk in the darkness, we lie and do not live by the truth.** John knew, as does every perceptive pastor, that Christians sometimes feign spirituality while engaging in acts of disobedience. The Apostle Paul had to deal with a case of incest in the Corinthian assembly (1 Cor. 5:1-5) and laid down a list of sins for which church members should come under church discipline (1 Cor. 5:9-13). Spurious claims to fellowship with God have been a tragic reality throughout the history of the church.

A Christian who says he is in fellowship with God (who "is Light") but who is disobeying Him (walking "in the darkness") is lying (cf. 1 John 2:4). Ten times John used "darkness" to refer to sin (John 1:5; 3:19; 12:35 [twice]; 1 John 1:5-6; 2:8-9, 11 [twice]).

1:7. There can be only one sphere of real communion with God—the light itself. Thus John insisted that this is where a Christian will find that communion: **But if we walk in the light, as He is in the light, we have fellowship with one another.** It is strange that many commentators have understood the expression "with one another" as a reference to fellowship with other Christians. But this is not what the author is discussing here. The Greek pronoun for "one another" *(allēlōn)* may refer to the two parties (God and the Christian) named in the first part of the statement. John's point is that if Christians live in the light where God is, then there is mutual fellowship between Himself and them. That is, they have fellowship with Him and He has fellowship with them. The light itself is the fundamental reality which they share. Thus true communion with God is living in the sphere where one's experience is illumined by the truth of what God is. It is to live open to His revelation of Himself in Jesus Christ. As John soon stated (v. 9), this entails believers' acknowledging whatever the light reveals is wrong in their lives.

It is significant that John talked of walking *in* the light, rather than *according to* the light. To walk *according to* the light would require sinless perfection and would make fellowship with God impossible for sinful humans. To walk *in* it,

however, suggests instead openness and responsiveness to the light. John did not think of Christians as sinless, even though they are walking in the light, as is made clear in the last part of this verse. For John added that **the blood of Jesus, His Son, purifies us from every sin.** This statement is grammatically coordinate with the preceding one, "We have fellowship with one another." The statement of verse 7, in its entirety, affirms that two things are true of believers who walk in the light: (a) they are in fellowship with God and (b) they are being cleansed from every sin. So long as there is true openness to the light of divine truth, Christians' failures are under the cleansing power of the shed blood of Christ. Indeed, only in virtue of the Savior's work on the cross can there be any fellowship between imperfect creatures and the infinitely perfect God.

1:8. But when a believer is experiencing true fellowship with God he may then be tempted to think or say that he is, at that moment at least, free from sin. John warned against this self-deluding conception. **If we claim to be without sin, we deceive ourselves and the truth is not in us** (cf. v. 6; 2:4). If Christians understand the truth that God's Word teaches about the depravity of the human heart, they know that just because they are not *conscious* of failure does not mean that they are free from it. If the truth is "in" them as a controlling, motivating influence, this kind of self-deception will not take place. Whether someone claims to be "without sin" for a brief period of time or claims it as a permanent attainment, the claim is false.

1:9. In view of verse 8, Christians ought to be ready at all times to acknowledge any failure which God's light may expose to them. Thus John wrote, **If we confess our sins, He is faithful and just and will forgive us our sins and purify us from all unrighteousness.** Though the NIV's translation "our sins" (after the words "forgive us") is quite admissible, "our" is not in the Greek text. The phrase *(tas hamartias)* contains only an article and noun and it is conceivable that the article is the type which grammarians call "the article of previous reference." If so, there is a subtle contrast between this expression and the "all unrighteousness" which follows it. John's thought might be paraphrased: "If we confess our sins, He . . . will forgive the sins we confess and moreover will even cleanse us from *all* unrighteousness." Naturally only God knows at any moment the full extent of a person's unrighteousness. Each Christian, however, is responsible to acknowledge (the meaning of "confess," *homologōmen*; cf. 2:23; 4:3) whatever the light makes him aware of, and when he does so, a complete and perfect cleansing is granted him. There is thus no need to agonize over sins of which one is unaware.

Moreover, it is comforting to learn that the forgiveness which is promised here is both absolutely assured (because God "is faithful") and also is in no way contrary to His holiness (He is "just"). The word used here for "just" *(dikaios)* is the same one which is applied as a title to Christ in 2:1 where it is translated "the Righteous One." *Dikaios* is also used of God (either the Father or the Son) in 2:29 and 3:7. Obviously God is "just" or "righteous" when He forgives the believer's sin because of the "atoning sacrifice" which the Lord Jesus has made (see 2:2). As is already evident from 1:7, a Christian's fellowship with God is inseparably connected with the effectiveness of the blood which Jesus shed for him.

In modern times some have occasionally denied that a Christian needs to confess his sins and ask forgiveness. It is claimed that a believer already has forgiveness in Christ (Eph. 1:7). But this point of view confuses the perfect position which a Christian has in God's Son (by which he is even "seated . . . with Him in the heavenly realms" [Eph. 2:6]) with his needs as a failing individual on earth. What is considered in 1 John 1:9 may be described as "familial" forgiveness. It is perfectly understandable how a son may need to ask his father to forgive him for his faults while at the same time his position within the family is not in jeopardy. A Christian who never asks his heavenly Father for forgiveness for his sins can hardly have much sensitivity to the ways in which he grieves his Father. Furthermore, the Lord Jesus Himself taught His followers to seek forgiveness of their sins in a prayer that was obviously intended for daily use (cf. the expression "give us today our daily bread" preceding "forgive us our debts," Matt. 6:11-12). The teaching that a Christian should not ask God for daily forgiveness is an aberration. Moreover, confession of sin is *never* connected by John with the acquisition of eternal life, which is always conditioned on faith. First John 1:9 is not spoken to the unsaved, and the effort to turn it into a soteriological affirmation is misguided.

It may also be said that so long as the idea of walking in the light or darkness is correctly understood on an experiential level, these concepts offer no difficulty. "Darkness" has an ethical meaning (*Theological Dictionary of the New Testament*, s.v. "*skotos*," 7:444). When a believer loses personal touch with the God of light, he begins to live in darkness. But confession of sin is the way back into the light.

1:10. However, after a believer sins, he should not deny that sin. **If we claim we have not sinned, we make Him out to be a liar and His Word has no place in our lives.** This statement should be read in direct connection with verse 9. When a Christian is confronted by God's Word about his sins, he should admit them rather than deny them. To deny one's personal sin in the face of God's testimony to the contrary, is to "make" God "out to be a liar." By contradicting His Word, a person rejects it and refuses to give it the proper "place" in his life.

2:1. Some of John's readers might have thought his insistence on the sinfulness of Christians somehow would discourage holiness. The opposite was John's intention as he affirmed: **My dear children, I write this to you so that you will not sin.** He addressed them affectionately as an apostle with a fatherly concern (The Gr. word for "children" ["dear" is not in the Gr.] is *teknia* [lit., "little born ones"], used seven times by John in this epistle [vv. 1, 12, 28; 3:7, 18; 4:4; 5:21] and once in his Gospel [John 13:33]. A similar word *tekna* ["born ones"] occurs in John 1:12; 11:52; 1 John 3:2, 10 [twice]; 5:2; 2 John 1, 4, 13; and 3 John 4. On the other hand *paidia* ["children"] occurs only twice in 1 John [2:13, 18].)

The statements in 1:8, 10 about believers' sinful tendencies do not encourage sin; they actually put perceptive Christians on guard against it. If a believer tries to make the claims denounced in 1:8 and 10, then he is most likely to fail to recognize and reject sin. But sin is nevertheless a reality, however much John wished his readers would not commit it. Accordingly he assured them, **But if anybody does sin, we have One who speaks to the Father in our defense—Jesus Christ the Righteous One.** John did not want his readers to sin, but he knew that none of them was perfect and that all would need the help available from their Advocate.

The words "One who speaks . . . in our defense" translate a single term *(parakleton).* Its essential meaning is captured by the KJV's familiar "Advocate." John is the only New Testament writer to use it of the Holy Spirit (four times in his Gospel: John 14:16, 26; 15:26; 16:7). In these four verses the NIV renders it "Counselor" each time (cf. KJV's "Comforter"). The thought here in 1 John 2:1 is of a defense attorney who takes up the case of his client before a tribunal. The way in which the advocacy of the Lord Jesus works for His sinning people is admirably illustrated in His prayer for Peter (Luke 22:31-32). In anticipation of Peter's approaching denial, Jesus asked the Father to prevent Peter's faith from collapsing. He also had in mind Peter's future helpfulness to his Christian brethren. There is no reason to suppose that Christ must ask God to keep a Christian from going to hell as a result of his sin. Eternal life is fully guaranteed to those who have trusted Jesus for it (John 3:16; 5:24; etc.). But the consequences of a believer's failure, his restoration, and future usefulness are all urgent matters which Jesus takes up with God when sin occurs. His own personal righteousness (He is "the Righteous One"; cf. 1 John 1:9, God is "just") is what uniquely suits Christ for His role as a Christian's Advocate after he sins.

2:2. If God extends mercies to a sinning believer—and the believer does not reap the full consequences of his failure in his personal experience—that fact is not due to the merits of that believer himself. On the contrary, the grace obtained through the advocacy of Christ is to be traced, like all of God's grace, to His all-sufficient sacrifice on the cross. Should any sinning believer wonder on what grounds he might secure God's mercy after he has failed, the answer is found in this verse. So adequate is Jesus Christ as God's **atoning Sacrifice** that the efficacy of His work extends **not** merely to the **sins** of Christians themselves, **but also** to **the sins of the whole world.** In saying this, John was clearly affirming the view that Christ genuinely died for everyone (cf. 2 Cor. 5:14-15, 19; Heb. 2:9). This does not mean, of course, that everyone will be saved. It means rather that anyone who hears the gospel *can* be saved if he so desires (Rev. 22:17). In context, however, John's point is to remind his readers of the magnificent scope of Christ's "atoning sacrifice" in order to assure them that His advocacy as the Righteous One on their behalf is fully consistent with God's holiness.

In recent times there has been much scholarly discussion of the Greek word *hilasmos,* which the NIV renders as "atoning Sacrifice." (The word occurs in the NT only here and in 1 John 4:10.) Some say the term is not the placating of God's wrath against sin, but rather is an "expiation" or "cleansing" of sin itself. But the linguistic evidence for this interpretation is not persuasive. The view has been capably discussed and refuted by Leon Morris in *The Apostolic Preaching of the Cross* (Grand Rapids: Wm. B. Eerdmans Publishing Co., 1965, pp. 125–85).

God's wrath against sin may not be a concept congenial to the modern mind, but it is thoroughly biblical. *Hilasmos* could be fittingly rendered "propitiation" (cf. the noun *hilastērion,* "propitiation," in Rom. 3:25 and the verb *hilaskomai,* "to propitiate," in Luke 18:13 and Heb. 2:17). The Cross has indeed propitiated (satisfied) God and has met His righteous demands so thoroughly that His grace and mercy are abundantly available to both saved and unsaved alike.

B. *Basic principles of knowing God (2:3–11)*

John's transition (v. 3) to the subject of knowing God may seem more abrupt than it really is. In ancient thought, the concept of "light" readily suggested the idea of "vision," "perception," or "knowledge." It seems obvious that a life of fellowship with God in the light ought to lead to knowing Him. Of course in a sense all true Christians know God (John 17:3), but sometimes even genuine believers can be said not to know God or

Christ (John 14:7-9). Furthermore, Jesus promised His disciples a special self-disclosure that was predicated on their obeying His commands (John 14:21-23). It is clear that such an experience involves the knowledge of God. Finally, fellowship naturally leads to knowing the One with whom that fellowship takes place. Even on the level of human experience this is true. If a father and son live apart, they will not know each other as well as if they lived together, even though their parent-child relationship continues to exist.

It would be wrong, therefore, to read 1 John 2:3-11 as if John had left the subject of fellowship with God behind. On the contrary, the subject of knowing God is its logical continuation.

2:3. For readers who wish to decide whether their experience of fellowship with God has led them really to know Him in a personal way, John gave a simple test: **We know that we have come to know Him if we obey His commands.** The two occurrences of the word "know" (*ginōskō*) in this verse are the first of 23 times John used this word in this epistle. (A synonym, *oida*, occurs six times: 3:2; 5:15 [twice], 18-20.) As often in Johannine usage, the word "Him" might refer either to God or to Christ. For John, Jesus is so closely linked with the Father that a precise distinction between the Persons of the Godhead sometimes seems irrelevant. Fellowship is with both the Father and the Son (1:3) and to know One of Them intimately is to know the Other. But obedience is the condition for such knowledge (cf. John 14:21-23). It is also the means by which a Christian can be sure that he has really "come to know" his Lord (cf. "obey His commands" in 1 John 3:22, 24; 5:2-3).

2:4. It follows, therefore, that **the man who says, I know Him, but does not do what He commands is a liar.** As in 1:6, someone may profess a fellowship with God which his life shows he does not possess. John was not afraid to call this kind of claim what it really is: a lie. Furthermore, it may be said of the same person that **the truth is not in him.** The idea is similar to the statements made earlier about false claims (1:6, 8, 10). In such a person the truth is not a dynamic, controlling influence. He is seriously out of touch with spiritual reality.

2:5-6. On the other hand, obedience to God's **Word** ("His commands," v. 3) results in a rich and full experience of God's love: **God's love is truly made complete in him.** The Greek expression "the love of God" (rendered "God's love") could mean either His love for a Christian or a Christian's love for God. But the NIV rendering is perhaps the best, particularly in light of John 14:21-23. In that passage an obedient disciple is promised a special experience of the love of the Father and Son. Since a Christian is already the object of God's saving love, this additional, experiential realization of the divine affection may be properly said to make God's love complete in him (cf. 1 John 4:12, 17). That is to say, an obedient believer has a deep, full-orbed acquaintance with "God's love." Since God is love (4:16), to know God intimately is to know His love intimately.

John then added, **This is how we know we are in Him: Whoever claims to live in Him must walk as Jesus did.** (The translators have supplied the word "Jesus" which is represented in the original by a pronoun.) In these statements, John used two other expressions ("in Him" and "live in Him") which further his thought. As with the connection he makes between obedience and the knowledge of God, here too the Upper Room Discourse (John 13-16) is the seedplot from which these ideas come. The concept involved is derived especially from the Parable of the Vine and the Branches (John 15:1-8). The vine-branch relationship is an image of the discipleship experience. Jesus said, "This is to My Father's glory, that you bear much fruit, showing yourselves to be My disciples" (John 15:8). In 1 John 2:5-6 discipleship is also in view, as is seen from the reference to the imitation of Christ in verse 6. Moreover, the Greek term rendered in the NIV by "live" *(menō)* is the same verb used in John 15:4 where the NIV translates it "remain."

It would be a mistake to equate the concept of being "in Him" as John uses it here with the Pauline concept of being "in Christ." For Paul, the words "in Christ" describe a Christian's permanent position in God's Son with all its attendant privileges. With John, the kind of relationship pictured in the vine-branch imagery describes an experience that can be ruptured (John 15:6) with a resultant loss of fellowship and fruitfulness. Thus here in 1 John, the proof that a person is enjoying this kind of experience is to be found in a life modeled after that of Jesus in obedience to His Word. In short, 2:5-6 continues to talk about the believer's fellowship with God.

2:7. Verses 3-6 introduce the issue of obedience, though it was surely implicit also in 1:5-10. But John's insistence on obeying God's commands as a test of one's personal intimacy and knowledge of Him leads to a natural question: Which commands did John have in mind? The answer is offered here. John did **not** have in mind some **new** obligation which his readers had never heard. On the contrary the **command** foremost in his mind was **an old one, which you have had since the beginning** (cf. 2 John 5). No doubt John thought here especially of the command to love one another (cf. 1 John 2:9-11). He emphasized his point by adding that **this old command is the message** (*logos*, lit., "word"; cf. 1:5; 3:11) which **you have heard** (the majority of mss. add again "from the beginning"). Whatever innovations the readers might be confronting because of the doctrines of the antichrists, their real responsibility was to a commandment which they had heard from the very start of their Christian experience (cf. "heard" and "from the beginning" in 1:1; 2:24; 3:11).

John's affectionate concern for them is seen in his use of *Agapētoi*, literally, "Beloved" and here rendered **Dear friends.** He used the same word in 3:2, 21; 4:1, 7, 11 and *Agapēte* ("Dear friend") in 3 John 2, 5, 11.

2:8. Yet Jesus had called that commandment "new" (John 13:34) and John pointed out that it had not lost its freshness. It is really still **a new command and its truth is seen in Him and you.** This last assertion, somewhat freely rendered by NIV, seems to mean that the command to love came to realization first in Jesus Himself and then in His followers. The next phrase, **because the darkness is passing and the true light is already shining,** is best related back to the claim that he was after all writing a new command to them. His point was that the command to love (which Jesus and His followers exhibit) belongs to the new Age of righteousness which has begun to dawn. It does not belong to the old Age of darkness which was passing away. Christ's Incarnation brought a light into the world which can never be extinguished. The love He manifested and taught His disciples to manifest is a characteristic of the Age to come. It is the darkness of the present world and all its hatred which is destined to disappear forever (cf. 1 John 2:17a).

In speaking this way, John gave to the terms "light" and "darkness" a slant differing slightly from what they had in chapter 1. There light was defined in terms of the fundamental character of God (1:5). In that sense, the light has been shining as long as there has been a revelation of God to man. But here John wrote of the Incarnation in particular as the point at which the light began to shine. The new Age has dawned and its true character can now be defined in terms of the special revelation God has made of Himself in His Son. And above all, that revelation is a revelation of divine love.

2:9. It follows that **anyone who claims to be in the light but hates his brother is still in the darkness.** This warning is clearly intended for Christians as the words "his brother" plainly show. An unsaved person can indeed hate a brother of physical kin, but since he has no spiritual kin he cannot really hate his (spiritual) brother. If John thought that no Christian could hate another Christian, there was no need to personalize the relationship with the word "his." But the opinion, held by some, that a true Christian could never hate another Christian is naive and contrary to the Bible and experience. Even so great a man as King David was guilty of murder, which is the final expression of hate. John was warning his readers against a spiritual danger that is all too real (cf. 1:8, 10). And he was affirming that a Christian who can hate his fellow Christian has not genuinely escaped from the darkness of this present passing Age. To put it another way, he has much to learn about God and cannot legitimately claim an intimate knowledge of Christ. If he really knew Christ as he ought, he would *love* his brother.

2:10-11. By contrast, **whoever loves his brother lives in the light** of the new Age which has dawned in Christ (cf. v. 8). **There is nothing in him** (in one who loves his brother) **to make him stumble.** Hatred is a kind of internal "stumbling block" which can lead to disastrous spiritual falls. But the calamities to which hatred leads are avoided by one who loves his brother.

This is not so, however, for one who **hates his brother.** Such a person **walks around in the darkness** and **he does not know where he is going, because the darkness has blinded him** (cf. v. 9). A Christian who harbors hatred for a fellow Christian has lost all real sense of direction. Like a man wandering aimlessly in the dark, he faces potentially grave dangers.

III. The Purpose of the Epistle (2:12-27)

In the prologue John had expressed the general aim and goal of his letter. Now he told his audience the specific concerns which motivated the letter. In that sense he articulated the precise purpose of this epistle.

A. In light of the readers' spiritual conditions (2:12-14)

In the light of all the warnings John gave (1:5–2:11), his readers might think that he was fundamentally dissatisfied with their spiritual conditions. But this was not so. John now assured them that he wrote because of the spiritual assets which they possessed.

2:12-13a. In describing these assets, the author addressed his readers as **dear children . . . fathers,** and **young men.** Some have suggested that John here divided his readers by chronological age-groups. Others say he did so by their spiritual maturity. If either explanation is adopted, the sequence—which makes "fathers" the middle term—is somewhat strange. Moreover, elsewhere John addressed *all* his readers as "children" (vv. 1, 28; 3:7, 18; 5:21). It seems best (with C.H. Dodd and I.H. Marshall) to view the terms of address as referring to all the readers in each case. Then each experience ascribed to them is appropriate to the category named.

Thus, thought of as "children," the readers had experienced the forgiveness that their heavenly Father grants to His own. As "fathers" they had an experience that touches eternity past, since they **have known Him who is from the beginning.** In the light of 2:3-6, this implies they have truly experienced fellowship with God. (Here again [cf. v. 3] the word "Him" could refer to either the Father or the Son; the distinction was not important to John. His readers knew both.) As "young men," the readers had engaged in spiritual warfare and had **overcome the evil one,** Satan (cf. "evil one" in v. 14; 3:12; 5:18-19).

Thought of in this way, the sequence "children," "fathers," and "young men" is meaningful. The readers knew what it was to have sins forgiven and then have fellowship with the Eternal One. As a result they were like vigorous young men who had defeated satanic assaults.

2:13b-14. The attainments of the readers were then reiterated, but with some subtle variations. Thought of as **children** again, it can be said that they **have known the Father.** Unlike newborn infants (*teknia* ["little born ones"], v. 12; see comments on v. 1), who can scarcely recognize their fathers, these people (*paidia*, "children"; cf. v. 18)—through fellowship—have come to know their divine Parent. But what can be added to the experience of knowing the Eternal One? In calling them **fathers** again, John simply repeated the attainment mentioned earlier without changing it. Then viewing them once more as **young men,** the writer implied growth in strength. In verse 13, he had simply spoken of victory over Satan. Now he wrote, **You are strong, and the Word of God lives in you, and you have overcome the evil one.** By repeating the three categories under which he here addressed his audience, John suggested not only that they possessed spiritual attainments worthy of being called children, fathers, and young men, but also that they possessed these attainments in ample measure.

B. In light of the world's allurements (2:15-17)

The writer was not dissatisfied with the spiritual state of his readers. Much less did he question or doubt their salvation, as some expositors of this epistle imply. On the contrary, his readers may even be viewed as having matured in the faith. John wrote precisely because their present state was so good. But he wished to warn them about dangers which always exist, no matter how far one has advanced in his Christian walk.

2:15. He turned now to a warning. **Do not love the world or anything in the world.** The "world" *(kosmos),* thought of here as an entity hostile to God (cf. 4:4), is always a seductive influence which Christians should continually resist (cf. John 15:18-19; James 4:4. In other NT verses "world" *[kosmos]* means people, e.g., John 3:16-17.) The world competes for the love of Christians and one cannot both love it and the Father at the same time. **If anyone loves the world, the love of the Father is not in him.** As James also had told his Christian readers, "Friendship with the world is hatred toward God" (James 4:4).

2:16. The reason love for the world is incompatible with love for God is that **everything in the world . . . comes not from the Father but from the world.** The world thus conceived is a system of values and goals from which God is excluded. In describing "everything in the world," John specified its contents under three well-known phrases that effectively highlight the world's false outlook. Men of the world live for **the cravings of sinful man.** "Cravings" translates *epithymia,* which is used twice in this verse and once in the next verse. The NIV translates it differently each time: "cravings," "lust," "desires." In the New Testament the word usually, though not always, connotes desires that are sinful. The expression "sinful man" translates the Greek *sarx* (lit., "flesh"). The phrase refers particularly to illicit bodily appetites. The expression **the lust** *(epithymia)* **of his eyes** points to man's covetous and acquisitive nature. **The boasting of what he has and does** paraphrases the Greek *hē alazoneia tou biou* (lit., "the pretension of human life"), which signifies a proud and ostentatious way of life. (*Alazoneia* is used only here in the NT.) Christians ought to have nothing to do with such worldly perspectives as these.

2:17. After all, **the world and its desires** *(epithymia)* **are temporary and pass away, but the man who does the will of God lives forever.** The word "lives" renders the characteristic Johannine word *menō* (cf. 1:6). It suggests, as almost always in this epistle, the "abiding life" of fellowship with God. But here is obviously the additional thought that the life lived in God's fellowship, rejecting the sinful things of this passing world, is a life that has no real ending. A person whose character and personality are shaped by obedience to God will not be affected by the passing away of the world and its vain desires. It is a Johannine way of saying, "Only one life, 'twill soon be past; only what's done for Christ will last."

C. In the light of the deceptions of the last hour (2:18-23)

2:18. John's general warning against the world is now followed by a warning against one of its end-time manifestations. The false teachers who were present were worldly to the core (cf. 4:5). The readers knew about the predicted advent of **the Antichrist** and needed to be alerted to the appearance of **many** who would display his traits of hostility toward God's Christ. This is a clear indication that history has entered a climactic era: **the last hour.** Despite the lapse of centuries since John wrote, the climax of all things impends in a special way. The stage has been set for history's final drama.

2:19. Of the false teachers John had in mind, he wrote, **They went out from us.** The word "us" here is most naturally taken as the apostolic first person plural of this epistle (see 1:1-5; 4:6). "Us" contrasts with the "you" in 2:20-21, which referred to the readers. It does not make sense that the false teachers had left the churches to which the readers belonged. If they had, how were they still a problem? On the other hand if, like the legalists of Acts 15, they had seceded from the apostolic churches of Jerusalem and Judea, then they were a particular threat to the readers because they came to them claiming roots in the soil out of which Christianity arose. Thus John was eager to deny any connection with them.

They did not really belong to us paraphrases an expression more literally rendered, "they were not of us." The writer's point was that these men did not really share the spirit and perspective of the apostolic circle, for if they had their secession would not have taken place. Heresy in the Christian church, whether on the part of its saved members or unsaved people in it, always unmasks a fundamental disharmony with the spirit and doctrine of the apostles. A man in touch with God will submit to apostolic instruction (cf. 1 John 4:6).

2:20-21. The readers were well fortified against the antichrists, however, since they had **an anointing from the Holy One** (i.e., from God). The "anointing" is no doubt the Holy Spirit since, according to verse 27, the anointing "teaches." This clearly suggests that the "anointing" is conceived of as a Person. Jesus Himself was "anointed" with the Holy Spirit (cf. Acts 10:38). (For the possibility that the term suggests that the church leaders are in view, see the *Introduction*.) As a result of their "anointing," the readers (perhaps primarily the church leaders) had adequate instruction in **the truth** of God. John wrote them precisely **because** their apprehension of **the truth** was correct and **because . . . the truth** should never be confused with a **lie.**

2:22-23. The antichrists are liars for they deny **that Jesus is the Christ,** that is, God's Son and the appointed Savior (cf. John 4:29, 42; 20:31). This denial involves also a denial of **the Father.** Any claim they might make to having the Father's approval is false. **One** cannot have **the Father** without **the Son.** To reject One is to reject the Other.

D. *In light of the readers' responsibilities to abide (2:24-27)*

2:24. The readers must **see that what** they **have heard from the beginning** (cf. 1:1; 2:7; 3:11) **remains in** them. **If it does** (NIV paraphrases here), they **will remain in the Son and in the Father.** The term translated "remain" is again *menō*, which the NIV renders as "live" and "lives" in 2:6, 10, 14, 17. John's point was that if the readers would resist the lies of the antichrists and let the truth they had heard from the beginning "abide" (or "be at home") in them, they would continue to "abide" in the fellowship of God the Father and God the Son.

2:25-26. They could also continue to rest on the divine promise of **eternal life.** As John later insisted (5:9-13; cf. 5:20), they could be sure that they possessed this on the basis of God's testimony to that fact. It may well be that the antichrists denied that the readers were actually saved, since John went right on to say, **I am writing these things to you about those who are trying to lead you astray** (cf. 3:7). Coming as they evidently did from the apostolic churches of Judea, these men apparently sought to undermine the readers' conviction that Jesus is the Christ and that they had eternal life through Him. John's insistence that his readers genuinely know God and know His truth (2:12-14, 21) was part of his strategy for fortifying them against the antichrists.

2:27. The readers did not need teaching from the antichrists or, for that matter, from anyone. Their **anointing . . . received from** God, **remains in** them **and** was a sufficient Teacher. This, along with verses 12-14, may imply that John's readers were relatively spiritually mature, since the immature need human teachers (cf. Heb. 5:12). This is appropriate if John were addressing church leaders, but it would also suit a congregation that had long been in the faith. Unlike the antichrists, who may have claimed some form of inspiration, the readers' **anointing** was **real, not counterfeit.** They needed to **remain** (*menete*, "abide") **in Him** (the pronoun can refer to **the anointing**) and rely fully on His continuing instruction.

IV. The Body of the Epistle (2:28–4:19)

In the section just completed (2:12-27), John wrote both to assure his readers of the validity of their spiritual experiences and to warn them against the antichrists who denied that validity. In what may be described as the body of his letter, John then explored the true character and consequences of that form of experience which the readers already had and needed to maintain.

A. *The theme stated (2:28)*

2:28. Many commentators see a major break here. The words **continue in Him** involve again the Greek verb *menō* ("abide") which has already occurred 10 times in verses 6-27. (John used *menō* 66 of the 112 times it occurs in the NT: 40 in John, 23 in 1 John, and 3 in 2 John.) In accord with his basic theme about fellowship (1 John 1:3), John once more enjoined the "abiding" life. But now he introduced the new thought of being **confident** before Christ **at His coming.** The Greek words rendered "be confident" are literally "have confidence." The latter is *parrēsia*, a word that can signify a bold freedom of speech. John used it again in 3:21; 4:17; 5:14. If the readers would maintain their fellowship with God, they would enjoy a genuine boldness of speech when they would meet their Lord. How this can be so is the subject of 2:29–4:19. Should a believer fail to abide in Him, however, there is the possibility of shame when Christ comes. This intimates divine disapproval at the judgment seat of Christ, referred to in 4:17-19. The NIV's **unashamed before Him** might be more literally rendered: "not be ashamed before Him." The possibility is real but does not, of course, suggest the loss of salvation.

B. Discerning the children of God (2:29–3:10a)

At this point John began to develop a line of thought which culminates in the acquisition of the boldness of which he had just spoken (2:28; cf. 4:17-19). The fellowship with the apostolic circle and with God which he had in mind (cf. 1:3) requires discerning the way the lives of God's children are manifested in their actions. John was moving toward the thought that when one's life is properly manifested, God Himself is manifested in it (4:12-16).

2:29. This verse introduces for the first time in 1 John the explicit thought of new birth. Since the readers **know that He** (God the Father or God the Son) **is righteous,** they would also **know that everyone who does what is right has been born of Him** (the pronoun here probably refers to God the Father who regenerates). (The phrase "born of God" occurs in 3:9; 4:7; 5:1, 4, 18 [twice].) The statement has nothing to do with the readers' individual assurance of salvation. It is rather an assertion that when they see real righteousness ("what is right" translates *tēn dikaiosynēn*) exhibited, they can be sure that the person who exhibits it is a child of God. This righteousness, of course, for John can only mean the kind that Christ had enjoined. It has nothing to do with mere humanistic kindness and morality. The converse of John's statement does not follow, namely, that everyone who is born of God does righteousness. John knew that Christians can walk in the darkness and are susceptible to sin (1:6, 8; 2:1). He was writing here of the way one can see the new birth in the actions of others.

3:1. This verse begins with the word *idete* ("behold, look at"), not translated in the NIV. The writer had just told the readers how to see the reality of new birth in righteous behavior; now he invited them to contemplate the greatness of the divine love which that reality displays. Behold **how great is the love the Father has lavished on us, that we should be called children of God.** (The words **and that is what we are,** rightly omitted by most mss., are probably a scribal addition.) In the Bible the word "called" indicates that this is what one actually is (cf. "called to be holy," lit., "called saints" [1 Cor. 1:2]). Believers are "called children of God" because they are the born-ones (*tekna*) of "the Father." The perception to which John invited his readers is, however, lost on the world. Since the **world . . . did not know Him** (God or Christ), it can hardly be expected to recognize believers as His children. This kind of discernment about others is a distinctively Christian perception.

3:2-3. But even for Christians, this perception is a spiritual one. Though **now we are children of God,** there is no physical evidence of this that an eye can see. The physical changes in Christians await the coming of Christ. **But we know that when He appears, we shall be like Him** (cf. 1 Cor. 15:52-54; Phil. 3:21). Such a transformation will result from seeing **Him as He is.** But pending that event it is already true that **everyone who has this hope in Him** (the pronoun probably refers to Christ, the Object of this hope) **purifies himself, just as He is pure.** Here the writer probably continued to refer to the new birth. One who sets his hope by faith on the Son of God experiences an inward purification that is as complete as Christ's own purity ("just as He is pure"). John thus prepared the ground for the assertions he would soon make (1 John 3:6, 9). New birth involves a perfect purification from sin.

3:4. John now wrote about sin which stands in opposition to the purity he had just referred to in verse 3. The NIV renders his statement: **Everyone who sins breaks the law** (*tēn anomian poiei*, "does lawlessness"); **in fact, sin is lawlessness** (*anomia*). Usually in the Greek New

Testament *anomia* is a general term like the English word "wickedness," which has some prominence in eschatological contexts (cf. Matt. 7:23; 13:41; 24:12; 2 Thes. 2:7). So its use here so soon after the references to the antichrists may be significant. The writer probably intended it to be a strongly pejorative description of sin. It seems likely, in view of 1 John 3:7, that the antichrists had a softened view of sin which John wished to refute. A person who sins does what is wicked, and sin *is* wickedness, John was insisting. (Lit., the first clause in v. 4 is, "Everyone who commits wickedness.") Sin must not be taken lightly.

3:5-6. The seriousness of sin is further underscored by the consideration that Christ **appeared so that He might take away our sins. And in Him is no sin.** The Incarnation brought into the world the One who is totally sinless and who had as an objective the removal of sin from the lives of His own (cf. John 1:29; Heb. 9:28a). It follows logically from this that a person who is ("abides") *in* a sinless Person must himself be sinless, for he has a sinless, regenerate nature.

This is the inescapable logic of the text. But a different point is suggested by the NIV's rendering: **No one who lives** (*menōn*, "abides") **in Him keeps on sinning. No one who continues to sin has either seen Him or known Him.** A widely held explanation of this verse is that a believer "does not sin habitually," that is, sin is not his way of life. However, the Greek text has no words to represent phrases such as "keeps on" or "continues to" or "habitually." These phrases are based on an understanding of the Greek present tense which is now widely in dispute among New Testament scholars (see, e.g., S. Kubo, "1 John 3, 9: Absolute or Habitual?" *Andrews University Seminary Studies* 7. 1969:47–56; C.H. Dodd, *The Johannine Epistles*, pp. 78–81; I. Howard Marshall, *The Epistles of John*, p. 180). It cannot be shown anywhere in the New Testament that the present tense can bear this kind of meaning *without the assistance of other words*. Such a view is invalid for this verse and also for 1 John 3:9. Nor is John saying that sinless perfection must be achieved, and that those who fail to do so lose their salvation. Such a notion is foreign to John's argument and to all of Scripture.

John's point is simple and straightforward. Sin is a product of ignorance and blindness toward God. "No one who sins has seen Him or known Him" (v. 6b).

Sin can never come out of seeing and knowing God. It can never be a part of the experience of abiding in Christ. "No one who abides in Him sins" (v. 6a). But though the meaning of this is not really open to question, there has seemed to be an inconsistency between such assertions and John's earlier insistence that a believer can never claim to be without sin (1:8). The solution to this problem has been suggested by the statement in 3:3 in which the purification of the one "who has this hope in Him" is comparable in its nature to the purity of Christ ("just as He is pure"). From this it follows that the regenerate life is, in one sense, an essentially and fundamentally sinless life. For the believer sin is abnormal and unnatural; his whole bent of life is away from sin.

The fact remains, however, that Christians do not experience the sinless life perfectly on this earth; hence 1:8, 10 remain true. The two ideas are not really incompatible. The Christian still experiences a genuine struggle with the flesh and overcomes its impulses only by the help of the Holy Spirit (cf. Gal. 5:16-26).

Paul's thinking also conforms with this view. In his struggle with sin he was able to conclude, "Now if I do what I do not want to do, it is no longer I who do it, but it is sin living in me that does it" (Rom. 7:20). In this way Paul could perceive sin as not a real part of what he was at the most inward level of his being (cf. Rom. 7:25). When he wrote, "I no longer live, but Christ lives in me" (Gal. 2:20), he implied the same thing. If Christ alone really lives, sin can be no part of that experience. Insofar as God is experienced by a believer, that experience is sinless. (Cf. comments on 1 John 3:9.)

3:7-8. These verses suggest strongly that the doctrine of the antichrists involved a confusion between sin and righteousness. Perhaps the antichrists felt free to sin while at the same time denying their guilt and claiming to behave righteously. John warned against such ideas: **Do not let anyone lead you astray.** (The Gr. verb "lead astray," *planaō*, used also in 2:26, is the same word rendered "deceive" in 1:8.) **He who does what is**

right is righteous, just as He is righteous (cf. 1:9; 2:1, 29). Only righteousness springs from a righteous nature. By contrast, **He who does what is sinful is of the devil.** It would be wrong to water this assertion down. All sin, of whatever kind or degree, is satanic in nature. This is **because the devil has been sinning from the beginning** (cf. John 8:44). Sin originated with Satan and is his constant practice. To take part in sin at all is to take part in his activity. It is also opposing the work of **the Son of God** who came (**appeared;** cf. 1 John 3:5; Heb. 9:28a) **to** put an end (*lysē*, **destroy**) to that activity, **the devil's work.** Even the smallest sin runs counter to the work of Christ. Believers are to *overcome* "the evil one" (1 John 2:13-14), here called "the devil," and not to *participate* in what he is.

3:9. As was pointed out in connection with verse 6, adding such phrases as "continue to" and "go on" to John's statements about sinning is not justified on the basis of the Greek text. As before, the statements are absolute. **One who is born of God** (cf. 2:29; 4:7; 5:1, 4, 18) does not **sin** precisely **because God's seed remains in him,** and he cannot sin **because he has been born of God.** "God's seed" is His nature, given to each believer at salvation (John 1:13; 2 Peter 1:4). The point here is that the child partakes of the nature of his Parent. The thought of a sinless Parent who begets a child who only sins a little is far from the author's mind. As always, John dealt in stark contrasts. All sin is devilish (1 John 3:8); it does not stem from the believer's regenerate nature, God's seed, but the child of God cannot and does not sin. The explanation here is the same as that given in verse 6. The "new man" (or "new self"; Eph. 4:24; Col. 3:10) is an absolutely perfect new creation. By insisting on this point, John was seeking to refute a false conception about sin. Sin is not, nor ever can be, anything but satanic. It can never spring from what a Christian truly is at the level of his regenerate being.

3:10a. Literally, the first phrase of this verse is, "By this are manifest **the children of God** and **the children of the devil."** The words "by this" probably refer back to the whole previous discussion. By sharply differentiating between sin and righteousness, John made plain the fundamental way in which God's children are manifest over against the children of the devil. The key to his idea is the word "manifest" in which the ideas presented in 2:29 and 3:1 are touched again. Because a child of God is sinless at the core of his being, he can never be "manifest" through sin as can a child of the devil. While an unsaved person can display his true nature through sin, a child of God cannot. When a Christian sins, he *conceals* who he really is rather than making it *manifest*. If the readers perceive someone doing real righteousness, then—but only then—can they perceive this action as a true product of new birth (2:29) and can thus behold God's love (3:1). This consideration is crucial to John's advancing argument.

C. Discerning love for the brethren (3:10b-23)

John now left behind the subject of new birth which he did not mention again until 4:7. The function of the section that begins here is to define righteousness primarily in terms of Christian brotherly love and to show how such love properly expresses itself.

1. WHAT LOVE IS NOT (3:10B-15)

3:10b. Rather than taking verse 10a as introductory to verse 10b, it is better to regard 10a as the conclusion of the previous paragraph and 10b as the beginning of a new one. The words **a child** in 10b are not in the Greek. Thus the statement would better read, **Anyone who does not do what is right is not . . . of God.** The Greek expression for "of God" (*ek tou theou*) need mean no more than that a person so described does not find the source of his actions in God. He is "not . . . of God" in what he does. A failure to perform righteousness and a failure to **love** one's **brother** can never be traced to God. John had already said that all sin can be traced to the devil (v. 8). John also used this phrase *ek tou theou* ("of God") seven other times (4:1-4, 6-7; 3 John 11).

By joining together the idea of righteousness (mentioned in 1 John 2:29–3:7) with love (not mentioned in vv. 2-9), John formed a bridge to a new discussion. He now considered love as the appropriate expression of the regenerate life of which he had been speaking. Love is righteousness in action.

3:11-12. John here made it plain that his admonitions were directed to Christians. **This is the message you** (Christians) **have heard from the beginning: We** (Christians) **should love one another.** But before telling his audience precisely what love is, he first told them what it is not. It is most certainly **not** the kind of action **Cain** exhibited toward **his brother** Abel. Cain **murdered** his brother (Gen. 4:8) and in that action he was of **the evil one** (*ek tou ponērou*; **belonged to** is misleading). The reason for this murder was Cain's jealous resentment of his brother's superior righteousness (Gen. 4:2-7). In saying this, John touched a sensitive nerve, since hatred toward another Christian is often prompted by a feeling of guilt about one's **own** life as compared with that person's. It is well to remember that such reactions are satanic, as John bluntly affirmed here.

3:13. Such reactions of hatred and murder (vv. 11-12) are also worldly, since **the world hates** Christians. That fact should **not** surprise the readers (called **brothers** only here in 1 John) at all, however. What else can the world be expected to do? It is hatred among believers that is so abnormal, and against which John was fundamentally warning. In that sense it is right to treat this verse as more or less parenthetical.

3:14. In contrast with the world, however, John stated, **We know that we have passed from death to life, because we love our brothers.** The first "we" of this statement is quite emphatic in the original and may mean "we, the apostles." But even if it does, the writer no doubt intended that the readers apply this comment to themselves. Love for one's brothers is evidence that he has entered God's sphere of life (cf. John 13:35).

The expression translated "passed from death to life" occurs elsewhere only in John 5:24 (there trans. "crossed over from death to life") where it refers to conversion. But a phrase which is used only twice in John's writing can hardly be said to have a fixed meaning. The context here must decide its significance. The statements of 1 John 3:14b-15 suggest that the spheres of "death" and "life" are here treated as experiential and determined by one's actions. If so, the issue of conversion is not in view here.

The statement, **Anyone who does not love** (the majority of the mss. add "a brother" or "his brother") **remains in death,** is considered under verse 15.

3:15. This verse is usually taken to mean that a true Christian cannot hate his fellow Christian, since hatred is the moral equivalent of murder. But this view cannot stand up under close scrutiny.

To begin with, John speaks of **anyone who hates his brother.** If John had believed that only an unsaved person can hate another Christian, the word "his" unnecessarily personalizes the relationship (cf. comments on 2:9). But it is an illusion to believe that a real Christian is incapable of hatred and murder. David was guilty of the murder of pious Uriah the Hittite (2 Sam. 12:9) and Peter warned his Christian readers, "If you suffer, it should not be as a murderer" (1 Peter 4:15; more lit., "Let none of you suffer as a murderer"). The view that 1 John 3:15 cannot refer to the saved is totally devoid of all realism. The solemn fact remains that hatred of some other believer is the spiritual equivalent of murder (Matt. 5:21-22), as a lustful eye is the spiritual equivalent of adultery (Matt. 5:28).

John insisted then that **no murderer has eternal life** abiding **in him.** The NIV does not translate the Greek participle *menousan* ("abiding"), which is a crucial word here. John does *not* say that someone who hates his brother does not *possess* eternal life, but rather that he does not have it *abiding* in him. But since for John, Christ Himself is eternal life (John 14:6; 1 John 1:2; 5:20), John's statement is saying that no murderer has *Christ* abiding in him. Thus once more the experience of "abiding" is what John had in view.

Hatred on the part of one Christian toward another is thus an experience of moral murder. As John had indicated in 3:14b, he held that a Christian who fails to love his brother "remains (*menei*) in death." He is thus experientially living in the same sphere in which the world lives (see v. 13). Because he is a murderer at heart he can make no real claim to the kind of intimate fellowship with God and Christ which the word "abide" suggests. Eternal life (i.e., Christ) is not at home in his heart so long as the spirit of murder is there. Such a person is disastrously out of touch with his Lord and he experiences only death. (Cf. Paul's statement, "For if you live according to the sinful nature, you will die" [Rom. 8:13].) John's words were surely grim. But no service is rendered to the church by denying their applicability to believers. The experience of the Christian church through the ages shows how urgently they are needed. Hate, unfortunately, is not confined to unsaved people.

2. WHAT LOVE IS (3:16-18)

3:16. In stark contrast with hatred stands the true character of Christian **love.** So far is it from the spirit of murder that its essence lies in giving one's life for others rather than taking lives. This was exemplified in **Jesus Christ** who **laid down His life for us.** With this as a model, Christians should be prepared to make similar sacrifices **for their brothers.**

3:17-18. Yet the opportunity to sacrifice one's life for another may not arise. But **material possessions** (as food and clothes) help sustain life and, **if** a Christian's love is real, he cannot see **his brother in need** without having **pity on him.** "Pity" (*splanchna*) suggests a deep-seated emotional concern or affectionate sympathy (also used in Luke 1:78; 2 Cor. 6:12; 7:15; Phil. 1:8; 2:1; Phile. 7, 12, 20). The true test of love is not one's verbal profession of it (loving **with words or tongue**), but his willingness to help and thus to **love . . . with actions and in truth.**

3. WHAT LOVE DOES FOR BELIEVERS (3:19-23)

3:19-20. The statement, **This then is how we know that we belong to the truth,** probably refers back to verses 17-18. By practical acts of love in which the needs of others are met, Christians can have a basic assurance that they are participating experientially in the truth. (The NIV's "we belong to the truth" paraphrases the Gr. "we are of the truth"; cf. "of God" [v. 10] and "belonged to the evil one" [v. 12].)

The rest of verse 19 and all of verse 20 are difficult in the original, but probably should be translated, "And we shall persuade **our hearts** before Him that, if **our hearts condemn us,** God **is greater than our hearts,** and **knows** all things." It is precisely in the sphere of a believer's love for other Christians, in which Christ has set him so high a standard, that he may feel deeply his own inadequacy and failure. But if his heart condemns him, he can remind himself that **God** takes account of those things which at the moment his heart ignores. If he has been engaged in the kind of practical acts of love which John enjoined, his guilt-ridden heart can be persuaded by realizing that God is well aware of his fundamental commitment to the truth. The passage clearly recalls Peter's response to the Lord's final query, "Do you love Me?" Peter replied, "Lord, You know all things; You know that I love You" (John 21:17).

3:21-22. Once a condemning heart has been silenced by resting on God's knowledge of all things, there comes a new **confidence before God.** "Confidence" here translates *parrēsia*, which John had not used since his thematic statement in 2:28 (cf. 4:17; 5:14). The halfway point in his argument had now been reached. As a result of active participation in the truth by real deeds of love, Christians can calm their disapproving **hearts** and achieve boldness in prayer, and their prayers will be answered because they, as believers, are consciously subject to God's will (they **obey His commands** [cf. 2:3] **and do what pleases Him**). This presumes, of course, that the requests themselves are made in subjection to God's will (5:14-15).

3:23. The writer had declared that a confident and effective prayer life is founded on obedience to God's "commands" (v. 22). Now those commands are summed up in a single **command** consisting of faith and **love.** The phrase **believe in the name of His Son** contains the epistle's first direct reference to faith. The Greek here contains no word for "in" so the expression could be rendered "believe the name of His Son." In this context it certainly includes the faith in Christ's name which true Christian prayer involves (see John 14:12-15; 16:24).

First John 3:23 furnishes a kind of climax to the paragraph beginning in verse 18. As a Christian actively engages in deeds of love (v. 18) and as he achieves boldness before God in prayer (v. 21), he is doing what God commands (cf. 2:3; 3:24; 5:2-3): living a life of confidence in the name of Christ which is undergirded by love (3:23; cf. v. 14; 4:7, 11, 21). Since faith and love, thus conceived, go together, this kind of life is seen as obedience to a single "command."

D. Discerning the indwelling God (3:24–4:16)

Since the thematic statement of 2:28, John's argument has passed through two stages: (1) the one born of God is manifested only through righteousness (2:29–3:10a), and (2) this righteousness takes the form of a Christlike love for the brethren that leads to boldness in prayer (3:10b-23). Now John showed that this kind of life is the manifestation of the indwelling God.

1. DISCERNING THE SPIRIT OF TRUTH (3:24–4:6)

3:24. Two new themes appear in this verse. The first theme is the epistle's first reference to God, or Christ, abiding in each obedient believer. **Those who obey His commands** (cf. 2:3; 3:23; 5:2-3) **live** (*menei*, "abide") **in Him, and He in them.** That the abiding life involves this mutuality is made plain in the Parable of the Vine and the Branches (John 15:4-5, 7).

The second new idea is the epistle's first of six explicit references to the Holy Spirit (cf. 1 John 4:2, 6, 13; 5:6, 8; cf. "the Holy One" in 2:20). The way a believer can verify that God **lives** (*menei*, "abides") **in** him is **by the** operation of God's **Spirit** in his life. John then showed that God's Spirit is the Spirit of both faith (4:1-6) and love (4:7-16)—the two aspects of the two-part "command" given in 3:23.

4:1-3. To begin with, **the Spirit of God** must be distinguished from false spirits. This is particularly necessary **because many false prophets have gone out into the world.** The touchstone by which these **spirits** (false prophets) are to be tested is their attitude toward the incarnate person of **Jesus Christ.** The failure to acknowledge (*homologei*, "confess"; cf. 1:9; 2:23; 4:15) **that Jesus Christ has come in the flesh is** precisely what exposes the spirit of **the antichrist, which** John had already warned his readers about (2:18-27; cf. 2 John 7).

4:4-6. Up to now, the writer assured his **dear children** (*teknia*; cf. comments on 2:12), the readers, that they had **overcome** these antichrists. The readers had successfully resisted the antichrists (false prophets) by means of **the One who is in** them (no doubt another reference to the Spirit; cf. 3:24; 4:2). Reliance on God is the secret of all victory whether over heresy or any other snare. The indwelling One—the Holy Spirit who indwells every believer (3:24; 4:13; Rom. 8:9) and is thus "the One who is in you"—**is** mightier **than the one who is in the world,** namely, Satan (cf. 1 John 5:19). He is called "the prince of this world" (John 12:31); "the god of this Age" (2 Cor. 4:4); and "the ruler of the kingdom of the air" (Eph. 2:2).

The antichrists **are from the world and . . . speak from the viewpoint of the world.** For this reason they get a good hearing from **the world.** It is always true that satanically inspired thought has a special appeal to worldly minds. But people who **are from God** (*ek tou theou*, "of God"; cf. 1 John 4:4, "from God"; v. 5, "from the world"; and 3:12, "belonged to the evil one") **listen to** the apostles. The pronouns which begin verses 4-6 (**You . . . They,** and **We**) are emphatic in the original and evidently mark off three groups: the readers, the antichrists, and the apostles. Each one who can be described as "from God" (i.e., actuated and influenced by God) and thus **knows God listens to** the apostolic voice. In the history of the church, apostolic doctrine has always been the means by which **the Holy Spirit of truth and the spirit of falsehood** can be effectively distinguished. True Christianity is apostolic Christianity.

2. DISCERNING THE GOD OF LOVE (4:7-16)

4:7-8. The writer now returned to the subject of **love** which, like faith in God's Son (v. 13), is a product of the Spirit. As a confession of the incarnate person of Christ marks one off as being actuated by God (i.e., "from God", vv. 4, 6) so does love, since **love comes from God.** Hence, one **who loves** (in the Christian sense of that term) **has been born of God** (cf. 2:29; 3:9; 5:1, 4, 18) **and he knows God.** Love stems from a regenerate nature and also from fellowship with God which issues in knowing Him (see 2:3-5). The absence of **love** is evidence that a person **does not know God.** Significantly, John did not say such a person is not born of God. In the negative statement only the last part of the positive one (in 4:7) is repeated. Since

God is love, intimate acquaintance with Him will produce love. Like light (1:5), love is intrinsic to the character and nature of God, and one who is intimately acquainted with God walks in His light (1:7).

4:9-11. If one wishes to know **how God has demonstrated His love,** he need only look at the fact that God **sent His One and only Son into the world that we might** obtain eternal life thereby ("One and only" translates *monogenē*, "only born one," which also is used in John 1:14, 18; 3:16.) Moreover, this **love** was **not** a response to man's **love,** but an initiative on God's part (1 John 4:10). By it the **Son** became **an atoning Sacrifice** (*hilasmon*, "propitiation"; see comments on 2:2) **for our sins.** Nothing less than God's love in Christ is the model for the **love** Christians should have toward **one another.**

Important to John's argument is his reference to God's love in 4:9 as His love **among us.** In verses 12-16 he showed how this love, experienced among Christians, can make God visible to them.

4:12-13. In His divine nature and essence, **God** has never been **seen** by any living man (cf. John's similar statement, John 1:18). Yet in the experience of mutual **love** among believers, this invisible **God** actually **lives in us and His love is made complete in us.** The term "lives" once again renders John's characteristic word (*menō*) for the abiding life. As in 1 John 2:5, the idea of God's love reaching completeness in a believer may suggest a deep and full experience of that love (cf. 4:17).

The statement in verse 13 is intimately related to the ideas just expressed. **We know that we live** (*menomen*, "we abide") **in Him and He in us, because He has given us of His Spirit.** The mutual abiding of a believer in God and God in that believer (cf. John 15:4-7) is indicated by that believer's experience of the Spirit. The Greek for "of His Spirit" (*ek tou pneumatos*) suggests participation in the Spirit of God, literally, "He has given us *out of* His Spirit." The same construction occurs in 1 John 3:24. When a believer loves, he is drawing that love from God's Spirit (cf. Rom. 5:5), who is also the Source of his confession of Christ (1 John 4:2). Thus both the faith and the love enjoined in the dual "command" of 3:23 are products of the Spirit's operation in a believer. A believer's Spirit-led obedience becomes the evidence that he is enjoying the mutual abiding relationship with God that John wrote about.

4:14. The apostle now reached a climactic point in his argument. He had just written that "if we love each other," then the God whom no one has seen abides "in us and His love is made complete in us." The result of this experience is that **we have seen and testify that the Father has sent His Son to be the Savior of the world.** Since the first person plural in verses 7-13 is clearly meant to include the readers, the "we" of this verse includes them as well. The indwelling God, whose presence is manifested in the midst of a loving Christian community, thus becomes in a sense truly visible to the eye of faith. Though no one "has seen" (*tetheatai*, "beheld") God (v. 12), believers who abide in Him (v. 13) "have seen" (*tetheametha*, "behold") the Son as He is manifested among loving Christians. Christians who behold this manifestation have in fact "seen" and can "testify" to the fundamental truth that "the Father has sent the Son to be the Savior of the world." This great truth can be put on display through the instrumentality of Christian love.

With these words, John reached the goal he had announced in the prologue (1:1-4), namely, that his readers might share the apostles' experience. The apostles had "seen" (*heōrakamen*) the "life which was with the Father and . . . appeared to us" (1:2). In a loving Christian community, the believers can see that too. The term "Life" in 1:2, though it refers to Christ incarnate, nevertheless was carefully chosen by the writer. What his readers could witness is the renewed manifestation of that Life in their fellow Christians. But, as he had argued ever since 2:29, the "life" which Christians possess by new birth is inherently sinless and can only be manifested through righteousness and Christlike love. But when that occurs, Christ whom the apostles saw in the flesh is, in a real but spiritual sense, "seen" again (4:14).

4:15-16. Under the circumstances just described, confession (cf. 1:9; 2:23; 4:3) **that Jesus is the Son of God** is a sign that the confessor enjoys a mutual abiding relationship with **God.** The section is rounded off by the assertion, **We know and rely on** (lit., "have come to believe") **the love God has for us.** Living in the atmosphere of mutual Christian love produces a personal knowledge of God's love and fresh experience of faith in that love. Since **God is love** (cf. v. 8), one who **lives in love lives** (*menei*, "abides") **in God** and has God abiding with him. The last part of verse 16 ought to be taken as the conclusion of the paragraph, rather than the start of a new one. John again affirmed the reality of the abiding experience enjoyed by all Christians who love.

E. *The theme realized (4:17-19)*

The writer now returned to the theme of boldness (*parrēsia*) at the Second Advent, which he had introduced at 2:28. At the midpoint of his argument, he had spoken of boldness in prayer (3:21-22), but now he went a step further. Loving Christians can even have boldness at the judgment seat of Christ when their Lord returns.

4:17. This verse might be rendered, literally, "In this respect love **is** made complete with **us,** namely, **that we** should have boldness in **the day of** judgment." The writer was not referring here to a final judgment in which the eternal destiny of each believer hangs in balance. There is no such **judgment** for a believer (John 5:24). But a believer's life will be assessed at the judgment seat of Christ (1 Cor. 3:12-15; 2 Cor. 5:10). Yet even on that solemn occasion, a believer may **have confidence** (*parrēsian;* cf. 1 John 2:28; 3:21; 5:14) that God will approve the quality of his life if, through **love,** that believer while **in this world** becomes **like Him.** An unloving Christian is *unlike* his Lord and may anticipate rebuke and loss of reward at the judgment seat. But a loving believer is one in whom the work of God's love has been **made complete** (cf. the same words in 2:5; 4:12), and the fruit of that is boldness before the One who will judge him. In this way he achieves the goal of confidence and no shame before Him, expressed in 2:28.

4:18-19. If a believer looks forward with trepidation to the judgment seat of Christ, it is because God's **love** has not yet reached completeness in Him. The words here rendered **perfect** are no different in force from the idea of "completeness" expressed in 2:5 and 4:12. The matured experience of God's **love** (reached in the act of loving one another) is incompatible with **fear** and expels **fear** from the heart.

The words **fear has to do with punishment** are literally, "fear has punishment." Fear carries with it a kind of torment that is its own punishment. Ironically, an unloving believer experiences punishment precisely because he feels guilty and is afraid to meet his Judge. Such fear prohibits a completed love (one **who fears is not made perfect in love**). But a Christian who loves has nothing to fear and thus escapes the inner torment which a failure to love can bring. Nevertheless a believers' love is essentially derivative.

We love (the majority of mss. add "Him") **because He first loved us.** A believer who loves other believers also loves God, and in facing his Judge he is simply facing One whom he loves. There is no fear in such an experience; yet he recognizes that his love for God originated in God's love for him.

V. Conclusion (4:20–5:17)

The high watermark of the epistle was reached in 4:11-19. But the experience described there, with its astounding concept of boldness on the day of judgment, can be reached only in a most practical way. In his conclusion, John crystallized what he meant by love and how that love can be realized in one's life.

A. *Love clarified (4:20–5:3a)*

The brief but climactic statement of 4:19 mentioned love *for* God for the first time (following most Gr. mss.). But a claim to love God cannot be substituted for love for other believers. This furnished John with his point of departure.

4:20-21. Anyone who claims to **love God, yet hates his brother** makes a false claim: **he is a liar.** John often pointed up false claims by using the word "liar": 1:10; 2:4, 22; 4:20; 5:10 (cf. "lie" in 1:6). **Love** for the unseen **God** (cf. 4:12) can only be concretely expressed by **love** for one's visible Christian **brother.** Furthermore, God's **command** (v. 21; cf. 2:3; 3:23-24; 5:3) has joined together the two kinds of **love**—love for **God** and love for one's **brother.**

5:1-3a. If one asks who his Christian

brother or sister is, the answer is that **everyone who believes that Jesus is the Christ is born of God** (cf. "born of God" in 3:9; 4:7; 5:4, 18). Whether or not a believer exhibits an admirable life, he should be an object of his fellow Christian's love. This love does not spring from something lovable in the person himself, but from his paternity, since **everyone who loves the Father loves His child as well.** Moreover, **love** for God's **children** is not mere sentiment or verbal expression (cf. 3:18), but is inseparable from **loving God and** obeying **His commands** (5:2; cf. 2:3; 3:22, 24; 5:3).

If a further question is asked about what it means to **love . . . God,** the answer is, **to obey His commands.** Thus the apostle, by this series of statements, reduces love for God and one's fellow Christians to its fundamental character. A person who obeys God's commands is doing what is right, both toward God and toward his fellow believers and is thus loving both God and them. But it must be remembered that this includes the willingness to sacrifice for one's brother (cf. 3:16-17).

B. Love empowered (5:3b-15)

If love for God and one's fellow Christians is at its core obedience to God's commands, how can these be carried out? Are they beyond the capacity of a believer? In this section John pointed to faith as the secret of a victorious, obedient life.

5:3b-5. As a matter of fact, God's **commands are not burdensome** (cf. Matt. 11:30). This is because the principle of victory resides in **everyone born of God.** Every such person **has** already **overcome the world** (cf. 1 John 4:4). His **faith** in Christ, by which he was regenerated, constitutes a victory over the world system which is satanically blinded to the gospel (cf. 2 Cor. 4:3-4). **Who is it then that overcomes the world? Only he who believes that Jesus is the Son of God.** With these words, the writer affirmed that a believer is a world-conqueror by means of his faith in Christ. This suggests that such faith is the secret of his continuing victory and, for that reason, obedience to God's commands need not be burdensome.

5:6-8. But the object of this faith must always be **the One who came by water and blood—Jesus Christ.** It is simplest to take the term "water" as a reference to the baptism of Jesus by which His public ministry was initiated (Matt. 3:13-17; Mark 1:9-11; Luke 3:21-22). "Blood" would then refer to His death, by which His earthly work was terminated. John's insistence that **He did not come by water only, but by water and blood,** suggests that he was refuting a false notion of the type held by Cerinthus (see *Introduction*). Cerinthus taught that the divine Christ descended on the man Jesus at His baptism and left Him before His crucifixion. Thus he denied that one Person, Jesus Christ, came by both water and blood. Cerinthus was doubtless not alone in such views, which John regarded as utterly false and contrary to the true testimony of the Holy **Spirit.** Indeed, **there are three that testify: the Spirit, the water, and the blood; and the three are in agreement.** The Spirit's witness may be thought of as coming through the prophets (including John the Baptist). The Spirit's witness, then, was augmented by the historical realities involved in "the water" and "the blood." Both the baptism and the crucifixion of Jesus are strongly attested historical facts (cf. John 1:32-34; 19:33-37). All three witnesses ("water" and "blood" are personified) "are in agreement" that a single divine Person, Jesus Christ, was involved in these events.

5:9-12. One therefore has no reason for not accepting **God's testimony** to the person of Christ. If **man's testimony** can be accepted when adequately attested (Deut. 19:15), God's testimony, being **greater,** ought also be accepted. The NIV's words, **because it is the testimony of God, which He has given about His Son,** are perhaps better taken as commencing a new thought which involves a slight ellipsis. It might be paraphrased "Here then is God's testimony about His Son (which we ought to accept because of its greatness)."

But before specifying the content of God's testimony (which is done in 1 John 5:11-12), John paused parenthetically to remark that accepting this testimony internalizes it for the one who believes. Each believer **has** God's truth **in his heart.** By contrast, **anyone who** disbelieves **God has made Him out to be a liar** (cf. 1:10). For John there was no middle ground, no suspension of opinion. One either believes or he impugns God's veracity.

Having said this, John returned to the content of **the testimony,** which is that **God has given us eternal life** (cf. 5:13, 20) **and this life is in His Son. He who has the Son has life; he who does not have the Son of God does not have life.** In the light of 2:25-26 (see comments there), John's statement of God's testimony is probably directed against a claim by some antichrists that the readers did not really have eternal life through God's Son. But God has directly affirmed that eternal life is precisely what He has given in His Son. To deny this is to call Him a liar.

5:13. John wrote **these things . . . so that** his believing readers would **know** that they had eternal life (cf. vv. 12, 20). The words "these things" are often wrongly taken to refer to the whole epistle. But similar expressions in 2:1, 26 refer to the immediately preceding material and the same is true here. What John had just written about God's testimony (5:9-12) aims to assure his readers that, despite anything the antichrists have said, believers do indeed possess eternal life. It may be pointed out, in fact, that the assurance of one's salvation always rests fundamentally and sufficiently on the direct promises that God makes to that believer. In other words, one's assurance rests on the testimony of God.

After the words **that you have eternal life,** most Greek manuscripts add the words found in the KJV: "and that ye may believe on **the name of the Son of God."** Perhaps this statement seemed redundant to some early scribe or editor and for that reason was eliminated from his manuscript. But it actually prepares the ground for the discussion about prayer which follows by inviting continued faith in God's Son on the part of those who already have received eternal life through Him. Prayer too is an expression of trust in the name of God's Son (see comments on 3:23).

5:14-15. One who believes in the name of Jesus Christ has an **assurance** (*parrēsia*) **in approaching God** in prayer (cf. 3:21). Requests made in accordance with God's will are heard by Him and a believer can be certain of receiving answers to them. Naturally, Christians today discern God's will through the Scriptures and ask accordingly. But the unit of thought that commences with 5:3b has focused on the truth that God's commands are not a burden because faith in God's Son is the secret of spiritual victory over the world. In this context, then, it is natural to suppose that John was thinking especially, though not exclusively, of a Christian's right to **ask** God for help in keeping His commands. That kind of prayer is transparently **according to His will.** Thus in victorious living a Christian is relieved of any burden through prayer that is based on faith in the name of God's Son.

C. Love practiced (5:16-17)

But if a Christian's own needs may be met by prayerful reliance on the name of Jesus, what about the needs of other Christians? Extending his discussion of prayer, John once again wove together his dual theme of faith and love. A Christian who truly loves his brother and sister cannot be indifferent to their spiritual needs.

5:16. Verses 16-17 have been much discussed. But they should not have occasioned as much difficulty as they have. Sometimes a Christian may sin so seriously that God judges that sin with swift physical death: "a sin that leads to death." Ananias and Sapphira are cases in point (Acts 5:1-11). But most of the sins which one **sees** a Christian **brother commit** are not of such a nature, as their common occurrence shows. For these, a believer ought to **pray,** knowing that any sin—if continued in long enough—is a threat to a fellow Christian's life (cf. James 5:19-20; also cf. Prov. 10:27; 11:19; 13:14; 19:16). Thus the restoration of a brother may secure a prolonging of his physical life.

The words, **a sin that does not lead to death,** can be easily misunderstood. All sin ultimately leads to death, but the expression "that does not lead to death" (*mē pros thanaton*) should be understood in the sense, "not punished by death." The distinction is between sins for which death is a rapid consequence and sins for which it is not.

When a Christian sees another Christian sin in a way that is not fatal, **he** is instructed to pray for him **and God will give him life.** (The word "God" is not in the original, but it is properly supplied, as in the NIV.) However, John reminded his readers that **there is . . . sin that leads to** (i.e., "is punished by") **death.** There is no need for the word **a** before "sin." John was not likely thinking of only one kind of sin. The New Testament example cited earlier (Acts 5:1-11) was a flagrant violation of the sanctity of the Christian community. It is not necessary for a Christian to be absolutely sure which flagrant sins are punishable by swift death as long as he can recognize many which are not. He *is* commanded to pray regarding sins which are not punishable by swift death. Even for other sins, where a greater seriousness seems attached to them, Christians have the freedom to pray. John's words about fatal sin are, **I am not saying that he should pray about that.** But this clearly does not forbid prayer even in the most serious cases. But naturally in such cases believers will submit their prayers to the will of God. In contrast, with regard to sins not punished swiftly by death, Christians, on the basis of this verse, should be able to pray with confidence.

5:17. This verse affirms that there is genuine scope for the kind of prayer John enjoined in verse 16. **All wrongdoing** (*adikia*, "unrighteousness") **is sin,** but out of this broad spectrum **there is sin that does not lead** (swiftly) **to death.** This passage has suffered a great deal by the concentration of expositors on the question of what kind of sin is directly punished by death. John's emphasis, however, is on sin *not* thus punished. It is for this that a believer should pray. When he does so, he is demonstrating his love for his brother and is thus obeying the frequently repeated command of this letter to do so. At the same time, he is exercising faith in the name of God's Son, since his loving request for his brother is in Jesus' name. Prayer for one's sinning brother is therefore in obedience to the single two-pronged command of 3:23.

VI. Epilogue (5:18-21)

In a brief epilogue, the Apostle John sought to reinforce some of the basic truths in his epistle. The "we" which runs throughout the epilogue (six times) is probably fundamentally apostolic, as it was also in the prologue (1:1-4; cf. the "we" of John 21:24). But no doubt the writer hoped and expected that his readers could fully identify with the assertions he was making. Each verse in 1 John 5:18-20 begins with "we know" (*oidamen*).

5:18. As in 3:6, 9 (see comments there) the words **continue to** are not justified by the original. John was affirming that **anyone born of God** is a person whose true, inward nature is inherently sinless. (Cf. "born of God" in 2:29; 3:9; 4:7; 5:1, 4.)

The additional statement about **the one who was born of God** is not, as often suggested, a reference to Christ. John nowhere else referred to Christ in this way; and he was still writing about regenerate people. On this view, the word "himself" should be read in place of **him.** John thus affirmed that "the one who has been born of God *keeps himself*" (there is no word for **safe** in the original). This restates the truth of 3:9 in a slightly different form. A believer's new man (or "new self"; Eph. 4:24; Col. 3:10) is fundamentally impervious to sin and hence **the evil one** (cf. 1 John 2:13-14; 3:12), Satan, **does not touch him.**

5:19. A regenerate person's new nature is inherently sinless (v. 18) because God's "seed" is in him (3:9). Knowledge of this truth is coupled with the conviction that **we know that we are . . . of God** (in the Gr., **children** does not occur). This assurance (founded for each believer on God's testimony [5:9-13]) is accompanied by a realization that **the whole world is under the control of the evil one** (cf. v. 18). John was seeking in these summarizing statements to reinforce the readers' consciousness that they are distinct from the satanically controlled world system and basically free from its power. They need not listen to the worldly ideas advanced by the antichrists (3:7-8). Nor need they succumb to worldly desires (cf. 2:15-17).

5:20. Moreover, the coming of **the Son of God has** granted to believers an **understanding** which makes possible a knowledge of God. John and his circle were **in Him who is true** (and so were his readers as they continued to "abide"). But to abide in God is also to abide in **His Son Jesus Christ.** For that matter, Jesus Christ Himself **is the true God** (cf. John 1:1, 14) **and eternal life** (cf. 1 John 1:2; 2:25; 5:11-13). With this grand affirmation of the deity of Christ, John concluded his summary of apostolic truths which stand against the falsehoods of the antichrists.

5:21. That the final admonition of the letter should be, **Dear children** (*teknia*, "born-ones"; cf. 2:1, 12, 28; 3:7, 18; 4:4), **keep yourselves from idols,** has seemed surprising. But there is no need to take "idols" in a figurative sense. In the Greco-Roman world of John's day, any moral compromise with worldly perspectives was likely to lead to some involvement with idolatry, since idolatry permeated pagan life at every level. To adhere to "the true God and eternal life" (5:20)—and to seek to express one's basically sinless nature as a child of God—would necessarily mean avoiding idolatry and the moral laxness which went with it. The apostle's closing admonition was thus relevant to his initial readers.

BIBLIOGRAPHY

Barker, Glenn W. "1, 2, 3 John." In *The Expositor's Bible Commentary*, vol. 12. Grand Rapids: Zondervan Publishing House, 1981.

Brooke, A.E. *A Critical and Exegetical Commentary on the Johannine Epistles.* The International Critical Commentary. Edinburgh: T. & T. Clark, 1912.

Brown, Raymond E. *The Epistles of John.* The Anchor Bible. Garden City, N.Y.: Doubleday & Co., 1983.

Burdick, Donald W. *The Epistles of John.* Everyman's Bible Commentary. Chicago: Moody Press, 1970.

Dodd, C.H. *The Johannine Epistles.* New York: Harper & Row, 1946.

Marshall, I. Howard. *The Epistles of John.* The New International Commentary on the New Testament. Grand Rapids: Wm. B. Eerdmans Publishing Co., 1978.

Mitchell, John G. *Fellowship: Three Letters from John.* Portland, Ore.: Multnomah Press, 1974.

Pentecost, J. Dwight. *The Joy of Fellowship: A Study of First John.* Grand Rapids: Zondervan Publishing House, 1977.

Stott, John R.W. *The Epistles of John: An Introduction and Commentary.* The Tyndale New Testament Commentaries. Grand Rapids: Wm. B. Eerdmans Publishing Co., 1964.

Vaughan, Curtis. *1, 2, 3 John: A Study Guide.* Grand Rapids: Zondervan Publishing House, 1970.

Vine, W.E. *The Epistles of John: Light, Love, Life.* Grand Rapids: Zondervan Publishing House, 1970.

Westcott, Brooke Foss. *The Epistles of St. John: The Greek Text and Notes.* 1882. Reprint. Grand Rapids: Wm. B. Eerdmans Publishing Co., 1966.

Wiersbe, Warren W. *Be Real.* Wheaton, Ill.: SP Publications, Victor Books, 1972.

2 JOHN
Zane C. Hodges

INTRODUCTION

Second John is a brief epistle which could have been written on a single sheet of papyrus of standard size. The preservation of this brief letter is no doubt a tribute to its spirituality and inspiration.

Authorship. The authorship of 2 John has been traditionally assigned to the Apostle John. But the writer identifies himself only as "the elder." This title is not likely to refer to the office of an elder in a local church. It might simply be an affectionate designation (*presbyteros*, "the old man"; cf. 1 Tim. 5:1-2; 1 Peter 5:5; 3 John 1) by which the author was known to his readers. However, some ancient evidence exists that the term "elder" could be used to designate any apostle or other original witness to the life and teachings of the Lord Jesus. In view of the manifest similarity in style and content between 1 and 2 John, the arguments that point to apostolic authorship for the larger epistle carry force for the smaller one as well. There is no adequate reason for doubting the correctness of the traditional ascription of 2 John to the Apostle John.

Background. The letter is addressed "to the chosen lady and her children" (v. 1; cf. vv. 4-5). No personal names are found in it, and the suggestion that the recipient was named either Eklecta (from *eklektē*, the word rendered "chosen") or Kyria (the word rendered "lady") carries little conviction. In this respect 2 John stands in contrast with 3 John, which contains the personal names of three people. It has therefore been suggested that the apostolic writer adopted a literary form in 2 John, in which a particular Christian church is personified as "the chosen lady" and its members are called "her children." The personification of nations and cities as female personages is common in the Bible (cf. "the daughter of Zion"), and the Christian church is often referred to as "the bride of Christ" (cf. Eph. 5:22-33; 2 Cor. 11:2; Rev. 19:7).

The conclusion that 2 John is addressed to a church is further supported by the observation that in the Greek the writer drops the singular number for his pronouns after verse 5 and uses a singular again only in verse 13. Indeed, the general nature of the epistle's content is most appropriate to a community. Thus, while the possibility that a particular Christian woman is addressed cannot be totally excluded, it is preferable to treat the letter as addressed to a church. If so, the problems confronted by this church do not differ much from the ones confronted by the readers of 1 John. Here too the author warned against antichrists (2 John 7; cf. 1 John 2:18, 22). The error of which they were guilty was, as also in 1 John, a denial of the person of Christ (2 John 7; cf. 1 John 2:22-23; 4:1-3). The epistle likewise insists on obedience to God's commands, especially the command to love one another (2 John 5-6; cf. 1 John 2:3-9; 3:14-18, 23; 4:7, 11, 20-21).

Date. No independent data is available on which to base the date of the writing of 2 John. But the situation presupposed in this letter is similar to what evidently lies behind 1 John. This therefore makes possible a date approximately the same as that suggested for the larger epistle. On this assumption, 2 John may also belong in the period before the outbreak of the Jewish war against the Romans in Palestine, in A.D. 66. A date in the early 60s is thus the most probable guess.

OUTLINE

I. Preamble (vv. 1-3)
II. Body of the Epistle (vv. 4-11)

2 JOHN

  A. The truth practiced (vv. 4-6)
  B. The truth protected (vv. 7-11)
III. Farewell (vv. 12-13)

COMMENTARY

I. Preamble (vv. 1-3)

The epistle begins in the way ancient letters usually began. The writer announced himself, stated the identity of the recipient(s), and offered a greeting. But, as noted in the *Introduction*, John did not specifically name "the chosen lady" and the text reads naturally if a church were addressed. The preamble stresses that "truth" and "love" are the two major concerns of this letter ("truth": vv. 1 [twice], 2-4; "love": vv. 1, 3, 5-6 [twice in v. 6]) and of 3 John.

Vv. 1-2. The elder (see "Authorship" in the *Introduction*) commenced his communication by asserting that he loved this church (**the chosen lady;** cf. "dear lady," v. 5) **and** its members (**her children;** cf. v. 4) **in the truth.** So in fact did **all who know the truth.** This seems to suggest that the church addressed was well known in Christian circles. (It is called "chosen" because it was composed of God's elect, i.e., Christians.) The love of John and others for this community of believers was founded and predicated on God's truth. It arose **because of the truth, which lives in us and will be with us forever.** Christian love is by no means mere sentimentalism or humanistic compassion, but is motivated by a knowledge of the truth which has been revealed in Christ. Truth is the basis of love. It is precisely this truth, on account of which the church is loved, that the church must be careful to guard.

V. 3. Instead of just wishing **grace, mercy, and peace** for his readers, John announced that they would be experiencing these things **in truth and love** (cf. v. 1). (Interestingly Paul and Peter in the greetings in their epistles include only grace and peace, except for 1 and 2 Tim., which include "grace, mercy, and peace." See the chart, "Paul's Introductions to His Epistles" at Rom. 1:1-7.) But the qualities of truth and love are precisely the ones John enjoined his readers to maintain. If they do maintain them, then they can expect to enjoy the "grace, mercy, and peace" which come **from God the Father and from Jesus Christ.** The fact that these blessings stem from both the Father and the Son affirms the deity of Christ. **The Father's Son** is an unusual expression (cf. "the Father and the Son" in 2 John 9). God's blessings—favor (*charis*), compassion (*eleos*), and inner harmony and tranquility (*eirēnē*)—are enjoyed in an atmosphere where "truth" and "love" are in control. John had written that truth "will be with us" (v. 2). Now he added that grace, mercy, and peace **will be with us.**

II. Body of the Epistle (vv. 4-11)

Getting to his point immediately, John expressed his concerns (a) that the church would continue to be obedient to God and (b) that the believers would resist all inroads by false teachers. These two objectives, of course, are inseparable.

A. The truth practiced (vv. 4-6)

V. 4. Evidently John had encountered members of this church (**some of your children;** cf. v. 1) somewhere and was delighted (**it has given me great joy;** cf. 3 John 3-4) to observe their obedience to the truth. He used their fidelity, which he had observed, as a positive starting point. What they were doing (**walking in the truth;** cf. 3 John 3-4) was precisely what **the Father commanded.** To walk in the truth is to be obedient to the truth God has made known. John wanted the whole church to do the same.

V. 5. In his final reference to the church under personification (until v. 13), John enjoined it as a **dear lady.** What he wrote to the church was not some **new** requirement **but one** the church has **had from the beginning** (cf. v. 6). (For the same idea, see 1 John 2:7.) It is nothing other than the command **that we love one another.** As in the larger epistle, the apostle encouraged his readers to follow the old ways as he sought to help them resist the innovations of the antichrists (2 John 7).

V. 6. But what does it mean to "love one another"? The answer: **This is love, that we walk in obedience to His commands.** As he had also done in 1 John 5:2-3a, John defined Christian love in terms of obedience to God. A Christian who truly seeks God's best for his brothers and sisters can only do so by obeying what God has commanded him to do. Love undirected by God's revealed will may easily degenerate into unwise, sentimental activity. Believers who are "walking in the truth" (2 John 4), that is, living in response to what God has revealed, love each other. Brotherly love is part of the truth God has revealed and commanded.

The latter part of verse 6 is difficult in the original. The NIV rendering could be essentially correct (though the words **in love** interpretively render the Gr. *en autē*, "in it"). An alternative rendering would be, "And this is the command, that you walk in it as you have heard from the beginning." Under this construction of the text, John was affirming that obeying God's commands meant adhering to what had been commanded in the form in which it was expressed **from the beginning**. Taken in this way, the writer's words were designed to warn against any "reinterpretation" of God's will, such as the antichrists might propose.

The movement from the plural "commands" (v. 6a) to the singular **command** (v. 6b) is natural for this author (cf. 1 John 3:22-23). The many specifics of God's will can be thought of as a single obligation.

B. *The truth protected (vv. 7-11)*

V. 7. This verse is more closely linked in thought with verse 6 than the English rendering suggests. A Greek conjunction meaning "because" (*hoti*) has been left untranslated. The reason for John's previous admonition is that **many deceivers, who do not acknowledge Jesus Christ as coming in the flesh, have gone out into the world.** As in the first epistle, the apostle expressed his concern that many false teachers had arisen (cf. 1 John 2:18; 4:1). These teachers were "deceivers" (*planoi*, "ones who lead astray"; cf. *planaō*, "lead astray," in 1 John 2:26; 3:7). Their very number (as well as a probable variety of erroneous ideas) made them a substantial threat to Christian churches such as this one. What bound the false teachers and their views together was their unbelief and rejection of Christ's Incarnation.

The present participle "coming" (in the phrase "coming in the flesh") focuses on the principle involved in the Incarnation: Jesus taking on (coming in) and continuing with a human nature (cf. 1 John 4:2). This truth about "Jesus Christ . . . coming in the flesh" is what the deceivers denied. Some taught that Jesus' body was not truly human; it only appeared that way. That, of course, contradicted the truth of the Incarnation, that Jesus Christ is both fully God and fully human (Col. 2:9).

Such a denial marks that person as a **deceiver** as well as an **antichrist**. (See comments on 1 John 2:18). The word **the** before "deceiver" and "antichrist" could be misunderstood. The English article "a" (rather than "the") is sometimes appropriate for rendering the Greek definite article when an unnamed individual is in view. John did not mean to say here that "any such person" is *the* unique, end-time figure known as the Antichrist.

V. 8. Because of the appearance of these deceivers, the readers needed to **watch out** for the disastrous spiritual effects which any compromise with their ideas could lead to. The danger is not loss of salvation, of course, but loss of reward. The NIV uses the second person verb (**you**) for all three of the statements in this verse. But "we" (following most mss.) is preferred: "that we lose not those things which we have wrought, but that we receive a full reward" (KJV). Early scribes and editors may have altered the "we" to "you" in these places to avoid the suggestion that the apostle could share in a loss of reward. But the author's touch was both delicate and humble. He regarded himself as a co-laborer with his readers and their loss would be shared by him if they did not effectively resist false doctrine. The antichrists were a threat to the work of the Lord in which he and they were mutually engaged. It should be noted that the phrase **be rewarded fully** shows that failure by the readers would not totally deprive them of reward. God would not forget what they had done for Him (cf. Heb. 6:10). But the fullness of their reward (cf. 1 Cor. 3:11-15) was threatened by the subversion of the antichrists.

V. 9. The danger is now spelled out clearly. **Anyone who runs ahead** (*proagōn*; most mss. read "turns aside," *parabainōn*) **and does not continue in the teaching of Christ does not have God.** These words suggest strongly that the apostle was thinking here of defection from the truth by those who had once held to it. The word "continue" renders the Greek verb *menō*, familiar because of its frequent use (23 times) in 1 John in reference to the "abiding" life. A person who "does not continue" in a thing has evidently once been in it. The New Testament writers were realists about the possibility of true Christians falling prey to heresy and warned against it (cf. comments on the Book of Heb.). John had just cautioned his readers about possible loss of reward (2 John 8). They were thus now (v. 9) cautioned not to "overstep" the boundaries of sound doctrine, but to "remain" where they were, to "continue in the teaching (*didachē*; cf. v. 10) of (i.e., about) Christ." To deviate from the truth is to leave God behind. God is not with a person who does so. What such a person does, he does without God. This, of course, does not suggest loss of salvation. Instead it points to a doctrinal deviation, with its accompanying disobedience.

In contrast with the defector from the truth, **whoever continues in the teaching has both the Father and the Son.** This says that God is with those who persist in the true doctrine about Christ. (Here may also be another subtle affirmation of the deity of Christ; cf. v. 3.) But John no doubt had more in mind than mere creedal orthodoxy. He used *menō*, his characteristic word in the Johannine Epistles for the life of fellowship with the Father and Son, for the second time in verse 9. The roots of its significance in these letters are in texts such as John 8:31 and 15:1-7. For John, a person who "continues in the teaching" is one who "abides" or "makes his home" there. His connection with the truth is vital and dynamic, so he has a dynamic relationship with God whose commands he obeys (cf. John 14:21-23 for another expression of this kind of relationship). "Abiding" and obedience are inseparable in Johannine thought.

Vv. 10-11. But "continuing" in the truth about Jesus Christ calls for a firm response against those who have become purveyors of false doctrine. Hence John added, **If anyone comes to you and does not bring this teaching, do not take him into your house or welcome him.** In the Greco-Roman world of John's day, a traveling philosopher or religious teacher was a familiar phenomenon. Christian preachers also traveled and relied on local believers for support and hospitality (3 John 5-8). But the readers of 2 John were urged to be discriminating. If someone "comes" to them (the implication is "in the role of a traveling teacher") without also bringing sound doctrine (*didachēn*), he should be refused help. The Greek verb for "bring" is *pherō* ("to carry"), which continues the travel motif. If the truth is not part of his "baggage," he should receive no hospitality from those who are loyal to that truth. (By contrast, hospitality *is* to be shown to true believers [3 John 5, 8].) But a deceiver is not even to be given a greeting of welcome, since to do so would be to share **in his wicked** (*ponērois*, "evil"; cf. "the evil one" [*to ponēron*], 1 John 2:13-14) **work.** "Welcome him" (2 John 10-11) is literally, "Say 'Greetings' to him." In Greek "greetings" here is *chairein*, related to *chairō*, "to rejoice, be glad." *Chairein* was used as a cordial address of welcome or farewell, something like "I am glad to see you" or "I wish you well" (cf. Acts 15:23; 23:26; James 1:1).

To some modern minds these instructions seem unduly rigid and harsh. A great part of the problem, however, lies in the modern inclination to be highly tolerant of religious differences. One must frankly face the fact that the New Testament writers did not share this spirit of toleration. Their commitment to the truth and their consciousness of the dangers of religious error called forth many stern denunciations of false teachers. Not surprisingly, this modern age, having a diminishing sense of the dangers of heresy, has lost its convictions about the truth.

But the passage ought not to be taken beyond the writer's intent. He was thinking about false teachers actively engaged in disseminating error. In this activity they are not to be helped at all. Even a word of greeting might tend to give them a sense of acceptance that could be misconstrued. The readers were to make plain from their aloofness that they in no way condoned the activities of these men. The same must be true today. But John did not directly address the question of how efforts should be made to win such people to a recognition of the truth. Yet it is clear that any such efforts must be conducted so that they are not confused with any form of approbation.

III. Farewell (vv. 12-13)

The author's farewell is similar to his words in 3 John 13 (cf. "I have much to write you"; "I do not want to use [do so with] pen and ink"; "I hope to visit [see] you"; "talk . . . face to face"). Like the format of the letter as a whole, such conclusions were probably conventional. But this in no way suggests that they were insincere.

V. 12. John indicated that he had **much to write to** them **but** preferred **face-to-face** communication. He anticipated a **visit** soon, when he would have more to say to them. Such a personal visit would make his **joy** (*chara*) **complete**. What he might have written if he had not been planning to see them can perhaps be surmised from the contents of 1 John. Indeed, in some respects, 2 John reads like a condensed version of the first epistle. It is likely that the author would have amplified his admonitions in ways similar to what he had done in the larger letter.

V. 13. John gave farewell **greetings from the children of your chosen sister.** *If* this letter were written to an actual Christian woman, one would expect the greetings to come from her sister, not from her sister's children. Because of the anonymity of the references to people, once again it seems easiest to construe this as a greeting sent by the members ("children," cf. v. 1) of a "sister" church to the church to which John was writing (see the *Introduction*)—both "lady" churches having been "chosen" (elected) by God's sovereign grace. As such it gives testimony to the network of Christian interest and concern which united the members of different churches in the earliest years of the faith.

BIBLIOGRAPHY

See Bibliography on 1 John.

3 JOHN

Zane C. Hodges

INTRODUCTION

Third John is a personal letter written to a specific person, a man named Gaius. If, as seems probable, 2 John was written to a church, 3 John and Philemon are the only personal letters in the New Testament. The Pastoral Epistles (1 and 2 Tim., Titus), though addressed to individuals, were probably intended for public reading. Thus the Apostle John's epistle to Gaius is a precious fragment of early Christian correspondence. Its spiritual character is evident.

Authorship. As in 2 John, the writer called himself simply "the elder." In all probability this suggests not only his seniority (*presbyteros* means "old man") but also his authority as an eyewitness to the life of Christ. (See the *Introduction* to 2 John.) The style of the epistle is manifestly the same as that of both 1 and 2 John, and efforts to deny that a single author produced all three carry no conviction. The ancient opinion that the Apostle John wrote this letter, as well as the other two, may be readily accepted. The arguments that support apostolic authorship of 1 John carry over to this tiny epistle by virtue of the clear stylistic ties. Moreover, the self-confident authority of the writer of 3 John (cf. v. 10) also befits an apostle.

Background. Where Gaius (v. 1) lived is not specified. It is likely that he belonged to a church somewhere in Roman Asia (western Turkey). Tradition assigns the Apostle John a role in this area, as does the Book of Revelation. The writer seems to have been urging Gaius to show hospitality to Demetrius (v. 12) who was evidently a traveling Christian preacher (vv. 5-8). Demetrius was probably also the bearer of the letter.

The Apostle John apparently needed to appeal directly to Gaius for the support of Demetrius, since the church was dominated by a man named Diotrephes who did not extend a welcome to traveling brethren (vv. 9-10). Indeed, Diotrephes even sought to excommunicate those who offered such men their hospitality. If Gaius was a member of this same church, he might possibly have run a risk of incurring Diotrephes' wrath as well. But conceivably Gaius was a man of some means who could not be easily driven from the church. The suggestion that Gaius belonged to a different church than did Diotrephes does not seem probable in the light of verse 9 with its simple reference to "the church."

Diotrephes may possibly be an early (and unfavorable) example of a monarchical bishop. Out of the earliest ecclesiastical situation in which a body of elders of equal authority ruled the congregations, a system emerged in which one man assumed prominence over the other elders and became the "bishop" (though this title was originally synonymous with that of elder). This process must often have happened almost imperceptibly when a man of strong character gained ascendancy over the rest of the leadership. But in the church to which Gaius evidently belonged, the process had led to the prominence of a self-willed and authoritarian individual. Diotrephes' reasons for refusing to receive traveling brethren were not spelled out specifically by John. No doubt Diotrephes rationalized his conduct in some way. But the apostle made it plain that what Diotrephes did was wrong (cf. v. 11). He expected to correct the situation when he arrived (v. 10).

Date. As with 2 John, no independent data exists on which to base a date for the writing of 3 John. It is simplest to suggest a date for all three epistles sometime in the early 60s of the Christian era.

3 JOHN

OUTLINE

I. Salutation (vv. 1-4)
II. Body of the Epistle (vv. 5-12)
  A. Commendation of Gaius (vv. 5-8)
  B. Condemnation of Diotrephes (vv. 9-11)
  C. Recommendation of Demetrius (v. 12)
III. Farewell (vv. 13-14)

COMMENTARY

I. Salutation (vv. 1-4)

V. 1. The elder (see "Authorship" under *Introduction*) briefly greeted the recipient of this letter affectionately. This salutation is unlike most New Testament Epistles, in that it lacks the usual wish for grace and peace. However, the farewell includes "Peace to you" (v. 14).

My dear friend translates the Greek *tō agapētō* ("the beloved"), related to the verb *agapō* (**I love**). The spirit of Christian love prevailed in the elder's attitude toward **Gaius**. It is precisely this same spirit which was to dictate Gaius' attitude toward traveling preachers such as Demetrius. Three times more the writer addressed Gaius with this same significant term of address (vv. 2, 5, 11).

Moreover, the apostle's love for Gaius was **in the truth**, that is, it was genuine and in accord with God's truth. In the same way Gaius was to express his Christian love by a hospitality that supported the truth (cf. v. 8). As in John's two earlier epistles, the thought of this letter is dominated by concern for truth and love in Christian experience ("truth": vv. 1, 3 [twice], 4, 8, 12; "true": v. 12; "love": vv. 1, 6).

V. 2. The elder was pleased with Gaius' spiritual condition and wished that he might get **along** equally **well** on a physical level. As verses 2-6 show, Gaius was evidently an outstanding spiritual man. The words **I pray that you may enjoy good health and that all may go well with you** are not a mere conventional expression of good wishes. The apostle was concerned for the temporal well-being of others, and not only for their spiritual welfare. He must surely have learned this from Jesus whose concern for people's physical troubles is attested in all four Gospels. Certainly this is a biblical warrant for Christians today to pray for the temporal needs of their spiritual peers.

V. 3. The elder was glad (cf. v. 4) **to have** learned from **some brothers** about Gaius' loyalty to the truth. The words, **tell about your faithfulness to the truth,** somewhat paraphrase the Greek which more literally reads, "witness to your truth." The apostle was saying he had heard that Gaius was a man of truth. Quite possibly the "brothers" who brought this testimony to John had enjoyed Gaius' hospitality, the same thing which the writer apparently urged on behalf of Demetrius (v. 10). The words, **and how you continue to walk in the truth,** elaborate what the "brothers" had said about Gaius. Gaius' style of life (his "walk") was consistent with God's truth.

V. 4. Nothing made John happier (cf. v. 3) **than to hear that** his **children** were **walking in the truth.** This wording is similar to that in 2 John 4. It is possible that by referring to Gaius as one of his "children," John meant that Gaius was a convert of his (cf. Paul's use of this idea in 1 Cor. 4:14; Gal. 4:19; Phil. 2:22). On the other hand the elderly apostle may simply have thought of those to whom he ministered from a paternal perspective, with fatherly concern.

II. Body of the Epistle (vv. 5-12)

After praising the general conduct of Gaius, the writer moved directly to a matter that concerned him. Those who go forth to preach the truth need the support of Christians in the places where they travel. Unlike Diotrephes, Gaius gave this kind of assistance and the apostle wished to assure him that this was the proper course of action. This contrasts, interestingly, with the emphasis in 2 John 10-11 on *not* giving hospitality to false teachers.

A. Commendation of Gaius (vv. 5-8)

V. 5. Addressing Gaius again as "beloved" (**dear friend**; cf. vv. 1, 2, 11), the writer commended his hospitality to Christians who came his way. The NIV adopts a form of text in which **brothers** and **strangers** are equated. But many manuscripts read, "for the brothers and for strangers." Read in this way, the writer would refer to the traveling preachers as "the brothers," while also asserting that Gaius' hospitality did not stop there but extended also to "strangers" (probably esp. Christians) who happened to be in the vicinity. (Regarding Christian responsibility to entertain strangers, see Heb. 13:2.) About this course of conduct, the apostle declared, **You are faithful in what you are doing.** That is to say, such conduct is praiseworthy because it is an act of fidelity to the truth of God. Again, as in 2 John 1-2, love stems from truth.

V. 6. The report of Gaius' hospitality (**your love**) had reached **the church** where John now was. This may well have been the church at Jerusalem if the epistle was written before A.D. 66 (cf. *Introduction* to 1 John for a discussion of the possibility that the first epistle was written before that date). Undoubtedly, if this is so, Gaius would have been pleased to know that the highly respected Jerusalem congregation had heard of his service to the servants of God. But John now followed up this encouragement with an exhortation: **You will do well to send them on their way in a manner worthy of God.** The words "you will do well" are idiomatic in the original and virtually equal to "please." The verb for "send . . . on their way" (*propempsas*) no doubt carried in general usage the connotation of making adequate provisions for one's guests, both while they stayed and at the time of their departure. The force of the apostle's words was to enjoin on Gaius an openhanded generosity toward the traveling brethren. Nothing less than such generosity would be "worthy of God," who expressed His supreme generosity in the giving of His Son.

V. 7. The reason for such behavior (the verse begins in the Gr. with the untranslated "for," *gar*) is that those whom Gaius should help have gone out **for the sake of the Name.** The "Name" here is, of course, that of Jesus which was now exalted above every name (Phil. 2:9-11). To go out on behalf of that Name was a supreme honor (cf. Acts 5:41 for the honor of suffering for it). Naturally, it was inappropriate for those who did so to seek support from those who did not believe in or honor that Name. Thus the Lord's servants **went out, receiving no help from the pagans.** Even in the present day, there is something unseemly in a preacher of the gospel soliciting funds from people to whom he offers God's free salvation.

V. 8. But the fact that faithful Christian preachers sought no help from the unsaved meant that Christians were under a special obligation to assist them. By extending the needed help (showing **hospitality to such men**), Christians such as Gaius could **work together for the truth.** This last phrase might be better rendered "be fellow workers with the truth" (NASB). The thought is of partnership with what the truth accomplishes in people's hearts and lives. It was a noble objective for Gaius to follow.

B. Condemnation of Diotrephes (vv. 9-11)

V. 9. Not everyone shared this worthy objective, however. John stated, **I wrote to the church, but Diotrephes, who loves to be first, will have nothing to do with us.** The simple reference to "the church" suggests strongly that this was the church to which Gaius belonged. It sounds as if Gaius may not have known about John's letter to the church. It may well be that Diotrephes had suppressed it and kept it from the church's attention. Diotrephes, John observed, was motivated by a love for preeminence in the church. He was not the last church leader to be so motivated. The temptation to use a role in the Christian assembly as a means of self-gratification remains a real one that all servants of God need to resist. As a result of his personal ambitions, Diotrephes resisted the apostle's wishes. The expression, "will have nothing to do with us," may also be translated, "does not welcome us as guests." The apostle was probably thinking of Diotrephes' refusal to accord hospitality to the traveling brethren (cf. v. 5) who came to the church (perhaps with the letter just mentioned), and he took Diotrephes' rejection of the brothers as a rejection of himself. Quite possibly Diotrephes did not present himself as a personal opponent of John, but in rejecting John's representatives he was rejecting John (cf. John 13:20).

V. 10. The writer, however, knew that he could deal with this matter in person. **So if I come, I will call attention to what he is doing.** This assertion should probably be taken as an understatement. The verb (*hypomnēsō*) means basically "to remind" or "to call to mind." Here the phrase might be translated, "I will call his works to mind" with the manifest implication that Diotrephes' works would be dealt with appropriately.

Diotrephes, the writer asserted, had been guilty of three things. First, he was **gossiping maliciously about us.** These words are literally "bringing false charges (*phlyarōn,* used only here in the NT) against us with evil (*ponērois*) words." No doubt that self-willed leader did his best to tear down the reputation of those whom he was not prepared to receive (as in v. 9, the "us" may refer chiefly to John's representatives).

But Diotrephes went beyond mere talk, wrong as that was. **Not satisfied with that, he refuses to welcome the brothers.** This was his second wrongdoing. His malicious prattle no doubt laid the groundwork for actual refusal of hospitality (in contrast with Gaius' hospitality). And, third, like many other ecclesiastical dictators since his time, Diotrephes did all he could to enforce his will on others: **He also stops those who want to do so and puts them out of the church.** Using his self-acclaimed authority, having a prominent position (v. 9), he forced other believers to be inhospitable or, if they weren't, even prevented them from gathering with the church.

Perhaps Gaius already knew most of these facts. It is likely that John was indirectly reminding him of the potential difficulties he faced in welcoming men who served the truth. But Gaius' obvious dedication to hospitality (vv. 5-6) suggests that he was a man of some means and probably in a good position to resist the authority of Diotrephes. He would be further encouraged by John's promise that he would deal with Diotrephes when he arrived.

V. 11. At any rate, Gaius was **not to imitate what is evil but what is good.** Diotrephes' behavior was to be avoided, not copied. One's conduct clearly reflects one's relationship with God. **Anyone who does what is good is from God.** The words "from God" translate the Greek phrase *ek tou theou,* which occurs a number of times in 1 John (e.g., 3:10; 4:1-4, 6-7). It suggests that the source of one's actions or attitudes is in God. Conversely, **anyone who does what is evil has not seen God.** With this, the statement of 1 John 3:6 should be compared (see the discussion on that verse). The assertion should not be watered down. Evil never arises from a real spiritual perception of God but is always a product of darkness of heart and blindness toward Him. John was not questioning Diotrephes' salvation, but he *was* affirming that Diotrephes' conduct manifested real blindness toward God. Gaius was to be careful to shun such an experience as this.

C. *Recommendation of Demetrius (v. 12)*

V. 12. If Gaius would indeed "imitate what is . . . good" (cf. v. 11), he would extend hospitality to **Demetrius.** This is not explicitly requested, but seems the obvious implication of John's recommendation of Demetrius. In accordance with the Jewish law of witnesses (Deut. 19:15), the apostle adduced a threefold testimony to the character of Demetrius. (1) He was **well spoken of by everyone** who knew him. (2) He was also vouched for **by the truth itself.** Here the truth is personified as a "witness" and John no doubt meant that Demetrius' character and doctrine were in such conformity with that truth that the truth itself virtually spoke on his behalf. (3) As a third line of testimony, John wrote, **we also speak well of him, and you know that our testimony is true.** John himself could personally attest the worth of this man. Thus Gaius had no reason to hesitate showing Demetrius the kind of hospitality he had shown others. (The Demetrius of this letter is not to be confused with the Demetrius of Acts 19:24, an enemy of the gospel.)

III. Farewell (vv. 13-14)

Vv. 13-14a. John was now finished with what he wished to say in this short letter, but he still had **much to write** to Gaius. He *could* have said much more in writing, but (as he had also written in 2 John) he hoped to be able **soon** to communicate those things **face to face.**

V. 14b. The apostle wished Gaius **peace** and passed on **greetings** from **the friends here.** Similarly, he wanted Gaius to **greet the friends there by name.** The use of the term "friends" twice in these closing statements is perhaps one final reminder to Gaius that Christians in every place are or should be a network of friends who are ready to help one another whenever a need arises. It is part of the genius of Christianity that one can meet people whom he has never seen before, in places far from home, and discover through a shared faith an immediate bond of friendship.

BIBLIOGRAPHY

See Bibliography on 1 John.

JUDE
Edward C. Pentecost

INTRODUCTION

Authorship. The writer of the Epistle of Jude, the last of the "General Epistles," introduced his letter with one simple declaration about himself: "Jude, a servant of Jesus Christ, and a brother of James" (v. 1).

Who was this Jude? Three possibilities exist. The author may be either (a) Judas, a half brother of Christ, or (b) Judas, the apostle, or (c) Judas, a leader in the early church of Jerusalem. This latter Judas was sent to Antioch with Paul, Barnabas, and Silas (Acts 15:22). His surname was Barsabbas, indicating that he could have been a brother of Joseph Barsabbas, who was one of two "nominees" to replace Judas Iscariot (Acts 1:23). Thus he would have been known in the church. But little other evidence points to this individual as the author of this epistle.

As to whether he was the Apostle Jude, verse 17 in his letter seems to indicate that he did not consider himself to be an apostle, though modesty could have led him to write as he did. However, the important subject that he wrote about would probably have called for his identifying himself with the other apostles, for authority's sake, if he really was an apostle.

The most probable identification is that the author Jude was a half brother of Christ, a son of Joseph and Mary after Jesus. The term "servant" would be fitting, for though at first Jesus' brothers did not believe in Him (John 7:5), yet later they saw the resurrected Christ and were convinced (Acts 1:14). Among these was Judas, who did not consider himself worthy to call himself a "brother" but just a "servant" of Jesus Christ.

The James referred to by Jude as his brother was thus also a half brother of the Lord (Matt. 13:55; Mark 6:3), as well as a leader of the church at Jerusalem (Acts 15:13), and author of the epistle bearing his name (James 1:1).

Jude wrote with a heart of love and understanding, and with a note of concern and authority. He wanted to write on a joyful theme, "about the salvation we share" (Jude 3), but was compelled to write a much more somber epistle. His love for believers whom he saw endangered by encroaching adversaries moved him to turn from the more pleasant theme to sound a solemn warning.

Style. Jude wrote in a dynamic style, using many figures of speech (e.g., shepherds, clouds, and trees, v. 12; and waves and stars, v. 13).

Jude frequently wrote in triads, with some commentators discerning as many as 18 such series. Outstanding among them are his introduction: "Jude . . . servant . . . brother" (v. 1); his address: "to those . . . called . . . loved . . . kept" (v. 1); his greetings: "mercy, peace, and love" (v. 2); his description of the apostates: "godless men . . . change the grace of our Lord . . . deny Jesus Christ" (v. 4); his examples of other apostates who were judged: "people out of Egypt . . . angels . . . Sodom and Gomorrah and the surrounding towns" (vv. 5-7); his description of these heretical "dreamers": "pollute their own bodies . . . reject authority . . . slander celestial beings" (v. 8); his description elaborated: "taken the way of Cain . . . rushed for profit into Balaam's error . . . destroyed in Korah's rebellion" (v. 11).

Then Jude went beyond the triad, adding figure on figure, to emphasize his denouncement of the apostates. He called them "blemishes . . . [selfish] shepherds . . . clouds without rain . . . autumn trees without fruit . . . wild waves . . . wandering stars" (vv. 12-13).

In other trilogies Jude said these "grumblers and fault-finders" "follow their own evil desires . . . boast about themselves . . . and flatter others" (v. 16), and were characterized as those who "divide you . . . follow mere natural instincts . . . do not have the Spirit" (v. 19). Jude's readers were to "be merciful . . . snatch others from the fire . . . to others show mercy" (vv. 22-23).

Jude frequently referred to the Old Testament. He spoke of the Exodus (v. 5), the death of many Israelites in the wilderness (v. 5), Sodom and Gomorrah (v. 7), Moses' body (v. 9), Cain (v. 11), Balaam (v. 11), Korah (v. 11), Enoch (v. 14), and Adam (v. 14).

Date. Scholars disagree on the date of the writing of this book because Jude did not directly identify either the assembly he addressed the epistle to or the exact heretical group about whom he was writing. Most commentators, however, assign the date between A.D. 67 and 80. Jude was probably influenced by Peter, who wrote his second epistle about A.D. 67-68. (Peter predicted that false teachers *would* arise [2 Peter 2:1; 3:3], but Jude stated that they *have* "slipped in among you" [Jude 4].) And the antinomian Gnostic heresy (to which Jude may have been responding), was beginning to make its influence felt in the first century.

Purpose. One thought characterizes this epistle: beware of the apostates. In keeping with this warning, Jude proceeded to sound an exhortation to his readers to "contend for the faith" (v. 3). The heresy of Gnosticism had raised its head. "Here, in an undeveloped form, are all the main characteristics which went to make up later Gnosticism—emphasis on knowledge which was emancipated from the claims of morality; arrogance toward 'unenlightened' church leaders; interest in angelology; divisiveness; lasciviousness" (Michael Green, *The Second Epistle General of Peter and the General Epistle of Jude,* p. 39).

The incipient Gnostics against whom Jude warned were denying the lordship of Christ (v. 4), exercising sinful license (vv. 4, 8, 16), rebelling against authority (vv. 8, 11, 18), giving in to their own desires (vv. 16, 19), being concerned only with gain for themselves (vv. 11-12, 16), being divisive (v. 19), fault-finding (v. 16), and boasting (v. 16).

Gnosticism declared that the spirit was good and the material was evil. Therefore the spiritual was to be cultivated and fed, with freedom to pursue its good inclinations. In addition Gnostics felt free to give vent to the desires of the flesh. Thus the heart of this apostasy was that it turned the grace of God into license and lasciviousness. Jude wrote to warn of this dual apostasy of wrong conduct and false doctrine.

Original Readers. The tone of the letter demonstrates that the original recipients may have been Christian Jews of Palestine who were gathered into local fellowships. The references made to Old Testament incidents and to extrabiblical literature identified the recipients as people who would understand these references with no need for explanation. Egypt, Sodom and Gomorrah, Moses, Cain, Balaam, Korah, Enoch, Adam, and the fallen angels all point to a people familiar with Old Testament history and possibly apocryphal literature.

Application. The book is a solemn warning to Christians everywhere, since all are subject to the same doctrinal and practical errors. Though its theme regarding apostasy was specifically directed to first-century Jewish Christians, its message is applicable to all Christians. All believers need to avoid the pitfalls of denying Christ's lordship, promiscuously following the fleshly desires, rejecting authority, being divisive, and living for self.

OUTLINE

I. Salutation (vv. 1-2)
II. Warnings concerning Apostates (vv. 3-4)
III. Warnings concerning the Peril of Apostasy (vv. 5-16)
   A. Examples of apostates in the past (vv. 5-7)
      1. Egypt (v. 5)
      2. Angels (v. 6)
      3. Sodom and Gomorrah (v. 7)
   B. Actions of apostates in the present (vv. 8-16)
      1. Rejecting authority (vv. 8-10)
      2. Walking in error (v. 11)
      3. Leading falsely (vv. 12-13)
      4. Pleasing self (vv. 14-16)

IV. Guidelines for Avoiding Apostasy (vv. 17-23)
   A. Remembering the teaching of the apostles (vv. 17-19)
   B. Nurturing themselves (vv. 20-21)
   C. Being merciful to others (vv. 22-23)
V. Victory over Apostasy (vv. 24-25)

COMMENTARY

I. Salutation (vv. 1-2)

V. 1. The author introduced himself simply as **Jude, a servant of Jesus Christ and a brother of James.** He made no appeal to his readers on the basis of his personal authority. He was satisfied with being identified as a "servant" (*doulos*, "bondslave") of Jesus Christ. (For a discussion of the identity of this Jude, see the *Introduction*.)

Jude's epistle was directed **to those who have been called, who are loved by God the Father, and kept by Jesus Christ.** This threefold description of the people of God is one of many triads in this letter. The first expression "to those who have been called" reflects on the past—God's sovereign call to salvation in His electing grace (cf. Rom. 1:6; 8:30; 1 Cor. 1:24; Eph. 4:4; 2 Peter 1:3). The phrase "who are loved by God the Father" refers to the present. The verbal form of "loved" indicates that God's love was manifested in the past but also continues in the present. His third description, "kept by Jesus Christ," expresses the most positive assurance regarding the future, for He preserves those who trust Him till His coming (1 Thes. 5:23; 2 Tim. 1:12; 1 Peter 1:5; Jude 24). The calling is the active work of the Holy Spirit; the love emanates from the Father (cf. 2 Cor. 13:14); and the keeping work is the ministry of the Son. Thus the entire Godhead is included in Jude's salutation. The knowledge of God's calling, loving, and keeping brings believers assurance and peace during times of apostasy.

Each of these points in Jude's address seem to be alluded to later in the epistle: the calling may be hinted at in the words "the salvation we share" (v. 3), the love of God is mentioned in verse 21, and the keeping power of Jesus may be implied in the words, "as you wait for the mercy of our Lord Jesus Christ to bring you to eternal life" (v. 21; cf. v. 24).

V. 2. The divine provisions of **mercy, peace, and love** included in Jude's greeting are needed by Christians living in the licentious atmosphere of apostate teaching. God's mercy can sustain them in times of difficulty (Heb. 4:16); His peace can give a subtle calmness when evil abounds (Rom. 15:13; Phil. 4:7); and His love can protect and assure believers in the face of peril (Rom. 5:5; 1 John 4:12, 15-16).

The nature of the salutation reflects the writer's attitude. Jude's choice of words introduces his deep-seated compassion and heartfelt concern for his readers. He longed for them to know in the fullest measure God's "mercy, peace, and love." Jude overflowed with love for the believers while warning them about those who were making their way into the church to destroy it, those who knew nothing of God's mercy, peace, or love.

II. Warnings concerning Apostates (vv. 3-4)

Vv. 3-4. Wishing **to write** of the more pleasant theme of **salvation,** Jude was forced by his concern to write on an urgent and abhorrent theme. Circumstances had arisen that demanded immediate action, thus presenting an emergency situation. Jude addressed himself to a recognized problem, and exhorted the believers to respond with positive determination.

Jude got directly to the point: **I . . . urge you to contend for the faith.** Then he proceeded to tell his readers why he was so concerned. Godless men had **secretly slipped in among** them. They had joined the assemblies of believers, pretending to belong with them when actually they were enemies.

Jude's words were written to those who shared faith and salvation. His words were a warning to the believers to beware of those apostates who had made their way into local assemblies and would destroy if possible the foundation of faith on which the church was built.

"The faith" that God had **once for all entrusted to the saints** is the body of truths taught by the apostles. The term "the faith," used also in Galatians 1:23 and 1 Timothy 4:1, refers to things believed. The false teachings of the apostates called for the believers to contend (*epagōnizesthai*, "agonize earnestly") with all diligence in defense of those truths, which ungodly men were trying to destroy. In effect Jude said, "Let us hold firmly to the faith we profess" (Heb. 4:14).

The intrusion of the libertines refers to outsiders who would poison the church and who should be rejected. These apostates were not followers of Christ who had erred, but intruders who did not belong and who sought to wreck the believers' faith.

The **condemnation** of these men, which **was written about long ago,** may refer to Old Testament prophecies (e.g., Isa. 8:19-22; Jer. 5:13-14). Their end is also predicted in the New Testament (e.g., 2 Thes. 2:6-10; 2 Peter 2:3).

Two characteristics identify these **godless** (*asebeis*, "irreverent"; cf. Jude 15) apostates: perverting God's **grace,** and rejecting God's Son.

Claiming liberty in Christ, they interpreted His grace as **license** to do what their flesh desired with no inhibitions. Their libertinism turned grace into barbarous licentiousness. These antinomians declared that since the flesh was not created by God, it was proper to give in to its desires. Not surprisingly, this perversion in practice was accompanied by a perversion in doctrine—a denial of the person and authority of **Jesus Christ.**

III. Warnings concerning the Peril of Apostasy (vv. 5-16)

Jude first warned his readers of the peril of apostasy by citing three examples from the past of apostates who were destroyed (vv. 5-7), and then by describing the upcoming judgment on present apostates (vv. 8-16).

A. Examples of apostates in the past (vv. 5-7)

1. EGYPT (V. 5)

V. 5. Egypt is mentioned as a reminder of the fact that most Israelites who left Egypt were not faithful. An entire generation perished in the wilderness because of their unbelief (cf. Heb. 3:16-19).

2. ANGELS (V. 6)

V. 6. Among the **angels** were those who had remained in their first abode and had been obedient to God. But others rebelled and left **their** first **positions of authority** and are now **in darkness, bound . . . for judgment on the Great Day.**

Jude's source of information for this statement is debated. Some feel that this may refer to Genesis 6:1-4, and that "the sons of God" who cohabited with "the daughters of men" on earth were the angels who left "their positions of authority" in disobedience to God. (But see the comments on Gen. 6:1-4.) Others feel Jude was making use of the apocryphal Book of Enoch. Since Jude did not identify his source, any decision is only conjecture. The way Jude referred to the angels gives reason to believe that this truth was well accepted by his readers and thus needed no further explanation.

3. SODOM AND GOMORRAH (V. 7)

V. 7. Jude's third illustration, of **Sodom and Gomorrah and the surrounding towns,** serves as a dreadful example of what happens to those who turn from God to follow their own lustful natures. The fate of the unbelievers in those two cities (Gen. 19:1-29) foreshadows the fate of those who deny God's truth and ignore His warnings. The punishment by fire on the perverse inhabitants of Sodom and Gomorrah illustrates the **eternal fire** of hell, which will be experienced by false teachers.

B. Actions of apostates in the present (vv. 8-16)

1. REJECTING AUTHORITY (VV. 8-10)

V. 8. Jude returned to the apostates within the church, altering the order of his historical references in verses 5-7. Those who **pollute their own bodies** are like Sodom and Gomorrah. "Pollute" is *miainousin*, literally, "defile, deprave" used elsewhere only in Titus 1:15 and Hebrews 12:15. Those who **reject authority** are like the unbelieving Israelites who rejected the authority of both Moses and Yahweh. Those who **slander celestial beings** recall the angels who abandoned their home. These three actions reveal their inner attitudes of physical immorality (cf. Rom. 1:24, 26-27; Eph. 4:19), intellectual insubordination, and spiritual irreverence. As **dreamers,** they are unrealistic in thinking their ways will bring satisfaction.

V. 9. The archangel Michael was sent to bury Moses' body, but according to Jewish tradition (the pseudepigraphical book, The Assumption of Moses), **the devil** argued with the angel about **the body,** apparently claiming the right to dispose of it. But Michael, though powerful and authoritative, **did not dare** dispute with Satan, so he left the matter in God's hands, saying, **The Lord rebuke you!** The false teachers Jude spoke of had no respect for authority or for angels. The apostates' slandering of celestial beings (v. 8) stands in arrogant contrast to the chief angelic being, Michael, who would not dare slander Satan, chief of the fallen angels.

V. 10. Whereas Michael did not dare accuse the devil, these apostates, by contrast spoke **abusively** against what **they** did **not understand.** This abusive speech may refer to their slandering of angels (v. 8). Their understanding was debased, for it followed only natural animal instinct. The apostates' only "reasoning" was like that of **unreasoning animals.** Rather than comprehending what was above them (the angels), they really understood only what was below them (the animals). Jude thus demolished their Gnostic claim to superior knowledge. And their understanding—polluting "their own bodies" (v. 8)—was, like the sin of Sodom, self-destructive.

2. WALKING IN ERROR (V. 11)

V. 11. Again Jude returned to one of his triads. The apostates erred in three respects so Jude said, **Woe to them!**

They have taken the way of Cain. This may mean either that they, like Cain, (a) disobediently devised their own ways of worship, (b) were envious of others, or (c) hated others with a murderous spirit (cf. 1 John 3:12).

They have rushed for profit into Balaam's error. Balaam, under the guise of serving God, encouraged others to sin, while at the same time seeking to gain monetarily from their error (2 Peter 2:15-16; Num. 22:21-31). Similarly the false leaders of Jude's day, greedy for money, led others into sin without recognizing the danger of their actions.

They have been destroyed in Korah's rebellion. Korah led a revolt against Moses and Aaron, not acknowledging that God had delegated authority to them (Num. 16). So their rebellion was actually against God Himself. Likewise the men of whom Jude spoke (perhaps local church leaders) rebelled against God's authority and as a result would be destroyed suddenly. That destruction was so certain that Jude stated in the past tense that "they have been destroyed."

3. LEADING FALSELY (VV. 12-13)

V. 12. Jude pointed out how craftily the apostates had moved into the church. They had made their way into the **love feasts**—which were the closest celebrations of believers—meals (indicated by the words **eating with you**), which were probably followed by the Lord's Supper. Yet these false teachers, though participating outwardly, were inwardly denying the Lord (v. 4b). This is the most outrageous blasphemy possible. Such men were thus **blemishes** that marred the inner beauty of the church. Furthermore they were intruding (cf. "secretly slipped in among you," v. 4a) **without the slightest qualm** or inhibition. "Blemishes" is *spilades* ("stains"); cf. the verb form *espilōmenon* ("stained") in verse 23. In staining others (v. 12) they stained themselves (v. 23).

In addition these unbelievers had taken a shepherding role, but did not function as **shepherds.** Instead of feeding the flock of God, they selfishly would **feed only themselves.** How unthinkable for a shepherd not to feed his sheep—which was his major responsibility! Their leadership was false, for it was deceptive, hardened, and selfish.

As leaders, these apostates were **clouds without rain, blown along by the wind.** This is the first of four vivid comparisons from nature in verses 12-13. These men had no water for thirsty souls; they only pretended that they did. And they were soon gone, unstable as wind-driven clouds.

As leaders these apostates were spiritually dead. A tree in the **autumn** (the time of gathering fruit from fruit **trees**) without fruit appears (or is) dead, and a fruitless tree that is **uprooted** is dead forever—thus it is **twice dead.** The dead condition of apostate leaders was indicated by two things: (a) they did not bear spiritual fruit in others, and (b) they were without spiritual roots themselves, and thus faced judgment.

V. 13. Like **wild waves of the sea,** raging back and forth and producing only froth on the shore, these apostates spewed their foam with nothing solid, edifying, helpful, or nourishing. What they produced was only **shame,** which their actions caused.

Wandering stars (i.e., "shooting" stars), move across the sky, shining briefly, and then vanish without producing light or giving direction. Fixed stars help guide navigators, but wandering stars are useless to them. If any shipmaster would be stupid enough to follow one, he would be led astray. Similarly the prominence of apostate leaders is short-lived, useless, and false. They do lead unwary followers astray, pretending to be what they are not. They will therefore be swallowed up into the **blackest darkness** forever; eternal judgment is certain for them.

These apostates were not unfruitful believers, who would not receive rewards in heaven at the judgment seat of Christ. Instead they were impostors who would be judged according to their evil deeds.

4. PLEASING SELF (VV. 14-16)

Vv. 14-15. The judgment on apostates, already mentioned in verses 4-7, 13, was now confirmed by a reference to a pre-Flood prophecy made by **Enoch, the seventh from Adam** (Gen. 5:4-20). However, scholars have puzzled over the absence of any reference in the Old Testament to this prophecy attributed to Enoch. Since Jude's statement is similar to a passage in the apocryphal Book of Enoch (1:9)—written prior to 110 B.C. and thus probably known by the early Christians—many assume that Jude is quoting from that book. Others suggest that the difference between Jude's words and the Book of Enoch indicate that Jude received the information about Enoch directly from God, or that under divine inspiration he recorded an oral tradition. None of these views affects the doctrine of inspiration adversely. If Jude quoted the apocryphal book, he was affirming only the truth of that prophecy and not endorsing the book in its entirety (cf. Paul's quotation of the Cretan poet Epimenides, in Titus 1:12).

Enoch's prophecy pointed to the glorious return of Christ to the earth with **thousands upon thousands of** His angels (**holy ones**) (Matt. 24:30; 2 Thes. 1:10), when **His** purpose will be **to judge everyone** (2 Thes. 1:7-10) **and to convict all the ungodly** with unanswerable evidence that their actions, manners, and words have been **ungodly** (*asebeis*, "irreverent"; cf. Jude 4). Jude's fourfold use of this word **ungodly** reinforces his description of their nature. Rather than being true spiritual leaders, they had spoken **harsh words** (cf. "speak abusively" in v. 10) against Jesus Christ whom they denied.

V. 16. Here Jude described the apostates in a fourfold way. These descriptions justify Enoch's calling them "ungodly." (a) They were **grumblers and faultfinders** who faulted others but saw no flaws in themselves; (b) they lustfully followed **their own evil desires** (cf. vv. 8, 10, 18-19); (c) they bragged **about themselves** (the word *hyperonka*, used only here and in 2 Peter 2:18, means to be "puffed up" or "swollen"); and (d) they flattered **others,** currying favor only when it was to **their own** evil advantage to do so. Vocally discontented, sinfully self-centered, extravagantly egotistical, and deceptively flattering—such are apostates, then and today.

Thus in unflinching terms Jude clearly identified the apostates, while at the same time exposing their character in order to warn believers of their true nature and their final destiny. He was laying the groundwork to call his readers to action against these ungodly men and their practices.

IV. Guidelines for Avoiding Apostasy (vv. 17-23)

Having identified the apostates in expressive language, Jude gave the believers guidelines on how to avoid the apostates' errors. It is not enough to recognize false teachers; it is also necessary to avoid falling into their errors.

A. *Remembering the teaching of the apostles (vv. 17-19)*

Vv. 17-19. Jude told his readers to **remember what the apostles** had **foretold** about **scoffers.** At Ephesus, Paul warned of the "savage wolves" that would come in to destroy the flock and distort the truth (Acts 20:29-30). He sounded similar warnings of apostasy to Timothy (1 Tim. 4:1; 2 Tim. 3:1-5; 4:3-4). Peter had addressed the same issue (2 Peter 2:1-3; 3:3-4). The quotation in Jude 18 is a loose rendering of Peter's words in 2 Peter 3:3, and at the same time it summarized Paul's warnings.

As stated in Jude 18-19, these intruders (a) scoffed (cf. vv. 10-15), (b) followed **their own ungodly desires** (cf. v. 16) and **mere natural instincts** (cf. vv. 10, 16), and (c) sought to **divide** believers. Such men obviously did **not have the** Holy **Spirit** and thus were not born again (Rom. 8:9).

B. Nurturing themselves (vv. 20-21)

Vv. 20-21. In addition to remembering what the apostles had said about the apostates, Jude's readers were to give attention to themselves. Here is the heart of his message: **build yourselves up in your most holy faith . . . pray in the Holy Spirit, keep yourselves in God's love** and **wait for** Christ's return. (The NIV seems to suggest four exhortations, but the Greek has three parallel participles—building, praying, expecting—and one command, keep. The evident contrast of these actions to the scoffers was introduced by the words **But you.** And for the third time Jude addressed his readers as **dear friends** (vv. 3, 17, 20).

Personal edification ("build yourselves up") comes from progressing in the knowledge of "your most holy faith." This "faith that was once for all entrusted to the saints" (v. 3) was the teaching of the apostles now recorded in the Scriptures, to be studied (Acts 20:32; 2 Tim. 2:15).

Praying in the Holy Spirit is not speaking in tongues, but is "praying out of hearts and souls that are indwelt, illuminated, and filled with the Holy Spirit" (George Lawrence Lawlor, *Translation and Exposition of the Epistle of Jude*, p. 127). It is praying in the power of the Holy Spirit (cf. Eph. 6:18).

Keeping oneself "in God's love" (Jude 21) does not indicate that salvation depends on one's own efforts, for that would contradict other Scripture passages (e.g., v. 24). Instead, a believer is nurtured as he is occupied with God's love for him, and is in fellowship with Him (cf. John 15:9-10, "remain in My love").

Waiting (*prosdechomenoi*, "looking expectantly") for the blessed hope, the return of Christ for His church, is a fourth means of personal nurture. Waiting for that event is waiting **for the mercy of our Lord Jesus Christ** in the sense that the Rapture will be the consummating evidence of His mercy. Jude added that it will **bring you to eternal life,** that is, to enjoying never-ending life in God's own presence (cf. 1 Peter 1:5, 9, 13).

C. Being merciful to others (vv. 22-23)

Vv. 22-23. Because the words of the apostates were confusing, probably many believers were in **doubt** as to whether to follow them. Such persons, Jude wrote, should not be slandered or criticized. They should be dealt with in love and mercy—the same way in which the Lord dealt with them (cf. v. 21). They needed encouragement, not criticism. They needed to be built up, not torn down.

Others—those who are unsaved—were about to fall into the fire, the eternal fire of hell (cf. v. 7). Jude exhorted his readers to **snatch** them **from the fire and save them.**

To still others, a third group, believers should **show mercy.** But they were to do so in an attitude of **fear,** that is, caution, lest they become contaminated by the sin of "the most abandoned heretic" (Michael Green, *The Second Epistle General of Peter and the General Epistle of Jude*, p. 188). Such persons are so corrupt that the stench of death has polluted them and even their **clothing,** as it were, reeks with the odor of **corrupted flesh** (cf. comments on "stained" in v. 12).

In his short epistle, Jude gave seven commands to believers:

1. Earnestly contend for the faith (v. 3).
2. Remember the teaching and warning of the apostles (v. 17).
3. Build yourselves up in the most holy faith (v. 20).
4. Pray in the Holy Spirit (v. 20).
5. Keep yourselves in the love of God (v. 21).
6. Look for the mercy of the Lord to bring you to eternal life (v. 21).
7. Show mercy to Christians who are doubting, snatch unbelievers from the fire, and cautiously show mercy to the corrupt (vv. 22-23).

V. Victory over Apostasy (vv. 24-25)

Vv. 24-25. In this final paragraph Jude exploded with a most elevated doxology, answering the unexpressed question, "But who will deliver us from the apostates and the apostasy into which they lead the unsuspecting?" His proclamation was, praise be **to Him who is able to keep you from falling.** Victory over apostasy is found in Jesus Christ! He is the One who will "keep" believers. Christ will **present** believers to His Father **without fault and with great joy**—joy both for Himself and for them (Heb. 12:2; 1 Peter 1:8). Here is the greatest theme of victory to be sounded, the highest note of praise and adoration possible, and the greatest assurance for the redeemed. Jude attributes to God—to **the only God our Savior . . . glory, majesty, power, and authority,** which are all available to believers through the Victor, **Jesus Christ our Lord.** And this exalted position is true of God in eternity past, in the present, and for all eternity in the future.

Thus Jude fulfills his heart's desire of writing in the most joyful terms (Jude 3), for in Christ there is hope in victory, which gives believers joy and confidence.

BIBLIOGRAPHY

Bigg, Charles. *A Critical and Exegetical Commentary on the Epistles of St. Peter and St. Jude.* The International Critical Commentary. Edinburgh: T.&T. Clark, 1902.

Blum, Edwin A. "Jude." In *The Expositor's Bible Commentary*, vol. 12. Grand Rapids: Zondervan Publishing House, 1981.

Coder, S. Maxwell. *Jude.* Everyman's Bible Commentary. Chicago: Moody Press, 1967.

Green, Michael. *The Second Epistle General of Peter and the General Epistle of Jude: An Introduction and Commentary.* The Tyndale New Testament Commentaries. Grand Rapids: Wm. B. Eerdmans Publishing Co., 1968.

Ironside, H.A. *Exposition of the Epistle of Jude.* Rev. ed. New York: Loizeaux Brothers, n.d.

Lawlor, George Lawrence. *Translation and Exposition of the Epistle of Jude.* Nutley, N.J.: Presbyterian and Reformed Publishing Co., 1976.

Lenski, R.C.H. *The Interpretation of the Epistles of St. Peter, St. John and St. Jude.* Minneapolis: Augsburg Publishing House, 1966.

MacArthur, John, Jr. *Beware the Pretenders.* Wheaton, Ill.: Scripture Press Publications, Victor Books, 1980.

Manton, Thomas. *An Exposition on the Epistle of Jude.* Reprint. London: Banner of Truth Trust, 1978.

Mayor, Joseph B. *The Epistle of St. Jude and the Second Epistle of St. Peter.* London: Macmillan Co., 1907. Reprint. Minneapolis: Klock & Klock Christian Publishers, 1978.

Pettingill, William L. *Simple Studies in the Epistles of James, First and Second Peter, First, Second and Third John and Jude.* Findlay, Ohio: Fundamental Truth Publishers, n.d.

Plummer, Alfred. *The General Epistles of St. James and St. Jude.* The Expositor's Bible. New York: Hodder & Stoughton, n.d.

Sadler, M.F. *The General Epistles of James, Peter, John, and Jude.* 2d ed. London: George Bell & Sons, 1895.

Wand, J.W.C., ed. *The General Epistles of St. Peter and St. Jude.* London: Methuen & Co., 1934.

Wolff, Richard. *A Commentary on the Epistle of Jude.* Grand Rapids: Zondervan Publishing House, 1960.

REVELATION
John F. Walvoord

INTRODUCTION

Importance. The Book of Revelation is important because it is the last inspired book of the Bible to be written and is rightly positioned as the New Testament's final book. As the New Testament opens with the four Gospels relating to the first coming of Christ, so the Book of Revelation closes the New Testament with the general theme of the second coming of Christ. The Book of Revelation is also the climax of many lines of revelation running through both Testaments, and it brings to conclusion the revelation of many prophecies yet to be fulfilled.

The second coming of Christ and the years immediately preceding it are revealed in Revelation more graphically than in any other book of the Bible. The Book of Daniel describes in detail the period from Daniel's time to Christ's first coming and speaks briefly of the Tribulation and Christ's rule on earth. But the Book of Revelation amplifies the great end-time events with many additional details, culminating in the new heaven and the new earth.

Authorship. As the opening verses in Revelation plainly state, the book was written by John. From the first century to the present, orthodox Christians have almost unanimously agreed that he is the Apostle John. Dionysius was the first to dispute the Johannine authorship, and did so on the grounds that he disagreed with the book's theology and found many inaccuracies in its grammar. These objections were disregarded in the early church by most of the important fathers such as Justin Martyr, Irenaeus, Tertullian, Hippolytus, Clement of Alexandria, and Origen. (For a full discussion see John F. Walvoord, *The Revelation of Jesus Christ*, pp. 11-4.) Practically all scholars today who accept the divine inspiration of the Book of Revelation also accept John the Apostle as its author. However, Erasmus, Luther, and Zwingli questioned the Johannine authorship because it teaches a literal 1,000-year reign of Christ.

Date. Most evangelical scholars affirm that Revelation was written in A.D. 95 or 96. This is based on accounts of the early church fathers that the Apostle John had been exiled on Patmos Island during the reign of Domitian who died in A.D. 96. John was then allowed to return to Ephesus.

Because of a statement by Papias, an early church father, that John the Apostle was martyred before A.D. 70, the Johannine authorship has been questioned. However, the accuracy of this quotation from Papias has been seriously challenged by statements by Clement of Alexandria and Eusebius who affirm that the book was written by John on Patmos in A.D. 95 or 96.

Inspiration and Canonicity. Those accepting John the Apostle as the author universally recognize the divine inspiration of Revelation and its rightful place in the Bible. Because its style differs from that of other New Testament books, acceptance of Revelation by early Christians was delayed by a rising opposition to premillennialism. The doctrine of the literal 1,000-year reign of Christ was rejected by some church leaders in the third and fourth centuries. The evidence, however, shows that orthodox theologians readily accepted the book as genuinely inspired. Early fathers who recognized the book as Scripture include Irenaeus, Justin Martyr, Eusebius, Apollonius, and Theophilus, the bishop of Antioch. By the beginning of the third century the book was widely quoted as Scripture. The fact that the Book of

REVELATION

Revelation complements other inspired Scripture such as the Book of Daniel has confirmed its divine inspiration.

Style. Like the Old Testament Books of Daniel and Ezekiel, Revelation uses symbolic and apocalyptic forms of revelation extensively. The fact that symbols must be interpreted has led to many diverse interpretations. In most cases, however, the meaning of the symbolic revelation is found by comparing it with previous prophetic and apocalyptic revelation in the Old Testament. This has led many interpreters to view the Book of Revelation as presenting realistic predictions of the future. Its apocalyptic and symbolic character sharply contrasts with books of similar nature written outside the Bible which are classified as Pseudepigrapha. While many of these extrabiblical books are almost impossible to understand, Revelation, by contrast, presents a sensible view of the future in harmony with the rest of Scripture (cf. Walvoord, *Revelation,* pp. 23-30).

Interpretation. Because of its unusual character, Revelation has been approached from a number of interpretive principles, some of which raise serious questions concerning its value as divine authoritative revelation.

The allegorical or nonliteral approach. This form of interpretation was offered by the Alexandrian school of theology in the third and fourth centuries. It regards the entire Bible as an extensive allegory to be interpreted in a nonliteral sense. The allegorical interpretation of the Bible was later restricted largely to prophecy about the Millennium by Augustine (354–430), who interpreted Revelation as a chronicle of the spiritual conflict between God and Satan being fulfilled in the present Church Age. A liberal variation of this in modern times considers Revelation simply as a symbolic presentation of the concept of God's ultimate victory.

The preterist approach. A more respected approach is known as the preterist view which regards Revelation as a symbolic picture of early church conflicts which have been fulfilled. This view denies the future predictive quality of most of the Book of Revelation. In varying degrees this view combines the allegorical and symbolic interpretation with the concept that Revelation does not deal with specific future events. Still another variation of the preterist view regards Revelation as setting forth principles of divine dealings with man, without presenting specific events.

The historical approach. A popular view stemming from the Middle Ages is the historical approach which views Revelation as a symbolic picture of the total church history of the present Age between Christ's first and second comings. This view was advanced by Luther, Isaac Newton, Elliott, and many expositors of the postmillennial school of interpretation and has attained respectability in recent centuries. Its principal problem is that seldom do two interpreters interpret a given passage as referring to the same event. Each interpreter tends to find its fulfillment in his generation. Many have combined the historical interpretation with aspects of other forms of interpretation in order to bring out a devotional or spiritual teaching from the book. The preceding methods of interpretation tend to deny a literal future Millennium and also literal future events in the Book of Revelation.

The futuristic approach. The futuristic approach has been adopted by conservative scholars, usually premillenarians, who state that chapters 4–22 deal with events that are yet future today. The content of Revelation 4–18 describes the last seven years preceding the second coming of Christ and particularly emphasizes the Great Tribulation, occurring in the last three and one-half years before His coming.

Objections to this view usually stem from theological positions opposed to premillennialism. The charge is often made that the Book of Revelation would not have been a comfort to early Christians or understood by them if it were largely futuristic. Adherents of the futuristic school of interpretation insist, on the contrary, that future events described in Revelation bring comfort and reassurance to Christians who in the nature of their faith regard their ultimate victory as future. The futuristic interpretation, however, is demanding of the expositor as it requires him to reduce to tangible prophetic events the symbolic

Purpose. The purpose of the Book of Revelation is to reveal events which will take place immediately before, during, and following the second coming of Christ. In keeping with this purpose the book devotes most of its revelation to this subject in chapters 4–18. The Second Coming itself is given the most graphic portrayal anywhere in the Bible in chapter 19, followed by the millennial reign of Christ described in chapter 20. The eternal state is revealed in chapters 21–22. So the obvious purpose of the book is to complete the prophetic theme presented earlier in the prophecies of the Old Testament (e.g., Dan.) and the prophecies of Christ, especially in the Olivet Discourse (Matt. 24–25). Along with the predictive character of the Book of Revelation is extensive revelation in almost every important area of theology. In addition, many verses suggest practical applications of prophetic truths to a Christian's life. Specific knowledge and anticipation of God's future program is an incentive to holy living and commitment to Christ.

Application. In addition to passages that suggest practical application of prophetic truth, chapters 2–3 are especially important for they consist of messages to seven local churches which appropriately represent the entire church. The pointed message of Christ to each of these churches is the capstone to New Testament Epistles dealing with the practical life of those committed to the Christian faith. On the one hand believers are exhorted to holy living, and on the other hand unbelievers are warned of judgments to come. The book provides solid evidence that the righteous God will ultimately deal with human sin and bring to consummation the salvation of those who have trusted in Christ. A solemn warning is given to those who are unprepared to face the future. A day of reckoning, when every knee will bow to Christ (Phil. 2:10), is inevitable in the divine program. Because of its broad revelation of events to come as well as its pointed exhortation to righteousness, the book pronounces blessing on those "who hear it and take to heart what is written in it, because the time is near" (Rev. 1:3).

OUTLINE

I. Introduction: "What You Have Seen" (chap. 1)
   A. Prologue (1:1-3)
   B. Salutation (1:4-8)
   C. The Patmos vision of Christ glorified (1:9-18)
   D. The command to write (1:19-20)
II. Letters to the Seven Churches: "What Is Now" (chaps. 2–3)
   A. The letter to the church in Ephesus (2:1-7)
   B. The letter to the church in Smyrna (2:8-11)
   C. The letter to the church in Pergamum (2:12-17)
   D. The letter to the church in Thyatira (2:18-29)
   E. The letter to the church in Sardis (3:1-6)
   F. The letter to the church in Philadelphia (3:7-13)
   G. The letter to the church in Laodicea (3:14-22)
III. The Revelation of the Future: "What Will Take Place Later" (chaps. 4–22)
   A. The vision of the heavenly throne (chap. 4)
   B. The seven-sealed scroll (chap. 5)
   C. The opening of the six seals: the time of divine wrath (chap. 6)
   D. Those who will be saved in the Great Tribulation (chap. 7)
   E. The opening of the seventh seal and the introduction of the seven trumpets (chaps. 8–9)
   F. The mighty angel and the little scroll (chap. 10)
   G. The two witnesses (11:1-14)
   H. The sounding of the seventh trumpet (11:15-19)
   I. The seven great personages of the end times (chaps. 12–15)
   J. The bowls of divine wrath (chap. 16)
   K. The fall of Babylon (chaps. 17–18)
   L. The song of hallelujah in heaven (19:1-10)
   M. The second coming of Christ (19:11-21)
   N. The millennial reign of Christ (20:1-10)

O. The judgment of the great white throne (20:11-15)
P. The new heaven and the new earth (21:1–22:5)
Q. The final word from God (22:6-21)

COMMENTARY

I. Introduction: "What You Have Seen" (chap. 1)

A. Prologue (1:1-3)

1:1. The opening words, **The revelation of Jesus Christ,** indicate the subject of the entire book. The word "revelation" is a translation of the Greek *apokalypsis,* meaning "an unveiling" or "a disclosure." From this word comes the English "apocalypse." The revelation was given to John to communicate to others, **His servants,** and it prophesies **what must soon take place,** rather than relating a historic presentation as in the four Gospels. The word "soon" (*en tachei;* cf. 2:16; 22:7, 12, 20) means that the action will be sudden when it comes, not necessarily that it will occur immediately. Once the end-time events begin, they will occur in rapid succession (cf. Luke 18:8; Acts 12:7; 22:18; 25:4; Rom. 16:20). The words, **He made it known,** are from the Greek verb *esēmanen,* meaning "to make known by signs or symbols," but the verb also includes communication by words. The angel messenger is not named but some believe he was Gabriel, who brought messages to Daniel, Mary, and Zechariah (cf. Dan. 8:16; 9:21-22; Luke 1:26-31). The reference to **John** as a **servant** (*doulos,* which normally means "slave") is the term used by Paul, James, Peter, and Jude (cf. Rom. 1:1; Phil. 1:1; Titus 1:1; James 1:1; 2 Peter 1:1; Jude 1) in speaking of their positions as God's servants.

1:2. John faithfully described what **he saw** as **the Word of God and the testimony of Jesus Christ.** What John saw was a communication from—and about—Jesus Christ Himself.

1:3. The prologue concludes with a blessing on each individual **who reads the** book as well as on **those who hear it and take to heart what is written in it.** The implication is that a reader will read this message aloud to an audience. Not only is there a blessing for the reader and the hearers, but there is also a blessing for those who respond in obedience.

John concluded his prologue with **the time is near.** The word "time" (*kairos*) refers to a period of time, that is, the time of the end (Dan. 8:17; 11:35, 40; 12:4, 9). The end time, as a time period, is mentioned in Revelation 11:18 and 12:12. In 12:14 the word "time" means a year (cf. Dan. 7:25); and the phrase "time, times, and half a time" means one year ("time") plus two years ("times") plus six months ("half a time"), totaling three and one-half years—the length of the time of "the end." Revelation 1:3 includes the first of seven beatitudes in the book (1:3; 14:13; 16:15; 19:9; 20:6; 22:7, 14).

The prologue presents concisely the basic facts underlying the entire book: its subjects, purpose, and angelic and human channels. It is most important to observe that the book was primarily intended to give a practical lesson to those who read and heed its contents.

B. Salutation (1:4-8)

1:4-6. This salutation—like Paul's salutations in his epistles and the salutation of John himself in 2 John—specifies the book's destination. The recipients of this message were **the seven churches in the Roman province of Asia** in Asia Minor (Rev. 1:11; chaps. 2 and 3). The words **grace and peace** concisely summarize both a Christian's standing before God and his experience. "Grace" speaks of God's attitude toward believers; "peace" speaks both of their standing with God and their experience of divine peace.

The salutation is unusual in that it describes God the Father as the One **who is, and who was, and who is to come** (cf. 1:8). **The seven spirits** probably refers to the Holy Spirit (cf. Isa. 11:2-3; Rev. 3:1; 4:5; 5:6), though it is an unusual way to refer to the third Person of the Trinity. Of the three Persons in the Trinity, **Jesus Christ** is here mentioned last, probably because of His prominence in this book. He is described as **the faithful Witness,** that is, the source of the revelation to be given; **the Firstborn from the dead** (cf. Col. 1:18), referring to His historic resurrection; **and the Ruler of the kings of the earth,** indicating His prophetic role after His second coming (chap. 19).

The Seven "Beatitudes" in Revelation

"Blessed is the one who reads the words of this prophecy, and blessed are those who hear it and take to heart what is written in it, because the time is near" (1:3).

"Then I heard a voice from heaven say, 'Write: "Blessed are the dead who die in the Lord from now on. "Yes,' says the Spirit, 'they will rest from their labor, for their deeds will follow them' " (14:13).

"Behold, I come like a thief! Blessed is he who stays awake and keeps his clothes with him, so that he may not go naked and be shamefully exposed" (16:15).

"Then the angel said to me, 'Write: "Blessed are those who are invited to the wedding supper of the Lamb!" ' And he added, 'These are the true words of God' " (19:9).

"Blessed and holy are those who have part in the first resurrection. The second death has no power over them, but they will be priests of God and of Christ and will reign with Him for a thousand years" (20:6).

"Behold, I am coming soon! Blessed is he who keeps the words of the prophecy in this book" (22:7).

"Blessed are those who wash their robes, that they may have the right to the tree of life and may go through the gates into the city" (22:14).

Christ's resurrection was **from the dead**. As the "Firstborn," He is the first to be resurrected with an everlasting body, which is a token of other selective resurrections including those of saints who die in the Church Age (Phil. 3:11), the Tribulation martyrs (Rev. 20:5-6), and the wicked dead of all ages (20:12-13). In His dying on the cross Christ **who loves us** is the One who **freed us from our sins by His blood** (some Gr. mss. have the word "washed" instead of "freed"). Believers are now **a kingdom and priests** with the purpose now and forever of serving God. This prompted John to express a benediction of praise and worship culminating with **Amen** (lit., "so be it").

1:7-8. Readers are exhorted to **look** for **He is coming**. This is His second coming which will be **with the clouds** (cf. Acts 1:9-11). **Every eye will see Him, even those who pierced Him**. Though the literal executioners and rejectors of Christ are now dead and will not be resurrected until after the Millennium, the godly remnant of Israel "will look on [Him], the One they have pierced" (Zech. 12:10). This godly remnant will represent the nation.

Christ's second coming, however, will be visible to the entire world including unbelievers, in contrast with His first coming at His birth in Bethlehem and in contrast with the future Rapture of the church, which probably will not be visible to the earth as a whole. The present tense of the expression "He is coming" (Rev. 1:7) points to the future Rapture of the church (John 14:3). John again appended the word **Amen**. The salutation closes with a reminder of Christ as the eternal One, **the Alpha and the Omega**, the first and last letters of the Greek alphabet (also used in Rev. 21:6; 22:13). He is further described as the One **who is, and who was, and who is to come** (cf. 4:8; 11:17), **the Almighty**. The Greek word for "Almighty" is *pantokratōr*, "the all-powerful One." It is used 10 times in the New Testament, 9 of them in Revelation (2 Cor. 6:18; Rev. 1:8; 4:8; 11:17; 15:3; 16:7, 14; 19:6, 15; 21:22). The major revelation of the entire book is referred to in these salutation verses.

C. The Patmos vision of Christ glorified (1:9-18)

The location of the dramatic revelation of Christ recorded in this book was the island of Patmos, a small island in the Aegean Sea southwest of Ephesus and between Asia Minor and Greece. According to several early church fathers (Irenaeus, Clement of Alexandria, and Eusebius), John was sent to this island as a prisoner following his effective pastorate at Ephesus. Victorinus, the first commentator on the Book of Revelation, stated that John worked as a prisoner in the mines on this small island. When the Emperor Domitian died in A.D. 96, his successor Nerva let John return to Ephesus. During John's bleak days on Patmos, God gave him the tremendous revelation embodied in this final book of the Bible.

1:9-11. This section begins with the expression **I, John.** This is the third reference to John as the human author in this chapter and the first of three times in the book when he referred to himself as I (cf. 21:2; 22:8). This contrasts with his reference to himself in 2 John 1 and 3 John 1 as an elder and his indication in John 21:24 that he was a disciple.

In these opening chapters addressed to the seven churches of Asia, John described himself as a **brother** who was **patient** in his **endurance** of **suffering.** His suffering had come because of his faithful proclamation of and faith in **the Word of God and the testimony of Jesus.** (Some Gr. texts add "Christ" after Jesus.) "The testimony of Jesus" means John's testimony *for* and *about* Jesus, not a testimony given *by* Jesus. Like many other well-known writers of Scripture (Moses, David, Isaiah, Ezekiel, Jeremiah, and Peter), John was writing from a context of suffering because of his commitment to the true God.

John's revelation occurred **on the Lord's Day** while he **was in the Spirit.** Some have indicated that "the Lord's Day" refers to the first day of the week. However, the word "Lord's" is an adjective and this expression is never used in the Bible to refer to the first day of the week. Probably John was referring to the day of the Lord, a familiar expression in both Testaments (cf. Isa. 2:12; 13:6, 9; 34:8; Joel 1:15; 2:1, 11, 31; 3:14; Amos 5:18, 20; Zeph. 1:7-8, 14, 18; 2:3; Zech. 14:1; Mal. 4:5; 1 Thes. 5:2; 2 Peter 3:10). "In the Spirit" could also be rendered "in [my] spirit" (cf. Rev. 4:2; 17:3; 21:10). That is, he was projected forward in his inner self in a vision, not bodily, to that future day of the Lord when God will pour out His judgments on the earth.

The stirring events beginning in Revelation 4 are the unfolding of the day of the Lord and the divine judgments related to it. The idea that the entire Book of Revelation was given to John in one 24-hour day seems unlikely, especially if he had to write it all down. Being transported prophetically into the future day of the Lord, he then recorded his experience.

Hearing **a loud voice like a trumpet,** John was instructed to write on a scroll what he saw and heard and send it to seven churches located in Asia Minor. This is the first of 12 commands in this book for John to write what he saw, a command which seems related to each preceding vision (cf. 1:19; 2:1, 8, 12, 18; 3:1, 7, 14; 14:13; 19:9; 21:5). One vision, however, was not to be recorded (10:4).

Each of these churches was an autonomous local church and the order of mention is geographical in a half-moon circle beginning at Ephesus on the coast, proceeding north to Smyrna and Pergamum, then swinging east and south to Thyatira, Sardis, Philadelphia, and Laodicea. (For more information on these seven churches see comments on chaps. 2-3).

1:12-16. Hearing **the voice** behind him, John **turned ... to see** its source. What he **saw** was **seven golden lampstands.** Apparently these were individual lampstands rather than one lampstand with seven lamps as was true of a similar piece of furniture in the tabernacle and the temple.

Among the lampstands John saw **Someone "like a Son of Man,"** an expression used in Daniel 7:13 to refer to Christ. The description was that of a priest **dressed in a** long **robe ... with a golden sash around his chest.** The whiteness of His hair corresponded to that of the Ancient of Days (cf. Dan. 7:9), a reference to God the Father. God the Son has the same purity and eternity as God the Father, as signified by the whiteness of **His head and hair.** The **eyes like blazing fire** described His piercing judgment of sin (cf. Rev. 2:18).

This concept is further enhanced by **His feet** which **were like bronze glowing**

in a furnace (cf. 2:18). The bronze altar in the temple was related to sacrifice for sin and divine judgment on it. **His voice** was compared to the roar **of rushing waters. His face** glowed with a brilliance **like the sun shining.** John noticed that **in His right hand He held seven stars,** described in verse 20 as the angels or messengers of the seven churches. Significantly Christ held them in His right hand, indicating sovereign possession. Speaking of Christ's role as a Judge, John saw a **sharp double-edged sword** coming **out of His mouth.** This type of sword (*rhomphaia,* also referred to in 2:12, 16; 6:8; 19:15, 21) was used by the Romans in a stabbing action designed to kill. Jesus Christ was no longer a Baby in Bethlehem or a Man of sorrows crowned with thorns. He was now the Lord of glory.

1:17-18. John stated, **When I saw Him, I fell at His feet as though dead.** Paul was struck to the ground in a similar way when he saw Christ in His glory (Acts 9:4). Previously John had put his head on Jesus' breast (cf. John 13:25, KJV). But now John could not be this familiar with the Christ of glory.

John received reassurance from Christ in the words, **Do not be afraid.** Christ stated that He is the eternal One, **the First and the Last** (cf. Rev. 1:8; 2:8; 21:6; 22:13), and the resurrected One, the **Living One,** who though once **dead** is now alive **forever and ever!** Here Christ affirmed that He alone has **the keys of death and hades** that is, authority over death and the place of the dead (cf. John 5:21-26; 1 Cor. 15:54-57; Heb. 2:14; Rev. 20:12-14). Though the glorified Christ is to be reverenced, faithful believers like John can be sure they are accepted by the Son of God. The Christian's death and resurrection are both in His hands. This picture of Christ glorified contrasts with the portrayal of Christ as a Man in the four Gospels (cf. Phil. 2:6-8), except for His transfiguration (Matt. 17:2; Mark 9:2).

D. *The command to write (1:19-20)*

1:19-20. Following the revelation of Christ in glory, John was again commanded to **write.** The subject of his record has three tenses: (a) what he had already experienced: **what you have seen;** (b) the present experiences: **what is now;** and (c) the future: **what will take place later.** This appears to be the divine outline of Revelation. What John was told to write was first a record of his experience (chap. 1), now history. Then he was to write the present message of Christ to seven churches (chaps. 2–3). Finally, the main purpose of the book being prophetic, he was to introduce the events preceding, culminating in, and following the second coming of Christ (chaps. 4–22).

The chronological division of the Book of Revelation is much superior to many other outlines in which interpreters often seize on incidental phrases or manipulate the book to fit their peculiar schemes of interpretation. This outline harmonizes beautifully with the concept that most of Revelation (beginning in chap. 4) is future, not historic or merely symbolic, or simply statements of principles. It is significant that only a futuristic interpretation of Revelation 4–22 has any consistency. Interpreters following the allegorical approach to the book seldom agree among themselves on their views. This is also true of those holding to the symbolic and historical approaches.

In Revelation a symbol of vision is often presented first, and then its interpretation is given. So here **the seven stars** were declared to be **the angels** or messengers **of the seven churches, and the seven lampstands are the seven churches** themselves. The Book of Revelation, instead of being a hopeless jumble of symbolic vision, is a carefully written record of what John saw and heard, with frequent explanations of its theological and practical meanings.

Revelation, with assistance from such other symbolic books as Daniel and Ezekiel, was intended by God to be understood by careful students of the entire Word of God. Like the Book of Daniel, it will be better understood as history unfolds. Though timeless in its truth and application, it is a special comfort to those who need guidance in the days leading up to Christ's second coming.

Before unfolding the tremendous prophetic scenes of chapters 4–22, Christ first gave a personal message to each of the seven churches with obvious practical applications to His church today.

REVELATION

LOCATIONS OF THE SEVEN CHURCHES

II. Letters to the Seven Churches: "What Is Now" (chaps. 2–3)

As stated in Revelation 1:11 Christ sent a message to each of seven local churches in Asia Minor. The order of scriptural presentation was geographic. A messenger would naturally travel the route from the seaport Ephesus 35 miles north to another seaport Smyrna, proceed still farther north and to the east, to Pergamos, and then would swing further to the east and south to visit the other four cities (1:11).

There has been much debate as to the meaning of these messages for today. Obviously these churches were specially selected and providentially arranged to provide characteristic situations which the church has faced throughout its history. Just as Paul's epistles, though addressed to individual churches, are also intended for the entire church, so these seven messages also apply to the entire church today insofar as they are in similar situations. There were many other churches such as those at Colosse, Magnesia, and Tralles, some larger than the seven churches mentioned in Asia Minor, but these were not addressed.

As the contents of the letters are analyzed, it is clear that they are, first, messages to these historic local churches in the first century. Second, they also constitute a message to similar churches today. Third, individual exhortations to persons or groups in the churches make it clear that the messages are intended for individuals today. Fourth, some believe that the order of the seven churches follows the order of various eras in church history from the first century until now.

There are some remarkable similarities in comparing these letters to the seven churches to the movement of church history since the beginning of the apostolic church. For instance, Ephesus seems to characterize the apostolic church as a whole, and Smyrna seems to depict the church in its early persecutions. However, the Scriptures do not expressly authorize this interpretation, and it should be applied only where it fits naturally. After all, these churches all existed simultaneously in the first century.

Though each message is different, the letters have some similarities. In each one Christ declared that He knows their works; each one includes a promise to those who overcome; each one gives an exhortation to those hearing; and each letter has a particular description of Christ that related to the message which follows. Each letter includes a commendation (except the letter to Laodicea), a rebuke (except the letters to Smyrna and Philadelphia), an exhortation, and an encouraging promise to those heeding its message. In general these letters to the seven churches address the problems inherent in churches throughout church history and are an incisive and comprehensive revelation of how Christ evaluates local churches.

This portion of Scripture has been strangely neglected. While many turn to the epistles of Paul and other portions of the New Testament for church truth, often the letters to these seven churches, though coming from Christ Himself and being climactic in character, are completely ignored. This neglect has contributed to churches today not conforming to God's perfect will.

A. The letter to the church in Ephesus (2:1-7)

1. DESTINATION (2:1)

2:1. At the time this letter was written, **Ephesus** was a major city of Asia Minor, a seaport, and the location of the great temple of Artemis (cf. Acts 19:24, 27-28, 34-35), one of the seven wonders of the ancient world. Paul had visited Ephesus about A.D. 53, about 43 years before this letter in Revelation was sent to them. Paul remained in Ephesus for several years and preached the gospel so effectively "that all the Jews and Greeks who lived in the province of Asia heard the word of the Lord" (Acts 19:10). This large city was thoroughly stirred by Paul's message (Acts 19:11-41), with the result that the silversmiths created a riot because their business of making shrines of Artemis was threatened.

The church accordingly had a long history and was the most prominent one in the area. The pastor or messenger of the church was addressed as **the angel** (*angelos*). The word's principal use in the Bible is in reference to heavenly angels (William F. Arndt and F. Wilbur Gingrich, *A Greek-English Lexicon of the New Testament*. Chicago: University of Chicago Press, 1957, pp. 7-8). But it is also used to refer to human messengers (cf. Matt. 11:10; Mark 1:2; Luke 7:24, 27; 9:52).

Christ was holding **seven stars in His right hand** and walking **among the seven golden lampstands.** The "stars" were the angels or messengers of the churches and the "lampstands" were the seven churches (1:20).

2. COMMENDATION (2:2-3)

2:2-3. Christ commended those in the Ephesian church for their **hard work . . . perseverance,** their condemnation of **wicked men,** and their identification of **false** apostles. (False teachers were present in each of the first four churches; cf. vv. 2, 6, 9, 14-15, 20.) In addition they were commended for enduring **hardships** and **not** growing **weary** in serving God. In general this church had continued in its faithful service to God for more than 40 years.

3. REBUKE (2:4)

2:4. In spite of the many areas of commendation, the church in Ephesus was soundly rebuked: **Yet I hold this against you: you have forsaken your first love.** The order of words in the Greek is emphatic; the clause could be translated, "Your first love you have left." Christ used the word *agapēn*, speaking of the deep kind of love that God has for people. This rebuke contrasts with what Paul wrote the Ephesians 35 years earlier, that he never stopped giving thanks for them because of their faith in Christ and their love (*agapēn*) for the saints (Eph. 1:15-16). Most of the Ephesian Christians were now second-generation believers, and though they had retained purity of doctrine and life and had maintained a high level of service, they were lacking in deep devotion to Christ. How the church today needs to heed this same warning, that orthodoxy and service are not enough. Christ wants believers' hearts as well as their hands and heads.

4. EXHORTATION (2:5-6)

2:5-6. The Ephesians were first reminded to **remember the height from which you have fallen!** They were told to **repent** and to return to the love they had left. Similar exhortations concerning the need for a deep love for God are frequently found in the New Testament (Matt. 22:37; Mark 12:30; Luke 10:27; John 14:15, 21, 23; 21:15-16; James 2:5; 1 Peter 1:8). Christ stated that one's love for God should be greater than his love for his closest relatives, including his father, mother, son, and daughter (Matt. 10:37). Paul added that love for God should even be above one's love for his or her mate (1 Cor. 7:32-35). In calling the Ephesian believers to repentance Christ was asking them to change their attitude as well as their affections. They were to continue their service not simply because it was right but because they loved Christ. He warned them that if they did not respond, the light of their witness in Ephesus would be extinguished: **I will ... remove your lampstand from its place.** The church continued and was later the scene of a major church council, but after the 5th century both the church and the city declined. The immediate area has been uninhabited since the 14th century.

One additional word of commendation was inserted. They were commended because they hated **the practices of the Nicolaitans.** There has been much speculation concerning the identity of the Nicolaitans, but the Scriptures do not specify who they were. They apparently were a sect wrong in practice and in doctrine (for further information see Henry Alford, *The Greek Testament,* 4: 563-65; Merrill C. Tenney, *Interpreting Revelation,* pp. 60-1; Walvoord, *Revelation,* p. 58).

5. PROMISE (2:7)

2:7. As in the other letters, Christ gave the Ephesian church a promise addressed to individuals who will hear. He stated, **To him who overcomes, I will give the right to eat from the tree of life, which is in the paradise of God.** The tree of life, first mentioned in Genesis 3:22, was in the Garden of Eden. Later it reappears in the New Jerusalem where it bears abundant fruit (Rev. 22:2). Those who eat of it will never die (Gen. 3:22). This promise should not be construed as reward for only a special group of Christians but a normal expectation for all Christians. "The paradise of God" is probably a name for heaven (cf. Luke 23:43; 2 Cor. 12:4—the only other NT references to paradise). Apparently it will be identified with the New Jerusalem in the eternal state.

This encouragement to true love reminded them again of God's gracious provision for salvation in time and eternity. Love for God is not wrought by legalistically observing commands, but by responding to one's knowledge and appreciation of God's love.

B. *The letter to the church in Smyrna (2:8-11)*

1. DESTINATION (2:8)

2:8. The second letter was addressed to **Smyrna,** a large and wealthy city 35 miles north of Ephesus. Like Ephesus, it was a seaport. In contrast to Ephesus, which today is a deserted ruin, Smyrna is still a large seaport with a present population of about 200,000. Christ described Himself as **the First and the Last, who died and came to life again.** Christ is portrayed as the eternal One (cf. 1:8, 17; 21:6; 22:13) who suffered death at the hands of His persecutors and then was resurrected from the grave (cf. 1:5). These aspects of Christ were especially relevant to the Christians at Smyrna who, like Christ in His death, were experiencing severe persecution.

The name of the city, Smyrna, means "myrrh," an ordinary perfume. It was also used in the anointing oil of the tabernacle, and in embalming dead bodies (cf. Ex. 30:23; Ps. 45:8; Song 3:6; Matt. 2:11; Mark 15:23; John 19:39). While the Christians of the church at Smyrna were experiencing the bitterness of suffering, their faithful testimony was like myrrh or sweet perfume to God.

2. COMMENDATION (2:9)

2:9. What a comfort it was to the Christians in Smyrna to know that Christ knew all about their sufferings: **I know your afflictions and your poverty—yet you are rich!** Besides suffering persecution, they were also enduring extreme poverty (*ptōcheian* in contrast with *penia*, the ordinary word for "poverty"). Though extremely poor, they were rich in the wonderful promises Christ had given them (cf. 2 Cor. 6:10; James 2:5). They were being persecuted not only by pagan Gentiles but also by hostile Jews and by Satan himself. Apparently the local Jewish synagogue was called the **synagogue of Satan** (cf. Rev. 3:9). (Satan is mentioned in four of the seven letters: 2:9, 13, 24; 3:9.) In the history of the church the most severe persecution has come from religionists.

3. REBUKE

Notable is the fact that there was no rebuke whatever for these faithful, suffering Christians. This is in striking contrast with Christ's evaluations of five of the other six churches, which He rebuked. Smyrna's sufferings, though extremely difficult, had helped keep them pure in faith and life.

4. EXHORTATION (2:10A)

2:10a. The word of Christ to these suffering Christians was an exhortation to have courage: **Do not be afraid** (lit., stop being afraid) **of what you are about to suffer.** Their severe trials were to continue. They would receive further **persecution** by imprisonment and additional suffering **for 10 days.** Some have taken these words "for 10 days" as a symbolic representation of the entire persecution of the church; others think it refers to 10 persecutions under Roman rulers. The most probable meaning is that it anticipated a limited period of time for suffering (cf. Walvoord, *Revelation*, pp. 61-2). Scott finds precedence in Scripture that 10 days means a limited period of time (Walter Scott, *Exposition of the Revelation of Jesus Christ*, p. 69). He cites Genesis 24:55; Nehemiah 5:18; Jeremiah 42:7; Daniel 1:12; Acts 25:6. Alford holds the same position, citing Numbers 11:19; 14:22; 1 Samuel 1:8; Job 19:3 (*The Greek Testament*, 4:567).

The problem of human suffering, even for a limited time, has always perplexed faithful Christians. Suffering can be expected for the ungodly, but why should the godly suffer? The Scriptures give a number of reasons. Suffering may be (1) disciplinary (1 Cor. 11:30-32; Heb. 12:3-13), (2) preventive (as Paul's thorn in the flesh, 2 Cor. 12:7), (3) the learning of obedience (as Christ's suffering, Heb. 5:8; cf. Rom. 5:3-5), or (4) the providing of a better testimony for Christ (as in Acts 9:16).

5. PROMISE (2:10B-11)

2:10b-11. In their suffering the believers at Smyrna were exhorted, **Be faithful, even to the point of death.** While their persecutors could take their physical lives, it would only result in their receiving **the crown of life.** Apparently up to this time none had died, but this could be expected. Later Polycarp, having become the bishop of the church in Smyrna, was martyred, and undoubtedly others were also killed (cf. Robert Jamieson, A. R. Fausset, and David Brown, *A Commentary Critical, Experimental and Practical on the Old and New Testaments*. Grand Rapids: Wm. B. Eerdmans Publishing Co., 1945. 6:662). "The crown of life" is one of several crowns promised to Christians (cf. 1 Cor. 9:25; 1 Thes. 2:19; 2 Tim. 4:6-8; 1 Peter 5:4; Rev. 4:4). The crown of life is also mentioned in James 1:12. Believers are encouraged to be faithful by contemplating what awaits them after death, namely, eternal life.

As in all the letters, an exhortation is given to the individuals who will listen. The promise is given to overcomers, referring in general to all believers, assuring them that they **will not be hurt at all by the second death** (cf. Rev. 20:15).

The reassuring word of Christ to Smyrna is the word to all suffering and persecuted Christians. As stated in Hebrews 12:11, "No discipline seems pleasant at the time, but painful. Later on, however, it produces a harvest of righteousness and peace for those who have been trained by it."

C. *The letter to the church in Pergamum (2:12-17)*

1. DESTINATION (2:12)

2:12. The third church was in **Pergamum** or Pergamos, about 20 miles inland from Smyrna. Like Ephesus and Smyrna it was a wealthy city, but it was wicked.

REVELATION

People in its pagan cults worshiped Athena, Asclepius, Dionysus, and Zeus. Pergamum was famous for its university with a library of about 200,000 volumes, and for manufacturing parchment resulting in a paper called *pergamena*. The atmosphere of this city was adverse to any effective Christian life and testimony.

Anticipating Christ's rebuke for their being tolerant of evil and immorality, John described **Him** as the One **who has the sharp, double-edged sword** (also mentioned in 1:16; 2:16; 19:15, 21). The sword is a symbolic representation of the Word of God's twofold ability to separate believers from the world and to condemn the world for its sin. It was the sword of salvation as well as the sword of death.

2. COMMENDATION (2:13)

2:13. Following the same order as in the two preceding letters, commendation is given first. Christ recognized the difficulty of their situation. They lived **where Satan has his throne.** This may refer to the great temple of Asclepius, a pagan god of healing represented in the form of a serpent. Further recognition of Satan is indicated at the close of the verse. Pergamum was **where Satan lives.** The saints there were commended for being true, **even** when **Antipas** (which means "against all") was martyred. Nothing is known of this incident. The Christians at Pergamum had been true to God under severe testing but had compromised their testimony in other ways, as seen in the next two verses.

3. REBUKE (2:14-15)

2:14-15. They had been guilty of severe compromise by holding **the teaching of Balaam** and **the teaching of the Nicolaitans.** Balaam had been guilty of counseling King **Balak** to cause Israel **to sin** through intermarriage with heathen women and through idol-worship (cf. Num. 22-25; 31:15-16). Intermarriage with heathen women was a problem in Pergamum where any social contact with the world also involved worship of idols. Usually meat in the marketplace had been offered to idols earlier (cf. 1 Cor. 8).

They were also condemned for following the Nicolaitans' teaching. Earlier the Ephesian church had been commended for rejecting what appears to be a moral departure (cf. Rev. 2:6). Some Greek manuscripts add here that God hates the teaching of the Nicolaitans, as also stated in v. 6. Compromise with worldly morality and pagan doctrine was prevalent in the church, especially in the third century when Christianity became popular. So compromise with pagan morality and departure from biblical faith soon corrupted the church.

4. EXHORTATION (2:16)

2:16. Christ sharply rebuked the church with the abrupt command, **Repent therefore!** They were warned, **Otherwise, I will soon come to you and will fight against them with the sword of My mouth.** He promised that the judgment would come "soon" (*tachys*) which also means "suddenly" (cf. 1:1; 22:7, 12, 20). Christ would contend with them, using the sword of His mouth (cf. 1:16; 2:12; 19:15, 21). This again is the Word of God sharply judging all compromise and sin.

5. PROMISE (2:17)

2:17. The final exhortation to individuals, as in the messages to other churches, is again addressed to those who are willing to **hear.** Overcomers are promised **hidden manna** and **a white stone with a new name written on it.** The "hidden manna" may refer to Christ as the Bread from heaven, the unseen source of the believer's nourishment and strength. Whereas Israel received physical food, manna, the church receives spiritual food (John 6:48-51).

Scholars differ as to the meaning of the "white stone." Alford is probably right in saying that the important point is the stone's inscription which gives the believer "a new name," indicating acceptance by God and his title to glory (*The Greek Testament,* 4:572). This may be an allusion to the Old Testament practice of the high priest wearing 12 stones on his breastplate with the names of the 12 tribes of Israel inscribed on it. Though believers at Pergamum may not have had precious stones or gems of this world, they had what is far more important, acceptance by Christ Himself and assurance of infinite blessings to come. Taken as a whole, the message to the church in Pergamum is a warning against compromise in morals or teaching and against deviating from the purity of doctrine required of Christians.

D. The letter to the church in Thyatira (2:18-29)

1. DESTINATION (2:18)

2:18. Thyatira, 40 miles southeast of Pergamum, was a much smaller city. Thyatira was situated in an area noted for its abundant crops and the manufacture of purple dye. The church was small, but it was singled out for this penetrating letter of rebuke.

In keeping with what follows, Christ is introduced as **the Son of God, whose eyes are like blazing fire and whose feet are like burnished bronze.** This description of Christ is similar to that in 1:13-15, but here He is called the Son of God rather than the Son of Man. The situation required reaffirmation of His deity and His righteous indignation at their sins. The words "burnished bronze," which describe His feet, translate a rare Greek word *chalkolibanō*, also used in 1:15. It seems to have been an alloy of a number of metals characterized by brilliance when polished. The reference to His eyes being "like blazing fire" and the brilliant reflections of His feet emphasize the indignation and righteous judgment of Christ.

2. COMMENDATION (2:19)

2:19. Though much was wrong in the church at Thyatira, believers there were commended for their **love ... faith ... service, and perseverance** (cf. 2:2). And the Thyatira Christians were doing **more** as time went on (in contrast to the Ephesus church which did less). But despite these evidences of Christian life and testimony, the church at Thyatira had serious problems.

3. REBUKE (2:20-23)

2:20-23. Jesus' major condemnation concerned **that woman Jezebel,** who claimed to be **a prophetess** and taught believers to take part in the **sexual immorality** that accompanied pagan religion and to eat **food sacrificed to idols.** What was acceptable to that local society was abhorred by Christ. Their departure from morality had gone on for some time (v. 21). The church in Thyatira may have first heard the gospel from Lydia, converted through Paul's ministry (Acts 16:14-15). Interestingly now a woman, a self-claimed "prophetess," was influencing the church. Her name "Jezebel" suggests that she was corrupting the Thyatira church much like Ahab's wife Jezebel corrupted Israel (1 Kings 16:31-33). Christ promised sudden and immediate judgment, called her sin **adultery** and promised that all who followed her would **suffer intensely.** He also promised, **I will strike her children dead,** meaning that suffering would extend also to her followers. The judgment would be so dramatic that **all the churches** would **know that** Christ is the One **who searches hearts and minds.**

4. EXHORTATION (2:24-25)

2:24-25. After His condemnation, Christ extended a word of exhortation to the godly remnant who existed in the church in Thyatira, implying that the rest of the church was apostate. The remnant He called **the rest of you in Thyatira ... you who do not hold to her teaching and have not learned Satan's so-called deep secrets.** On this godly remnant He imposed one simple instruction: **only hold on to what you have until I come.** Perhaps because the church was small, Christ did not command them to leave it but to remain as a godly testimony. Judgment on Jezebel and her followers would come soon and would purge the church. In modern times Christians who find themselves in apostate local churches can usually leave and join another fellowship, but this was impractical under the circumstances in Thyatira.

The parallels between Thyatira and other apostate churches throughout church history are clear. Some compare Thyatira to believers in the Middle Ages when Protestantism separated from Roman Catholicism and attempted a return to purity in doctrine and life. The prominence of Jezebel as a woman prophetess is sometimes compared to the unscriptural exaltation of Mary. The participation in idolatrous feasts can illustrate the false teaching that the Lord's Supper is another sacrifice of Christ. In spite of the apostasy of churches in the Middle Ages, there were churches then which, like the church of Thyatira, had some believers who were bright lights of faithfulness in doctrine and life.

REVELATION

5. PROMISE (2:26-29)

2:26-27. Christ promises believers who are faithful that they will join Him in His millennial **rule** (Ps. 2:8-9; 2 Tim. 2:12; Rev. 20:4-6). The word in verse 27 translated "rule" (*poimanei*) means "to shepherd," indicating that they will not simply be administering justice but will also, like a shepherd using his rod, be dealing with his sheep and protecting them as well. Though Psalm 2:9 refers to Christ's rule, John's quotation of it here relates the ruling (shepherding) to the believer who overcomes. Believers will have authority just as Christ does (1 Cor. 6:2-3; 2 Tim. 2:12; Rev. 3:21; 20:4, 6). Christ **received** this **authority from** His **Father** (cf. John 5:22).

2:28. In addition, the faithful will receive **the morning star,** which appears just before the dawn. The Scriptures do not explain this expression, but it may refer to participation in the Rapture of the church before the dark hours preceding the dawn of the millennial kingdom.

2:29. The letter to Thyatira closes with the familiar exhortation to **hear what the Spirit says to the churches.** Unlike the earlier letters, this exhortation follows rather than precedes the promise to overcomers, and this order is followed in the letters to the last three churches.

E. The letter to the church in Sardis (3:1-6)

1. DESTINATION (3:1A)

3:1a. The important commercial city of **Sardis** was located about 30 miles southeast of Thyatira, on an important trade route that ran east and west through the kingdom of Lydia. Important industries included jewelry, dye, and textiles, which had made the city wealthy. From a religious standpoint it was a center of pagan worship and site of a temple of Artemis, which ruins still remain (cf. comments on 2:1 regarding another temple of Artemis). Only a small village called Sart remains on the site of this once-important city. Archeologists have located the ruins of a Christian church building next to the temple. In addressing the message to the church Christ described Himself as the One **who holds the seven spirits of God and the seven stars,** similar to the description in 1:4. Here Christ said He holds them, speaking of the Holy Spirit in relation to Himself (Isa. 11:2-5; cf. Rev. 5:6). As in 1:20 the seven stars, representing the pastors of the churches, were also in His hands (cf. 2:1).

2. COMMENDATION (3:1B)

3:1b. The only word of approval is in actuality a word of rebuke as Christ declared that they had **a reputation** for **being alive** and apparently were regarded by their contemporaries as an effective church.

3. REBUKE (3:1C, 2B)

3:1c, 2b. Christ quickly stripped away their reputation of being alive by declaring, **you are dead.** Like the Pharisees, their outer appearance was a facade hiding their lack of life (cf. Matt. 23:27-28). Christ added, **I have not found your deeds complete in the sight of My God.** They were falling far short of fulfilling their obligations as believers.

4. EXHORTATION (3:2A, 3)

3:2a, 3. They were exhorted to **wake up** from their spiritual slumber and to **strengthen** the few evidences of life they still had. He exhorted them to **remember ... obey ... and repent.** He warned them that if they did not heed this exhortation, He would **come** on them **like a thief,** that is, suddenly and unexpectedly.

5. PROMISE (3:4-6)

3:4-6. While this church as a whole was dead or dying, Christ recognized a godly remnant **in the Sardis** church who had **not soiled their clothes** with sin. He promised that true believers will **be dressed in white** (cf. v. 18), symbolic of the righteousness of God, that their names will remain in **the book of life,** and that He will acknowledge them as His own **before** His **Father and His angels.**

The statement that their names will not be erased from the book of life presents a problem to some. But a person who is truly born again remains regenerate, as John said elsewhere (John 5:24; 6:35-37, 39; 10:28-29). While this passage may imply that a name could be erased from the book of life, actually it only gives a positive affirmation that their names will not be erased (cf. Walvoord,

Revelation. pp. 82, 338). Six times John referred to the book of life (Rev. 3:5; 13:8 [cf. comments there]; 17:8; 20:12, 15; 21:27).

The letter also concludes with the exhortation to **hear what the Spirit says to the churches.** The letter to Sardis is a searching message to churches today that are full of activity and housed in beautiful buildings but are so often lacking in evidences of eternal life. Christ's word today is to "remember," "repent," and "obey," just as it was to the church in Sardis.

F. *The letter to the church in Philadelphia (3:7-13)*

1. DESTINATION (3:7)

3:7. The city of **Philadelphia** was 28 miles southeast of Sardis. It was located in an area noted for its agricultural products but afflicted with earthquakes which destroyed the city several times, most recently about A.D. 37. The city was named for a king of Pergamum, Attalus Philadelphus, who had built it. "Philadelphus" is similar to the Greek word *philadelphia,* meaning "brotherly love," which occurs seven times in the Bible (Rom. 12:10; 1 Thes. 4:9; Heb. 13:1; 1 Peter 1:22; 2 Peter 1:7[twice]; Rev. 3:7). Only here is it used of the city itself. Christian testimony continues in the city in this present century.

Christ described Himself as the One **who is holy and true, who holds the key of David,** and who is able to open or shut a door which no one else could open or shut. The holiness of Christ is a frequent truth in Scripture (1 Peter 1:15), and being holy He is worthy to judge the spiritual life of the Philadelphia church. "The key of David" seems to refer to Isaiah 22:22, where the key of the house of David was given to Eliakim who then had access to all the wealth of the king. Christ earlier had been described as the One who holds "the keys of death and hades" (Rev. 1:18). The reference here, however, seems to be to spiritual treasures.

2. COMMENDATION (3:8-9)

3:8. As in the messages to the other churches, Christ stated, **I know your deeds.** In keeping with the description of His authority to open and close doors (v. 7), He declared, **See, I have placed before you an open door that no one can shut.** There is no word of rebuke, though Christ said, **I know that you have little strength.** These words, however, become a basis for His commendation that **you have kept My word and have not denied My name.**

3:9. Christ referred to their enemies as the **synagogue of Satan** (cf. 2:9). They were Jews who opposed the believers' Christian testimony. False religion has always been a formidable antagonist against true Christian faith. The day will come, however, when all opponents of the faith will have to acknowledge the truth (cf. Isa. 45:23; Rom. 14:11; Phil. 2:10-11). Then Christ declared, **I will make them come and fall down at your feet and acknowledge that I have loved you.**

3. PROMISE (3:10-12)

3:10. The church in Philadelphia received no rebuke from Christ. Instead they were commended and given a promise because they had been willing to **endure patiently.** The promise was, **I will also keep you from the hour of trial that is going to come upon the whole world to test those who live on the earth.** This is an explicit promise that the Philadelphia church will not endure the hour of trial which is unfolded, beginning in Revelation 6. Christ was saying that the Philadelphia church would not enter the future time of trouble; He could not have stated it more explicitly. If Christ had meant to say that they would be preserved *through* a time of trouble, or would be *taken out* from within the Tribulation, a different verb and a different preposition would have been required.

Though scholars have attempted to avoid this conclusion in order to affirm posttribulationism, the combination of the verb "keep" (*tērein*) with the preposition "from" (*ek*) is in sharp contrast to the meaning of keeping the church "through" (*dia*), a preposition which is not used here. The expression "the hour of trial" (a time period) makes it clear that they would be kept *out of* that period. It is difficult to see how Christ could have made this promise to this local church if it were God's intention for the entire church to go through the Tribulation that will come on the entire world. Even though the church at Philadelphia would go to glory via death long before the time of trouble would come, if the church here is taken to be typical of the body of Christ standing true to the faith, the promise seems to go beyond the Philadelphia church to all those who are believers in Christ (cf. Walvoord, *Revelation*, pp. 86-8).

3:11. Additional promises were given. Christ promised, **I am coming soon,** a concept repeated often in the Book of Revelation. The thought is not simply that of coming soon but coming suddenly or quickly (cf. 1:1; 2:16). They were exhorted in the light of His coming to continue to **hold on to what** they have.

3:12. Everyone who is an overcomer will become **a pillar in the temple of ... God.** This is of course symbolic of the permanent place in heaven for believers, referred to here as the temple of God. The entire New Jerusalem will be the ultimate temple (21:22). In contrast to earthly temples and earthly pillars which fall, believers will continue forever in the temple. Christ specified that He was referring to **the city of My God,** that is, the New Jerusalem (cf. 21:2). He repeated His promise: **I will also write on him My new name** (cf. 2:17; 14:1; 19:12). Because believers have identified with Christ by faith, He will identify Himself with them.

4. EXHORTATION (3:13)

3:13. The letter closed with the familiar appeal, **hear what the Spirit says to the churches.** The promise given to the Philadelphia church and the challenge to continue to be faithful is certainly God's Word to His whole church today.

G. The letter to the church in Laodicea (3:14-22)

1. DESTINATION (3:14)

3:14. The wealthy city of **Laodicea** was located on the road to Colosse about 40 miles southeast of Philadelphia. About 35 years before this letter was written, Laodicea was destroyed by an earthquake, but it had the wealth and ability to rebuild. Its main industry was wool cloth. There is no record that Paul ever visited this city, but he was concerned about it (Col. 2:1-2; 4:16).

In addressing the church Christ introduced Himself as **the Amen, the faithful and true Witness, the Ruler of God's creation.** The word "Amen," meaning "so be it," refers to the sovereignty of God which is behind human events (cf. 2 Cor. 1:20; Rev. 1:6). In speaking of Himself as "the faithful and true Witness" Christ was repeating what He had said earlier (1:5; 3:7). As "the Ruler of God's creation" Christ existed before God's Creation and is sovereign over it (cf. Col 1:15, 18; Rev. 21:6). This description was in preparation for the stern word of rebuke which Christ would give the church in Laodicea.

2. REBUKE (3:15-17)

3:15-16. No word of commendation was extended to the Laodicean church. They were pictured as utterly abhorrent to Christ because they were **lukewarm.** This was addressed to the church and also to the messenger or the pastor whom some believe was Archippus (Col. 4:17). It is improbable, however, that Archippus, if he had been the pastor of the church, was still living. In referring to the church as "lukewarm" Christ had in mind that this was its permanent situation. In their feasts as well as in their religious sacrifices people in the ancient world customarily drank what was either hot or cold—never lukewarm. This rebuke would have been especially meaningful to this church, for water was piped to the city from Hierapolis, a few miles north. By the time the water reached Laodicea, it was lukewarm!

3:17. Their being lukewarm spiritually was evidenced by their being content with their material **wealth** and their being unaware of their spiritual poverty. Christ used strong words to describe them: **wretched, pitiful, poor, blind, and naked.**

3. EXHORTATION (3:18-19)

3:18-19. They were urged to buy not ordinary gold, but **refined** gold, referring to that which would glorify God and make them truly rich. Through its banking industry the city had material wealth. But the church lacked spiritual richness. Though they had beautiful clothes, they were urged to wear **white clothes** (cf. v. 4), symbolic of righteousness which would cover their spiritual **nakedness.** As wool was a major product of the area, Laodicea was especially

THE LETTERS TO THE SEVEN CHURCHES

	Christ	Commendation	Rebuke	Exhortation	Promise
Ephesus (2:1–7)	Holds the seven stars in His right hand and walks among the seven golden lampstands.	Deeds, hard work, perseverance. Does not tolerate wicked men. Endures hardships. Hates the practices of the Nicolaitans.	Has forsaken her first love.	Remember; repent; do the things you did at first.	Will eat from the tree of life.
Smyrna (2:8–11)	The First and the Last, who died and came to life again.	Suffers persecution and poverty.	—	Do not be afraid. Be faithful, even to the point of death.	Will receive a crown of life; will not be hurt by the second death.
Pergamum (2:12–17)	Has the sharp, double-edged sword.	Remains true to Christ; does not renounce her faith.	People there hold the teachings of Balaam and of the Nicolaitans.	Repent.	Will receive hidden manna and a white stone with a new name on it.
Thyatira (2:18–29)	The Son of God, whose eyes are like blazing fire and whose feet are like burnished brass.	Deeds, love, faith, service, perseverance, doing more than at first.	Tolerates Jezebel with her immorality and idolatry.	Repent; hold on to what you have.	Will have authority over the nations; the morning star.
Sardis (3:1–6)	Holds the seven spirits of God and the seven stars.	Deeds; reputation of being alive.	Dead.	Wake up! Strengthen what remains. Remember what you received, obey it, repent.	Will be dressed in white; will be acknowledged before My Father and His angels.
Philadelphia (3:7–13)	Holy and true, holds the key of David.	Deeds, keeps Christ's word and does not deny His name, endures patiently.	—	Hold on to what you have.	Those who overcome will be pillars in the temple; the name of God, of the New Jerusalem, and of Christ's new name, will be written on them.
Laodicea (3:14–22)	The Amen, the faithful and true Witness, the Ruler of God's creation.	—	Lukewarm, neither cold nor hot. Wretched, pitiful, poor, blind, and naked.	Buy from Christ refined gold, white clothes, and eye salve. Be earnest, and repent.	Overcomers will eat with Christ; will rule with Christ.

famous for a black garment made out of black wool. What they needed instead was pure white clothing.

Then Christ exhorted them to put **salve . . . on** their **eyes.** A medical school was located in Laodicea at the temple of Asclepius, which offered a special salve to heal common eye troubles of the Middle East. What they needed was not this medicine but spiritual sight. The church at Laodicea is typical of a modern church quite unconscious of its spiritual needs and content with beautiful buildings and all the material things money can buy. This is a searching and penetrating message. To all such the exhortation is **be earnest, and repent.** Christ rebuked them because He loved them, which love would also bring chastisement on this church.

4. PROMISE (3:20-22)

3:20-21. Dramatically Christ pictured Himself as standing outside and knocking on a **door.** In a familiar painting the latch is not shown but is assumed to be on the inside. The appeal is for those who hear to open the door. To them Christ promised, **I will go in and eat with him, and he with Me.** With Christ on the outside, there can be no fellowship or genuine wealth. With Christ on the inside, there is wonderful fellowship and sharing of the marvelous grace of God. This was an appeal to Christians rather than to non-Christians. This raises the important question concerning the extent of one's intimate fellowship with Christ. To those who respond, Christ promises to give the right to **sit with** Him **on** His **throne** and share His victory.

3:22. Once again the invitation to listen and respond is given: **He who has an ear, let him hear what the Spirit says to the churches.**

The letters to the seven churches are a remarkably complete treatment of problems that face the church today. The recurring dangers of losing their first love (2:4), of being afraid of suffering (2:10), doctrinal defection (2:14-15), moral departure (2:20), spiritual deadness (3:1-2), not holding fast (v. 11), and lukewarmness (vv. 15-16) are just as prevalent today as they were in first-century churches. Because these letters come from Christ personally, they take on significance as God's final word of exhortation to the church down through the centuries. The final appeal is to all individuals who will hear. People in churches today would do well to listen.

III. The Revelation of the Future: "What Will Take Place Later" (chaps. 4-22)

In keeping with the divine outline given in 1:19, God unfolded to John the details of the future, "what will take place later." This includes the stirring events leading up to the second coming of Christ (chaps. 4-18); then the Second Coming itself (chap. 19); then the aftermath, the millennial kingdom (chap. 20); and finally the New Jerusalem and the new heaven and new earth (chaps. 21-22). It is obvious that the central truth is the second coming of Christ in chapter 19, just as the central feature of the four Gospels was the first coming of Christ.

While many interpretations of the Book of Revelation have been suggested, the only views which provide a cogent understanding are those which consider the book, beginning with chapter 4, as referring to future events. Any other system of interpretation gets lost in a maze of conflicting opinions.

While the events portrayed in this futuristic section are not necessarily all in strict chronological order, they are all yet future. As such, they present a more graphic picture of the future, given in more detail, than is found in any other part of the Bible. Such a revelation is a fitting climax to all the biblical prophecies relating to human history, which are properly centered in the person and work of Jesus Christ.

The revelation of the future opens with a vision of heaven (chaps. 4-5). Beginning in chapter 6 the seven seals, as they are broken, constitute the main chronological movement of the Great Tribulation, leading up to the second coming of Christ. The seven trumpets give the details of events which will follow the breaking of the seventh seal. Likewise in chapter 16 the seven bowls of the wrath of God unfold the content of the seventh trumpet.

The order is climactic, and as the period approaches the second coming of Christ, events occur with increasing rapidity and greater devastation. Once Christ's second coming is revealed, the concluding chapters briefly summarize the wide expanse of future events—chapter 20 relating to the millennial kingdom, and chapters 21–22 describing the new heaven and the new earth.

It is obvious that the main purpose of the Book of Revelation is to present the second coming of Christ and accompanying events and to alert the people of God as well as the world as a whole to the importance of being prepared for God's coming judgment.

A. The vision of the heavenly throne (chap. 4)

1. THE INVITATION (4:1)

4:1. John saw the vision of the heavenly throne after he heard the revelation of the messages to the churches. The time sequence is indicated by the expression **after this** (*meta tauta*, in the NASB, "after these things").

John saw **a door ... open in heaven** and heard a **voice** inviting him, **Come up here, and I will show you what must take place after this.** The words "what must take place after this" are similar to those in 1:19, "what will take place later." Whereas 1:19 indicates that the events *will* take place later, in 4:1b the Greek word *dei* is used, which means that the events *must* occur. This points not only to the future but also to the sovereign purpose of God. The similarity of the two expressions confirms the threefold chronological outline given in 1:19. Both the revelation and its fulfillment are chronologically subsequent to chapters 1–3.

2. THE HEAVENLY THRONE (4:2-3)

4:2-3. John stated that immediately he **was in the Spirit** (or "in [my] spirit"; cf. 1:10; 17:3) meaning that experientially he was taken up to heaven though his body was actually still on the island of Patmos. **In heaven** he saw a great **throne** with One **sitting on it** who **had the appearance of jasper and carnelian.** This jasper (cf. 21:18) is a clear stone in contrast to the opaque jasper stones known today; it may have resembled a diamond. The carnelian, also known as ruby (the NIV trans. it "ruby" in the OT), and sardius, were a ruby-red color. The jasper and the carnelian were the first and last of the 12 gemstones worn on the high priest's breast (cf. Ex. 28:17-21). Jasper and sardius were used in relation to the king of Tyre (Ezek. 28:13) and will be in the foundation of the New Jerusalem (Rev. 21:19-20). The throne's overall appearance was one of great beauty and color, enhanced by **a rainbow, resembling an emerald,** which **encircled the throne.** The green color of the emerald added further beauty to the scene.

3. THE 24 ELDERS (4:4)

4:4. Around the principal **throne** were **24** lesser **thrones** on which were **seated ... 24 elders. They were dressed in white** and were wearing **crowns of gold on their heads.** The crowns were similar to those given victors in Greek games (*stephanos*), in contrast with the crown of a sovereign ruler (*diadēma*, "diadem"). The crowns seem to indicate that the elders had been judged and rewarded.

There has been much speculation on the identity of the elders. The two major views are (1) that they represent the church raptured prior to this time and rewarded in heaven, or (2) that they are angels who have been given large responsibilities. The number 24 is the number of representation, illustrated in the fact that in the Law of Moses there were 24 orders of the priesthood. (For further discussion of the identity of the 24 elders see the comments on 5:8-10.)

4. THE SEVEN SPIRITS OF GOD (4:5)

4:5. The impressive scene of heaven was enhanced by **flashes of lightning, rumblings, and peals of thunder.** Thunder is mentioned eight times in Revelation (4:5; 6:1; 8:5; 11:19; 14:2; 16:18; 19:6). John also saw **seven lamps** which **were blazing.** These seven lamps were said to be **the seven spirits of God.** These should be understood to represent the Holy Spirit rather than seven individual spirits or angels, with the concept of the sevenfold character of the Spirit (Isa. 11:2-3; cf. Rev. 1:4; 5:6). With God the Father seated on the throne and the Holy Spirit represented by the seven lamps, the stage was then set for the revelation (chap. 5) of Christ Himself as the slain Lamb.

14 Doxologies in the Book of Revelation

References	The One(s) Giving the Praise	The One(s) Receiving the Praise
4:8	4 living creatures	God the Father
4:11	24 elders	God the Father
5:9–10	24 elders and 4 living creatures	The Lamb (Christ)
5:12	Many angels	The Lamb
5:13	Every creature	God the Father and the Lamb
7:10	Tribulation martyrs	God the Father and the Lamb
7:12	Angels, 24 elders, and 4 living creatures	God the Father
11:16–18	24 elders	God the Father
15:3–4	Tribulation saints	God the Father and the Lamb
16:5–6	Angel	God the Father
16:7	"The altar"	God the Father
19:1–3	A great multitude	God the Father
19:4	24 elders and 4 living creatures	God the Father
19:6–8	A great multitude	God the Father

5. THE FOUR LIVING CREATURES (4:6-8)

4:6-8. A sea of glass, clear as crystal, was **before the throne** and reflected all the brilliant colors of the entire heavenly scene (cf. 15:2). **In the center** of the picture **four living creatures** were compared to **a lion . . . an ox . . . a man** and **a flying eagle.** Each of the . . . **creatures had six wings and was covered with eyes all around.** They were said to be continually praising God as the **holy . . . Almighty** (*pantokratōr*; cf. 1:8; 11:17; 15:3; 16:7, 14; 19:6, 15; 21:22), and eternal One (**who was, and is, and is to come;** cf. 1:8; 11:17). This is the first of 14 doxologies in the Book of Revelation (see the chart).

Many interpretations have been given of the four living creatures. As the Holy Spirit was seen symbolically in the seven lamps, probably the four living creatures symbolically represent the attributes of God including His omniscience and omnipresence (indicated by the creatures being full of eyes)—with the four animals bringing out other attributes of God: the lion indicating majesty and omnipotence; the ox, typical of faithful labor and patience; man, indicating intelligence; and the eagle, the greatest bird, representing supreme sovereignty.

Another possible view is that they represent Christ as revealed in the four Gospels: in Matthew, the lion of the tribe of Judah; in Mark, the ox as the servant of Yahweh; in Luke, the incarnate human Jesus; and in John, the eagle as the divine Son of God. Another alternative is that the four living creatures are angels (cf. Isa. 6:2-3), who extol the attributes of God.

6. WORSHIP IN HEAVEN (4:9-11)

4:9-11. The worship by the four **living creatures** is attended by **the 24 elders** also worshiping the One **on the throne** and attributing to God **glory and honor and power** (cf. 5:12-13) and acknowledging that He is the Creator and Sustainer of the universe (cf. John 1:3; Eph. 3:9; Col. 1:16-17; Heb. 1:2-3; Rev. 10:6; 14:7). **They lay their crowns before the throne** in ascribing all glory to Him as the Sovereign.

B. The seven-sealed scroll (chap. 5)

1. THE SEVEN-SEALED SCROLL INTRODUCED (5:1)

5:1. All of chapter 4 is an introduction to the main point of chapters 4-5, that is, to introduce the **scroll** with its **seven seals.** The symbolic presentation showed a scroll or a rolled-up parchment with seven seals affixed to the side in such a way that if unrolled the seven seals would need to be broken one by one.

2. THE QUESTION, "WHO IS WORTHY?" (5:2-5)

5:2-5. John **saw a mighty angel** (cf. 10:1; 18:21) and heard him ask **in a loud voice, Who is worthy to break the seals and open the scroll?** This is the first of 20 times "loud voice" occurs in Revelation. The last is in 21:3. The Greek word rendered "scroll" is *biblion*, from which is derived the word "Bible." When no one was found to be worthy, John **wept and wept** (lit., "kept on shedding many tears"). **One** of the 24 **elders,** however, told him not to weep, and introduced him to **the Lion of the tribe of Judah, the Root of David** (cf. Isa. 11:1; Rev. 22:16). The elder informed John that He had **triumphed,** that is, had already achieved victory, and that He alone was **able to** break the **seals** and **open the scroll.**

3. THE LAMB (5:6-7)

5:6-7. Though introduced as a "Lion" (v. 5), what John **saw** was **a Lamb** that appeared to have been **slain** or sacrificed. Yet the Lamb was **standing in the center of the throne.** About Him were the **24 elders** and **the four living creatures.** The Lamb **had seven horns and seven eyes.**

The Lion and the Lamb surely refer to Christ, with the Lamb referring to His first coming and His death and the Lion referring to His second coming and His sovereign judgment of the world. This is the only place in Revelation where Christ is called a Lion, whereas the word "Lamb" (*arnion*, "a small or young lamb") is found 27 times in Revelation and elsewhere in the New Testament in only John 21:15. But two similar words for a sacrificial lamb are used in the New Testament: *arēn*, found only in Luke 10:3, and *amnos*, which occurs four times (John 1:29, 36; Acts 8:32; 1 Peter 1:19).

Since horns symbolize strength (1 Kings 22:11), the "seven horns" represent the authority and strength of a ruler (Dan. 7:24; Rev. 13:1). The "seven eyes," defined as **the seven spirits of God** (cf. Zech. 3:9; 4:10) symbolically represent the Holy Spirit (cf. Rev. 1:4, 4:5). Because He alone is worthy, the Lamb **took the scroll from the right hand of Him who sat on the throne** (cf. Dan. 7:9, 13-14).

4. THE WORSHIP OF THE LAMB (5:8-14)

5:8. When the scroll was **taken** by the Lamb, **the 24 elders fell down before the Lamb** in worship. Each elder **had a harp and golden bowls full of incense,** which was interpreted as **the prayers of the saints** (cf. Ps. 141:2). While the angels presented the prayers, they were not priests or mediators. Only the harp (lyre) and the trumpet are mentioned as musical instruments in heavenly worship in the Book of Revelation.

5:9-10. In **a new song** the 4 creatures and 24 elders ascribed worthiness to the Lamb **to take the scroll** and break the **seals,** stating that the Lamb had been **slain** and had **purchased men for God from every tribe and language and people and nation.** Those He purchased with His **blood** were made **a kingdom and priests to serve our God** (cf. 1:6), and to **reign on the earth.** "Purchased" is from the verb *agorazō*, "to redeem." (See the chart, "New Testament Words for Redemption," at Mark 10:45.)

A textual problem exists in these verses. The Greek text used by the KJV indicates that the new song is sung by those who themselves have been redeemed: "Thou . . . has redeemed *us* to God . . . and hast made *us* unto our God kings and priests, and *we* shall reign on the earth."

The NIV, however, reads, "You purchased *men* for God. . . . You have made *them* to be a kingdom and priests to serve our God, and *they* will reign on the earth." If the KJV is correct, the 24 elders must represent the church or saints in general. If their song is impersonal as in the NIV and they simply are singing that Christ is the Redeemeer of all men, it opens the possibility that the 24 elders could be angels, though it does not expressly affirm it.

While scholars differ on this point, it would seem that since the elders are on thrones and are crowned as victors, they represent the church rather than angels. Angels have not been judged and rewarded at this point in the program of God. But angels soon join the creatures and the elders in praising the Lamb (5:11-12). The two different interpretations here should not mar the beauty of the picture and the wonder of this song of praise.

5:11-12. The **elders** were joined by the hosts of **angels** in heaven who added their words of praise **in a loud voice.** The words **they sang** are literally "they said" (*legontes*). This is in contrast to verse 9 where the 24 elders "sang" (*adousin*). In the angels' praise they ascribed **power and wealth and wisdom and strength and honor and glory and praise** to God.

5:13-14. Every creature in heaven and on earth and under the earth and on the sea and all that is in them joined the heavenly throng in words of praise to God. In this final act of praise **the four . . . creatures said Amen,** and the 24 **elders fell** prostrate in worship.

With the heavenly vision of chapters 4–5, the stage was set for the dramatic events to follow, the opening of the seven seals. It is clear from this revelation that heaven is real, not imagined. These two chapters reveal the indescribable glory and infinite majesty of the Godhead in heaven. The following chapters reveal this sovereign power of God expressed in judgment on a wicked world sunk in unprecedented depths of sin and blasphemy. Though believers today do not have the privilege of sharing John's vision or a similar one granted to Paul (2 Cor. 12:1-3), every believer can take the word pictures of Scripture here and anticipate the glory and the wonder of the heavenly scene that he will someday see with his own eyes.

C. The opening of the six seals: the time of divine wrath (chap. 6)

1. THE FIRST SEAL (6:1-2)

Five important questions must be answered before the events of chapter 6 can be understood: *Are the events which begin with the breaking of the first seal past or future?* Though many have tried to find fulfillment in the past (see *Introduction*), there are solid reasons for believing that the revelation concerns events yet future.

The vision in chapters 4–5 is described in 4:1 as "after this," that is, after the revelation to the seven churches which is described in 1:19 as "what is now," in contrast to "what will take place later." Since the scroll in 5:1 is "sealed," the clear implication is that the seals are broken at a time after chapter 5. All attempts to find fulfillment of the seals in history have failed to yield any uniform interpretation with no two commentators agreeing. Actually there is no sequence in history that clearly corresponds to these events. So it may be concluded that they are yet future.

A second question arises: *What is the relationship of the seals to the Rapture of the church?* In the letter to Thyatira the Rapture is pictured as yet future (2:25, 28) and the Rapture is in view in the letter to the church in Philadelphia (3:10-11). Beginning in chapter 6, however, there is no reference whatever to the churches or to the Rapture that is described in familiar passages (e.g., 1 Cor. 15:51-58; 1 Thes. 4:13-18). Since neither the Rapture nor the church are the subject of Revelation 6–18, many conclude that the Rapture of the church takes place before the events beginning in chapter 4 and thus precedes the Tribulation (for full discussion see Charles C. Ryrie, *Revelation*; Charles C. Ryrie, *The Final Count-*

down; and John F. Walvoord, *The Rapture Question*).

A third question: *What is the relationship of the seals to Daniel 9:27?* Israel's program, concluding in the 70th week of Daniel, is best understood as related to the scenes here described in Revelation. Though some have tried to find historic fulfillment of Daniel 9:27, nothing in history really corresponds to it; so it is better to consider the last seven years as the final period leading up to the Second Coming and therefore still future.

A fourth question: *Does Revelation deal with the entire seven years anticipated in Daniel 9:27 or only with the last three and one-half years, often referred to as "the Great Tribulation" or "a time of great distress"?* (Jer. 30:7; Dan. 12:1; Matt. 24:21) Because the Great Tribulation is specifically mentioned in Revelation 7:14 and the same period is called "the great day of their wrath" (6:17), there seems to be clear identification of Daniel 9:27 with the events of Revelation. Most expositors assume that the events beginning in Revelation 6 cover the whole seven-year period. The Book of Revelation, however, never uses a seven-year figure but frequently refers to three and one-half years or 42 months (11:2; 13:5). Because the events of chapter 6 and afterward seem to coincide with the Great Tribulation rather than with the time of peace in the first half of the seven years (1 Thes. 5:3), there are good reasons for concluding that these great events are compacted in the last three and one-half years before Christ's return to the earth. Certainly at least by the fourth seal (Rev. 6:7-8), the events described anticipate a time of unprecedented trouble.

A fifth question: *What is the relationship of the events of Revelation to Christ's sermon on the end times?* (Matt. 24–25) As J. Dwight Pentecost points out (*Things to Come*, pp. 280-82), the order of events in Revelation and the order of events in Matthew are strikingly similar: (a) war (Matt. 24:6-7; Rev. 6:3-4), (b) famine (Matt. 24:7; Rev. 6:5-6), (c) death (Matt. 24:7-9; Rev. 6:7-8), (d) martyrdom (Matt. 24:9-10, 16-22; Rev. 6:9-11), (e) the sun and the moon darkened with stars falling (Matt. 24:29; Rev. 6:12-14), (f) divine judgment (Matt. 24:32–25:26; Rev. 6:15-17). It should be obvious that the events of Revelation have their background in previous prophecies, which aids in interpreting John's symbolic revelation. The evidence points to the conclusion that it describes the final period (probably the final three and one-half years) climaxed by the second coming of Christ to set up His kingdom (for further discussion, see Walvoord, *Revelation*, pp. 123-28; also cf. comments on Matt. 24–25).

6:1-2. As John **watched** the events after the opening of **the first . . . seal** by **the Lamb**, he saw **a white horse** with **a rider** holding **a bow,** wearing a victor's **crown** (*stephanos*), and going forth to conquer. Because Christ in His second coming is pictured (19:11) as riding on a white horse, some have taken it that this rider in 6:2 also must refer to Christ, as the white horse is a symbol of victory. Roman generals after a victory in battle would ride a white horse in triumph with their captives following. The chronology, however, is wrong, as Christ returns to the earth **as a conqueror** not at the beginning of the Tribulation but at the end of the Tribulation. Also the riders on the other horses obviously relate to destruction and judgment which precede the second coming of Christ by some period of time.

A better interpretation is that the conqueror mentioned here is the future world ruler, sometimes referred to as Antichrist though Revelation does not use this term. He is probably the same person as the ruler of the people mentioned in Daniel 9:26. This ruler has a bow without an arrow, indicating that the world government which he establishes is accomplished without warfare (see comments on Rev. 13:4). The future world government begins with a time of peace but is soon followed by destruction (1 Thes. 5:3). In general, the seals, trumpets, and bowls of divine wrath signal the terrible judgments of God on the world at the end of the Age, climaxing in the second coming of Christ.

2. THE SECOND SEAL (6:3-4)

6:3-4. With the breaking of **the second seal** a **red** horse appeared with a **rider** empowered **to take peace from the earth** (cf. "the red dragon," 12:3; the "scarlet beast," 17:3). In contrast with the first rider who has a bow without an arrow this second rider carried **a large**

sword. This again was a picture of political power with the rider as the world ruler.

3. THE THIRD SEAL (6:5-6)

6:5-6. With the opening of **the third seal** a **black horse** was revealed with a **rider** carrying **a pair of scales in his hand.** At the same time **a voice** was heard from **among the four living creatures saying, A quart of wheat for a day's wages, and three quarts of barley for a day's wages, and do not damage the oil and the wine!** "A day's wages" refers to a silver coin, the Roman denarius, worth about 15 cents, which was the normal wage for a worker for an entire day. So this passage is saying that in that food shortage an entire day's work would be required to buy either a quart of wheat or three quarts of barley. If one bought wheat, it would be enough for one good meal; if he bought barley, it would be enough for three good meals but nothing would be left for buying oil or wine. Famine is the inevitable aftermath of war. This will be a major cause of death in the Great Tribulation. The black color of the horse speaks of famine and death.

4. THE FOURTH SEAL (6:7-8)

6:7-8. A **pale horse** was introduced when **the fourth seal was opened.** "Pale" is literally a pale green (cf. the same word used of vegetation in Mark 6:39; Rev. 8:7; 9:4). John stated that the rider's name was **Death** and that **hades was following close behind him.** Here is the aftermath of war, famine, and death. With war and famine people fall prey to a plague and the wild beasts of the earth. The startling fact is revealed that **a fourth of the earth,** or approximately a billion people by today's population figures, will be killed by these means. It should be obvious that this is not a trivial judgment but a major factor in the Great Tribulation, thus supporting the conclusion that the Great Tribulation has begun. The first four seals may be considered as a unit and a general description of the Great Tribulation as an unprecedented time of trouble (cf. Jer. 30:7; Dan. 12:1; Matt. 24:21-22).

5. THE FIFTH SEAL (6:9-11)

6:9. With the opening of **the fifth seal** John had another revelation of heaven itself and his attention was directed to **souls** pictured as **under the altar** and identified as those **who had been slain because of the Word of God and the testimony they had maintained.** (For "under the altar," see Ex. 29:12; Lev. 4:7.) These are obviously martyrs, mentioned in more detail in Revelation 7. This makes it clear that souls will be saved in the Great Tribulation, but many of them will be martyred.

6:10-11. They will cry out to the **Lord,** asking **how long** it will be before He will **avenge** them. In reply **each** is **given a white robe** and informed that the Tribulation is not over and that others must be martyred before God's judgment on the wicked and deliverance of the righteous occurs at the Second Coming. This passage shows that the time period is the Great Tribulation, but not its end.

Spirits without any substance could not wear robes. The fact that they will be given robes supports the concept that when believers die they are given temporary bodies in heaven which are later replaced by resurrection bodies at the time of resurrection (cf. 20:4).

6. THE SIXTH SEAL (6:12-17)

6:12-14. As **the sixth seal** opened, John recorded that **a great earthquake** occurred. More dramatic than the earthquake was the transformation of the heavens with **the sun** turning **black,** the **moon** turning **blood red,** and **stars** falling like **late figs from a fig tree.** The heavens appeared **like a scroll** being rolled up. At the same time, due to the earthquake, all the mountains and islands were moved from their places. Here again in the sequence of events, the end had not been reached as there was still another seal. But this was the most dramatic judgment thus far in this time of great distress before the Second Coming.

Many expositors have attempted to see a figurative fulfillment to this prophecy. It is preferable, however, to take this prediction literally. The trumpet and bowl judgments, to be revealed later in Revelation, also include great disturbances in the heavens and on the earth before Christ's second coming.

6:15-17. The practical effect of the judgment was fear in unbelievers from all walks of life. They called on **the mountains and the rocks** to **fall on** them and to **hide** them from God's **wrath.** Their fear was so great they would rather be killed by a falling mountain than to face the wrath of **the Lamb** and **Their wrath,** referring to the anger of the Triune God. Again this is not a picture of ordinary trouble but the period of greatest distress in world history.

Taken as a whole, chapter 6 is one of the most important and pivotal chapters in the entire book. It describes the first six seals and also introduces the seventh seal which consists of and introduces the seven trumpets and the seven bowls of the wrath of God in chapters 8–9; 16.

The contents of chapter 6 should put to rest the false teachings that God, being a God of love, could not judge a wicked world. It also raises the important question contained in the closing words of verse 17: **Who can stand?** Only those who have availed themselves of the grace of God before the time of judgment will be able to stand when God deals with the earth in this final period of great distress. Those who will be saved in the Great Tribulation are described in the next chapter.

D. Those who will be saved in the Great Tribulation (chap. 7)

1. THE SEALING OF THE 144,000 OF ISRAEL (7:1-8)

7:1-3. The question was raised in 6:17 whether any would be saved in the Tribulation. This is answered in this chapter, and two classes of the saved are mentioned specifically: (1) those who are saved in Israel, (2) those of all nations who, though saved spiritually, are martyred. **Four angels** were told to withhold judgment on **the earth** until the **servants of . . . God** were sealed (v. 3). The **seal on** their **foreheads** symbolizes protection and ownership and God's intention to protect the 12 tribes that are mentioned, much as He protected Noah from the Flood, Israel from the plagues of Egypt, and Rahab and her household in Jericho.

7:4-8. John heard the names of 12 **tribes** with **12,000** from each **tribe . . . sealed** and thus protected. The 12 tribes are not "lost" as some contend.

Attempts have been made to identify the 12 tribes here with the church, mostly to avoid the implication that this is literally **Israel.** The fact that specific tribes were mentioned and specific numbers from each tribe were indicated would seem to remove this from the symbolic and to justify literal interpretation. If God intended these verses to represent Israel literally, He would have used this means. Nowhere else in the Bible do a dozen references to the 12 tribes mean the church. Obviously Israel will be in the Tribulation, and though men do not know the identification of each tribe today, certainly God knows.

Much speculation has arisen about why the tribe of Dan is omitted. Joseph and one of his two sons, Manasseh, are listed, but Ephraim, Joseph's other son, is omitted. Thus if Dan were included, there would have been 13 tribes. According to J.B. Smith, Scripture contains 29 lists of the tribes of Israel in the Old and New Testaments and in no case are more than 12 tribes mentioned (*A Revelation of Jesus Christ*, p. 130). The tribe omitted was usually Levi, from which the priesthood came. Inasmuch as it is normal to have only 12 and not 13 tribes, the omission of Dan is not significant. Perhaps Dan was omitted here because it was one of the first tribes to go into idolatry (Jud. 18:30; cf. 1 Kings 12:28-29). However, Dan is mentioned in Ezekiel 48:2 in the millennial land distribution.

The most important fact taught here is that God continues to watch over Israel even in the time of Israel's great distress. There is no justification whatever for spiritualizing either the number or the names of the tribes in this passage, to make them represent the church.

2. THE MULTITUDE OF MARTYRS (7:9-17)

7:9-12. Then John saw a **multitude** of people **from every nation, tribe, people, and language,** who were **standing before the throne** (i.e., before God the Father) **and in front of the Lamb** (i.e., God the Son). This is the same group mentioned in 6:9, but here they were **wearing white robes** and **holding palm branches,** apparently signifying righteous triumph. As this multitude ascribed salvation to God and to the Lamb, **all the angels,** the 24 **elders, and the 4 living creatures** joined them in worship as they did in 5:9-10.

7:13-17. One of the 24 **elders** asked about the origin of those who stood **in white robes.** Is it not significant that if the

24 elders represent the church these described here are a different group of the saved? When John indicated that he did not know the answer (v. 14a) the elder himself answered the question as to who this multitude was and where they came from: **These are they who have come out of the Great Tribulation; they have washed their robes and made them white in the blood of the Lamb.**

It seems evident that these "who have come out of the Great Tribulation" have been martyred and were then safe in heaven. They were given the special privilege of being before God's **throne** and serving **Him day and night in His temple.** They were protected by God Himself and never again would they experience **hunger . . . thirst,** or **scorching heat,** with the implication that this was their experience of suffering on earth. They were under the special shepherd-care of **the Lamb** and were drinking from **springs of living water.** The narration concludes with the comforting truth that all their tears would be wiped away.

The two groups seen by John were the 144,000 Israelites and a great multitude from every nation, including some Israelites who were not thus protected and who were martyred in the Great Tribulation. A natural explanation of these two groups is that neither represents the church, the body of Christ in the present Age, because both groups are distinguished from the 24 elders and neither group is clearly identified with the church in this present dispensation.

The events of this chapter, like those in other chapters to follow, do not advance the narrative but are a pause in the description of the events to spotlight a concentrated revelation on a special feature, in this case the answer to the question of 6:17, "Who can stand?"

Though the chapters of Revelation are not all in chronological sequence, chapter 7 depicts a scene in heaven which precedes the second coming of Christ to the earth. Those seen in heaven were said to "come out of the Great Tribulation" (v. 14). The chapter accordingly indicates how they will be marvelously blessed in heaven after their trials on earth. The 144,000 will appear again (14:1-5), and the multitude of martyrs who were killed for refusing to worship the beast appear again at the time of the resurrection in 20:4. That they are not millennial saints should be evident from the fact that they will be in heaven before God's throne, and will have been resurrected.

E. *The opening of the seventh seal and the introduction of the seven trumpets (chaps. 8–9)*

1. THE OPENING OF THE SEVENTH SEAL (8:1)

8:1. The opening of **the seventh seal** is a most important event, confirmed by the fact that **there was silence in heaven**

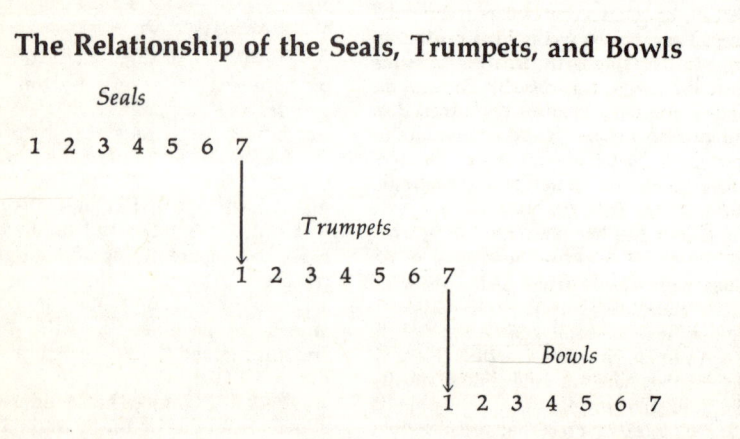

for about half an hour after it was opened. The contents of the seven trumpets indicate that they differ from the seven seals. W. Graham Scroggie states, "The trumpets, therefore, do not double back over all or some of the seals, but lie under the sixth seal, and proceed from it" (*The Great Unveiling*, p. 111). He also holds that the bowls of the wrath of God (chap. 16) "do not double back over the seal and trumpet judgments" (p. 112).

C.A. Blanchard holds the same position: "The series of three sevens are really included in one series of seven, that is, the seven trumpets are included under the seventh seal and the seven bowls are included under the seventh trumpet, so that we have in fact a single series in three movements" (*Light on the Last Days*, p. 58). The seventh seal accordingly is important because it actually includes all the events from 8:1 through 19:10.

2. THE SEVEN ANGELS AND THE SEVEN TRUMPETS (8:2)

8:2. As John observed the heavenly scene, he wrote that he **saw the seven angels** to whom **were given seven trumpets.** The fact that these are angels' trumpets distinguishes them from the trumpet of God (1 Cor. 15:52; 1 Thes. 4:16) and from other New Testament trumpets (Heb. 12:19; Rev. 1:10; 4:1).

3. THE GOLDEN CENSER (8:3-5)

8:3-5. Before the trumpets sounded, however, a dramatic introduction was given them by **another angel,** one in addition to the seven, who **stood** before **the golden altar** with **a golden censer.** In the Old Testament tabernacle a censer made of copper, probably heavy to handle, was used to carry coals from the brazen altar outside the tabernacle to the altar of incense inside. Later, in the temple, Solomon used censers made of gold (1 Kings 7:50; 2 Chron. 4:22).

This is the only reference to censers in the Book of Revelation, though golden bowls full of incense, which probably were not censers, are mentioned in Revelation 5:8. Like the golden bowls of 5:8, however, the golden censer offering incense here is symbolic of **the prayers of all the saints.**

This offering in heaven corresponds to the custom of offering incense on the altar of incense in both the tabernacle and the temple. The censer would hold the coals, and a separate vessel would carry the incense which was to be poured on the coals once the altar was reached. The resulting smoke was typical of prayer ascending **before God.**

In verse 5 **the angel** offered the incense on the coals before God, and then, taking **the censer** with the **fire** still in it, he threw it **on the earth.** As a result there were **thunder, rumblings, flashes of lightning, and an earthquake.** The picture is one of ominous anticipation.

4. THE FIRST TRUMPET (8:6-7)

8:6-7. As **the first angel sounded his trumpet . . . hail and fire mixed with blood . . . was hurled down upon the earth,** resulting in **a third of the earth** being **burned up,** including **the trees** and **all the green grass.** This devastating judgment, like that announced by most of the trumpets, primarily affected a third of the earth.

5. THE SECOND TRUMPET (8:8-9)

8:8-9. As **the second . . . trumpet** sounded, **something like a huge mountain, all ablaze, was thrown into the sea.** The result was that **a third of the sea turned into blood,** and this caused **a third of the living creatures in the sea** to die, and also **a third of the ships were destroyed.** It is best to interpret these events literally though the description of the sea being turned into blood may be the language of appearance as in the mention of blood after the first trumpet blast. Reference to blood as a divine judgment is found in the plagues of Egypt (cf. Ex. 7:14-22).

Obviously the results of these judgments are literal. The sea turned to blood results in the death of a third of the sea creatures, and the blazing mountain cast into the sea results in destruction of a third of the ships. The mountain is probably best understood as being a literal large body that fell from heaven. Since the results are literal, it is reasonable to take the judgments as literal also.

6. THE THIRD TRUMPET (8:10-11)

8:10-11. The judgment following **the third . . . trumpet** was similar to that of the second. But here the mass falling from heaven to earth was **a great star, blazing like a torch.** This fell **on a third of the rivers and on the springs of water;** in other words, waters other than the oceans.

The **star** was named **Wormwood.** Wormwood is a bitter desert plant mentioned only here in the New Testament. It is mentioned seven times in the Old Testament where it represents sorrow and bitter judgment (Deut. 29:18; Prov. 5:4; Jer. 9:15; 23:15; Lam. 3:15, 19; Amos 5:7).

Though many have attempted to interpret the third trumpet symbolically, it seems best to consider it as a large meteor or star falling on the earth from heaven and turning the water, as indicated, into bitterness so that people who drank it **died.** The contrast found in the Cross of Christ is symbolized in the sweetening of the waters of Marah (Ex. 15:23-25) and the turning of bitter judgment into sweet mercy, bringing life and hope. The third trumpet is another awesome judgment resulting in great loss of life.

7. THE FOURTH TRUMPET (8:12)

8:12. At the sound of **the fourth . . . trumpet** the light of the sky was reduced by one third. Without **a third of the sun** a third of the day was lacking normal light, and a third of the night was without light from **the moon** and **the stars.** Again the best interpretation is literal. Just as the first three trumpets dealt with a third of the earth, so the fourth trumpet dealt with a third of the heavens.

8. ANNOUNCEMENT OF THE FINAL THREE TRUMPETS (8:13)

8:13. Warning was given that the next three trumpets would be more severe and devastating than those which preceded them. The triple **woe** announced by **an eagle** warned of coming judgment. Eagles are also mentioned in 4:7 and 12:14.

9. THE FIFTH TRUMPET (9:1-11)

9:1-6. The events after the sounding of **the fifth . . . trumpet** are given considerable explanation, implying that this is a most important step in God's progressive and increasing judgments on the earth. Because of the **he** in verse 2 and "king" in verse 11, the **star** that fell **to the earth** was a person rather than a fragment of a star (cf. Isa. 14:12-17; Luke 10:18). Even in modern terminology it is customary to speak of an unusual athlete or performer as a star. This star, probably representing Satan cast out of heaven at the beginning of the Great Tribulation (Rev. 12:9), **was given the key to the shaft of the Abyss** ("bottomless pit," KJV). The "Abyss" (*abyssos*) is the home of demons (cf. Luke 8:31; Rev. 9:11; 11:7; 17:8; 20:1, 3; in Rom. 10:7 it is translated "deep"). Satan will be confined for a thousand years in the Abyss during the reign of Christ on earth (Rev. 20:1-3).

Here the star (Satan) used his key to allow demons in the Abyss to come out and afflict the earth. Visually this event was represented as a great **smoke,** darkening the sky and **the sun. Out of the smoke** came creatures called **locusts** with the deadly sting of **scorpions.** While they were harmless to natural vegetation and trees, they stung **people who did not have the seal of God on their foreheads.**

In chapter 7 the 144,000 of Israel were sealed, and protection from the plague was extended to all who knew the Lord in that day (cf. Eph. 1:13-14; 2 Tim. 2:19). In the Old Testament locusts were a fearful plague, for they were able to reduce the land to starvation by eating up all green vegetation (Ex. 10:12-20; Joel 1:4-7). These locusts, however, did not eat vegetation, but had the power to torment people **for five months** (cf. Rev. 9:10). Thus they might be demons who appeared in the form of locusts. This is confirmed by the fact that they came from the Abyss, the home of demons (Luke 8:31). Their demonic control over people was such, however, that though the victims desired to die they could not take their own lives.

9:7-11. The description of **the locusts** compared to **horses prepared for battle** is awesome: **human faces . . . crowns of gold . . . women's hair . . . lions' teeth,** ironlike **breastplates,** and **wings** that sounded like horse-drawn **chariots rushing into battle.**

Obviously John was describing what he saw but did not interpret each characteristic. The picture is one of Satan's awesome supernatural power and the demon world especially in relation to unbelievers.

Unlike the previous judgments which apparently were short in time this judgment extended for five months (v. 10; cf. v. 5). This is important as it refutes clearly the notion that all these judgments will occur in a brief span of time immediately before the second coming of Christ.

The demons had a ruler **over them** whose **Hebrew** name **is Abaddon** and whose **Greek** name is **Apollyon.** Both words mean "destroyer." Though Satan is sometimes portrayed as an angel of light (2 Cor. 11:14), here Satan and his demons are seen for what they really are, destroyers of people. This judgment confirms what was already intimated in preceding judgments, that the Great Tribulation, as Christ described it, will be a time of "great distress, unequaled from the beginning of the world until now—and never to be equaled again" (Matt. 24:21).

10. THE SIXTH TRUMPET (9:12-21)

9:12. The fifth trumpet described as **the first woe** is now to be followed by the two final trumpets, also called "woes" (cf. 8:13).

9:13-15. The sixth . . . trumpet seems to relate to the final military conflict described in 16:12-16 (cf. Dan. 11:40-45). At the sounding of the sixth trumpet John **heard a voice coming from the horns of the golden altar that is before God. The sixth angel** was then instructed to **release the four angels . . . bound** by the **Euphrates** River. These **four angels** are clearly demons, as holy angels are not bound. The release of these four is minutely timed at a particular **hour and day and month and year,** and they **kill a third** of the world's population.

The fourth seal (Rev. 6:7-8) resulted in a fourth of the earth's people being killed. Here a third of the remainder were put to death. These two judgments alone, disregarding all intervening judgments, would account for the death of half the earth's population. This fact is to be taken literally as it confirms the statement by Daniel (Dan. 12:1) and the words of Christ (Matt. 24:21) that the Great Tribulation will be without precedent and would end in the death of all mankind if it were not stopped by His second coming (Matt. 24:22).

9:16. The loosing of the four angels (not the same as the four angels of 7:1) resulted in releasing an army of **200 million . . . mounted troops.** Most interpreters do not take the number literally, though there is good evidence that all other numbers in Revelation are literal. Even if taken symbolically, this figure clearly represents an overwhelming military force. Years ago Red China claimed to have an army of 200 million (cf. *Time,* May 21, 1965, p. 35).

Some interpreters say these millions are demons, but demons are not normally marshaled as a military force. The fact that John **heard the number,** as obviously he could not visually count 200 million men, seems to lend credence to the concept that this is literal and predicts that an army will come from the East crossing the dried-up Euphrates River (16:12).

Great dams have already been placed across the Euphrates River to divert water for irrigation so that at times the riverbed is dry or partially so. A large invasion from the East and North in the end times is predicted in Daniel 11:44.

9:17-19. The horses and their **riders** had **breastplates** of red, dark blue, and **yellow.** The lionlike **heads of the horses** imply something other than natural horses. Furthermore, John declared, **out of their mouths came fire, smoke, and sulfur.** Some have taken this as a picture of modern warfare including the use of armed vehicles such as tanks. Whether symbolic or literal, the passage certainly implies terrible destruction and an awesome invading force. The results are twice stated and include the death of **a third of mankind** (vv. 15, 18).

9:20-21. Though the judgment was devastating and obviously from God, it did not bring men to repentance, and they continued to worship **demons** and their representation in **idols** and kept on murdering and participating in the occult (**magic arts,** *pharmakeiōn,* from which is derived "pharmacies"; cf. Gal. 5:20; Rev. 18:23; 21:8; 22:15), **their sexual immorality,** and thievery.

The trumpet judgments clearly grew in a crescendo, becoming worse and more devastating. In spite of the clear evidence of God's power to judge the world, no evidence was given John that there would be any change of heart on the part of the great mass of humanity. Though the sixth judgment produced fear, it did not produce repentance.

F. The mighty angel and the little scroll (chap. 10)

1. THE INTRODUCTION OF THE ANGEL HOLDING THE SCROLL (10:1-4)

Chapter 7 dealt parenthetically with the 144,000 and the many martyrs, without advancing chronologically the events of the Great Tribulation. Similarly 10:1-11:14 give additional information as a background to the seal, trumpet, and bowl judgments.

Another angel was introduced, apparently not one of the seven angels sounding the trumpets. Some believe this angel was Christ, pointing to the angel mentioned in 8:3 as also probably a representation of Christ as a priest. But though Christ appeared frequently as the Angel of Jehovah in the Old Testament (e.g., Gen. 16:13; 24:7; 31:11, 13; Jud. 6:22), there is no evidence that this person was other than a mighty angel (cf. Rev. 5:2), perhaps Michael the archangel.

10:1-4. This **angel**, however, was pictured dramatically as **robed in a cloud**, having **a rainbow above his head**, his face brilliant with glory **like the sun**, and with **his legs ... like fiery pillars.** John added that the angel held **a little scroll** and stood with **his right foot on the sea and his left foot on the land.** At the same time he shouted **like the roar of a lion.** The scene is certainly one to inspire awe, and when this angel **shouted, the voices of the seven thunders spoke.** John was forbidden to record **what the seven thunders** said. While Revelation is primarily designed to reveal and not to conceal God's purpose and future events, some revelation was kept hidden as illustrated by God's prohibiting John to write what "the voices" of the seven thunders said.

In contrast with the seven-sealed scroll (*biblion*) held by the Lamb (5:1), this angel held a small scroll (*biblaridion*, also used in 10:9-10). This scroll apparently contained the angel's written order for the mission he was about to fulfill.

2. THE ANNOUNCEMENT OF THE IMPENDING END (10:5-7)

10:5-7. The dramatic introduction of this angel (in vv. 1-4) was a preparation for the pronouncement which followed in verses 5-7. Solemnly swearing by God the eternal Creator, the angel declared, **There will be no more delay!** The KJV rendering, "There shall be time no longer," has been mistakenly interpreted as an abolishment of the present time system with its sequence of events. But this is not the thought of the passage, as the NIV translation is accurate. The clear reference to God as Creator (cf. 4:11; 14:7) answers evolutionary speculation as to the origin of the earth, and it also affirms the omnipotence of God in dealing with the world in judgment when the time is ripe.

Announcement was made that **the seventh ... trumpet** would bring about the accomplishment of **the mystery of God.** This mystery had been previously announced to God's **prophets.** The reference, therefore, is not to hidden truth but to the fulfillment of many Old Testament passages which refer to the glorious return of the Son of God and the establishment of His kingdom of righteousness and peace on the earth. While God's purposes are not necessarily revealed in current events where Satan is allowed power and manifestation, the time will come when Satan no longer will be in power and the predictions of the Old Testament prophets will be fulfilled. Then all will know the Lord and the truth about Him (Jer. 31:34). Here again is evidence that the seventh trumpet introduces the seven bowl judgments of God's wrath described in Revelation 16.

3. THE EATING OF THE SCROLL (10:8-11)

10:8-11. John obeyed the angel's instruction to **eat** the scroll, and though it was **sweet** (like **honey**) in his **mouth**, it soured in his **stomach.** The angel then added that John would **prophesy again.**

What does this incident mean? Though no interpretation was given John, it is evident that in partaking of the book he was appropriating what the book states (cf. Jer. 15:16). The scroll seems to symbolize the Word of God and divine revelation in general, for John was told to deliver the Word faithfully.

To John the Word of God was indeed sweet with its revelation of the grace of God and its many precious promises that belong to believers. As such it sharply contrasted with his circumstances on Patmos Island. David stated, "The ordinances of the Lord are sure and altogether righteous. They are more precious than gold, than much pure gold; they are sweeter than honey, than honey from the comb" (Ps. 19:9-10). Though the Word is sweet to believers, it will be bitter to unbelievers when it brings divine judgment on them.

G. *The two witnesses (11:1-14)*

While it is clear that 11:1-14 continues the parenthetical section begun in 10:1, an amazing variation of interpretations of this portion of Scripture have been offered. Alford calls this chapter "one of the most difficult in the whole Apocalypse" (*The Greek Testament,* 4:655).

The best guideline to follow in interpreting this section is to take each fact literally. In line with this principle, a literal temple will be in existence during the Great Tribulation, and the city should be considered the literal city Jerusalem in keeping with its identification in 11:8. The time periods of 42 months (v. 2) and three and one-half days (vv. 9, 11) again should be considered literally. The earthquake will kill literally 7,000 individuals, and the two witnesses should be considered as two individual men.

1. THE MEASURING OF THE TEMPLE (11:1-2)

11:1-2. John **was given a reed,** a lightweight **rod,** to be used as a measuring instrument. John was instructed to **measure the temple** and **the altar** but not **the outer court,** meaning he was to measure the holy place and the holy of holies. While others could come into the outer court, only priests could enter into those two temple rooms. The explanation was given that this would be under the control of **the Gentiles** who would **trample on the holy city for 42 months.**

Why should John measure the temple? Measurement is usually taken of one's possessions, and the temple belonged to God. In a similar way the temple of Ezekiel 40 was measured and the New Jerusalem was measured (Rev. 21:15-17). The temple here will be constructed so that orthodox Jews can offer sacrifices according to the Mosaic Law in the period in the first half of the seven-year period known as Daniel's 70th week. At the beginning of the 42-month Great Tribulation, however, the sacrifices will stop and the temple will be desecrated and become a shrine for the world ruler of the Great Tribulation who will put an idol in it and proclaim himself to be God (cf. Dan. 9:27; 12:11; 2 Thes. 2:4; Rev. 13:14-15).

John was also instructed, however, to count the worshipers who came to the temple. Here the thought seems to be that God will evaluate both the temple and those in it.

The tendency of some is to spiritualize the 42-month length of the Great Tribulation, but this should be taken as a literal period, as confirmed by the 1,260 days of 11:3 which are 42 months of 30 days each. From this it is also clear that "the times of the Gentiles" (Luke 21:24) will not end until the second coming of Christ to the earth to set up His kingdom. Though Jews may possess Jerusalem temporarily, as they have in this century, they will lose possession in the Great Tribulation.

Some believe that the 42 months refer to the first half of Daniel's 70th week (Dan. 9:27). While it is not clear, the evidence surrounding this passage in Revelation seems to refer to the final three and one-half years. This also seems to be confirmed by the fact that in the first half of the last seven years the Jews will actually possess the city of Jerusalem and worship in their temple, whereas here the context indicates that this is the period when Gentiles will tread down the Holy City, implying ill treatment of the Jews and desecration of the temple.

2. THE MINISTRY OF THE TWO WITNESSES (11:3-6)

11:3-6. It was revealed to John that the **two witnesses** would be empowered by God to serve as prophets for 1,260 days or 42 months. They would be **clothed in sackcloth** and would be called **two olive trees** and **two lampstands.**

Numerous and varied interpretations have been given concerning the two witnesses. Some have suggested that they are not literal individuals. However, in view of the fact that they die and are resurrected, the implication is that they are actual people.

Another problem is their identification. A common interpretation is that they are Moses and Elijah because the judgments inflicted by Moses and Elijah in the Old Testament are similar to those of these two witnesses (11:5-6). Further support is given the identification of Elijah because of the prediction (Mal. 4:5) that he will appear "before that great and dreadful day of the Lord comes." Christ said this prophecy of Elijah was partially fulfilled in His lifetime (Matt. 17:10-13; Mark 9:11-13; cf. Luke 1:17). And both Moses and Elijah were involved in the transfiguration (Matt. 17:3), which anticipated the Second Coming. But a problem with this suggested identity is that Moses had already died once. Some have identified the two witnesses as Enoch and Elijah inasmuch as they did not die but were translated (cf. Heb. 9:27).

While there is room for considerable discussion of these various views, the fact is that the passage does not identify the two witnesses, and they probably do not have historic identification.

The description of the two witnesses as olive trees and lampstands has an Old Testament background (Zech. 4:2-14). The two witnesses in this passage were Joshua the high priest and Zerubbabel the governor. Their connection to the lampstands was that they were empowered by the Holy Spirit, symbolized by the olive oil. In a similar way the two witnesses of Revelation 11 will be empowered by the Holy Spirit.

Like prophets of old the two witnesses will be able to do supernatural miracles, and fire will destroy those who will try to harm them (Rev. 11:5). Like Elijah they will have power to stop rain, and will have power like Moses to turn water into blood and to bring on plagues (v. 6). In the midst of the unbelief, apostasy, and satanic power of the Great Tribulation these two witnesses will be a threat to the entire wicked world for a literal period of 1,260 days.

3. THE DEATH OF THE TWO WITNESSES (11:7-10)

11:7-10. With the ministry of the two witnesses ended, God permitted **the beast that comes up from the Abyss** (cf. 9:1-2, 11; 17:8; 20:1, 3) to overcome them. The beast, that is, the Antichrist, is mentioned nine other times in Revelation (13:1; 14:9, 11; 15:2; 16:2; 17:3, 13; 19:20; 20:10). After the witnesses were killed, their bodies were left unburied in Jerusalem, **figuratively called Sodom and Egypt,** because of the people's apostasy and rejection of God.

For three and one-half days the whole world gloated over their dead **bodies.** This implies some worldwide display, now made possible by television. Their deaths were considered a great victory for the world ruler and Satan, and were celebrated by people **sending each other gifts.**

4. THE RESURRECTION OF THE TWO WITNESSES (11:11-12)

11:11-12. After three and one-half days in the street, however, suddenly the two witnesses were resurrected and **stood on their feet.** They responded to the invitation, **Come up here,** and **went up to heaven in a cloud, while their enemies looked on** with great fear.

5. THE RESULTING JUDGMENT OF GOD ON JERUSALEM (11:13-14)

11:13-14. At the same moment an **earthquake** occurred in Jerusalem with **a 10th of the city** collapsing and **7,000 people were killed.** In contrast with previous judgments where revolt and rebellion against God continued, **the survivors were terrified and gave glory to the God of heaven.** So ended **the second woe,** leaving only the seventh trumpet, the final and **third woe,** to come.

H. *The sounding of the seventh trumpet (11:15-19)*

11:15. Though the full results from the sounding of **the seventh . . . trumpet** are only introduced here and not brought to finality (as they will be in chap. 16), the introduction of the seventh trumpet itself is dramatic. As the trumpet sounded, voices were heard in heaven: **The kingdom of the world has become the kingdom of our Lord and of His Christ, and He will reign forever and ever.** (Cf. predictions of the earthly kingdom of Christ in Ezek. 21:26-27; Dan. 2:35, 44; 4:3; 6:26; 7:14, 26-27; Zech. 14:9.) The fact that this will be fulfilled at the Second Coming makes it clear that the period of the seventh trumpet chronologically reaches to Christ's return. Therefore the seventh trumpet introduces and includes the seven bowl judgments of the wrath of God revealed in chapter 16. In contrast with previous trumpets where a single voice was heard, here a mighty chorus from heaven joined in the proclamation.

11:16-18. After this announcement, **the 24 elders,** who appear frequently (4:4, 10; 5:5-6, 8, 11, 14; 7:11, 13; 11:16; 14:3; 19:4) and **who were seated on their thrones before God,** were seen by John as falling **on their faces** to worship **God.** Their song of praise indicates that the time had come for God to judge **the nations,** to judge **the dead,** and to reward God's **servants.**

God was described as the **Almighty** (*pantokratōr*; also used in 1:8; 4:8; 15:3; 16:7, 14; 19:6, 15; 21:22), eternal (**who is and who was;** cf. 1:8; 4:8), and possessing **power** (*dynamin*) (11:17). In general their hymn of praise anticipates the second coming of Christ and the establishment of His rule on earth.

11:19. The chapter closes with another dramatic incident. John wrote, **Then God's temple in heaven was opened.** At the same time John was able to look into the **temple** where he saw **the ark of His covenant.** This refers to the heavenly temple rather than to a temple on earth. The corresponding results in the earth, however, included **lightning . . . thunder, an earthquake, and a great hailstorm** (cf. 8:5).

The dramatic introduction of the events relating to the seventh trumpet concluded here and will be resumed in chapter 16. Chronologically the time was close to Christ's second coming.

I. The seven great personages of the end times (chaps. 12-15)

Though the seventh trumpet was recorded in 11:15 as sounding, the details of what will come out of the seventh trumpet are not revealed until chapter 16. Accordingly chapters 12-15 view the prophecies of the end time from another perspective and introduce the great personages who are involved in the second half of the seven-year period.

Many have pointed out that seven personages appear in chapters 12-13: (1) a woman clothed with the sun, representing Israel (12:1-2); (2) the red dragon with seven heads and 10 horns, representing Satan (12:3-4); (3) the male Child, representing Christ (12:5-6); (4) the archangel Michael, casting Satan out of heaven (12:7-12); (5) the offspring of the woman, persecuted by the dragon (12:13-17); (6) the beast out of the sea, the future world dictator (13:2-10); (7) the beast out of the earth, the false prophet (13:11-18). These chapters do not advance the narrative chronologically, but present events and situations that are concurrent with the soundings of the trumpets. Chronological progress of events resumes in chapter 16.

1. THE FIRST PERSONAGE: A WOMAN CLOTHED WITH THE SUN (12:1-2)

12:1-2. The first great personage to appear was **a woman clothed with the sun, with the moon under her feet and a crown of 12 stars on her head.** She was called **a great and wondrous sign** (*sēmeion mega,* lit., "a great sign"; cf. 13:13). Undoubtedly the sign provoked wonder, as indicated in the KJV and NIV, but the translation "a great sign" (NASB) is more accurate, since John did not use the Greek word for wonder (*teras*). This was the first of a series of events called "signs" or "miracles" (12:3; 13:13-14; 15:1; 16:14; 19:20). As signs they were symbols of something that God was about to reveal and usually contained an element of prophetic warning. Though this sign was seen in heaven, the events which followed obviously occurred on earth.

The woman symbolized Israel, as indicated by Genesis 37:9-11, where the sun and the moon referred to Jacob and Rachel, Joseph's parents. The stars in the woman's crown clearly related to the 12 sons of Jacob and identified the woman as Israel fulfilling the Abrahamic Covenant. J.B. Smith cites Isaiah 60:1-3, 20 as proof that the sun refers to Israel's future glory (*A Revelation of Jesus Christ,* p. 182).

Many commentaries are so intent on attempting to identify Israel as the church that they ignore these plain indications that the woman is Israel. Robert H. Mounce, for instance, makes the woman "the messianic community, the ideal Israel . . . the church (Rev. 12:17). The people of God are one throughout all redemptive history" (*The Book of Revela-*

tion, p. 236). While there is a unity of the people of God, this does not wipe out dispensational and racial distinctions.

The symbolism, while not referring specifically to Mary, the mother of Christ, points to Israel as the source of Jesus Christ. Thus it does not refer to the church. Wicked women are sometimes used to represent false religions, as in the case of Jezebel (2:20), the apostate church of the end time as a prostitute (17:1-7, 15, 18), and Israel as the unfaithful wife of Yahweh (Hosea 2:2-13). The church by contrast is pictured as the virgin bride (2 Cor. 11:2), the Lamb's wife (Rev. 19:7).

The woman was said to be **pregnant** and **about to give birth** (12:2). While in some sense this may be fulfilled in the birth of Christ to the Virgin Mary, the context seems to refer to the emerging nation of Israel in its suffering prior to the second coming of Christ. This is further supported by the verses which follow.

2. THE SECOND PERSONAGE: THE RED DRAGON WITH THE 7 HEADS AND 10 HORNS (12:3-4)

12:3-4. The second wonder (*semeion*, "sign"; cf. v. 1) **appeared in heaven**, though it actually related to scenes on earth. It was a great **red dragon**, having **7 heads and 10 horns, and 7 crowns on his heads.** From similar descriptions in Daniel 7:7-8, 24 and Revelation 13:1, this beast represented Satan's control over world empires in the Great Tribulation. Revelation 12:9 identifies the dragon as Satan. The color red might indicate the bloodshed related to this period. The 10 horns presented symbolically the 10 kings (see Dan. 7:24) who reigned simultaneously with the coming world ruler and who were mentioned both in Daniel 7:7 and Revelation 13:1.

The casting down of **a third of the stars out of the sky** seemed to imply satanic power which extended to the heavens and the earth. Satan was seen here to extend his power over those who opposed him spiritually or politically. The dragon's attempt to **devour** the newborn **Child** (12:4) seemed to point to Satan's attempts to destroy the Infant Jesus. Satanic opposition to Israel and especially to the messianic line is clear in both Testaments.

3. THE THIRD PERSONAGE: THE MALE-CHILD, CHRIST (12:5-6)

12:5-6. When the Child—described as **a Son, a male Child, who will rule all the nations with an iron scepter**—was born, He **was snatched up to God and to His throne.** The Child obviously is Jesus Christ (Ps. 2:9; Rev. 19:15). Alford states that "the Man-Child is the Lord Jesus Christ, *and none other*" (*The Greek Testament*, 4:668). The catching up of the Child referred to the Ascension, not to the later Rapture of the church though the same word for "snatched up" is used of the Rapture (1 Thes. 4:17; cf. Acts 8:39; 2 Cor. 12:2-4). The Rapture of the church would not constitute a deliverance of the Man-Child from Satan.

The deliverance itself took place when the woman **fled into the desert to a place prepared for her by God,** and she was preserved **for 1,260 days,** which was three and one-half years or 42 months of 30 days each. Matthew (24:16) referred to the flight of Israel at the beginning of the Great Tribulation (cf. Mark 13:14). References to both desert and mountains are not a contradiction as both were wilderness areas. In her desert hideout Israel was cared for perhaps as miraculously as Israel was in her wilderness journey from Egypt to the Promised Land.

The time period was 1,260 days, later described as "a time, times, and half a time" (cf. comments on Rev. 12:14). This action (vv. 5-6) followed what is described in verse 7 as a "war in heaven."

4. THE FOURTH PERSONAGE: SATAN CAST OUT OF HEAVEN (12:7-12)

12:7. Michael the archangel (cf. Jude 9) **and his angels** fought Satan **and his angels,** that is, demons. The time of this **war in heaven** was not indicated but the context refers to the end time. The efforts of some expositors to make this coincidental with the first coming of Christ, linking it with Luke 10:18, are not justified by the context in Revelation 12. Also Satan is most obviously active throughout the period of the Church Age (cf. Acts 5:3; 1 Cor. 5:5; 7:5; 2 Cor. 2:11; 11:14; 12:7; 1 Tim. 1:20; 1 Peter 5:8).

The concept that Satan is inactive in the present Age is a false conclusion based on an attempt to place the binding of Satan at the first coming of Christ (Rev. 20:1-3). However, the binding of Satan is still a future event that relates to the millennial kingdom.

12:8-9. The outcome of the war was that Satan **was hurled to the earth,** and his character was clearly revealed in the various titles ascribed to him: **the great dragon . . . that ancient serpent . . . the devil or Satan.** With him went the fallen **angels** of the demon world.

While the concept of Satan in heaven is difficult to comprehend, it is clear that he is now the accuser of saints (cf. Job 1:6; Rev. 12:10). Though Satan was defeated at the first coming of Christ (John 16:11), his execution was delayed and is in stages. Here (Rev. 12:8-9) he will be cast out of heaven in the middle of the Tribulation. Later he will be bound for the duration of the millennial kingdom (20:1-3). The devil will finally be thrown into the lake of burning sulfur (20:10) where the world ruler (Antichrist) and the false prophet will have been cast a thousand years earlier.

Satan and his activities in heaven and earth opposed Christ as Priest in heaven, as King in Satan's world rule in the Great Tribulation, and as the true Prophet by advancing the beast out of the earth (13:11), who was the false prophet (20:10). Satan was identified as that ancient serpent, alias the devil or Satan, and was declared to be the one who led the whole world astray. When he will be cast into the earth, all the fallen angels or demons will be cast down with him.

12:10-12. John then heard a hymn of praise uttered by **a loud voice in heaven.** Announcement was made of the coming demonstration of divine **salvation** and **power** with the advent of the millennial kingdom. Satan was characterized as the one who **accuses** believers **before our God day and night.** The principle by which he was overcome and cast out of heaven was **the blood of the Lamb** and **the word of their testimony.** Not only did Christ provide the victory, but also those who were martyred took part in that victory. Those in the heavens were called on to rejoice because of Satan's defeat, but the earth was warned that the devil was **filled with fury, because he** knew **that his time** was short. The devil knew that his time was limited to 1,260 days,

the period of the Great Tribulation. By no stretch of the imagination can these prophecies be spread to cover the whole Interadvent Age as some attempt to do.

5. THE FIFTH PERSONAGE: THE OFFSPRING OF THE WOMAN PERSECUTED BY THE DRAGON (12:13-17)

12:13-14. The woman introduced in verse 1 became the special object of Satan's persecution. She was given supernatural help symbolized by **the two wings of a great eagle** which enabled her **to fly to the place prepared for her in the desert.**

This hiding place was not clearly identified. Some suggest that it might be Petra, fortress capital of the Nabateans in Edom, south of the Dead Sea. This city has a narrow access which could easily be blocked but which opens up into a large canyon capable of caring for many thousands of people. Though Scripture is not specific, some believe the 144,000 of chapter 7 are to be preserved here. The Scriptures themselves speak of God's seal of protection on them.

The two wings probably do not refer to modern airplanes but rather to God's delivering power, and are a figure of speech taken from such Old Testament passages as Exodus 19:4 and Deuteronomy 32:11-12. The flight of Israel to a place of safety was also indicated in Matthew 24:16; Mark 13:14; and Luke 21:21.

Though Revelation 12:6, 14 referred to the refuge as a desert and the Synoptic passages referred to mountains, this is no contradiction as both desert and mountains are in a wilderness area. The length of time of her preservation was said to be **a time, times, and half a time.** This refers to the three and one-half years of the Great Tribulation with "a time" equaling one year, "times" equaling two years, and "half a time" indicating 6 months (cf. Dan. 7:25; 12:7 with the 42 months referred to in Rev. 11:2; 13:5). References to these specific time periods show that the Great Tribulation is *not* the entire present Age but the three and one-half years preceding the second coming of Christ.

12:15-17. Pursuing the woman, the devil as **the serpent** originated a flood to **sweep her away with the torrent,** but the

REVELATION

earth swallowed up the water. Some have taken this as a literal flood, but since Israel could flee in every direction the contour of the Holy Land does not lend itself to such a flood. Probably the flood represents Satan's effort to exterminate Israel. This is thwarted by the rough terrain which provides hiding places. In some way God assists the Israelites so that they are not completely destroyed, though Zechariah 13:8 indicates that "two-thirds will be struck down and perish."

Though only one-third of Israel in the land is thus preserved (of which the 144,000 of Rev. 7 are a portion), Satan the dragon continues to war against the rest.

Revelation 12 introduces four important persons and one group of people living at the end time: Israel, Satan, Christ, the archangel, and the remnant of Israel. In Revelation 13 two important persons complete the scene.

6. THE SIXTH PERSONAGE: THE BEAST OUT OF THE SEA (13:1-10)

a. The beast out of the sea introduced (13:1-2)

13:1-2. Chapter 13 presents a most important personage of the end time—**a beast coming out of the sea.** His **10 horns and 7 heads, with 10 crowns on his horns,** depict the revived Roman Empire, which was also represented by the fourth beast of Daniel, which also had 10 horns (Dan. 7:7-8; cf. Rev. 13:3; 17:3, 7). In Revelation 13 and 17 the beast is the world ruler, whereas in Daniel 7 the little horn on the beast was the world ruler.

The fact that the beast comes out from the sea indicates that he is a Gentile, for the sea of humanity is involved as his source (cf. Rev. 17:15).

Many have said that the beast refers to some character in past history, but the context clearly refers to the final three and one-half years before Christ's second coming. Under the control of this central ruler in the Middle East during the Great Tribulation will be 10 nations (cf. Dan. 7:24, "The 10 horns are 10 kings"). (For discussion of various alternative views, see Walvoord, *Revelation*, pp. 198-99.)

In Revelation 13:2 the beast was seen to gather in the symbolism of the three preceding empires—Greece (**a leopard,** cf. Dan. 7:6), Medo-Persia (**a bear,** cf.

Dan. 7:5), and Babylon (**a lion,** cf. Dan. 7:4). The power of the beast was derived from Satan himself: **the dragon gave the beast his power and his throne and great authority.** This accords with Paul (2 Thes. 2:9) who referred to "the lawless one" (i.e., the Antichrist, this first beast of Rev. 13) as working "all kinds of counterfeit miracles [*dynamei*], signs [*sēmeiois*], and wonders [*terasin*]."

b. The fatal wound of the beast (13:3)

13:3. The seven **heads of the beast** seem to represent important rulers, and one of them, probably the seventh, suffered **a fatal wound** caused by a sword (v. 14), which was subsequently **healed,** causing astonishment in the entire world.

Many have attempted to identify this beast as someone in the past or present who is to become the final world ruler. Among the suggestions have been Nero, Judas Iscariot, Mussolini, Hitler, Stalin, Kissinger, and many others; but such men obviously do not fit the details of this yet-future ruler.

What is the meaning of the fatal wound that is healed? Two possibilities seem to fit this description. Alford, for instance, sees the deadly wound as the destruction of "the Roman pagan Empire" by "the Christian Roman Empire," thus making it a matter of history rather than prophecy (*The Greek Testament*, 4: 675). The revival of the Roman Empire would then be its miraculous healing. Another plausible explanation is that the final world ruler receives a wound which normally would be fatal but is miraculously healed by Satan. While the resurrection of a dead person seems to be beyond Satan's power, the healing of a wound would be possible for Satan, and this may be the explanation. The important point is that the final world ruler comes into power obviously supported by a supernatural and miraculous deliverance by Satan himself.

c. The worship of Satan and the beast (13:4-6)

13:4-6. The supernatural character of **the beast** makes him the object of worship along with Satan, the source of his power. It has always been Satan's purpose to receive the worship due to

God alone, as stated in Isaiah 14:14: "I will make myself like the Most High." This is Satan's final form of counterfeit religion in which he assumes the place of God the Father, and the beast or the world ruler assumes the role of King of kings as a substitute for Christ. This situation is probably introduced at the beginning of the last three and one-half years when the Great Tribulation begins.

Recognizing the supernatural character of Satan and the ruler, the question is raised, **Who is like the beast? Who can make war against him?** (Rev. 13:4) This apparently explains how the beast could become world ruler without a war. His blasphemous assumption of the role of God continues **for 42 months,** during which time he blasphemes **God** as well as heaven and **those who live in heaven.**

d. *The worldwide power of the beast (13:7-8)*

13:7-8. The beast becomes a worldwide ruler, for his authority extends **over every tribe, people, language, and nation.** As predicted in Daniel 7:23, he does "devour the whole earth, trampling it down and crushing it."

In addition to achieving political domination over the entire world, he also abolishes all other religions and demands that everyone worship him (cf. 2 Thes. 2:4). **All inhabitants of the earth** worship **the beast** except for those whose names are recorded **in the book of life.** In the expression **the Lamb that was slain from the Creation of the world,** the words "from the Creation of the world" seem, as in the NIV margin, to relate to the time in eternity past when the names were written in the book of life, rather than to Christ's crucifixion, since He was not crucified when the world was created. As Paul wrote, those who were saved were foreordained to salvation before Creation (cf. Eph. 1:4).

Some hold that the book of life originally contained the names of every living person to be born in the world, and that the names of the unsaved get blotted out when they die. This interpretation stems from Revelation 3:5, where Christ promised the believers in Sardis that their names would not be erased from the book of life, and from 22:19, where a person who rejects the messages in the Book of Revelation is warned that "God will take away from him his share in the tree of life" (cf. "tree of life" in 2:7 and 22:2, 14 and "book of life" in 3:5; 17:8; 20:12, 15; 21:27). However, 13:8 probably means simply that those who are saved had their names written in the book of life in eternity past in anticipation of the death of Christ on the cross for them and that they will never be erased.

Taken together, verses 7 and 8 indicate the universal extent of the beast's political government as well as the final form of satanic religion in the Great Tribulation. Only those who come to Christ will be delivered from the condemnation that is involved.

e. *The exhortation to hear (13:9-10)*

13:9-10. In a format similar to the exhortation to the seven churches of Asia Minor (chaps. 2-3) this passage gave an invitation to individuals who would listen. The dream of many today, of a universal church and a universal religion, will be realized in the end time, but it will be satanic and blasphemous instead of involving worship of the true God. In such a situation, appeal can only be made to individuals who will turn from it to God. In every age God speaks to those who will hear, a concept mentioned frequently in the Gospels (Matt. 11:15; 13:9, 43; Mark 4:9, 23; Luke 8:8; 14:35).

In contrast with the invitation addressed to the seven churches where each exhortation was addressed "to the church," the mention of churches is notably absent here. This is another indication that the church has been raptured before the time of these events. Revelation, instead of being interpreted as addressed only to first-generation Christians facing persecution, is better understood as an exhortation to believers in all generations but especially those who will be living in the end time. Those who are willing to listen are reminded that their obedience to the Word of God may result in their **captivity** or martyrdom (Rev. 13:10), so the exhortation closes, **This calls for patient endurance** (*hypomonē*, "steadfastness, perseverance"; cf. 14:12) **and faithfulness on the part of the saints.**

7. THE SEVENTH PERSONAGE: THE BEAST OUT OF THE EARTH (13:11-18)

a. Introduction of the beast out of the earth (13:11-12)

13:11-12. In contrast with the first beast who came "out of the sea" (v. 1), the second beast came **out of the earth.** He was similar to the first beast (*thērion*, "a beast," was used of both personages). However, while the first beast was a Gentile, since he came from the entire human race as symbolized by "the sea" (v. 1), the second beast was a creature of the earth. Some have taken this as a specific reference to the Promised Land and have argued that he was therefore a Jew. There is no support for this in the context as the word for "earth" is the general word referring to the entire world (*gē*). Actually his nationality and geographic origin are not indicated, and he is apparently the one referred to as "the false prophet" in 19:20 and 20:10. (For a comprehensive discussion of the two beasts see Alford, *The Greek New Testament,* 4:678-79.)

The second beast **had two horns like a lamb, but he spoke like a dragon,** that is, like Satan. From this it can be gathered that he was a religious character whose role was to support the political ruler, **the first beast.** He had great **authority** apparently derived from Satan and the political ruler, and he **made the earth and its inhabitants worship the first beast,** the one **whose fatal wound had been healed.**

The false religious system, which was supported in this way imitated the divine Trinity. Satan seeks to take the place of God the Father; the first beast assumes the place of Jesus Christ, the Son, the King of kings; and the second beast, the false prophet, has a role similar to the Holy Spirit who causes Christians to worship God. This is Satan's final attempt to substitute a false religion for true faith in Christ.

b. The miracles of the beast (13:13-15)

13:13-15. To induce people to worship the first beast, the second beast performs **great and miraculous signs** (lit., "great signs," *sēmeia megala;* cf. "a great . . . sign" in 12:1), including **fire . . . from heaven.** People sometimes overlook the fact that, while God can do supernatural things, Satan within certain limitations can also perform miracles, and he used this **power** to the full in this situation to induce people to worship Satan's substitute for Christ. Accordingly the second beast **deceived the inhabitants of the earth.**

In addition to causing fire to come down from heaven, the second beast set up an image of the first beast. The image was probably set up in the first temple in Jerusalem which was taken over from the Jews. According to Paul (2 Thes. 2:4) the first beast actually sat in God's temple at times and received worship which properly belonged to God. Perhaps the beast's image was placed in the same temple to provide an object of worship when the beast himself was not there.

This image was mentioned frequently (Rev. 13:14-15; 14:9, 11; 15:2; 16:2; 19:20; 20:4). Whether the image was in the form of the world ruler, the first beast, or merely some object of worship is not clear, but it did seem to symbolize the power of the first beast.

The fact that the second beast could **give breath to the image of the first beast,** even making it **speak,** has created problems for expositors, for the Bible does not seem to indicate that Satan has the power to give life to an inanimate object. Only God is the Creator. So probably the beast's image is able to give an *impression* of breathing and speaking mechanically, like computerized talking robots today. There might be a combination of natural and supernatural powers to enable the beast out of the earth to accomplish his purpose. It apparently was quite convincing to people and induced them to worship the image.

The command to **worship the image** as well as the first beast was enforced by killing those who **refused to** do so. But there was a difference between the decree to put them to death and its execution. The problem of ferreting out everyone in the entire earth who would not worship the beast would naturally take time. Hitler, in his attempt to exterminate the Jews, took many months and never completed his task. The multitude of martyrs is referred to in 7:9-17.

c. The mark of the beast (13:16-18)

13:16-18. Enforcing his control over the human race and encouraging worship of the beast out of the sea, the second beast required **everyone . . . to receive a mark on his right hand or on his forehead,** and without this evidence that he had worshiped the beast **no one could buy or sell.** The need to buy or sell such necessities as food and clothing would force each person in the entire world to decide whether to worship the beast or to bear the penalty. Apparently the great majority worshiped the beast.

There has been much speculation on the insignia or "mark" of the beast, but it could be any of several kinds of identification. Countless attempts have been made to interpret the number 666, usually using the numerical equivalents of letters in the Hebrew, Greek, or other alphabets. As there probably have been hundreds of explanations continuing down to the present day, it is obvious that if the number refers to an individual it is not clear to whom it refers.

Probably the best interpretation is that the number six is one less than the perfect number seven, and the threefold repetition of the six would indicate that for all their pretentions to deity, Satan and the two beasts were just creatures and not the Creator. That six is **man's number** is illustrated in many instances in the Bible, including the fact that man should work six days and rest the seventh. (For further discussion of the many views cf. Mounce, *The Book of Revelation,* pp. 263-65; Smith, *A Revelation of Jesus Christ,* pp. 206-7; and Walvoord, *Revelation,* pp. 209-12.)

The practice of gematria, the attempt to find hidden meanings in numbers in Scripture, was prominent in the ancient world. Maybe John had in mind a particular person whom his close associates would be able to identify. Literature from the early church fathers, however, reveals the same confusion and variety of meanings that exist today, so probably it is best to leave this puzzle unsolved. Probably the safest conclusion is that of Thomas F. Torrance, "This evil trinity 666 apes the Holy Trinity 777, but always falls short and fails" (*The Apocalypse Today,* p. 86).

Chapter 13 is important because it introduces two of the main characters of Revelation: the beast out of the sea, the world dictator; and the beast out of the earth, the false prophet and chief supporter of the political ruler. There is no evidence that either of them is a Jew though some have identified one or the other as an apostate Jew based on the expression "the God of his fathers" (Dan. 11:37, KJV). However, the Hebrew word *'ĕlōhîm* is a general word for god, quite different from *Yahweh,* and there is no proof that in Daniel it refers to the God of Israel. In recent translations it is "gods" (cf. ASV, NASB, NEB, NIV, AND RSV). Thus while it has been popular to consider either the first or the second ruler of Revelation 13 as an apostate Jew, the supporting evidence is lacking. Both beasts are probably Gentiles inasmuch as this will be the final hour of the time of the Gentiles, when Gentiles will tramp underfoot the city of Jerusalem (Luke 21:24), and both rulers will persecute Jews as well as believing Gentiles.

Revelation 13, however, gives much insight into the character of the Great Tribulation. It will be a time of one world government and one world religion, with one world economic system. Those who will resist the ruler and refuse to worship him will be subject to execution, and the martyrs may outnumber the believers who survive. It will be Satan's final and ultimate attempt to cause the world to worship him and to turn them from the worship of the true God and Jesus Christ as their Savior.

This chapter also makes it clear that the postmillennial dream of a world getting better and better through Christian effort and gospel preaching is not supported in the Bible. Instead the final form of world religion will be apostate, satanic, and blasphemous. There are many indications today that the world is heading in this direction, with the corresponding conclusion that the coming of the Lord may be near.

8. THE RESULTING SCENE IN EARTH AND HEAVEN (CHAPS. 14-15)

a. The 144,000 on Mount Zion (14:1-5)

In chapters 14 and 15 various other details of the world scene in heaven and earth are introduced in preparation for the final series of seven bowl judgments in chapter 16 and the judgments in chapters 17-18.

14:1-2. First, another view is given of the **144,000** who were **standing on Mount Zion** with **the Lamb.** It is reasonable to conclude that this is the same group mentioned in 7:4-8, except that here they are in a later period of the Tribulation. Chronologically the vision anticipates the triumph of the 144,000 still intact at the time of Jesus Christ's return from heaven to earth. In contrast with many others who become martyrs, these people live through the period. But they are not the only ones to survive, as many Gentiles and Jews will turn to Christ in the end time and somehow escape martyrdom and be honored to welcome Christ at His return.

Again the scene in heaven is dramatic with a loud noise similar to **rushing waters . . . thunder,** and **harpists** (cf. "thunder" in 4:5; 6:1; 8:5; 11:19; 16:18; 19:6).

14:3-5. John wrote, **And they sang a new song before the throne and before the four living creatures and the elders.** These singers were apparently a heavenly group. They could be the multitude in white robes mentioned in 7:9-17. But there is no justification here for symbolizing Mount Zion as heaven. It is better to take the chorus as the 144,000 (cf. 14:1) who had not yet died and would still be on earth at the literal Mount Zion.

Reference to the purity of **the 144,000** could be recognition that during the difficult times of the Tribulation they could not have led normal married lives. Or it may refer to spiritual purity, often symbolized by virginity (cf. 2 Kings 19:21; Isa. 37:22; Jer. 18:13; 31:4, 21; Lam. 2:13; Amos 5:2). In 2 Corinthians 11:2 the concept of virginity is extended to the entire church, including both sexes.

Some people believe that the 144,000 will be evangelists in the Great Tribulation. But there is no indication that the 144,000 were preachers or prophets; their testimony was largely from their moral purity and the fact that they were not martyred like many others. **They follow the Lamb wherever He goes.** John further stated, **They were purchased from among men and offered as firstfruits to God and the Lamb.** The word "firstfruits" suggests that these converted Israelites precede many others who at the Lord's second coming will turn to Him (Zech. 12:10; Rom. 11:15, 26-27). They were also described as **blameless** (*amōmoi,* a word used of sacrificial animals without defect)

and as those who, living in a period of great satanic deception, were free from lying. The passage as a whole is a prophetic foreview of the triumph of the 144,000 when Christ returns.

b. The message of the three angels (14:6-12)

14:6-8. John was then given a vision of an angel carrying a message called **the eternal gospel.** The angel was commissioned to bring his message to every group of people **on the earth.** Because of the word "gospel," some have felt that this was a message of salvation or the good news of the coming kingdom. The context, however, seems to indicate otherwise, for the message is one of **judgment** and condemnation. The angel announced, **Fear God and give Him glory, because the hour of His judgment has come.** So the "eternal" message seems to be a message of God's righteousness and judgment rather than a message of salvation.

The first angel was followed by **a second angel** who announced that **Babylon the Great,** which intoxicated others with **her adulteries, has fallen.** This apparently is in anticipation of the description of that city (see comments on chap. 18).

14:9-12. A **third angel followed** with another judgment that worshipers of **the beast and his image** who receive **his mark** will be objects of God's wrath and will be destined for eternal torment along with Satan, the demon world, and all unsaved people. The everlasting character of this judgment is stated plainly in verse 11: **The smoke of their torment rises forever and ever,** and they will have **no rest.** Those who keep God's commandments and are faithful to Him will need **patient endurance** (v. 12; cf. 13:10). The doctrine of eternal punishment, though unpopular with liberal scholars and difficult to accept, is nevertheless clearly taught in the Bible. Jesus and the Apostle John say more on this subject than does all the rest of the Bible.

c. The blessing of the faithful saints (14:13)

14:13. After the solemn pronouncement of the third angel John **heard a voice from heaven** commanding him,

Write: **Blessed are the dead who die in the Lord from now on.** To this the Holy Spirit added the promise, **they will rest from their labor, for their deeds will follow them.**

This passage is often quoted in regard to God's general blessings on all Christians, but the context indicates that the blessing is especially for those who die in the Great Tribulation. For them it is a blessed release from persecution, torture, and trial and a deliverance into the glorious presence of the Lord.

d. The messages of the second group of three angels (14:14-20)

14:14-16. John in his vision next saw seated on **a white cloud** one **like a Son of Man** wearing **a crown of gold** and holding **a sharp sickle.** Though some have identified "a Son of Man" as an angel, it is more probable that it is Christ Himself who is frequently called "the Son of Man" (cf. 1:13). In the Book of Matthew alone this title is ascribed to Christ more than 25 times (Matt. 8:20; 9:6; 11:19; 12:8, 32; 13:41; etc.). The sickle in His hand suggests judgment. And this is supported by the messages of the three angels (Rev. 14:15-20).

An **angel** called out to Christ to **reap, because the harvest of the earth is ripe.** The ripeness is in the sense of withered or overripe (*exēranthē*). What follows is judgment as the **sickle** is **swung . . . over the earth.** Alford holds that verse 14 refers to the harvest of the saints, and that verses 15-16 describe judgment on the wicked (*The Greek New Testament,* 4: 691). But it is difficult to imagine a harvest of saints as being withered or overripe.

14:17-20. Another angel had **a sharp sickle,** and a fellow **angel** commanded him to **gather . . . clusters of grapes from the earth's vine, because its grapes are ripe.** Here a different word is used for ripe (*ēkmasan*), meaning "to be fully grown" or "in prime condition." The grapes were full of juice and ready for harvest. In obedience the angel **gathered** the **grapes and threw them into the great winepress of God's wrath. They were trampled** there **outside the city,** probably Jerusalem (cf. "the great city" in 11:8).

The custom was to produce grape juice by trampling on grapes in a winepress. The result here, however, is different. **Blood flowed out of the press rising as high as the horses' bridles for a distance of 1,600 stadia,** about 180 miles. While this distance may be literal and may designate the area of judgment as around the city of Jerusalem, it is of course impossible for the blood to reach a height where it would touch horses' bridles. What this affirms is a tremendous bloodletting in which blood is spattered as high as the bridles of horses. This is a graphic picture of a great slaughter (Isa. 63:1-3). Other Scriptures (e.g., Rev. 16:14; Dan. 11:40-45) make it clear that there will be a world war of tremendous scope underway at the time of the second coming of Christ, and this may be a partial fulfillment of these prophecies.

Taken as a whole, Revelation 14 on the one hand refers to the preservation of the 144,000 through the Great Tribulation. And on the other hand it graphically declares some of the terrible judgments that will be inflicted on the world which rejects Christ and follows Satan's substitute for the Lord.

William Kelly regards this chapter as an outline of major events at the end of the Age: (1) the appearance of the godly remnant of Israel; (2) a testimony to Gentiles; (3) the fall of Babylon; (4) the doom of the worshipers of the beast; (5) the blessedness of saints who are martyred; (6) the harvest; (7) the wrath of God on the world (*Lectures on the Book of Revelation,* p. 330).

e. The seven angels introduced (15:1-8)

15:1-2. With the background of the scene in heaven described in chapter 14, John then recorded more details of God's judgment. He wrote that he **saw in heaven another great and marvelous sign. Seven angels**—each having a plague which all together were described as **the seven last plagues**—were introduced as the final step in the outpouring of **God's wrath** on the earth. This final "sign" relates to the preceding great signs of the woman in 12:1 and the red dragon in 12:3. These seven angels should not be confused with the two groups of three angels in the preceding chapter (14:6-20) or with any other previous group of angels.

John also **saw what looked like a sea of glass mixed with fire.** This is probably the same sea that was described in 4:6. **Beside** this **sea** John saw the martyred dead, the same group described in 7:9-17.

15:3-4. The victorious saints **sang** with harps **the song of Moses ... and the song of the Lamb.** These may be two separate songs, the first referring to God's faithfulness to Israel and the second referring to their present situation in the Great Tribulation. Some, like Walter Scott, refer the song of Moses to Exodus 15 where Israel triumphed over the Egyptians (*Exposition of Revelation*, p. 315). Others, such as J.B. Smith, suggest that this is the song of Deuteronomy 32, which gives a comprehensive review of God's faithfulness to Israel (*A Revelation of Jesus Christ*, pp. 224-25). In this song in Revelation 15:3-4 God is praised for His great deeds, justice, truth (cf. 16:7), glory, and holiness (see 4:8 for a chart of the 14 doxologies in Rev.). Then a prediction is made that **all** the **nations** will **worship** God.

This description of praise to God and prediction of universal worship is in keeping with many other Scriptures and relates, of course, to the second coming of Christ and worship of God by the entire world in the millennial kingdom (Pss. 2:8-9; 24:1-10; 66:1-4; 72:8-11; 86:9; Isa. 2:2-4; 9:6-7; 66:18-23; Jer. 10:7; Dan. 7:14; Zeph. 2:11; Zech. 14:9). The awful hour of wickedness and blasphemy against God, which will characterize the period leading up to the Second Coming, will be followed by a full vindication of God's judgment and holiness in the next period.

15:5-8. As John continued to look at the heavenly vision, he saw **the temple** described as **the tabernacle of Testimony.** The allusion to a temple **in heaven** seems to be the heavenly counterpart of the earthly temple. As it was opened, **the seven angels with** their **plagues** exited from it. The **clean, shining linen** of the angels indicates their purity, and the **golden sashes around their chests** point to the glory of God.

John saw **one of the four living creatures** give the **seven golden bowls filled with the wrath of God** to the seven angels. When this was done, **smoke** filled **the temple,** making it impossible for anyone to **enter** it **until the seven plagues** were poured out on the earth (cf. Ex. 40:34-35). Taken as a whole, Revelation 15:5-8 presents a fearful picture of impending divine judgment on a wicked world. The judgments which are to be poured out (chap. 16) fully justify this ominous introduction.

J. The bowls of divine wrath (chap. 16)

Chronologically this chapter is close to the time of the second coming of Christ, and the judgments described fall in rapid succession. Alford says, "There can then be no doubt here, not only that the series reaches on to the time of the end, but that the whole of it is to be placed close to the same time" (*The Greek Testament*, 4:696). Daniel indicated that these closing days of the Tribulation will be a time of world war (Dan. 11:36-45). World events are now pictured by John as rapidly coming to their climax.

1. THE FIRST BOWL (16:1-2)

16:1-2. John recorded that he **heard a loud voice from the temple** instructing **the seven angels** to **pour out the seven bowls of God's wrath on the earth.** This is undoubtedly the voice of God speaking from His heavenly temple. The adjective translated "loud" (*megalēs*) is frequently used in this chapter (v. 17 also refers to the loud voice). But the same Greek word is used in connection with intense heat (v. 9), the great river Euphrates (v. 12), the great day of God Almighty (v. 14), a severe earthquake (v. 18), the great city (v. 19), Babylon the Great (v. 19), huge hailstones (v. 21), and a terrible plague (v. 21). The judgments being poured out are greater, more severe, more intense than anything that has happened in the preceding events. When **the first angel ... poured out his bowl** of wrath, it produced **ugly and painful sores** on those who had the beast's mark **and worshiped his image.**

The question has been raised as to whether the bowls of the wrath of God are chronologically subsequent to or identical with the seven trumpets of the angels. There is clearly much similarity between the trumpet judgments and the bowl judgments. They both deal with (a) the earth (8:7) or the land (16:2), (b) the sea (8:8; 16:3), (c) the rivers and springs of water (8:10; 16:4), and (d) the sun, moon, and stars (8:12) with only the sun mentioned in the bowl judgments (16:8-9). The fifth trumpet dealt with demon possession with the sun and sky darkened (9:1-3), which is similar to the fifth bowl in which darkness will cover the earth and sores will cause agony among men (16:10-11). The sixth trumpet deals with the river Euphrates (9:13-14), and the sixth bowl will dry up the Euphrates (16:12). The seventh trumpet implies that the Great Tribulation is coming to its end (11:15-19), and the seventh bowl of the wrath of God records a loud voice from heaven, saying, "It is done!" (16:17) with resulting destruction of the earth by earthquake and hail, which is also included in the seventh trumpet (11:18-19).

Similarities, however, do not prove identity, and a comparison of the trumpets with the bowls of God's wrath reveals striking differences even though the order of the judgments is the same. In the trumpet judgments, generally speaking, a third of the earth or heaven is afflicted, whereas in the bowl judgments the effects of the judgments are on the entire earth and are much more severe and final in character. Accordingly it seems best to follow the interpretation which has long been held in the church that the seven bowls are an expansion of the seventh trumpet, just as the seven trumpets are an expansion of the breaking of the seventh seal. The order is climactic and the judgments become more intensive and extensive as the time of the second coming of Christ approaches. All indications are that the bowl judgments fall with trip-hammer rapidity on a world that is reeling under previous judgments and a gigantic world war. Some bowl judgments are selective and extend only to the wicked (16:2, 8-11), and several affect parts of nature (sea, rivers, sun, etc.).

In the first bowl judgment people who followed the Antichrist received painful sores. Sores also come with the fifth bowl (vv. 10-11).

2. THE SECOND BOWL (16:3)

16:3. After the second trumpet blew (8:8-9), "a third of the sea turned into blood," killing "a third of the living creatures" and destroying "a third of the ships" (8:8-9). In **the second . . . bowl,** however, **every living thing in the sea died** (16:3). It is probable that the ocean here did not chemically correspond to human blood, but that it looked like blood and had the same effect in killing everything. Just as in the second trumpet, the blood here is analogous to the first plague in Egypt (Ex. 7:20-25). As most of the earth's surface is covered by the seas, this is a worldwide, tremendous judgment.

3. THE THIRD BOWL (16:4-7)

16:4-7. Just as the third trumpet made "a third of the waters" bitter (8:11), so **the third . . . bowl** extends the judgment of the second bowl on the sea to **rivers and springs** and **they became blood** (16:4). John heard the angel in charge of the waters proclaim that God the Holy One is **just in** His **judgments** (v. 5). For God's work in turning the waters to blood is in response to the shedding of **the blood of . . . saints and prophets** (v. 6). This is echoed by a word from the altar declaring the judgment just (v. 7; cf. 15:3).

4. THE FOURTH BOWL (16:8-9)

16:8-9. This judgment focused the **intense heat of the sun.** In response people **cursed . . . God** and **refused to repent** (cf. v. 11). By contrast, the fourth trumpet (8:12) darkened a third of the heavens but did not include additional intense heat. It is clear from this and other prophecies that dramatic changes in climate will occur in the Great Tribulation.

5. THE FIFTH BOWL (16:10-11)

16:10-11. This judgment was directed toward the beast's **throne,** imposed **darkness** on the earth, and inflicted painful **sores** (cf. v. 2) on people. Again they **cursed . . . God** and **refused to repent.** This is the last reference in Revelation to a failure to repent (cf. 2:21; 9:21; 16:9; cf., however, 16:21). The fifth bowl is similar to the fifth trumpet (9:1-11) in that both will bring darkness, but the fifth trumpet has to do with demon possession rather than physical pain.

6. THE SIXTH BOWL (16:12-16)

16:12. According to John's revelation, **the sixth angel poured out his bowl** and dried up the river Euphrates **to prepare the way for the kings from the**

East. There has been endless speculation about "the kings from the East," with many expositors trying to relate them to some contemporary leaders of their generation. A survey of 100 commentaries of the Book of Revelation reveals at least 50 interpretations of the identity of the kings of the East. The simplest and best explanation, however, is that this refers to kings or rulers from the Orient or East who will participate in the final world war. In the light of the context of this passage indicating the near approach of the second coming of Christ and the contemporary world situation in which the Orient today contains a large portion of the world's population with tremendous military potential, any interpretation other than a literal one does not make sense. Alford states it concisely: "This is the only understanding of these words which will suit the context, or the requirement of this series of prophecies" (Alford, *The Greek Testament,* 4:700).

This is related to the **great river Euphrates** because this is the water boundary between the Holy Land and Asia to the east (cf. comments on 9:12-16). While the implication is that the water is dried up by an act of God, the fact is that dams have been built across the Euphrates River in this century to divert water for irrigation so that there are times even today when there is little or no water in the Euphrates. The Euphrates River is frequently mentioned in Scripture (e.g., Gen. 15:18; Deut. 1:7; 11:24; Josh. 1:4). The drying up of this river is also predicted in Isaiah 11:15.

16:13-16. John was then given a symbolic and comprehensive view of the preparation for the final bowl of God's wrath. He **saw three evil spirits that looked like frogs** coming out of the mouths of Satan (**the dragon**) and the two beasts (Antichrist [13:1-10] and the false prophet [13:11-18]). One need not speculate on the identity of the three frogs, for verse 14 explains that **they are spirits of demons performing miraculous signs.** These demons go throughout the world influencing kings to assemble **for the battle on the great day of God Almighty** ("Almighty" [*pantokratōr*] is also used in 1:8; 4:8; 11:17; 15:3; 16:7; 19:6, 15; 21:22).

While the meaning of this symbolic presentation is clear, there is a major problem involved in what the demons do. The coming world government in the Great Tribulation will be established by the power of Satan (13:2). Here, however, Satan, the world ruler, and the false prophet unite in inciting the nations of the world **to gather** for the final world war. Actually the war is a form of rebellion against the world ruler. Why then should satanic forces be let loose to destroy the world empire which has just been created?

The answer seems to be in the events which follow. Satan, knowing that the second coming of Christ is near, will gather all the military might of the world into the Holy Land to resist the coming of the Son of Man who will return to the Mount of Olives (Zech. 14:4). Though the nations may be deceived in entering into the war in hope of gaining world political power, the satanic purpose is to combat the armies from heaven (introduced in chap. 19) at the second coming of Christ.

The war is said to continue right up to the day of the Second Coming and involves house-to-house fighting in Jerusalem itself on the day of the Lord's return (Zech. 14:1-3). The reference to "the battle" (*ton polemon,* Rev. 16:14) is probably better translated "the war" (NASB). Thus it is better to speak of "the war of Armageddon" (see v. 16) rather than the "the battle of Armageddon." The war will be going on for some time, but the climax will come at Christ's second coming. "Armageddon" comes from the Greek *Harmagedōn,* which transliterates the Hebrew words for Mount (*har*) of Megiddo. That mountain is near the city of Megiddo and the plain of Esdraelon, the scene of many Old Testament battles.

Accordingly John heard the warning coming from Christ Himself: **Behold, I come like a thief! Blessed is he who stays awake and keeps his clothes with him, so that he may not go naked and be shamefully exposed.**

Christ's return is often compared to the coming of a thief. It implies suddenness and unpreparedness as far as unbelievers are concerned. Just as Christians are not to be surprised by the Rapture of the church (1 Thes. 5:4), so believers at the time of the Second Coming will be anticipating His return. Blessing is promised to the one who is prepared for the coming of the Lord by being attired in the righteousness or clothing which God Himself supplies.

Taken as a whole, the sixth bowl of the wrath of God is preparation for the final act of judgment before the Second Coming, and is the later stage of development related to the river Euphrates, anticipated earlier (Rev. 9:14). The time factor between the sixth trumpet and the sixth bowl is comparatively short.

7. THE SEVENTH BOWL (16:17-21)

16:17-20. The seventh angel then **poured out his bowl into the air.** John heard **a loud voice from the throne, saying, It is done!** A similar pronouncement followed the seventh trumpet (11:15-19). Here also John saw **lightning** flashes and heard **thunder,** which was followed by **a severe earthquake (16:18).** John was then informed that this will be the greatest earthquake of all time (other earthquakes are mentioned in 8:5 and 11:19), and the resulting description indicates that it will affect the whole earth with the possible exception of the land of Israel. **The great city** which **split into three parts** refers to the destruction of **Babylon.** The most important event, however, is that **the cities of the nations collapsed.** The huge earthquake will reduce to rubble all the cities of the nations (Gentiles). The stage is thus being set for the second coming of Christ. Obviously in the collapse of the world's cities there will be tremendous loss of life and destruction of what is left of the world empire.

Though Jerusalem is mentioned in 11:8 as "the great city, which is figuratively called Sodom and Egypt, where also their Lord was crucified," "the great city" here is specifically Babylon, as indicated in 16:19. God will give Babylon **the cup filled with the wine of the fury of His wrath,** that is, she will experience a terrible outpouring of His judgment. Some have suggested that this city is Rome, but is called Babylon because of its spiritual declension. While this has been debated at length by scholars (cf. J.A. Seiss, *The Apocalypse,* pp. 381-82, 397-420), it is preferable to view "Babylon" as the rebuilt city of Babylon located on the Euphrates River, which will be the capital of the final world government (cf. Walvoord, *Revelation,* pp. 240-41).

In addition to the terrible earthquake and probably because of it, John recorded, **Every island fled away and mountains could not be found.** These verses (vv. 18-20), if taken literally, indicate topographical changes in the earth which eventually will also include great changes in the Holy Land in preparation for Christ's millennial kingdom.

16:21. In addition to the earthquake, **huge hailstones of about 100 pounds each** fell on people. Such huge masses of ice supernaturally formed would destroy anything left standing from the earthquake and would no doubt kill or seriously injure those they hit. In spite of the severity of the judgment and its cataclysmic character the hardness of human hearts is revealed in the final sentence: **And they cursed God on account of the plague of hail, because the plague was so terrible.**

The question is sometimes raised why eternal punishment is eternal. The answer is that people in the hardness of their hearts will not change; they deserve eternal punishment because they are eternally unrepentant. With the final destruction coming from the seventh bowl of the wrath of God, the stage will then be set for the dramatic and climactic second coming of Christ, revealed in chapter 19. Before this event, however, a future detailed description is given of Babylon in chapters 17-18.

K. The fall of Babylon (chaps. 17-18)

Babylon—the source of so many heathen and pagan religions which have opposed the faith of Israel as well as the faith of the church—is here seen in its final judgment. These chapters do not fall chronologically within the scheme of the seals, trumpets, and bowls of the wrath of God, and expositors have had difficulty in determining precisely the meaning of the revelation in these chapters.

In general, however, in chapter 17 Babylon is seen in its religious character climaxing in a world religion which seems to fit the first half of the last seven years preceding Christ's second coming. Chapter 17 also records the destruction of Babylon by the 10 kings (v. 16).

Chapter 18, by contrast, seems to refer to Babylon as a political power and as a great city and as the seat of power of the great world empire which will dominate the second half of the last seven years before Christ's return. Babylon, referred to about 300 times in the Bible, is occasionally viewed as a satanic religious program opposing the true worship of God, but primarily it is viewed as a political power with a great city bearing the name Babylon as its capital. The end times bring together these two major lines of truth about Babylon and indicate God's final judgment on it.

1. RELIGIOUS BABYLON DESTROYED (CHAP. 17)

17:1-2. One of the seven angels (in chap. 16) **who had** one **of the seven bowls** invited John to witness **the punishment of the great prostitute, who sits on many waters.** This evil woman symbolizes the religious system of Babylon, and the waters symbolize "peoples, multitudes, nations, and languages" (v. 15). The angel informed John that **the kings of the earth** had **committed adultery** with the woman; in other words, they had become a part of the religious system which she symbolized (cf. 14:8).

17:3-5. John was then taken in **the Spirit** (or better, "in [his] spirit," i.e., in a vision, not bodily; cf. 1:10; 4:2) to **a desert** where he saw the **woman** herself. She was **sitting on a scarlet beast that was covered with blasphemous names.** The beast **had 7 heads and 10 horns.** The beast is an obvious reference to the world government (13:1). The 10 horns are later defined (17:12) as 10 kings who had "not yet received a kingdom." The 7 heads seem to refer to prominent rulers of the yet-future Roman Empire.

The woman was dressed in purple and scarlet, and was glittering with gold, precious stones, and pearls. Her adornment is similar to that of religious trappings of ritualistic churches today. While purple, scarlet, gold, precious stones, and pearls can all represent beauty and glory in relation to the true faith, here they reveal a false religion that prostitutes the truth.

In her hand the woman **held a golden cup . . . filled with abominable things and the filth of her adulteries** (cf. "the wine of her adulteries" in v. 2). This confirms previous indications that her character and life are symbolic of false religion, confirmed by the words **written on her forehead: MYSTERY BABYLON THE GREAT THE MOTHER OF PROSTITUTES AND OF THE ABOMINATIONS OF THE EARTH.** The NASB and NIV are probably right in separating the word "mystery" from the title which follows because the word "mystery" is not a part of the title itself; it describes the title.

The Bible is full of information about Babylon as the source of false religion, the record beginning with the building of the tower of Babel (Gen. 10-11). The name "Babel" suggests "confusion" (Gen. 11:9). Later the name was applied to the city of Babylon which itself has a long history dating back to as early as 3,000 years before Christ. One of its famous rulers was Hammurabi (1728-1686 B.C.). After a period of decline Babylon again rose to great heights under Nebuchadnezzar about 600 years before Christ. Nebuchadnezzar's reign (605-562 B.C.) and the subsequent history of Babylon is the background of the Book of Daniel.

Babylon was important not only politically but also religiously. Nimrod, who founded Babylon (Gen. 10:8-12), had a wife known as Semiramis who founded the secret religious rites of the Babylonian mysteries, according to accounts outside the Bible. Semiramis had a son with an alleged miraculous conception who was given the name Tammuz and in effect was a false fulfillment of the promise of the seed of the woman given to Eve (Gen. 3:15).

Various religious practices were observed in connection with this false Babylonian religion, including recognition of the mother and child as God and of creating an order of virgins who became religious prostitutes. Tammuz, according to the tradition, was killed by a wild animal and then restored to life, a satanic anticipation and counterfeit of Christ's resurrection. Scripture condemns this false religion repeatedly (Jer. 7:18; 44:17-19, 25; Ezek. 8:14). The worship of Baal is related to the worship of Tammuz.

After the Persians took over Babylon in 539 B.C., they discouraged the continuation of the mystery religions of Babylon. Subsequently the Babylonian cultists moved to Pergamum (or Pergamos) where one of the seven churches of Asia

Minor was located (cf. Rev. 2:12-17). Crowns in the shape of a fish head were worn by the chief priests of the Babylonian cult to honor the fish god. The crowns bore the words "Keeper of the Bridge," symbolic of the "bridge" between man and Satan. This handle was adopted by the Roman emperors, who used the Latin title *Pontifex Maximus*, which means "Major Keeper of the Bridge." And the same title was later used by the bishop of Rome. The pope today is often called the *pontiff*, which comes from *pontifex*. When the teachers of the Babylonian mystery religions later moved from Pergamum to Rome, they were influential in paganizing Christianity and were the source of many so-called religious rites which have crept into ritualistic churches. Babylon then is the symbol of apostasy and blasphemous substitution of idol-worship for the worship of God in Christ. In this passage Babylon comes to its final judgment.

17:6. The woman symbolizing the apostate religious system, **was drunk with the blood of the saints.** This makes it clear that the apostate religious system of the first half of the last seven years leading up to Christ's second coming will be completely devoid of any true Christians. As a matter of fact the apostate church will attempt to kill all those who follow the true faith. John expressed his great astonishment at this revelation.

17:7-8. The angel explained the meaning **of the woman and of the beast** she was riding. **The beast . . . will come up out of the Abyss,** the home of Satan (11:7) and the place from which demons come (9:1-2, 11). This indicates that the power behind the ruler is satanic (cf. 13:4) and that Satan and the man he controls are closely identified. Their power is one. The fact that the beast **was, now is not, and will come up** in the future is another indication of what was introduced in 13:3. The supernatural survival and revival of both the world ruler and his empire will impress the world as being supernatural and will lead to worship of the beast and Satan. (On **the book of life** see comments on 3:5; 13:8. Also cf. 20:12, 15; 21:27.)

17:9-11. The angel informed John, **This calls for a mind with wisdom** (cf. 13:18). The truth that is being presented here symbolically requires spiritual insight to be understood, and the difficulty of correct interpretation is illustrated by the various ways it has been interpreted in the history of the church.

The angel informed John that the beast's **heads are seven hills on which the woman sits.** Many ancient writers, such as Victorinus, who wrote one of the first commentaries on the Book of Revelation, identified the seven hills as Rome, often described as "the city of seven hills." This identification has led to the conclusion this passage teaches that Rome will be the capital of the coming world empire. Originally Rome included seven small mountains along the Tiber River, and the hills were given the names Palatine, Aventine, Caelian, Equiline, Viminal, Quirimal, and Capitoline. Later, however, the city expanded to include the hill Janiculum and also a hill to the north called Pincian. While Rome is often referred to as having seven hills or mountains, different writers do not necessarily name the same seven mountains.

A close study of the passage does not support the conclusion that this refers to the city of Rome. Seiss, for instance, offers extensive evidence that the reference is to rulers rather than to physical mountains (*The Apocalypse*, pp. 391-94). This is supported by the text which explains, **They are also seven kings** (lit., "the seven heads are seven kings"). If the mountains represent kings, then obviously they are not literal mountains and refer not to a literal Rome but to persons.

This view is also supported by verse 10, **Five have fallen, one is, the other has not yet come; but when he does come, he must remain for a little while.** John was writing from his point of view in which five prominent kings of the Roman Empire had already come and gone, and one was then on the throne (probably Domitian, who caused the persecution which put John on the island of Patmos). The identity of the seventh king, the one to come after John's time, is unknown.

Verse 11 adds that the final world empire will be headed by **an eighth king. . . . The beast who once was, and now is not. . . . belongs to the seven and is going to his destruction.** The eighth king is obviously identical to the final world ruler, the man who heads up the final world empire destroyed by Christ at His second coming.

One possible explanation of the difference between the seventh and eighth beast is that the seventh beast itself is the Roman Empire marvelously revived in the end time, and the eighth beast is its final ruler. These verses show that in the end time, particularly during the first half of the last seven years, there will be an alliance between the Middle East ruler (the Antichrist) and the apostate world church of that time. This will come to a head, however, at the midpoint of the seven years, when that political power becomes worldwide.

17:12-14. Verse 12 explains that **the 10 horns . . . are 10 kings.** While many commentators have tried to identify 10 successive kings in the past, the passage itself indicates that they are contemporaneous kings who are heads of the countries which will form the original alliance in the Middle East that will support the future world ruler. They will receive authority **for one hour . . . as kings along with the beast.** While the 7 heads may be chronologically successive rulers of the Roman Empire who are singled out as prominent, the 10 horns by contrast are contemporaneous with each other, and as the text indicates they will receive political power for a brief time.

The 10 kings will unite their **power** to support **the beast** (v. 13), the Middle East ruler who will emerge in the end time and will make a covenant with Israel seven years before the second coming of Christ. Their antagonism to Christ is indicated throughout the entire seven years. And when Christ returns, these 10 kings will **war against** Him but will be defeated (v. 14). Interestingly Christ **the Lamb** is also the **Lord of lords and King of kings** (cf. 1 Tim. 6:15; Rev. 19:16).

17:15. Verse 1 stated that the woman "sits on many waters." These **waters** are now interpreted as **peoples, multitudes, nations, and languages.** This indicates that there will be one ecumenical world religious system, embracing all nations and languages.

17:16-18. The chapter closes with the dramatic destruction of the woman. **The beast** (the world ruler, the Antichrist) **and the 10 horns** (10 kings) **will hate the prostitute** and **will bring her to ruin.** While the exact time of this event is not given in this passage, it would seem to occur at the midpoint of the seven years when the beast will assume the role of world dictator by proclamation (Dan. 9:27; Matt. 24:15).

When the ruler in the Middle East takes on worldwide political power, he will also assume the place of God and demand that everyone worship him or else be killed (cf. Dan. 11:36-38; 2 Thes. 2:4; Rev. 13:8, 15). The world church movement, which characterizes the first half of the seven years leading up to the Second Coming, is thus brought to an abrupt end. It will be replaced by the final form of world religion which will be the worship of the world ruler, Satan's substitute for Christ.

This is part of God's sovereign purpose to bring evil leaders into judgment, **For God has put it into their hearts to accomplish His purpose by agreeing to give the beast their power to rule, until God's words are fulfilled.**

The final description of the woman is given in 17:18: **The woman you saw is the great city that rules over the kings of the earth.** The reference to the woman as a city is another link with ancient Babylon, this time regarded as a religious center for false religion. The apostate church represented by the woman was a combination of religious and political power. As stated in verse 5, the city and the woman are a "mystery," and are therefore a symbolic presentation. Verse 18, however, introduces the next chapter which seems to refer to Babylon more as a literal city than as a religious entity.

2. POLITICAL BABYLON DESTROYED (CHAP. 18)

18:1-3. Further revelation on the destruction of Babylon was made by **another angel coming down from heaven.** This contrasts with "one of the seven angels" mentioned in 17:1 and should not be confused with angelic representations of Christ. Angels do have great authority and often make pronouncements in the Book of Revelation. The power and glory of this angel was such that **the earth was illuminated by his splendor** (18:1).

The angel's message is summarized: **Fallen! Fallen is Babylon the Great!** The question has been raised as to whether or not this is another view of the same destruction mentioned in 17:16-17. A comparison of chapters 17 and 18 reveals that these are different events. The woman in chapter 17 was associated with the political power but was not the political power itself, and her destruction apparently brought no mourning from the earth. By contrast the destruction of Babylon in chapter 18 brings loud lamentation from the earth's political and economic powers. Instead of being destroyed and consumed by the 10 kings, here the destruction seems to come from an earthquake, and it is probable that this is an enlarged explanation of what was described in 16:19-21.

What is pictured here is a large prosperous city, the center of political and economic life. The judgment of God makes it **a home for demons and a haunt for every evil spirit, a haunt for every unclean and detestable bird. For all the nations have drunk the maddening wine of her adulteries.** This false religion is like a drug that drives men to madness. While it brought riches to **merchants**, it is now doomed for destruction.

18:4-8. Following the pronouncement of the angel, another voice from heaven instructed the people of God to leave the city so that they would escape the judgment to come on it (vv. 4-5). Babylon will receive **torture and grief** commensurate with her **glory and luxury**, in which she boasted that she was a **queen** (v. 7). **Death, mourning, and famine**, also **fire**, will come on the city **in one day** (v. 8).

18:9-20. When **kings** who were involved with the city see its destruction they will be grieved, and will cry, **Woe! Woe, O great city, O Babylon, city of power!** (v. 10) **Merchants** too will bemoan the city's downfall since they will no longer be able to carry on commerce with the city. The description in verses 12-13 indicates the great luxury and wealth of the city. This obviously refers to an economic and political situation rather than a religious one. The mourning of the merchants is similar to that of the kings: **Woe! Woe, O great city . . . !** (v. 16)

Sea captains . . . sailors, and others in navigational occupations will lament in similar fashion: **Woe! Woe, O great city . . . !** (v. 19) All three groups—kings, merchants, and sailors—speak of her destruction as sudden: **in one hour** (vv. 10, 17, 19). As the world mourns the destruction of Babylon, the saints are told to **rejoice** because **God has judged her for the way she treated you** (v. 20).

18:21-24. The final and violent destruction of the city is compared to throwing **a large millstone . . . into the sea** (v. 21). The lament follows that those who once characterized the city—**harpists and musicians, flute players and trumpeters**, and workmen **of any trade** (v. 22)—will not be seen in the city again. Nor will there be **light** and the joy of weddings (v. 23). The reason for her judgment is that by her **magic spell** (*pharmakeia;* cf. 9:21) **all the nations were led astray** from God (18:23; cf. 17:2), and she was guilty of murdering **prophets and . . . saints** (18:24; cf. 17:6).

The question remains as to what city is in view here. A common view is that it refers to the city of Rome, because of the prominence of Rome as the seat of the Roman Catholic Church and the capital of the ancient Roman Empire. Some find confirmation of this in the fact that the kings and sea merchants will be able to see the smoke of the burning of the city (18:9, 18).

Other evidence seems to point to the fact that it is Babylon itself, located on the Euphrates River, which in the end time will be converted into a ship-bearing river. When all the evidence is studied, the conclusion seems to point to Babylon being rebuilt as the capital of the world empire in the end time rather than to Rome in Italy. Bible expositors, however, continue to be divided on this question.

The events of chapter 17 will be fulfilled at the midpoint of the seven years, whereas the events of chapter 18 will occur at the end of the seven years, immediately before the second coming of Christ. The destruction of the city of Babylon is the final blow to the times of the Gentiles, which began when the Babylonian army attacked Jerusalem in 605 B.C. (cf. Luke 21:24).

With chapters 17 and 18 giving additional insight and information concerning the earth's major religious and political movements during that final seven years, the stage is now set for the

REVELATION

climax of the Book of Revelation—the second coming of Christ (chap. 19).

L. The song of hallelujah in heaven (19:1-10)

1. THE HALLELUJAH OF THE MULTITUDES IN HEAVEN (19:1-3)

Revelation 4-18 dealt primarily with the events of the Great Tribulation. Beginning in chapter 19 there is a noticeable change. The Great Tribulation is now coming to its end and the spotlight focuses on heaven and the second coming of Christ. For the saints and angels it is a time of rejoicing and victory.

19:1. Beginning in chapter 19 a chronological development is indicated by the phrase **after this** (*meta tauta*). Literally this phrase means "after these things," and refers to the events of chapter 18. Accordingly John **heard what sounded like the roar** of many people **in heaven** praising God, obviously because of the judgment on Babylon. Interpreters have shown much confusion in understanding the order of the events in chapters 19-20; thus it is important to note that this praise in 19:1 follows Babylon's destruction in chapter 18.

The word "roar" (*phōnēn*) is literally a "sound," modified by the adjective "great" (*megalēn*). This loud noise is from **a great multitude,** the same phrase used in 7:9 where the "great multitude" refers to the martyred dead of the Great Tribulation. For them in particular the judgment of Babylon is a great triumph. The Greek word for **Hallelujah** is *hallēlouia,* sometimes translated "alleluiah." The word "hallelujah" is derived from the similar Hebrew word in the Old Testament. It occurs in the New Testament only four times, all of them in Revelation 19 (vv. 1, 3-4, 6). This is the biblical "Hallelujah Chorus."

19:2-3. In expressing their praise of God, God's glory and power resulting from and caused by His salvation are mentioned along with the fact that **His judgments** are **true and just.** The destruction of **the great prostitute** (cf. 17:1, 4) is a proper act of vengeance for her martyring the **servants** of God (17:6). The judgment that is wrought on her, however, is only the beginning of the eternal punishment of the wicked, indicated in the statement that **the smoke from her goes up forever and ever.**

2. THE HALLELUJAH OF THE 24 ELDERS (19:4-5)

19:4-5. The 24 elders and the 4 living creatures also sing a hallelujah chorus. This is another reminder that the 24 elders, representing the church of the present Age, are distinguished from the Tribulation saints, described in verse 1 as "a great multitude." The 4 living creatures, previously introduced in 4:6-8, seem to refer to angels who praise God. Still another voice of praise, apparently coming from an angel, also praised God and exhorted **all you His servants** (19:5) to join in this praise.

3. THE PROPHETIC PROCLAMATION OF THE WEDDING OF THE LAMB (19:6-9)

19:6-8. The fourth and final hallelujah of this chapter, according to John, sounded like a **multitude** of people, **rushing waters,** and loud **thunder.** Here the rejoicing is prophetic for what is about to happen rather than for the judgment just executed.

The second coming of Christ is anticipated in the words, **for our Lord God Almighty reigns.** John used the word "Almighty" (*pantokratōr;* also in 1:8; 4:8; 11:17; 15:3; 16:7, 14; 19:15; 21:22). Along with the exhortation to **rejoice,** announcement is made that **the wedding of the Lamb has come, and His bride has made herself ready.**

In Scripture, marriage is often used to describe the relationship of saints to God. In the Old Testament Israel is pictured, as in Hosea, as the unfaithful wife of Yahweh who is destined to be restored in the future kingdom. In the New Testament, marriage is also used to describe the relationship between Christ and the church, but the illustration contrasts with the Old Testament, for the church is regarded as a virgin bride waiting the coming of her heavenly bridegroom (2 Cor. 11:2).

The **fine linen** with which the bride will be adorned is explained as representing **the righteous acts of the saints** (Rev. 19:8). (In the OT the high priest's clothing included linen: Ex. 28:42; Lev. 6:10; 16:4, 23, 32.) While some think this refers to the fact that the saints are justified by faith, the plural expression "the righteous acts" seems to refer to the righteous deeds wrought by the saints through the grace of God. Though all this has been made possible by the grace of God, the emphasis here seems to be on the works of the bride rather than on her standing as one who has been justified by faith.

This is the last of 14 outbursts of praise to God in the Book of Revelation by saints, angels, the 24 elders, and/or the 4 living creatures. The hymns or shouts of praise are in 4:8, 11; 5:9-10, 12-13; 7:10, 12; 11:16-18; 15:3-4; 16:5-7; 19:1-4, 6-8 (see the chart near 4:8).

19:9. The angel who commanded John to write (14:13) commanded him again to record the message, **Blessed are those who are invited to the wedding supper of the Lamb!**

One of the false interpretations that has plagued the church is the concept that God treats all saints exactly alike. Instead, a literal interpretation of the Bible distinguishes different groups of saints, and here the bride is distinguished from those who are invited to the wedding supper. Instead of treating all alike, God indeed has a program for Israel as a nation and also for those in Israel who are saved. He also has a program for Gentiles in the Old Testament who come to faith in God. And in the New Testament He has a program for the church as still a different group of saints. Again in the Book of Revelation the Tribulation saints are distinguished from other previous groups. It is not so much a question of difference in blessings as it is that God has a program designed for each group of saints which corresponds to their particular relationship to His overall program. Here the church, described as a bride, will be attended by angels and by saints who are distinct from the bride.

Expositors have debated whether the wedding will be in heaven or on earth. While the difference is not that important, the interpretive problem can be resolved by comparing the wedding described here to weddings in the first century. A wedding normally included these stages: (1) the legal consummation of the marriage by the parents of the bride and of the groom, with the payment of the dowry; (2) the bridegroom coming to claim his bride (as illustrated in Matt. 25:1-13 in the familiar Parable of the 10 Virgins); (3) the wedding supper (as illustrated in John 2:1-11) which was a several-day feast following the previous phase of the wedding.

In Revelation 19:9 "the wedding supper" is phase 3. And the announcement coincides with the second coming of Christ. It would seem, therefore, that the wedding supper has not yet been observed. In fulfilling the symbol, Christ is completing phase 1 in the Church Age as individuals are saved. Phase 2 will be accomplished at the Rapture of the church, when Christ takes His bride to heaven, the Father's house (John 14:1-3). Accordingly it would seem that the beginning of the Millennium itself will fulfill the symbolism of the wedding supper (*gamos*). It is also significant that the use of the word "bride" in 19:7 (*gynē*, lit., "wife,") implies that phase 2 of the wedding will have been completed and that all that remains is the feast itself. (The word commonly used for "bride" is *nymphē*; cf. John 3:29; Rev. 18:23; 21:2, 9; 22:17.)

All this suggests that the wedding feast is an earthly feast, which also corresponds to the illustrations of weddings in the Bible (Matt. 22:1-14; 25:1-13), and thus will take place on earth at the beginning of the Millennium. The importance of the announcement and invitation to the wedding supper, repeated in Revelation 22:17, is seen in the angel's remarks, **These are the true words of God.**

4. THE COMMAND TO WORSHIP GOD (19:10)

19:10. So impressive was the scene in heaven with the four great hallelujahs and the announcement of the coming wedding feast that John once again fell down to worship the angel, as he had done before (1:17). Then, however, he was worshiping Christ, which was proper. But here the angel rebuked him, urging him to worship only God and not him since he was **a fellow servant** with John. The angel added, **For the testimony of Jesus is the spirit of prophecy,** that is, the very nature or purpose of prophecy is to testify of Jesus Christ and to bring glory to Him. In the present Age one of the special functions of the Holy Spirit is to glorify Christ and to inform believers of "what is yet to come" (John 16:13). The tremendous revelation in the first 10 verses of Revelation 19 is a fitting introduction to what is about to be revealed, the second coming of Jesus

REVELATION

Christ, the subject of the entire book (1:1).

M. The second coming of Christ (19:11-21)

As John saw heaven open, he saw prophetically Christ's second coming and the events which will follow it. The second coming of Christ is a prominent doctrine in Scripture (Pss. 2:1-9; 24:7-10; 96:10-13; 110; Isa. 9:6-7; Jer. 23:1-8; Ezek. 37:15-28; Dan. 2:44-45; 7:13-14; Hosea 3:4-5; Amos 9:11-15; Micah 4:7; Zech. 2:10-12; 12; 14:1-9; Matt. 19:28; 24:27-31; 25:6, 31-46; Mark 13:24-27; Luke 12:35-40; 17:24-37; 18:8; 21:25-28; Acts 1:10-11; 15:16-18; Rom. 11:25-27; 2 Thes. 2:8; 2 Peter 3:3-4; Jude 14-15; Rev. 1:7-8; 2:25-28; 16:15; 22:20). So this is obviously a major event in the divine program.

Conservative interpreters of the Bible almost universally recognize this as a yet-future event, as indicated in orthodox creeds throughout the history of the church. Just as the first coming of Christ was literal and was fulfilled in history, so the second coming of Christ which is yet future will be fulfilled in the same literal manner.

Among conservative interpreters, however, the question has been raised whether the Rapture of the church, as revealed in such major passages as 1 Thessalonians 4:13-18 and 1 Corinthians 15:51-58, is fulfilled at the time of the second coming of Christ to the earth or, as pretribulationists hold, is fulfilled as a separate event seven years before His formal second coming to the earth.

It should be noted that none of the many details given in Revelation 19:11-21 corresponds to the Rapture of the church. In Revelation Christ returns, but in none of the Rapture passages is He ever pictured as touching the earth, for the saints meet Him in the air (1 Thes. 4:17).

Most significant is the fact that in Revelation 19–20 there is complete silence concerning any translation of living saints. In fact the implication of the passage is that saints who are on earth when Christ returns will remain on earth to enter the millennial kingdom in their natural bodies. If the Rapture were included in the second coming of Christ to the earth, one would expect to find reference to such a major event in Revelation 19. But no such reference is to be found. For these and many other reasons chapter 19 is a confirmation of the teaching that the Rapture of the church is a separate earlier event and that there is no translation of the living at the time of His second coming to the earth. (For further discussion see John F. Walvoord, *The Rapture Question*.)

1. THE REVELATION OF THE RIDER ON THE WHITE HORSE (19:11-13)

19:11-13. As John gazed into **heaven,** he saw Christ on **a white horse.** Though some have identified this rider with the rider in 6:2, the context is entirely different. In 6:2 the rider is the world ruler of the Great Tribulation, while here the rider is a ruler who obviously comes from heaven itself. The white horse is a sign of His coming triumph. It was customary for a triumphant Roman general to parade on the Via Sacra, a main thoroughfare of Rome, followed by evidences of His victory in the form of booty and captives (cf. 2 Cor. 2:14). The white horse is thus a symbol of Christ's triumph over the forces of wickedness in the world, the details of which follow.

The horse's **rider is called Faithful and True** for, as John declared, **With justice He judges and makes war.** His piercing judgment of sin is indicated in the words, **His eyes are like blazing fire** (cf. Rev. 1:14), and His right to rule is evidenced by the **many crowns** He is wearing. **Written on Him** is a name **that no one but He Himself knows,** suggesting that Christ is the ineffable, indescribable One. But actual titles are given for Him. Revelation 19:13 says, **His name is the Word of God** (cf. John 1:1, 14; 1 John 1:1), and Revelation 19:16 states that the name of His robe and on His thigh is KING OF KINGS AND LORD OF LORDS (cf. 1 Tim. 6:15; Rev. 17:14). The rider obviously is Jesus Christ, returning to the earth in glory. That He is coming as Judge is further supported by the fact that **He is dressed in a robe dipped in blood** (19:13; cf. Isa. 63:2-3; Rev. 14:20).

2. THE COMING OF THE KING AND HIS ARMIES OF HEAVEN (19:14-16)

19:14-16. The drama of the scene is further enhanced by the multitude of **the**

armies of heaven described as **riding on white horses and dressed in fine linen, white and clean** (cf. v. 8). In Christ's mouth was **a sharp sword** (cf. 1:16; 2:12, 16; 19:21) which He would use **to strike down the nations**. The word for "sword" (*rhomphaia*) was used of an unusually long sword and sometimes used as a spear, thus indicating a piercing action. In addition to using the sword for striking down, He will use **an iron scepter** for ruling (cf. Ps. 2:9; Rev. 2:27). Christ is also described as the One who **treads the winepress of the fury of the wrath of God Almighty** (cf. 14:19-20; and cf. "Almighty" in 1:8; 4:8; 11:17; 15:3; 16:7, 14; 19:6; 21:22). This scene is a dramatic indication of the awfulness of the impending judgment. Matthew 24:30 indicates that those on earth will be witnesses of this impressive scene.

The scene on earth is the final stage of the great world war that will be under way for many weeks. With armies battling up and down the Holy Land for victory, on the very day of the return of Christ there will be house-to-house fighting in Jerusalem itself (Zech. 14:2). Combatants will have been lured to the battle site by demons sent by Satan to assemble the armies of the world to fight the armies of heaven (cf. Rev. 16:12-16).

3. THE DESTRUCTION OF THE WICKED (19:17-21)

19:17-18. The armies of earth are no match for the armies from heaven. The sharp sword in Christ's mouth (v. 15) is symbolic of His authoritative word of command that destroys earth's armies by divine power. Millions of men and their horses will be destroyed instantly. In keeping with this, John recorded that he **saw an angel standing in the sun, who cried in a loud voice to all flying birds** to **gather together for the great supper of God** to eat the carcasses of **kings, generals,** horsemen, and all people slain by Christ.

19:19-21. The beast and his **armies** will gather to fight against Christ and His army. The outcome of this battle—referred to in 16:14 as "the battle on the great day of God Almighty"—is summarized in 19:19-21. The world rulers—**the beast** and **the false prophet**—will both be **captured.** Their former **miraculous** demonic power will no longer be sufficient to save them. Both of them will be **thrown alive into the fiery lake of burning sulfur.**

The wicked who have died throughout the history of the world up to this point are in hades (Luke 16:23). The fiery lake, a different place, was prepared for the devil and his angels (Matt. 25:41), and will not be occupied by human beings until later (Rev. 20:14-15).

The armies themselves will be killed by Christ's sword (19:21; cf. 1:16; 2:12, 16; 19:15). The number of dead will be so great that the vultures will have more than they can eat. The defeat of the earth's wicked will then be complete, and will be finalized as later judgments search out the unsaved in other parts of the earth and also kill them (cf. Matt. 25:31-45).

The same inspired Word of God which so wonderfully describes the grace of God and the salvation which is available to all who believe is equally plain about the judgment of all who reject the grace of God. The tendency of liberal interpreters of the Bible to emphasize passages dealing with the love of God and to ignore passages dealing with His righteous judgment is completely unjustified. The passages on judgment are just as inspired and accurate as those which develop the doctrines of grace and salvation. The Bible is clear that judgment awaits the wicked, and the second coming of Christ is the occasion for a worldwide judgment unparalleled in Scripture since the time of Noah's flood.

N. The millennial reign of Christ (20:1-10)

This chapter presents the fact that Christ will reign on earth for a thousand years. If this chapter is taken literally, it is relatively simple to understand what is meant. However, because many Bible interpreters have rejected the idea that there will be a reign of Christ on earth for a thousand years after His second coming, this chapter has been given an unusually large number of diverse interpretations, all designed to eliminate a literal millennial reign. In general there are three viewpoints, each with a number of variations.

The most recent view is what is known as *postmillennialism*. According to this view the thousand years represent the triumph of the gospel in the period *leading up to* the second coming of Christ. The return of Christ will follow the Millennium. Usually traced to Daniel Whitby, a controversial writer of the 17th century, this view has been advanced by other prominent scholars in the history of the church including Charles Hodge, A.H. Strong, David Brown, and more recently, Loraine Boettner. Basically it is an optimistic view that Christ will reign spiritually on earth through the work of the church and the preaching of the gospel. This view has largely been discarded in the 20th century, because many anti-Christian movements have prospered and the world has not progressed spiritually.

A second major view is *amillennialism*, which denies that there is any literal Millennium or reign of Christ on earth. The millennial reign of Christ is reduced to a spiritual reign in the hearts of believers. This reign is either over those on earth who put their trust in Him or over those in heaven. Both the amillennial and postmillennial views must interpret Revelation 20 in a nonliteral sense. Often there is wide difference among amillenarians in their interpretations of various passages in the Book of Revelation. Amillennialism historically had its first important advocate in Augustine who lived in the 4th and 5th centuries. Before Augustine, it is difficult to find one orthodox amillenarian. Modern advocates include such respected 20th-century theologians as Oswald Allis, Louis Berkhof, William Hendriksen, Abraham Kuyper, R.C.H. Lenski, and Gerhardus Vos.

A third form of interpretation is *premillennialism*, so named because it interprets Revelation 20 as referring to a literal thousand-year reign of Christ following His second coming. As the Second Coming occurs *before* the Millennium, it is therefore *pre*millennial. Twentieth-century advocates of this position include Lewis Sperry Chafer, Charles L. Feinberg, A.C. Gaebelein, H.A. Ironside, Alva McClain, William Pettingill, Charles C. Ryrie, C.I. Scofield, Wilbur Smith, and Merrill F. Unger. Other premillenarians can be found from the first century on, including Papias, Justin Martyr, and many other early church fathers. Arguments for this position are based on the natural sequence of events in chapter 20 following chapter 19, viewing them as sequential and as stemming from the second coming of Christ. Many passages speak of the second coming of Christ being followed by a reign of righteousness on earth (Pss. 2; 24; 72; 96; Isa. 2; 9:6-7; 11-12; 63:1-6; 65-66; Jer. 23:5-6; 30:8-11; Dan. 2:44; 7:13-14; Hosea 3:4-5; Amos 9:11-15; Micah 4:1-8; Zeph. 3:14-20; Zech. 8:1-8; 14:1-9; Matt. 19:28; 25:31-46; Acts 15:16-18; Rom. 11:25-27; Jude 14-15; Rev. 2:25-28; 19:11–20:6).

It should be evident that one's interpretation of Revelation 20 is an important decision that serves as a watershed for various approaches to prophetic Scripture. The approach taken in this commentary is that the events in chapter 20 follow chronologically the events in chapter 19. Many also believe that chapters 21-22 follow in chronological order (for more detailed discussion of various views, see Walvoord's *Revelation,* pp. 282-90; and *The Millennial Kingdom.* Grand Rapids: Zondervan Publishing House, 1959, pp. 263-75).

1. THE BINDING OF SATAN (20:1-3)

20:1-3. Chapter 20 begins with the familiar phrase, **And I saw an angel** (cf. 7:2; 8:2; 10:1; 14:6; 18:1; 19:17). The "and" with which this chapter begins suggests that it continues the sequence of events begun in 19:1, which is introduced with the words "after this." In chapter 19 the Greek has "and" at the beginnings of 15 verses (but it is omitted in the NIV in vv. 4, 8, 10-11, 13-16, and 21 and is trans. "then" in vv. 5-6, 9, and 19 and "but" in v. 20). The use of the word "and" (*kai*) often indicates action that follows in logical and/or chronological sequence. Accordingly there is no reason why chapter 20 should not be considered as describing events which follow chapter 19. "And" (*kai*) continues throughout chapter 20, beginning each verse except verse 5. There is thus no linguistic or grammatical suggestion that these events are anything other than events following the second coming of Christ and occurring in sequence.

In addition to the grammar which connects these incidents, there is also the causal connection of the events which follow naturally from the fact that Christ will have returned to the earth. In chapter 19 these events include casting the beast and the false prophet into the lake of burning sulfur and destroying their armies. Having disposed of the world ruler and the false prophet as well as the armies, it would be only natural that Christ should then turn to Satan himself, as He does in chapter 20.

Accordingly John saw an angel descend from **heaven** holding **the key to the Abyss** and **a great chain.** The angel grabbed Satan, **the dragon** (cf. 12:3-4, 7, 9, 13, 16-17; 13:2, 4, 11; 16:13), **that ancient serpent (12:9, 14-15), bound him, and threw him into the Abyss, and locked** it, in order to prevent Satan's work of **deceiving the nations any more** for **a thousand years.**

An important interpretive question is whether Satan was bound at the first coming of Christ, as is commonly advanced by amillenarians, or will be bound at His second coming, as is held by premillenarians. Revelation 20:1-3 rather clearly contradicts the amillennial interpretation that Satan was bound at the first coming of Christ. Throughout the Scriptures Satan is said to exert great power not only against the world but also against Christians (Acts 5:3; 1 Cor. 5:5; 7:5; 2 Cor. 2:11; 11:14; 12:7; 1 Tim. 1:20). If there is still any question whether this is so, it should be settled by the exhortation of 1 Peter 5:8: "Be self-controlled and alert. Your enemy the devil prowls around like a roaring lion looking for someone to devour."

Amillenarians answer this by saying that Satan is limited by the power of God. But this has always been true, as illustrated in the Book of Job and elsewhere. To describe Satan's present situation as being locked in the Abyss and unable to deceive the nations for a period of a thousand years is simply not factually true today, and it requires extreme spiritualization of the literalness of this passage as well as other New Testament references to Satan's activities and present power. This same power of Satan is further revealed in the Great Tribulation when he empowers the world ruler (Rev. 13:4). Satan will have been cast out of heaven at the beginning of the Great Tribulation and will then be more active than ever (Rev. 12:9, 13, 15, 17).

If Satan is actually deceiving the nations today, as the Scriptures and the facts of history indicate, then he is not now locked in the Abyss, and the thousand-year Millennium is still future. This interpretation is also supported by the final statement that after the thousand years, **he must be set free for a short time** (20:3). Here expositors again are at a loss to explain this except in a literal way, making possible a final satanic rebellion at the end of the millennial kingdom.

2. THE RESURRECTION AND REWARD OF THE MARTYRS (20:4-6)

20:4. Next in the series of revelations John recorded that he **saw thrones on which were seated those who had been given authority to judge.** In addition he **saw the souls of those who had been beheaded because of their** standing true to the Lord and His **Word** in the Great Tribulation. The fact that John could see them implies that they had received intermediate bodies in heaven and were awaiting their resurrections.

A distinction should be made between what John saw and what he received as revelation. Though he could see the souls, he was informed that they had been beheaded because they had refused to worship **the beast or his image** and would not receive **his mark.** What John saw was not all the souls in heaven but a particular generation of martyred dead who had been contemporaneous with the world ruler, the beast out of the sea (13:1). If the church were raptured prior to this event, as premillenarians teach, it would make sense to single out these martyred dead for resurrection. But if the church were not raptured, it would be most unusual to ignore all the martyrs of preceding generations, the church as a whole, and to specify this relatively small group.

John apparently was not told the identity of the individuals seated on the thrones. They evidently do not include the martyred dead themselves. Christ had predicted (Luke 22:29-30) that the 12 disciples would "eat and drink at My table in My kingdom and sit on thrones,

REVELATION

judging the 12 tribes of Israel." As the disciples are also a part of the church, the body of Christ, it would be natural for them to sit on these thrones.

According to the Scriptures a series of judgments is related to Christ's return. The beast and the false prophet will be cast into the fiery lake (Rev. 19:20), Satan will be cast into the Abyss (20:1-3), and then the martyred dead of the Great Tribulation will be judged and rewarded (v. 4). In addition, Israel will be judged (Ezek. 20:33-38), and the Gentiles will be judged (Matt. 25:31-46). These judgments precede and lead up to the millennial kingdom.

John stated that these martyred dead **came to life and reigned with Christ a thousand years.** Their coming to life suggests that they will be given resurrected bodies. In addition to receiving the visual revelation, John was informed as to the meaning and character of the judgment that was here taking place.

20:5. John was also informed that **the rest of the dead did not come to life until the thousand years were ended.** This refers to the resurrection of the wicked dead, discussed later (vv. 11-15). John stated that what he was seeing **is the first resurrection.** Posttribulationists refer to this as proof that the church will not be raptured before the Tribulation and that no resurrection has taken place prior to this point in fulfillment of God's prophetic program. It should be obvious, however, that in no sense could this be the number-one resurrection chronologically because historically Christ was the first to rise from the dead with a transformed, resurrected body. There was also the resurrection "of many" (Matt. 27:52-53) which took place when Christ died. In what sense then can this resurrection in Revelation 20:5 be "first"?

As the context which follows indicates, "the first resurrection" (vv. 5-6) contrasts with the last resurrection (vv. 12-13), which is followed by "the second death" (vv. 6, 14). It is first in the sense of *before.* All the righteous, regardless of when they are raised, take part in the resurrection which is first or before the final resurrection (of the wicked dead) at the end of the Millennium. This supports the conclusion that the resurrection of the righteous is by stages. Christ was "the Firstfruits" (1 Cor. 15:23), which was preceded by the token resurrection of a number of saints (Matt. 27:52-53). Then will occur the Rapture of the church, which will include the resurrection of dead church saints and the translation of living church saints (1 Thes. 4:13-18). The resurrection of the two witnesses will occur in the Great Tribulation (Rev. 11:3, 11). Then the resurrection of the martyred dead of the Great Tribulation will occur soon after Christ returns to earth (20:4-5). To these may be added the resurrection of Old Testament saints which apparently will also occur at this time, though it is not mentioned in this text (cf. Isa. 26:19-21; Ezek. 37:12-14; Dan. 12:2-3).

20:6. All those who share in the resurrection of the righteous are said to be **blessed and holy, and the second death has no power over them, but they will be priests of God and of Christ and will reign with Him for a thousand years.** While all the righteous will be raised before the Millennium, individuals will retain their identities and their group identifications such as Gentile believers and believers in Israel in the Old Testament, the church of the New Testament, and saints of the Tribulation.

It should be noted that the term "a thousand years" occurs six times in chapter 20. This was not something that could be seen visually; John had to be informed of it and the vision had to be interpreted as relating to a period of a thousand years. While amillenarians and others have tended to view this as nonliteral, there is no evidence to support this conclusion. This is the only chapter in Revelation where a period of a thousand years is mentioned, and the fact that it is mentioned six times and is clearly described as a period of time before which and after which events take place lead to the conclusion that it means a literal thousand-year period.

Since other time designations in Revelation are literal (e.g., "42 months," 11:2; 13:5; "1,260 days," 11:3; 12:6) it is natural to take "a thousand years" literally also. If the term "a thousand years" designates a nonspecific but long period of time, the present Age between Christ's two advents, as amillenarians hold, then one would expect John to say simply that Christ would reign "a long time," in contrast to the "short time" of Satan's release (20:3).

Events which precede the thousand years are (a) the second coming of Christ, (b) the beast and the false prophet thrown into the fiery lake, (c) the armies destroyed, (d) Satan bound and locked in the Abyss, (e) thrones of judgment introduced, and (f) the martyred dead of the Tribulation resurrected. These events revealed in their proper sequence make it clear that the thousand-year period follows all these events, including the second coming of Christ. The conclusion that the Second Coming is premillennial is clearly supported by a normal, literal interpretation of this text.

3. THE FINAL DOOM OF SATAN (20:7-10)

Apart from frequent mention of the thousand years, no details are given concerning the reign of Christ on earth except that it is a time of great blessing. Many Old Testament passages supply additional information about the Millennium. The main point of the revelation here is that the Millennium follows the Second Coming.

20:7-8. John was told what would happen at the conclusion of **the thousand years. Satan will be released from** the Abyss, **his prison,** and will make a final attempt to induce nations—called **Gog and Magog**—to come and **battle** with him against Christ. Satan's release will produce a worldwide rebellion against the millennial reign of Christ. The armies will be so vast in numbers that they are said to be **like the sand on the seashore.**

Who are these who will follow Satan? Those who survive the Tribulation will enter the Millennium in their natural bodies, and they will bear children and repopulate the earth (Isa. 65:18-25). Under ideal circumstances in which all know about Jesus Christ (cf. Jer. 31:33-34), many will outwardly profess faith in Christ without actually placing faith in Him for salvation. The shallowness of their professions will become apparent when Satan is released. The multitudes who follow Satan are evidently those who have never been born again in the millennial kingdom.

The question has been raised as to whether this war is the same one discussed in Ezekiel 38–39, where Gog and Magog are also mentioned (Ezek. 38:2). These are two different battles, for in the war of Ezekiel 38–39 the armies come primarily from the north and involve only a few nations of the earth. But the battle in Revelation 20:7-9 will involve all nations, so armies will come from all directions.

Furthermore nothing in the context of Ezekiel 38–39 is similar to the battle in Revelation, as there is no mention of Satan or of millennial conditions. In Revelation 20:7 the context clearly places the battle at the end of the Millennium, whereas the Ezekiel battle takes place in connection with end-time events.

Why then is the expression "Gog and Magog" used by John? The Scriptures do not explain the expression. In fact it can be dropped out of the sentence without changing the meaning. In Ezekiel 38 Gog was the ruler and Magog was the people, and both were in rebellion against God and were enemies of Israel. It may be that the terms have taken on a symbolic meaning much as one speaks of a person's "Waterloo," which historically refers to the defeat of Napoleon at Waterloo, Belgium, but has come to represent any great disaster. Certainly the armies here come in the same spirit of antagonism against God that is found in Ezekiel 38.

20:9. The armies will surround **the camp of God's people, the city He loves.** This could mean only Jerusalem, which will be the capital of the world government of Christ throughout the millennial kingdom (cf. Isa. 2:1-5). The result is immediate judgment. **Fire** will come **down from heaven** and devour them.

In contrast with Ezekiel 38, there is no mention of earthquake, hail, or other disasters. The only similarity is that in both cases there is fire from heaven, a frequent method of divine judgment on the earth (cf. Gen. 19:24; Ex. 9:23-24; Lev. 9:24; 10:2; Num. 11:1; 16:35; 26:10; 1 Kings 18:38; 2 Kings 1:10, 12, 14; 1 Chron. 21:26; 2 Chron. 7:1, 3; Ps. 11:6; etc.).

20:10. After Satan's followers will be destroyed, he will be **thrown into the lake of burning sulfur.** Being cast into the lake that was prepared for him and his angels is the final judgment on Satan (cf. Matt. 25:41). Most significant as a support of the doctrine of eternal punishment is the concluding statement, **They will be tormented day and night forever and ever.** The word "they" includes the devil, the beast, and the false prophet. The lake of burning sulfur is not annihilation, for the beast and false prophet are still there a thousand years after they experienced their final judgment (Rev. 19:20).

O. The judgment of the great white throne (20:11-15)

1. THE RESURRECTION AND JUDGMENT OF THE WICKED DEAD (20:11-13)

20:11. The final five verses of chapter 20 introduce the judgment at the end of human history and the beginning of the eternal state. John wrote, **I saw a great white throne.** The events here described clearly follow the thousand years of verses 1-6. The great white throne apparently differs from the throne mentioned more than 30 times in Revelation beginning with 4:2. It apparently is located neither in heaven nor earth but in space, as suggested by the statement, **Earth and sky fled from His presence, and there was no place for them.** It is not indicated who sits on this throne, but probably it is Christ Himself as in 3:21 (cf. Matt. 19:28; 25:31; John 5:22; 2 Cor. 5:10—though the throne in these references is not necessarily the same throne as in Rev. 20:11). While Christ is now seated on the throne in heaven and will be seated on the Davidic throne on earth in the Millennium (Matt. 25:31), this white throne judgment is a special situation.

The question has been raised as to whether the earth and the starry heavens as they are today will be destroyed at this point in the future or will be simply restored to a new state of purity. Many references in the Bible suggest that the earth and the heavens, as now known, will be destroyed (cf. Matt. 24:35; Mark 13:31; Luke 16:17; 21:33; 2 Peter 3:10-13). This is confirmed by the opening statement of Revelation 21, "the first heaven and the first earth had passed away."

The present universe was created like a gigantic clock which is running down, and if left to itself, would ultimately come to a state of complete inactivity. Inasmuch as God created the universe and set it in motion for the purpose of enacting the drama of sin and redemption, it would seem proper to begin anew with a new heaven and a new earth suitable for His eternal purpose and built on a different principle. The new heaven and new earth described in chapter 21 has no similarity to the present earth and heaven.

20:12. The purpose of establishing the great white throne is to judge the dead. John wrote that **the dead, great and small,** stood **before the throne.** From other Scriptures it seems that all the righteous dead have been raised, including Old Testament saints, the dead of the Great Tribulation, and the church saints, the body of Christ (see comments on v. 5). Thus it may be assumed that verses 11-15 refer to the judgment of the wicked dead, who according to verse 5 would not be resurrected until after the thousand years and will have no part in what is called "the first resurrection."

At that judgment John saw **books... opened,** including a book called **the book of life.** The text does not state clearly what these books are, but the first opened books may refer to human works and "the book of life" is the record of those who are saved (cf. 3:5; 13:8; 17:8; 20:15; 21:27). The fact that these dead have not been raised before is evidence in itself that they do not have eternal life and that their judgment is a judgment of their works.

All final judgments deal with works, whether the works of Christians rewarded at the judgment seat of Christ or the works of the unsaved which are in view here. The question of who is saved is determined not in heaven but in life on earth. What is revealed here is the *confirmation* of one's destiny by means of God's written records.

Some view the book of life as the record of all the living and that when the unsaved die their names are deleted from it. A better view is that the book is the record of those who are saved whose names were "written in the book of life from the creation of the world" (17:8). Regardless of which view is taken, at this time only the saved are in the book of life.

20:13. In order for the wicked **dead to be judged ... the sea ... death, and hades** will give up their dead. Those who are unsaved at the time of death go immediately to a state of conscious punishment described in the Old Testament as sheol and in the New Testament as hades. Neither sheol nor hades ever refer to the *eternal* state and should not be considered equivalent to the English word "hell," which properly is the place of eternal punishment. The lake of fire (vv. 14-15) referred to as "the fiery lake of burning sulfur" (19:20) is the same as gehenna (cf. Matt. 5:22, 29-30; 10:28; 18:9; 23:15, 33; Mark 9:43, 45, 47; Luke 12:5; James 3:6) and is translated "hell" in the NIV and KJV with the word "fire" added in several passages. Actually gehenna was originally a name for the place of burning refuse, located in the Valley of Hinnom south of Jerusalem. The term, however, goes far beyond this geographic background and refers to eternal punishment.

The statement "death and hades gave up the dead" means that the physical bodies of the unsaved will be joined with their spirits which have been in hades. The mention of "the sea" giving up its dead makes it clear that regardless of how far a body has disintegrated, it will nevertheless be resurrected for this judgment.

2. THE LAKE OF FIRE (20:14-15)

20:14-15. Following the great white throne judgment **death and hades were thrown into the lake of fire. The lake of fire is the second death,** the final destination of the wicked. The doctrine of eternal punishment has always been a problem to Christians who enjoy the grace of God and salvation in Christ. The Bible is clear, however, that the punishment of the wicked is eternal. This is confirmed in verse 10, where the beast and the false prophet are still in the lake of fire after the thousand years of Christ's millennial reign. Though the wicked dead will receive resurrection bodies, they will be quite unlike the resurrection bodies of the saints. The former people will continue to be sinful but will be indestructible and will exist forever in the lake of fire.

Though many have attempted to find some scriptural way to avoid the doctrine of eternal punishment, as far as biblical revelation is concerned there are only two destinies for human souls; one is to be with the Lord and the other is to be forever separated from God in the lake of fire. This solemn fact is motivation for carrying the gospel to the ends of the earth whatever the cost, and doing everything possible to inform and challenge people to receive Christ before it is too late.

P. *The new heaven and the new earth (21:1–22:5)*

1. THE NEW HEAVEN AND THE NEW EARTH CREATED (21:1)

21:1. The opening verses of chapter 21 describe the creation of the new heaven and the new earth, which chronologically follows the thousand-year reign of Christ described in chapter 20. Chapter 21 begins with the familiar words **I saw,** an expression repeated in verse 2 (cf. v. 22, "I did not see"). This new creation is described as **a new heaven and a new earth.** That it is a totally new heaven and a new earth, and not the present heaven and earth renovated, is supported by the additional statement, **for the first heaven and the first earth had passed away** (also see comments on 20:11). An amazingly small amount of information is given about the new heaven and the new earth. But one major fact is stated in this verse: **there was no longer any sea.**

In contrast with the present earth, which has most of its surface covered by water, no large body of water will be on the new earth. The Bible is silent, however, on any features of the first heaven except the statement in 21:23 that there will be no sun or moon and, by implication, no stars. The new heaven refers not to the abode of God, but to the earth's atmosphere and planetary space.

No landmarks whatever are given concerning the new earth, and nothing is known of its characteristics, vegetation, color, or form. The implication, however, is that it is round and is the residence of all who are saved. A few other references are found in Scripture in relation to the new earth, including Isaiah 65:17; 66:22; and 2 Peter 3:10-13.

Because in some of these passages the Millennium is also discussed, expositors have often confused the eternal state with the Millennium. However, the principle is well established in Scripture that distant events are often telescoped together. Examples of this are Isaiah 61:1-2 (cf. Luke 4:17-19), which speaks of the first and second comings of Christ together, and Daniel 12:2, which mentions the resurrection of the righteous and of the wicked together even though, according to Revelation 20:5, they will be separated by a thousand years. Sometimes even the chronological order is reversed, as in Isaiah 65:17-25 (vv. 17-19 refer to the new heaven and new earth whereas vv. 20-25 clearly refer to the Millennium). End-time events are all also brought in close proximity in 2 Peter 3:10-13, where the beginning and the end of the day of the Lord are mentioned in the same passage.

Though expositors have differed on this point, the principle that clear passages should be used to explain obscure passages supports the conclusion that the second coming of Christ is followed by a thousand-year reign on earth, and this in turn is followed by a new heaven and new earth, the dwelling place of the saints for eternity. With the absence of any geographic identification and the absence of a sea, the new earth will obviously be entirely different. By contrast, the sea is mentioned many times in relation to the Millennium (e.g., Ps. 72:8; Isa. 11:9, 11; Ezek. 47:8-20; 48:28; Zech. 9:10; 14:8). The evidence is conclusive that the new heaven and new earth are not to be confused with the Millennium.

2. THE NEW JERUSALEM DESCRIBED (21:2-8)

21:2. John's attention was then directed to a specific feature of the new heaven and new earth, namely, **the Holy City, the New Jerusalem, coming down out of heaven from God, prepared as a bride beautifully dressed for her husband.** The New Jerusalem is called "the Holy City," in contrast with the earthly Jerusalem (which spiritually was compared to Sodom in 11:8). As early as 3:12 the New Jerusalem was described as "the city of My God, the New Jerusalem, which is coming down out of heaven from My God." The fact that the New Jerusalem comes down from heaven and that it is not said to be created at this point has raised the question as to whether it has been in existence during the Millennium (see further discussion on this under 21:9).

Many expositors regard the promise of Christ in John 14:2, "I am going there to prepare a place for you," as referring to this city. The suggestion has been made that if the New Jerusalem is in existence during the millennial reign of Christ, it may have been suspended in the heavens as a dwelling place for resurrected and translated saints, who nevertheless would have immediate access to the earth to carry on their functions of ruling with Christ. J. Dwight Pentecost, for instance, quotes F.C. Jennings, William Kelly, and Walter Scott as supportng this concept of the New Jerusalem as a satellite city during the Millennium (*Things to Come.* Grand Rapids: Zondervan Publishing House, 1958, pp. 577-79). In the Millennium the New Jerusalem clearly does not rest on the earth, for there is an earthly Jerusalem and an earthly temple (Ezek. 40-48).

The New Jerusalem then will apparently be withdrawn from its proximity to the earth when the earth will be destroyed at the end of the Millennium, and then will come back after the new earth is created. Though this possibility of a satellite city has been disregarded by most commentators and must be considered as an inference rather than a direct revelation of the Bible, it does solve some problems of the relationship between the resurrected and translated saints to those still in their natural bodies in the Millennium, problems which otherwise are left without explanation.

Here, however, the New Jerusalem is described as it will be in the eternal state, and it is said to be "a bride beautifully dressed for her husband." Because the church is pictured in Scripture as a bride (2 Cor. 11:2), some have tried to identify the New Jerusalem's inhabitants as specifically the church saints, excluding saints of other dispensations. However, the use of marriage as an illustration is common in Scripture, not only to relate Christ to the church but also Yahweh to Israel. Though the city is compared to a beautifully dressed bride, it actually is a city, not a person or group of people.

21:3-4. Following this initial revelation of the New Jerusalem John wrote, I heard **a loud voice from the throne.** This is the last of 20 times that the expression "a loud voice" is used in Revelation (first used in 5:2).

The final revelation from heaven states that God will then dwell **with men, that the saints will be His people** and He will **be their God.** In eternity saints will enjoy a new intimacy with God which is impossible in a world where sin and death are still present. The new order will be without sorrow. God **will wipe every tear from their eyes,** and death with its mourning, and pain with its crying will vanish, **for the old order of things** will have **passed away.**

Some have wondered if grief and sorrow will exist for a while in heaven and then be done away with here at the establishing of the new order. It is better to understand this passage as saying that heaven will have none of the features that so characterize the present earth.

21:5-6. The dramatic change to the new order is expressed in the words, **I am making everything new!** This revelation is **trustworthy and true,** and John was instructed to write down that fact. The One bringing about the change is Christ, who calls Himself **the Alpha and the Omega** (cf. 1:8; 22:13), the first and last letters of the Greek alphabet, interpreted by the phrase **the Beginning and the End.**

Those who are **thirsty** are promised that they will be able **to drink without cost from the spring of the water of life.** Apparently this refers not to physical thirst but to a desire for spiritual blessings.

21:7-8. Christ explained that **he who overcomes will inherit all this, and I will be his God and he will be My son.** This expresses the intimate relationship between the saints and God in the eternal state.

By contrast, **those who practice** the sins of the unbelieving world will be excluded from the New Jerusalem and will be destined for the fiery lake of burning sulfur. This judgment is a righteous punishment for their sins, eight of which are itemized here. He adds, **This is the second death.**

It should be obvious that this passage is not affirming salvation by works, but rather is referring to works as indicative of whether one is saved or not. Obviously many will be in heaven who before their conversions were indeed guilty of these sins but who turned from them in the day of grace in trusting Christ as their Savior. Though works are the evidence of salvation or lack of it, they are never the basis or ground of it. Similar lists of sins are found elsewhere in Revelation (cf. v. 27; 22:15).

3. THE NEW JERUSALEM AS THE BRIDE (21:9-11)

21:9-11. One of the angels of chapter 16 who had poured out a bowl of wrath on the earth then invited John to see the New Jerusalem as a bride. **Come, I will show you the bride, the wife of the Lamb.** Carried by **the Spirit** to a high **mountain,** John saw the New Jerusalem **coming down out of heaven from God,** shining with **the glory of God.**

Expositors have raised questions about the additional revelation of the New Jerusalem, beginning in verse 9. Some believe that this section is a recapitulation and pictures the New Jerusalem as it will be suspended over the earth during the millennial reign of Christ. A preferred interpretation, however, is that the passage continues to describe the New Jerusalem as it will be in the eternal state. Obviously the city would be much the same in either case, but various indications seem to relate this to the eternal state rather than to the Millennium.

The overall impression of the city as a gigantic brilliant **jewel** compared to **jasper, clear as crystal** indicates its great beauty. John was trying to describe what he saw and to relate it to what might be familiar to his readers. However, it is evident that his revelation transcends anything that can be experienced.

The jasper stone known today is opaque and not clear (cf. 4:3). It is found in various colors, and John apparently was referring to the beauty of the stone rather than to its particular characteristics. Today one might describe that city as a beautifully cut diamond, a stone not known as a jewel in the first century.

As in the earlier references to the New Jerusalem as a bride, here again is a city, not a person or group of people. This is confirmed by the description of the city which follows.

REVELATION

4. THE NEW JERUSALEM AS A CITY (21:12-27)

21:12-13. John saw a gigantic city, "square" in shape (v. 16), and surrounded by **a great, high wall with 12 gates.** The 12 gates bore **the names of the 12 tribes of Israel.** The number 12 is prominent in the city with 12 gates and 12 **angels** (v. 12), 12 tribes of Israel (v. 12), 12 foundations (v. 14), 12 apostles (v. 14), 12 pearls (v. 21), 12 kinds of fruit (22:2), with the wall 144 cubits—12 times 12 (21:17), and the height, width, and length, 12,000 stadia, about 1,400 miles (v. 16). The city has walls north, south, east, and west with **three gates** on each side (v. 13) and with an angel standing guard at each gate (v. 12).

This is an entirely different situation from the earthly Jerusalem in the Millennium. But if the names of the gates corresponded to the millennial Jerusalem described in Ezekiel 48:31-34, the north side from east to west would have the gates named Levi, Judah, and Reuben. On the west side from north to south were Naphtali, Asher, and Gad; on the south side from east to west, Simeon, Issachar, and Zebulun; and on the east side from north to south, Joseph, Benjamin, and Dan. In contrast to Revelation 7:5-8, where Dan is omitted and Joseph and Manasseh are included, Ezekiel mentioned Dan but not Manasseh.

21:14-16. The **12 foundations** to the city's **wall** bore **the names of the 12 apostles of the Lamb.** The apostles were part of the church, the body of Christ. Thus both the church and Israel will be in the city; the former are represented by the apostles' names on the foundations (v. 14), and the latter by the names of Israel's 12 tribes on the gates (v. 12). The distinction between Israel and the church is thus maintained. An **angel** measured **the city** with **a measuring rod of gold,** about 10 feet in length. The city is **12,000 stadia in length** and width, approximately 1,400 miles on each side. Tremendous as is the dimension of the city, the amazing fact is that it is also 1,400 miles **high.**

Commentators differ as to whether the city is a cube or a pyramid. The descriptions seem to favor the pyramid form.

21:17-18. Surrounding this huge city is a wall **144 cubits** or 216 feet **thick.** The reference to **man's measurement** simply means that though an angel is using the rod, he is using human dimensions.

As John gazed at **the wall,** he saw that it was **made of jasper,** and that **the city** was made **of pure gold, as pure as glass.** John was using the language of appearance, for apparently both the jasper and the gold differ from these metals as they are known today. In verse 11 the jasper is translucent, and in verses 18 and 21 the gold is clear like glass.

21:19-21. The decorations of the **foundations** (with the apostles' names inscribed on them) include 12 stones involving different colors. The color of the **jasper** is not indicated. The **sapphire** was probably blue; the **chalcedony** comes from Chalcedon, Turkey and is basically blue with stripes of other colors. The **emerald** is a bright green; the **sardonyx** is red and white; and the **carnelian,** called a "sardius" in the NASB, is usually ruby-red in color, though it sometimes has an amber or honey color. In 4:3 the carnelian stone is coupled with the jasper to reflect the glory of God. The **chrysolyte** is a golden color, probably different from the modern chrysolyte stone which is pale green. The **beryl** is a sea green; the **topaz** is a transparent yellow-green; the **chrysoprase** is also green; the **jacinth** is violet in color; and the **amethyst** is purple. The stones together provide a brilliant array of beautiful colors. The gates resemble huge, single **pearls,** and **the street of the city was of pure gold, like transparent glass** (cf. 21:18).

While the beauty of the city may have symbolic meaning, no clue is given as to the precise interpretation. Since it is reasonable to assume that the saints will dwell in the city, it is best to take the city as a literal future dwelling place of the saints and angels.

21:22-27. John declared that he **did not see a temple in the city** because **God the Father and the Lamb** (God the Son) **are its temple.** There will be no need for light from the **sun** or **moon** because **the glory of God** will provide **the light.** As John explained, **the Lamb is its lamp.**

From the fact that the nations (the Gentiles) will be in the city (vv. 24, 26)—as well as Israel and the church—it is evident that the city is the dwelling place of the saints of all ages, the angels, and

God Himself. The description of the heavenly Jerusalem in Hebrews 12:22-24 itemizes all those mentioned here and adds "the spirits of righteous men made perfect," which would include all other saints not specifically mentioned.

John learned that the gates of the city will never **be shut,** and because God's glory will be present continually **there will be no night there. The glory and honor of the nations will be** in the city, and everything that is **impure . . . shameful, or deceitful** will be excluded (cf. Rev. 21:8; 22:15). The inhabitants will be **only those whose names are written in the Lamb's book of life.** It is interesting that in the six references to the book of life in Revelation only this one calls it "the Lamb's" (cf. 3:5; 13:8; 17:8; 20:12, 15).

Though the description of the city does not answer all questions concerning the eternal state, the revelation given to John describes a beautiful and glorious future for all who put their trust in the living God.

5. THE RIVER OF THE WATER OF LIFE (22:1-2A)

22:1-2a. In the opening verses of chapter 22 additional facts are given about the New Jerusalem. **The angel showed** John **the river of the water of life, as clear as crystal, flowing from the throne of God and of the Lamb.** While this may be a literal river, its symbolism is clear. Out of the throne of God will flow pure water, symbolic of the holiness and purity of God and the city. This reference to a river should not be confused with similar millennial situations such as those in Ezekiel 47:1, 12 and Zechariah 14:8. These refer to literal rivers flowing from the temple and from Jerusalem and will be part of the millennial scene. The river in Revelation 22:1 will be part of the New Jerusalem in the new earth. The water flows **down the middle of the great street of the city.** This apparently refers to a main thoroughfare in the New Jerusalem coming from the throne of God with the river being a narrow stream in the middle of the street. The KJV attaches the phrase "in the midst of the street" to the next sentence rather than to the river.

It is significant also that the Lamb is pictured on the throne (mentioned also in v. 3). This makes it clear that 1 Corinthians 15:24, which states that Christ "hands over the kingdom to God the Father after He has destroyed all dominion, authority, and power," does not mean that Christ's reign on the throne will end but that it will change its character. Christ is King of kings and Lord of lords (cf. Rev. 17:14; 19:16) for all eternity.

6. THE TREE OF LIFE (22:2B)

22:2b. As John contemplated the heavenly city, he saw **the tree of life, bearing 12 crops of fruit, yielding its fruit every month.** Interpreters have puzzled over this expression that the tree of life is **on each side of the river.** Some take this is as a group of trees. Others say that the river of life is narrow and that it flows on both sides of the tree. The tree of life was referred to in the Garden of Eden (Gen. 3:22, 24), where it was represented as perpetuating physical life forever. Adam and Eve were forbidden to eat of the fruit of this tree. Earlier in Revelation (2:7) the saints were promised the "right to eat from the tree of life, which is in the paradise of God."

While the literal and the symbolic seem to be combined in this tree, there is no reason why it could not be an actual tree with literal fruit. The practical effect would be to continue physical life forever. While the verse does not state that the fruit can be eaten, this is presumably the implication.

The tree's **leaves . . . are for the healing of the nations.** Based on this statement some have referred this situation back to the millennial times when there will be sickness and healing. However, another meaning seems to be indicated. The word "healing" (*therapeian*) can be understood as "health-giving." The English "therapeutic" is derived from this Greek word. Even though there is no sickness in the eternal state, the tree's fruit and leaves seem to contribute to the physical well-being of those in the eternal state.

7. THE THRONE OF GOD (22:3-4)

22:3-4. As if to remind the reader that healing as such is not necessary, John added, **No longer will there be any curse.** As the curse of Adam's sin led to illness requiring healing and death, so in the eternal state there will be no curse;

therefore no healing of illness is necessary.

As mentioned earlier, God and the Lamb are in the new city (21:22-23; 22:1). The New Jerusalem will be the temple of God (21:22), and the throne of God will also be in it. Then John wrote, **His servants will serve Him.** The highest joy and privilege of the saints in eternity will be to serve their blessed Lord, even though it is true that they will also reign with Him (2 Tim. 2:12; Rev. 5:10; 20:4-6). They will have a privileged place before the throne for **they will see His face.** The implication is that they are under the Lord's good favor and in His "inner circle." This intimacy is also indicated by the fact that **His name will be on their foreheads** (cf. 2:17; 3:12; 7:3; 14:1). Their freedom to be in the presence of God indicates that they will then be in their glorified bodies (cf. 1 John 3:2).

8. THE SAINTS' REIGN WITH GOD (22:5)

22:5. Once again John wrote that the glory and **light** of the New Jerusalem will be the presence of God, with no artificial illumination (cf. 21:23-24). And once again the statement is made that the servants of God will **reign** with Christ **forever** (cf. 20:6b).

Q. The final word from God (22:6-21)

1. THE CERTAINTY OF THE RETURN OF CHRIST (22:6-7)

22:6-7. Confirming both the truth and possibility of comprehending the prophecies previously given, the angel told John that the **words** of this book are **trustworthy and true.** The purpose of these communications is not to bewilder and confuse but to reveal many of **the things that must soon take place.**

This directly contradicts the point of view of many scholars that the Book of Revelation is an imponderable mystery for which no key is available today. This book is the Word of God and not the vague imaginations of John. In addition it is intended to describe future events. When taken in its literal, ordinary meaning, this is exactly what it does, even though much of Revelation is written in symbolic form. The Word of God was not given to be obscure. It was given to be understood by those taught by the Spirit.

The theme of Revelation is stated again in verse 7: **Behold, I am coming soon!** (cf. 1:7; 22:12, 20) Also He is coming quickly. The Greek word *tachy* may be translated "soon" (NIV) or "quickly" (NASB, ASV), and from the divine standpoint both are true. The coming of Christ is always soon from the standpoint of the saints' foreview of the future, and when it occurs, it will come suddenly or quickly. Accordingly a special blessing is pronounced on those who believe and heed the prophecy of the book. As stated earlier, this last book of the Bible, so neglected by the church and with its meanings confused by many expositors, contains more promises of blessing than any other book of Scripture. This reference to blessing is the sixth beatitude in the book (the seventh is in v. 14). The first blessing (in 1:3) is similar to this one in 22:7.

2. THE WORSHIP BY JOHN (22:8-9)

22:8-9. As this tremendous revelation was given to John, he once again **fell down to worship ... the angel.** Again he was rebuked and reminded that angels should not be worshiped because, like the saints, they are fellow servants. John was commanded to **worship** the Lord, not angels (cf. 19:10).

3. THE COMMAND TO PROCLAIM THE PROPHECY OF THE BOOK (22:10-11)

22:10-11. Daniel was told that his prophecies would be "sealed until the time of the end" (Dan. 12:9). But John was told **not** to **seal up the words of** these prophecies. Again it should be emphasized that the viewpoint of some scholars that the Book of Revelation is an impenetrable puzzle is expressly contradicted by this and other passages. Revelation, both via its plain statements and its symbols, is designed to reveal facts and events relating to the second coming of Christ.

The exhortation which follows has puzzled some. Those who do **wrong** and are **vile** are encouraged to **continue** to do so, and those who do **right** and are **holy** are encouraged to **continue** to do so (Rev. 22:11). The point here is not to condone what is evil, but to point out that if people do not heed this prophecy, they will continue in their wickedness.

On the other hand those who do heed the prophecy will continue to do what is right. Relatively speaking, **the time** of the Lord's return **is near** and no major changes in mankind's conduct can be expected.

4. THE COMING JUDGMENT AND REWARD (22:12)

22:12. The words with which this verse begins: **Behold, I am coming soon!** are the same as those at the beginning of verse 7. In connection with His return, which will be "soon" (cf. vv. 7, 20), a **reward** is promised to His saints for what they have **done** for Christ. The reference is to the judgment seat of Christ (2 Cor. 5:10-11). The final judgments of both the wicked and the righteous will be judgments of works. This is the joyous expectation of those who are faithful and the fear of those who have not been faithful.

5. THE ETERNAL CHRIST (22:13)

22:13. Once again Christ is described as **the Alpha and the Omega** (first and last letters of the Gr. alphabet), **the First and the Last, the Beginning and the End.** Christ is before all Creation and He will continue to exist after the present creation is destroyed. He is the Eternal One (cf. 1:4, 8, 17; 2:8; 21:6).

6. THE COMING BLESSING AND JUDGMENT (22:14-15)

22:14-15. The last of the seven beatitudes of Revelation is bestowed on the saints, **those who wash their robes.** They have access to the New Jerusalem and its **tree of life** (cf. v. 19). The other six beatitudes are in 1:3; 14:13; 16:15; 19:9; 20:6; 22:7. In the manuscripts followed by the KJV, the expression "those who wash their robes" is translated "that do His commandments." In both cases the words accurately describe the righteous.

By contrast, judgment is pronounced on those who are unsaved (**dogs** refers to people; cf. Phil. 3:2): **those who practice magic arts** (cf. Rev. 9:21; 18:23; 21:8), **the sexually immoral, the murderers, the idolaters, and everyone who loves and practices falsehood.** As in the similar description of the unsaved in 21:8, 27, the wicked works which characterize the unsaved are described. Though some saints have been guilty of these same practices, they have been washed in the blood of the Lamb and are acceptable to God. But those who refuse to come to the Lord receive the just reward for their sins. Though the world is excessively wicked, God will bring every sin into judgment. And the time for Christ's return may be drawing near, when this will be effected.

7. THE INVITATION OF THE SPIRIT AND THE BRIDE (22:16-17)

22:16-17. The entire Book of Revelation was delivered by Christ through His **angel** and is **for the churches.** Christ described Himself as **the Root and the Offspring of David, and the bright Morning Star.** Historically Christ comes from David (Matt. 1:1; cf. Isa. 11:11; Rev. 5:5). Prophetically His coming is like the morning star, the beginning of a bright new day. The Holy **Spirit** joined with **the bride,** the church, in extending an invitation to all who heed. Those who hear are encouraged to respond and also to extend the invitation to others. The wonderful promise is given that all those who are **thirsty** may **come** and will receive God's **free gift.**

This is the wonderful invitation extended to every generation up to the coming of Christ. Those who recognize their need and realize that Christ is the provider of salvation are exhorted to come while there is yet time before the judgment falls and it is too late. As the Scriptures make clear, the gift of eternal life (here called **the water of life;** cf. 22:1; John 7:37-39) is free. It has been paid for by the death of Christ on the cross and is extended to all who are willing to receive it in simple faith.

8. THE FINAL WARNING (22:18-19)

22:18-19. While on the one hand an invitation is extended to those who will listen, a word of warning is also given to those who reject the revelation of **this** final **book** of the Bible. A dual warning is given against adding to it or subtracting from it (cf. Deut. 4:2; 12:32; Prov. 30:6). How great will be the judgment of those who despise this book and relegate it to the mystical experiences of an old man, thereby denying that it is the inspired Word of God. Rejecting the Word of God is rejecting God Himself. And those who deny His promises of blessing and subtract from His truths will receive His judgment and will have no part in **the tree of life** or access to **the holy city** (cf. Rev. 22:14).

9. THE FINAL PRAYER AND PROMISE (22:20-21)

22:20-21. One further word of testimony was then given: **Yes, I am coming soon** (cf. vv. 7, 12). To this John replied in a brief prayer, **Amen. Come, Lord Jesus.**

With this tremendous revelation completed, a final word of benediction was pronounced. **The grace of the Lord Jesus be with God's people. Amen.** This expression, so common in other New Testament books, brings this final word from God to an end. For those who believe that Christ in His first coming provided salvation, there is the wonderful promise of His coming again to bring full and final deliverance. As the book began by introducing a revelation of Jesus Christ so it ends with the same thought that He is coming again.

Probably no other book of Scripture more sharply contrasts the blessed lot of the saints with the fearful future of those who are lost. No other book of the Bible is more explicit in its description of judgment on the one hand and the saints' eternal bliss on the other. What a tragedy that so many pass by this book and fail to fathom its wonderful truths, thereby impoverishing their knowledge and hope in Christ Jesus. God's people who understand and appreciate these wonderful promises can join with John in his prayer, "Come, Lord Jesus."

BIBLIOGRAPHY

Alford, Henry. *The Greek Testament.* Revised by Everett F. Harrison. 4 vols. in 2. Chicago: Moody Press, 1958.

Blanchard, Charles A. *Light on the Last Days.* Chicago: Bible Institute Colportage Association, 1913.

Ironside, H.A. *Lectures on the Book of Revelation.* New York: Loizeaux Brothers, 1930.

Kelly, William. *Lectures on the Book of Revelation.* London: W.H. Broom, 1874.

Mounce, Robert H. *The Book of Revelation.* The New International Commentary on the New Testament. Grand Rapids: Wm. B. Eerdmans Publishing Co., 1977.

Ryrie, Charles Caldwell. *Revelation.* Everyman's Bible Commentary. Chicago: Moody Press, 1968.

──────. *The Final Countdown.* Wheaton, Ill.: Scripture Press Publications, Victor Books, 1982.

Scott, Walter. *Exposition of the Revelation of Jesus Christ.* London: Pickering and Inglis, n.d.

Scroggie, W.G. *The Great Unveiling.* Reprint. Grand Rapids: Zondervan Publishing House, 1979.

Seiss, Joseph A. *The Apocalypse.* Grand Rapids: Zondervan Publishing House, 1957.

Smith, J.B. *A Revelation of Jesus Christ.* Scottdale, Pa.: Herald Press, 1961.

Swete, Henry Barclay. *Commentary on Revelation.* 3d ed. London: Macmillan & Co., 1911. Reprint. Grand Rapids: Kregel Publications, 1978.

Tenney, Merrill C. *Interpreting Revelation.* Grand Rapids: Wm. B. Eerdmans Publishing Co., 1957.

Torrance, Thomas F. *The Apocalypse Today.* Greenwood, S.C.: Attic Press, 1960.

Walvoord, John F. *The Revelation of Jesus Christ.* Chicago: Moody Press, 1966.

──────. *The Rapture Question.* Rev. ed. Grand Rapids: Zondervan Publishing House, 1979.

BIBLIOGRAPHY ON THE SEVEN CHURCHES IN REVELATION 2-3

Blaiklock, E.M. *The Seven Churches.* London: Marshall, Morgan & Scott, n.d.

Havner, Vance. *Repent or Else!* New York: Fleming H. Revell Co., 1958.

Loane, Marcus L. *They Overcame: An Exposition of the First Three Chapters of Revelation.* Grand Rapids: Baker Book House, 1981.

Morgan, G. Campbell. *A First Century Message to Twentieth Century Christians.* Westwood, N.J.: Fleming H. Revell Co., 1902.

Ramsay, W.M. *The Letters to the Seven Churches of Asia.* 4th ed. New York: Hodder and Stoughton, 1904. Reprint. Grand Rapids: Baker Book House, 1979.

Seiss, Joseph A. *Letters to the Seven Churches.* 1889. Reprint. Grand Rapids: Baker Book House, 1956.

Tatford, Frederick A. *The Patmos Letters.* Grand Rapids: Kregel Publications, 1969.

Trench, Richard Chenevix. *Commentary on the Epistles to the Seven Churches in Asia.* London: Macmillan & Co., 1867. Reprint. Minneapolis: Klock & Klock, 1978.

Yamauchi, Edwin M. *The Archaeology of New Testament Cities in Western Asia Minor.* Grand Rapids: Baker Book House, 1980. (Includes chapters on Ephesus, Pergamum, Sardis, and Laodicea.)

At David C Cook, we equip the local church around the corner and around the globe to make disciples. Come see how we are working together—go to **www.davidccook.com**. Thank you!

transforming lives together